WRITING THE LIVES OF PEOPLE AND THINGS, AD 500–1700

Writing the Lives of People and Things, AD 500–1700

A Multi-disciplinary Future for Biography

Edited by

ROBERT F.W. SMITH
University of Southampton, UK

GEMMA L. WATSON
University of Reading, UK

ASHGATE

Published by
Ashgate Publishing Limited
Wey Court East
Union Road
Farnham
Surrey, GU9 7PT
England

Ashgate Publishing Company
110 Cherry Street
Suite 3-1
Burlington, VT 05401-3818
USA

www.ashgate.com

British Library Cataloguing in Publication Data
A catalogue record for this book is available from the British Library

The Library of Congress has cataloged the printed edition as follows:
Names: Smith, Robert F. W., editor, author. | Watson, Gemma L., editor, author.
Title: Writing the lives of people and things, ad 500–1700 : a multi-disciplinary future for biography / edited by Robert F.W. Smith and Gemma L. Watson.
Description: Burlington, VT : Ashgate, 2015. | Includes bibliographical references and index.
Identifiers: LCCN 2015020321| ISBN 9781472450678 (hardcover) | ISBN 9781472450685 (ebook) | ISBN 9781472450692 (epub)
Subjects: LCSH: Biography as a literary form—History. | Historiography—History.
Classification: LCC CT31 .W75 2015 | DDC 907.2—dc23 LC record available at http://lccn.loc.gov/2015020321

ISBN: 9781472450678 (hbk)
ISBN: 9781472450685 (ebk – PDF)
ISBN: 9781472450692 (ebk – ePUB)

Printed in the United Kingdom by Henry Ling Limited, at the Dorset Press, Dorchester, DT1 1HD

Contents

List of Figures

List of Tables

Notes on Contributors

Natalie C. Aldred completed her PhD in English Literature at the University of Birmingham, England, in 2011. She is an independent researcher, and has taught at the Universities of Bath and Birmingham; as of April 2010 she has been employed as an Educational Support Worker for UK HE learners. Natalie specialises in the editing and bibliographical studies of early modern English vernacular texts, as well as book history, early book advertisements, sixteenth-century theatre history, digital humanities, and professional playwrights, notably William Haughton. Her articles, notes, and conference papers explore bibliography, editing, genre, biography, and printers. She is currently editing Haughton's *Englishmen for my Money* (for *Digital Renaissance Editions*), and co-producing, with Joshua McEvilla, an online catalogue of pre-1668 book advertisements in English periodicals. She is assistant editor of *The Literary Encyclopaedia*, on the Editorial Board of the *Map of Early Modern London* and contributes to the *Lost Plays Database*.

Kitrina Bevan recently completed a PhD in Law at the University of Exeter, specialising in medieval legal history. Her research focuses on concepts of legal and linguistic 'literacies' and considers the impact and influence that legal professionals and provincial administrators (such as town clerks and scriveners) had on access to justice in later medieval England. This research was supported by the Social Sciences and Humanities Research Council of Canada.

Gabriel Byng is a research fellow at Clare Hall, Cambridge University, and Director of Studies in History of Art at Clare College. He won scholarships from the Lightfoot, Ellen McArthur and Ochs Trusts for his doctoral work at Cambridge and won the Reginald Taylor and Lord Fletcher prize in 2013. He is widely published in peer-reviewed journals and is a trustee of the Mausolea and Monuments Trust and Caius House.

Justin M. Byron-Davies recently completed his doctoral studies at the University of Surrey, where he also worked as an Associate Tutor in the School of English and Languages. His thesis explores the influence of the book of Revelation on Julian of Norwich's *Revelations of Divine Love* and William Langland's *Piers Plowman*. He also has BA and MA degrees from Aberystwyth University.

Kirsty Day is a Teaching Fellow in Medieval History at the University of Leeds. Her research, which has been funded by the AHRC, examines the evidence for the female Franciscan dynastic communities that were established in Bohemia and the Polish duchies in the thirteenth century. She argues for the importance of these institutions – previously neglected due to Franciscan scholarship's androcentric and western-European focus – to the history of Franciscan identity construction.

Helen Draper is currently writing an interdisciplinary thesis on Mary Beale, co-supervised by the Institute of Historical Research and the Courtauld Institute of Art. The research places Beale and other women within the London art world, explores seventeenth-century ideas about portraiture and friendship, and relates them to the early modern preoccupation with self-definition and public identity. In 2012 Helen published an article on Beale's unique description of how to paint, and in autumn 2015 her paper 'Mary Beale and art's lost labourers: women Painter-Stainers' was published in *Early Modern Women: An Interdisciplinary Journal* (10:1).

Maria Kirk is a doctoral student at the University of Sussex studying for a PhD in Early Modern Literature and Culture. Her PhD project is funded by an AHRC Collaborative Doctoral Award and is jointly supervised by the University of Sussex and the National Trust. Her research focuses on the relationship between performance, consumption and collection in the early- to mid-seventeenth century, with specific reference to a collection of late-sixteenth and early-seventeenth century play quartos which are owned by the National Trust and kept at Petworth House in Sussex.

Toby F. Martin was awarded his PhD on the archaeology of Anglo-Saxon dress at the University of Sheffield in 2012. Since then, he has published his thesis as a monograph with Boydell and Brewer. From September 2013 Toby has been undertaking a junior research fellowship at the University of Oxford funded by the British Academy, extending the themes of his PhD into a wider European early medieval context.

Kathryn Maude is completing a PhD at King's College London, with Professor Clare Lees. Her thesis investigates a group of texts in Old English, Latin and Anglo-Norman directly addressed to women in the period 960–1160. These texts reflect the multilingual textual culture of the time, and also the range of material – historical, religious, legal and epistolary – written to and commissioned by women in this period.

Charles Nicholl is a travel writer and biographer. *The Reckoning: The Murder of Christopher Marlowe* won the Crime Writer's Association 'Gold Dagger' Award for Non-Fiction and the James Tait Black Memorial Prize. *Somebody Else: Arthur Rimbaud in Africa* won the Hawthornden Prize. His biographical studies of Shakespeare, Thomas Nashe and Leonardo da Vinci have been highly acclaimed. His most recent book, *Traces Remain,* was published by Penguin in 2012.

Ismini Pells has recently completed her PhD at the University of Cambridge, under the supervision of Dr David Smith. Her dissertation investigated the religious and political thought and military career of Philip Skippon, Sergeant-Major-General of the New Model Army. Ismini first became interested in Skippon through her involvement in the Honourable Artillery Company, of which Skippon was Captain-General during the years 1639–60. She is interested in all aspects of early modern military history but particularly the day-to-day life of soldiers on campaign and the relationship between soldiers and society.

Robert F.W. Smith is an independent researcher in early modern history, based in Norfolk. He completed a PhD at the University of Southampton in 2014. His research into the life of John Trussell of Winchester was funded by an AHRC award. He is currently training as an archivist.

Yolana Wassersug completed her PhD at the Shakespeare Institute, Stratford-upon-Avon (University of Birmingham) in 2014. Her doctoral thesis explores the function and representation of portraits on stage in English plays from 1558–1642. She is a part-time lecturer at Dalhousie University in Halifax, Canada.

Gemma L. Watson is a Post-Doctoral Research Assistant working in the Archaeology department at the University of Reading. She specialises in medieval material culture and interdisciplinary research. Her doctoral thesis explored the life of the fifteenth-century herald, Roger Machado, through the objects he owned and came into contact with. A permanent display on Roger Machado based on her research can be viewed at Southampton SeaCity Museum.

Katherine Weikert is a Lecturer in Early Medieval European History at the University of Winchester. Her research focuses on gender, social space, and authority in England and Normandy, c. 900–1200, with a special interest in female hostages and hostageships.

Foreword

'I esteem biography, as giving us what comes near to ourselves, what we can turn to use ....'

Samuel Johnson

This remarkably eclectic collection pursues the idea of biography – and, perhaps more importantly, the practice of biography – through a variety of approaches, disciplines and subject-matters. The actual people whose lives are discussed here are certainly various. The best known are the medieval mystic Julian of Norwich and the Restoration portrait-painter Mary Beale, but we also get to meet a Civil War soldier, a Puritan scholar, an Elizabethan printer, a Sussex churchwarden, a group of medieval provincial scriveners, and the intriguing Alice de Huntingfield, 'a daughter of the late Anglo-Norman gentry' whose brief and fragmentary curriculum vitae discloses a life of vicissitudes as 'hostage, wife and widow'.

As the title suggests, the collection also explores the 'lives' of material objects, and their interaction with the lives of those who made or owned or used them. Whether inanimate objects can truly be said to have a 'life' is a matter of philosophical debate, but they certainly have a story, if they can be made to tell it, and their survival as a marker of past proximities makes them a rich biographical source. A document is an obvious example: a text to be read, but also a physical object to be examined as a relic or vestige of the particular context in which it was produced. Thus we are invited to see how Philip Skippon's heavily annotated copy of the 'Breeches Bible' takes us into the mental world of a high-ranking officer in Cromwell's New Model Army; and how a bibliographical analysis of the 1616 edition of William Haughton's stage-comedy *Englishmen for my Money* throws light on the career and circumstances of its printer, William White. Other essays discover biographical resonances in a cache of Anglo-Saxon brooches, in some pew-carvings in a Suffolk church, in a collection of early books at Petworth House, and in the painted portraits in *Hamlet* – fictional objects, in this last case, though physically present on stage, and much commented on by characters who are looking at them through late Elizabethan eyes.

What links these disparate, multi-disciplinary studies is a strong sense of biography as a close-focus, microhistorical form of study, employing skills and procedures which are loosely described as 'forensic' (loose because the word correctly refers to criminal investigations). In this way these essays connect with a recent trend down the more commercial end of the life-writing business – the trend towards the biographical study, as distinct from the 'cradle to grave' life-story. This form gives us biography in a mode more miniaturist than monumental. It focuses on specific episodes or relationships or locations; it probes particular contexts; it pursues fine threads of connection and reverberation. And, in all of these, it is committed to the importance of detail – material, cultural, sociological, psychological – as a means to recover the presence of distant lives. In these challengingly precise areas of investigation, I suspect, lies the continuing relevance of biography for medievalists and early modernists.

I call this a recent trend in biography, but I am also struck by the way it goes right back to the first emergence of the English biographical tradition a little more than three centuries ago. Though it has many antecedents – Classical, Renaissance, ecclesiastical and indeed vernacular (chronicles, ballads, jest-books, etc.) – biography as we understand it today really began to take shape in the later seventeenth century. Its early pioneers were those diligent hunters of data and anecdote (with a preponderance of the latter) such as Anthony à Wood, Bishop Thomas Fuller and – pre-eminently – John Aubrey, the antiquarian and archaeologist whose voluminous biographical notes remained in manuscript at his death in 1697, and were eventually published under the title *Brief Lives* in the early nineteenth century. Aubrey, obsessively curious about people, and 'never off horseback' in his search for material, typifies a new sense of the biographer as one who actively gathers information, who studies the lives of others as if through a magnifying glass, who records their quirks and telling details, and who depicts them 'warts and all', as his contemporary, the miniaturist Samuel Cooper, famously did when he painted Cromwell in the 1650s.

The relish of readers for this sort of biographical intimacy is noted in the opening remarks of Nicholas Rowe's 'Some Account of the Life &c of Mr William Shakespear', which was published in 1709 and is generally considered the first 'joined-up' biography of Shakespeare:

> How fond do we see some people of discovering any little Personal Story of the great Men of Antiquity: their Families, the common Accidents of their Lives, and even their Shape, Make and Features have been the Subject of critical Enquiries. How trifling soever this Curiosity may seem to be, it is certainly very Natural; and we are hardly satisfy'd with an Account of any remarkable Person, 'till we have heard him describ'd even to the very Cloaths he wears.

One notes Rowe's rather ambivalent reaction – this interest in personal detail might be thought of as 'fond' (still close to its original meaning of 'foolish'), a 'trifling' kind of curiosity – and indeed the idea of the biographer as a faintly prying figure, an uninvited guest at the door of posterity, has persisted.

The first great heyday of English biography came a generation or two later, in the mid-eighteenth century, with Samuel Johnson and James Boswell (and some others of their circle, such as Edmond Malone and Arthur Murphy). In an essay written for *The Rambler* in 1750, Johnson discusses the importance of biographical detail, and of the kind of focus that detail brings. The true 'business of a biographer', he said,

> is often to pass slightly over those performances and incidents which produce vulgar greatness, to lead the thoughts into domestick privacies, and display the minute details of daily life, where exterior appendages are cast aside, and men excel each other only by prudence and by virtue. ... There are many invisible circumstances ... which are more important than publick occurrences ... but biography has often been allotted to writers who seem very little acquainted with the nature of their task, or very negligent about the performance. They rarely afford any other account than might be collected from publick papers, but imagine themselves writing a life when they exhibit a chronological series of actions or preferments; and so little regard the manners or behaviour of their heroes, that more knowledge may be gained of a man's real character by a short conversation with one of his servants, than from a formal and studied narrative, begun with his pedigree, and ended with his funeral.

Johnson's desire to avoid the broad brushstrokes of panegyric – the official or 'authorised' biography – is also expressed in his belief that the subjects of biography need not necessarily be the great and famous. Hence his warm praise of Pope's 'Epitaph on Mrs Corbet' ('Here rests a Woman, good without pretence,/ Bless'd with plain Reason and with sober Sense', etc.), of which he says:

> I have always considered this as the most valuable of Pope's epitaphs; the subject of it is a character not discriminated by any shining or eminent peculiarities yet that which really makes, though not the splendour, the felicity of life ... Of such a character, which the dull overlook and the gay despise, it was fit that the value should be made known and the dignity established.

Dr Johnson's more informal and more generously inclusive idea of biography is splendidly summed up in his comment, quoted at the beginning of this foreword, that biography is to be valued because it gives us something that 'comes near to ourselves', and that we 'can turn to use'. In a single, deceptively simple sentence Johnson conveys a powerful sense of life-writing as part of a repository of shared knowledge about human behaviour (his phrasing almost seems to anticipate the currently popular definition of culture as 'the stories we tell ourselves about ourselves'). His words are a short but rather majestic riposte to those columnists and conferencers who gather from time to time, like legacy-hunters round the bedside, to pronounce on the imminent death of biography in a postmodern landscape of digitised knowledge and historical ignorance.

Johnson's comment was recorded by James Boswell in his *Journal of a Tour to the Hebrides with Samuel Johnson*, which means, appropriately enough, that we know the precise biographical context of the utterance: it is the afternoon of Saturday 21 August 1773, and the Doctor is in post-prandial conversation with his host, the eccentric Lord Monboddo, at the latter's home – a 'poor old house [with] two turrets' – south of Aberdeen. It is also appropriate in that Boswell's *Journal* (published in 1786, two years after Johnson's death) was a kind of rehearsal or pilot for his *Life* of Johnson, on which he was then hard at work – a book considered by many to be the greatest of all English biographies.

Elsewhere in the *Journal* Boswell writes: 'I must again and again apologize to fastidious readers for recording such minute particulars. They prove the scrupulous fidelity of my journal. Dr Johnson said it was a very exact picture of a portion of his life'. The apology is, of course, feigned – or rather it is made in order to be immediately brushed aside. Boswell knows better than anyone that such 'minute particulars' are the indispensable raw material of that 'exact picture' of a person which we demand from biography. This is triumphantly evident in the *Life*, which 'comes near to ourselves' precisely by coming so near to Johnson, and is continuously evident in the long tradition of minute and painstaking biographical research which has followed, and to which this fine collection of essays belongs.

Charles Nicholl

Introduction

Robert F.W. Smith and Gemma L. Watson

This is a volume of essays which are biographical in nature. Already, some readers' eyebrows might be raised. Biography, it is often thought, needs defending, at least when attempted by academics. The disparaging attitudes of many in academia towards biography, the tendency to regard it as an 'unloved stepchild' to be 'shut outside with the riffraff', and the gloom that some biographers feel about the future of the method, have been surveyed by writers such as David Nasaw and Anne Chisolm.[1] Ray Monk, a successful biographer of Oppenheimer, Wittgenstein and Bertrand Russell, even put on a conference at the University of Southampton in 2012 which seriously posed the question 'Can Biography Survive?', and while many of the conference delegates were optimistic about the future of biography, it was generally quite a cautious optimism.

As the micro-historian Giovanni Levi has written, 'doubts about even the possibility of biography are a recurring factor'.[2] Given that biography has been practised since ancient times, and that biographical works such as Plutarch's *Lives* and Boswell's *Life* of Johnson are acknowledged to be among the classics of literature, this may seem absurd. On reflection, though, it is easy to understand why it is the case. As C.S. Lewis observed,

> most of the experiences in 'the past as it really was' were instantly forgotten by the subject himself. Of the small percentage he remembered (and never remembered with perfect accuracy) a smaller percentage was ever communicated even to his closest intimates; of this, a smaller percentage still was ever recorded; of the recorded fraction only another fraction has ever reached posterity.[3]

---

[1] David Nasaw, 'Introduction', *The American Historical Review* 114, no.3 (2009): 573–8. doi: 10.1086/ahr.114.3.662; Anne Chisolm, 'Has Biography Had Its Day?', *Lady Margaret Hall: The Brown Book 2010* (2010): 20–27.

[2] Giovanni Levi, 'The Uses of Biography', in *Theoretical Discussions of Biography: Approaches From History, Microhistory and Life Writing*, ed. Hans Renders and Binne De Haan (Netherlands: Brill, 2014), 63.

[3] C.S. Lewis, 'Historicism', in *Fern-seeds and Elephants*, ed. Walter Hooper (Glasgow: Fontana, 1975), 55.

In this he was making a point that many others have made: that the past is largely unknowable. At first glance this would indeed seem to be a formidable obstacle to the practice of biography.

In reality, however, this problem is no more insuperable for the life-writer than for the person living. Clearly we should make no pretence of 'completeness' in our biographies, but it is still possible to make true statements (and false ones) about the past, as Lewis would have acknowledged. A good analogy is the atom. We look around the room and see the desk, the chair, the stuffing from a shredded cushion scattered over the floor, the dog looking guiltily up at us from his basket. We would never imagine, if we did not know, that the chair, the desk, the cushion, the dog, are constructed from billions of atoms, each of which is 99.9 per cent empty space. And not knowing it would not prevent us from describing or drawing them in such a way as to make them comprehensible at the level of human reality. Even if 99.9 per cent of the history of a human life is unknowable to us, we can still make useful and meaningful statements about it.

This essay collection is predicated upon the belief that writing biography is still an important and valuable enterprise for academic writers about the past. Thomas Carlyle's famous aphorism, that 'history is the essence of innumerable biographies', may be a bit of a cliché nowadays, as one writer on Carlyle, Ann Rigney, has cautioned us.[4] But that only points to its perennial usefulness and the fact that Carlyle's maxim still has something to tell us. For one thing, as Rigney also argues, it cautions us against subordinating individuals to overarching meta-narratives, to societal forces or preconceived notions. Especially when dealing with periods of pronounced ideological conflict, such as the period of English history from the Reformation to the Civil War, the process of thematic history-writing has an inevitable tendency to set up opposed paradigms, imputing a polarisation between individuals and interests which was not really so distinctive as it seems. It is here that biography comes into its own, because it allows us to understand the actual procedure of life, which is invariably messy and complicated, and often not a matter of easy ideological definitions.

Carlyle's dictum encapsulates a fundamental truth: that history is not merely a chart of impersonal forces outworking through time, but a story of human lives which intersect, individuals who interact with one another. Since human lives are the medium in which history takes place, it follows that, as human lives are inevitably experienced chronologically, historical biography remains a useful primary means of understanding the reality of history as it was lived. There is also a view – which we share – that the ability to write medieval and Renaissance lives in any depth is a rare enough privilege that it should be done whenever possible.

---

[4]   Ann Rigney, 'The Multiple Histories of Thomas Carlyle', in *Victorian Keats and Romantic Carlyle: The Fusions and Confusions of Literary Periods*, ed. C.C. Barfoot (Amsterdam and Atlanta: Rodopi, 1999), 194.

Furthermore, as the early modern historian Robert Tittler has remarked, 'the unheralded events and people of an age often convey the tenor of the times just as usefully as the great and famous'.[5] In our view, there are no medieval or Renaissance subjects whatsoever who are unsuitable for biographisation.

There is one important theoretical question in medieval studies which it is essential to address in a book of this nature. As David Nasaw argues, 'the historian as biographer proceeds from the premise that individuals are situated but not imprisoned in social structures and discursive regimes'.[6] But it used to be doubted whether 'individuals' even existed in the Middle Ages; if they did not and were in fact 'discovered' only in the Renaissance then this would seem to be a significant impediment to writing biographical studies of medieval people, as many of the contributors to this volume do. However, during the revisionist era of historiography the 'revolt of the medievalists' led by David Morris and Caroline Walker Bynum pushed back the discovery of the individual by several centuries, and there is really no reason why we should continue to assume with Burckhardt and his followers that the individual ever went away.[7] This is a theory which has never been adequately proven, and relies heavily on lack of evidence. David Morris himself, in his revolutionary work, conceded that the surviving examples of tenth-century poetry 'indicate that tenth-century man was not a stranger to delicate and private feelings', and admitted that there may have been much more early medieval lyric poetry than has survived.[8] Morris amassed significant evidence that, during the high Middle Ages, people significantly developed their capacity to *express* individuality in sophisticated ways that we, today, can respond to; but the idea that this constituted a sea-change in the way they *regarded* themselves does not follow. The attitude of this collection is that, while the practical difficulty (in terms of the availability of sources) of writing the lives of medieval individuals may be greater than for early modern individuals, the theoretical difficulty is no greater.

Historians have become increasingly interested in groups of individuals.[9] The resulting prosopographical studies have been a self-conscious attempt to turn away from a tendency to focus on cradle-to-grave studies of major

---

[5]   Robert Tittler, *Townspeople and Nation: English Urban Experiences 1540–1640* (California: Stanford University Press, 2001), 121–2.

[6]   David Nasaw, 'Introduction': 577.

[7]   C. Morris, *The Discovery of the Individual, 1050–1200* (New York: Harper and Row, 1972); C.W. Bynum, 'Did the Twelfth Century Discover the Individual?', *Journal of Ecclesiastical History* 31 (1980), 1–17.

[8]   Morris, *Discovery of the Individual*, 33.

[9]   See, for example, the recent essay collection of Averil Cameron (ed.), *Fifty Years of Prosopography: The Later Roman Empire, Byzantium and Beyond*, (Oxford: Oxford University Press, 2003); K.S.B. Keats-Rohan (ed.), *Prosopography Approaches and Applications: A Handbook*, (Oxford: Unit for Prosopographical Research, 2007).

figures.[10] This is not to say that studies of major figures are no longer useful; at the other end of the scale from prosopography, the combination of micro-historical approaches with biography is proving fruitful. Two excellent books on Shakespeare, Charles Nicholl's *The Lodger*, and James Shapiro's *1599*, demonstrate the value of this approach, showing how the intensive study of one particular period in an individual life can result in a sense of immersion in a time and place, even when only traces remain in the documentary record. At its best, biography (along with prosopography) offers an unparalleled medium in which to make the transition from the particular to the universal, illuminating both in the process.[11] Biography, therefore, is no longer just the chronological narrative of an individual's life gained from the study of the documentary record, but encompasses wider concerns and uses a variety of different forms of evidence and interdisciplinary methodologies.

Biography is inherently interdisciplinary. Individual lives cannot be neatly bracketed within the confines of one discipline. Their traces may have been left to us in a variety of different ways other than the diaries and letters that are the standard fare of biographers: for instance in objects they created, owned, used and modified, places they lived in and visited, art and music they made, or literature they wrote. As a result, it makes sense that any analysis of a life takes this evidential multiplicity into consideration and adopts appropriate methodologies. Taking an interdisciplinary approach also enables biographers to overcome, to some extent, fragmentary evidence (something that is a particular problem for biographers of the medieval and early modern periods), allowing for an analysis of other types of evidence other than the traditional written sources. Many of this volume's contributors (Martin, Watson, Draper, Byng, Aldred, Pells, Kirk) have shown how inter/multi-disciplinary approaches can be harnessed to great effect with methodologies that look at objects, buildings or books/texts as objects in their biographies. This analysis of 'alternative' types of evidence has led them to have fresh insights and perspectives into historical lives, places, events and periods.

Neither is this volume solely concerned with the lives of human beings; it also encompasses the lives of things. Object biography considers the relationship between people and things, and has been used as a theoretical tool in social science, anthropology and archaeology for the past thirty years.[12] Its premise

---

[10]   David Bates, Julia Crick and Sarah Hamilton (eds), *Writing Medieval Biography, 750–1250* (Woodbridge: Boydell and Brewer, 2006), 9.

[11]   Charles Nicholl, *The Lodger: Shakespeare on Silver Street* (London: Penguin Books, 2008); James Shapiro, *1599: A Year in the Life of William Shakespeare* (London: Faber and Faber, 2005).

[12]   Examples include Arjun Appadura (ed.), *The Social Life of Things: Commodities in Cultural Perspective* (Cambridge: Cambridge University Press, 1986); Igor Kopytoff, 'The Cultural Biography of Things: Commoditization as Process', in *The Social Life of Things:*

is that objects do not just provide a stage setting for human action, but are integral to it. Objects are invested with meaning through the social interactions they are caught up in. These meanings change and are renegotiated through the life of an object. The purpose of an object biography is to illuminate that process by deconstructing the object's 'life' from manufacture to disposal, tracing its changing uses and meanings.[13] However, this theoretical approach has seldom been adopted within medieval archaeology. Rare examples include Chris Gerrard's paper on three objects found 'out of context' during fieldwork at Shapwick, Somerset, and Roberta Gilchrist's examination of medieval heirlooms.[14] Object biography is also discussed by Gilchrist in her study of the medieval life course, by Eleanor Standley in her work on medieval and early modern dress accessories, and by Richard Kelleher in a paper on the re-use of coins in medieval England and Wales.[15] Toby Martin adds to this short list in the present volume with his object biographical analysis of dress and identity in Anglo-Saxon England.

Nevertheless, a recent conference on *The Lives of Objects*, held at Wolfson College, Oxford, in September 2013, highlighted a continuing interest in object biography and its application to disciplines outside archaeology and anthropology. The increasing concern with the physicality of manuscripts and books has also meant an awareness of and interest in the 'lives' of these forms of material culture. For instance, the *Centre for Material Texts* was founded in 2009 at the University of Cambridge, its purpose to foster research into the physical forms of texts and the ways those forms have interacted with literary cultures and historical contexts. The Ashgate monograph series *Material Readings in*

Commodities in Cultural Perspective, ed. Arjun Appadura (Cambridge: Cambridge University Press, 1986); Janet Hoskins, *Biographical Objects: How Things Tell the Story of People's Lives* (New York: Routledge, 1998).

[13]   Chris Gosden and Yvonne Marshall, 'The Cultural Biography of Objects', *World Archaeology*, 31 (1999): 169–78.

[14]   Christopher Gerrard, 'Not All Archaeology is Rubbish: The Exclusive Life Histories of Three Artefacts from Shapwick, Somerset', in *People and Places: Essays in Honour of Mick Aston*, ed. Michael Costen (Oxford: Oxbow, 2007); Roberta Gilchrist, 'The Materiality of Medieval Heirlooms: From Sacred to Biographical Objects', in *Mobility, Meaning and Transformation of Things: Shifting Contexts of Material Culture Through Time and Space*, ed. H.P. Hahn and H. Weiss (Oxford: Oxbow Books, 2013).

[15]   Roberta Gilchrist, *Medieval Life: Archaeology and the Life Course* (Woodbridge: The Boydell Press, 2012); Eleanor R. Standley, *Trinkets and Charms: The Use, Meaning and Significance of Dress Accessories 1300–1700*, Oxford University School of Archaeology Monograph 78 (Oxford: Oxford University School of Archaeology, 2013); Richard Kelleher, 'The Re-Use of Coins in Medieval England and Wales *c.* 1050–1550: An Introductory Survey', *Yorkshire Numismatist*, 4 (2012): 183–200.

Early Modern Culture also provides a vehicle for studies considering the material forms of texts as part of investigations into early modern culture.

The contributors to this collection each have their own specialisms, their own disciplinary backgrounds, their own theories and attitudes. This collection is not an ideological monolith in that respect – the various essays within may come from different historiographical perspectives – and, on the grounds that diversity of thought is usually a strength, we do not feel that the collection as a whole suffers from it. What we do all have in common is a belief in biography as a valid method of writing about the past; a belief that, as Anne Chisolm has argued, 'biography has not had its day, and indeed never will while writers and readers remain interested in the ramifications of human behaviour, the interaction of character and behaviour and the delicate intricacies of the human heart'.[16]

The genesis of this collection dates back to the conference *Writing the Lives of People and Things, AD 500–1700*, which took place at Chawton House Library in March 2012. The conference brought together postgraduate students and early-career academics from across the humanities disciplines to discuss their research and their approaches to biography. Biography was also the theme of the 2013 Reuter Lecture and Masterclass hosted by the University of Southampton's *Centre for Medieval and Renaissance Culture*. The majority of the contributors to this collection gave papers to one or other of these events. Both the events themselves and this present volume demonstrate that biography is far from dead within academia, and is not seen by the next generation of academics as an inferior form of history or an 'unloved stepchild'. Instead, biography has a bright multi-disciplinary future.

Part I of this volume, 'Rescuing Forgotten Lives', contains research which will be new to almost all readers. Katherine Weikert examines the relevance of biography to the study of female hostageships in medieval England by reconstructing the elusive life and interesting times of Alice de Huntingfield. In rescuing the forgotten life of this hostage, wife and widow, we are given a new perspective on an unknown number of women who slip past the historical record and thus the historian's view. Next, Kitrina Bevan explores prosopography as an approach to the study of legal professionals by focusing on medieval scriveners. She applies a prosopographical methodology showing how it can be used as an innovative interdisciplinary research method to reveal some of the ways in which scriveners expressed their individual and group identities through the written word, and successfully demonstrates that there is much for us to learn about scriveners from the very documents that they produced. Robert F.W. Smith's study of the Renaissance scholar John Harmar in Chapter 3 deploys unpublished manuscript sources to supplement the well-known facts

---

[16]   Anne Chisolm, 'Has Biography Had Its Day?': 27.

of Harmar's public career with a comprehensive new narrative locating Harmar's life in the context of the communal life of Winchester College.

Part II, 'The Lives of Objects and Their Owners', contains four chapters featuring biographical approaches to material culture. Toby Martin's chapter applies the principles of object biography to demonstrate how the lives of objects intertwine with the lives and deaths of their owners, and even lives of nations. Martin examines the evidence for women's dress in the Anglian region of what was to become England in the fifth and sixth centuries, particularly focusing on the cruciform brooch. He argues that this type of brooch was a means by which a shared ethnic identity was displayed and constructed using biographical mechanisms. A large part of the value of these brooches stemmed from the way they were obtained at specific stages during the life courses of particular women. These brooches can also be seen as objects whose perceived value and authenticity lay in their own biographies. In Chapter 5 Gemma Watson combines archaeological with contemporary documentary evidence to write the microhistory of the little-known medieval herald, Roger Machado. She argues for the necessity of interdisciplinary research when looking at individual lives, as they touch on so many different aspects of the past.

Biographical uses of art are an important theme in Part II. In Chapter 6 Helen Draper shows how objects can become enmeshed in biography by examining the seventeenth-century artist Mary Beale's use of 'seen' and 'made' objects, including paintings, as a means of self-representation. Draper discusses Beale's exploration of likeness and identity as expressed in the painted and written objects she made, and concludes by demonstrating how Mary used such objects to manipulate her reputation and to further her career. Draper also describes how Mary's intimate circle of friends worked together to promote her respectable, and commercial, public persona. Draper shows how Beale's artistic reputation could have been informed by the objects she saw and the things she read. In the final chapter of the section, Yolana Wassersug examines how Shakespeare depicted characters undertaking biographical readings of portraits on the stage in *Hamlet*, situating her chapter within the context of post-Reformation visual culture in England. Wassersug asks how Shakespeare's Hamlet can learn about a person simply by looking at his or her face, and how far biography can be gleaned from a two-dimensional image. She posits that the Reformation was a period during which imagery in domestic spaces was highly meaningful, and could be used to inspire contemplative thought. She suggests that it was not uncommon to use portraits as interpretive tools rather than mere decoration in sixteenth- and seventeenth-century England, and that when viewed with a careful and discerning eye, portraits can give a biographer insight into the interior life of their subject.

Part III, 'The Life of the Book', also pertains to material culture, this time the materiality of books and its biographical applications. Inspired by the Renaissance conception of the Three Ages of Man (as famously depicted by

Titian in his painting of the same name), the three chapters in this section survey three 'ages' of the book: printing, reading (and annotation), and gathering into a collection. First of all, taking the largely neglected William White as a case study, Natalie Aldred strives towards a prosopography of an important early modern group, the printers, using the material output of White's printing house as a biographical source. Aldred shows how object (book) history informs and enriches our understanding of early modern printers, and as such, feeds into a wider discussion on the value and usefulness of non-traditional primary material in the reconstruction of historical lives. Aldred argues that although bibliographical studies are limited to the printers and typesetters involved, the results that they yield are rewarding biographically. As in the case of her case study, William White, such studies can be used to identify their role as trade printer or publisher, their economy of page setting and the productivity of their printing house. In addition, bibliographical studies of the texts that they printed can identify the size of the printing house and a minimum number of presses that they used.

Next, Ismini Pells, in a chapter that follows the best principles of the 'new biography' as expounded by Lois Banner, discusses the life of a seventeenth-century soldier, Philip Skippon, via his annotations to his Bible.[17] She looks at how Skippon's Bible helps us to reconstruct his personal religious ideology, how this religious ideology may have influenced Skippon's decision to pursue a military career in continental Europe and his personal worship and military conduct once he was there, and how his military experiences impacted upon his ideological development. Lastly, Maria Kirk writes the joint lives of a collection of early modern books and their collector – namely the Petworth House plays and Algernon Percy, the 10th Earl of Northumberland. Kirk's chapter demonstrates how much can be understood from the books themselves, about the way they interacted with the world around them at the time of their printing and purchase, what scars and signs they bear of their varied and multiple pasts, and what we can learn about how and why these pasts converged to form the current collection.

Part IV features two essays in group biography. Gabriel Byng and Kathryn Maude each seek to write the lives of collective institutions, specifically selected parishes in medieval England and a monastic community. Combining prosopography, architectural history and literary techniques, Byng offers a bold new historical methodology for understanding medieval parish communities by working towards a distilled 'ideal' biography of parish church patrons in East Anglia. Maude's subject is Wilton Abbey, a Benedictine convent in Wiltshire. Rather than attempting to tell the story of individual nuns at Wilton Abbey, her

---

[17] L.W. Banner 'Biography as History', *The American Historical Review*, 114: 3 (2009): 579–86.

chapter develops a collective biography of Wilton Abbey by focusing on it as a place and the interactions that people have with that place. Importantly, Maude strives to correct a potential deficiency of the move back to biography among medieval historians, arguing that privileging individuals in communities such as Wilton Abbey isolates biographical subjects from their true, communal form of life.

In the last Part, 'Representing Lives', two contributors engage directly with the element of artifice which is present in all life-writing. The richness and diversity of medieval European religious expression, and the attempts of religious authorities to control and channel it in the face of individual and communal manifestations of that diversity, are the themes of this section. In a chapter which should significantly reframe scholarship on the Franciscans and the Poor Clares, Kirsty Day interrogates the early *vitae* of St Clare of Assisi, arguing that both the medieval authors of these texts and, just as pertinently, modern scholars who have used them, have represented the life of Clare in a way which unduly privileges androcentric, Franciscan conceptions of religious life. By contrast, self-representation is the theme of the final chapter, which examines Julian of Norwich's *Revelations of Divine Love* alongside Margery Kempe's autobiographical *Book*. Justin Byron-Davies analyses the strategies which medieval female religious could employ to avoid the negative consequences of contravening Church orthodoxy whilst still conveying a personal vision in writings which were themselves intimate 'revelations' of self.

In his Foreword to this volume, Charles Nicholl quotes Dr Johnson, who esteemed biography 'as giving us what comes near to ourselves', and argues that his words are a riposte to those who hasten to read the last rites over the biographical genre.[18] Both scrupulously researched and humanly compelling, Nicholl's own works in the field of early modern biography have for more than one of the contributors to this collection been an inspiration, an example, and a spur to join in.[19] It is surely because of the powerful appeal of works like these, and of the stories they tell, that many of us have pursued a scholarly interest in the past at all. A.L. Rowse wrote movingly in *The Use of History* about the sudden transports the historian may experience: 'those moments when time falls away from us ... [and] our feeling for that man who has been dead for centuries is the feeling for ourselves'.[20] It is this feeling which keeps us coming back to the past. If future generations of students are to tread the same path that we and the

---

[18] James Boswell, *The Journal of a Tour to the Hebrides with Samuel Johnson* (London: Heineman, 1936), 55.

[19] For example: Charles Nicholl, *A Cup of News: The Life of Thomas Nashe* (London: Routledge & Kegan Paul, 1984); *The Reckoning: The Murder of Christopher Marlowe* (London: Vintage Books, 2002); *The Lodger: Shakespeare on Silver Street* (London: Penguin Books, 2008).

[20] A.L. Rowse, *The Use of History* (London: Hodder and Stoughton, 1946), 57.

other contributors to this volume have followed, we must make sure that there is always room in academia for histories which 'come near to ourselves'. It is in that hope and spirit that we offer up this collection of studies.

PART I
Rescuing Forgotten Lives

Chapter 1

The (Truncated) Life of
Alice de Solers Rufus née de Huntingfield:
Medieval Hostage, Wife and Widow

Katherine Weikert

The known facts of Alice de Huntingfield's life are slim, but they are these: Alice was probably born no later than 1192. She was a hostage to King John on behalf of her father by 16 September 1203 as a condition of her father's custodianship of Dover Castle. She was married to Richard de Solers, holder of the estate of Faccombe Netherton, Hampshire, in late 1203 or early 1204. Richard and presumably Alice fled for Normandy in either 1204 or 1205 as a part of King John's loss of Normandy. Alice is not heard from again until 1211 when Richard was dead, and Alice's father paid the king for her right to remarry along with a petition for dower from the properties of her deceased husband. By 1215 Alice was remarried to one Hugh, surname variously Rufus or de Rus, and the couple was contesting the ownership of Faccombe Netherton though they were not successful in claiming the estate. From here Alice de Solers Rufus née de Huntingfield disappears entirely from the written record. We have 12 years' confirmation of her existence.[1]

But these sparse facts represent a packed existence, particularly in her early life. In the space of only two years Alice had been hostage to a king, wife of a turncoat and part of a hurried exile to Normandy. Alice's hostageship to John on account of her father's custodianship fits perfectly with Adam Kosto's definition of a medieval hostage as a type of surety, 'a person deprived of liberty by a second person in order to guarantee an undertaking by a third person',[2] whilst her experience in the midst of the loss of Normandy demonstrates her potential greater importance as a '[pawn] in a complex, multilateral political game'.[3]

---

[1]   My thanks to Matthew Bennett, Stephen Church, Paul Hyams, Ryan Lavelle, Annette Parks and Emiliano Perra for comments on early versions of this chapter. Any remaining errors are, of course, my own.
    [2]   Adam J. Kosto, 'Hostages in the Carolingian World (714–840)', *Early Medieval Europe* 11, no. 2 (2002): 128.
    [3]   Kosto, 'Hostages', 140.

Outside the excellent recent work by Gwen Seabourne and Annette Parks on medieval female hostageship,[4] there has been little attention paid to the position of the female hostage in the Middle Ages. This is undoubtedly because of the paucity and opacity of the records surrounding such persons; the tracking of female hostages in the Middle Ages is never an easy prospect. Record-keeping that favoured male high-status hostages means that female hostages may simply be noted with nothing more than a line or two in a historical document, if that. The notice of Alice's hostageship, for example, appears as a single line in a Pipe Roll with no details of the hostageship nor any notice of her subsequent release. It is sometimes only the high status – and subsequently relatively well-known and well-documented – female hostages such as Eleanor of Brittany that can be held up for examination with any certainty. Indeed, Eleanor of Brittany appears roughly at the same time as Alice and some parallels can be drawn between the two in order to theorise on their experiences and positions.

There are, however, ways to 'find' female hostages in the Middle Ages and indeed ways to analyse their use and position. One such method, employed very ably by both Seabourne and Parks, is to build the foundation based upon patterns:[5] taking examples of known female hostages and holding them to the light in order to find similarities or differences and thus discern knowledge about the practice of female hostage-taking in the Middle Ages. Another way, undertaken here by myself as well as previously by both Seabourne and Parks, is to work around the subject in a form of a close biography.[6] By exploring not just the hostage herself but the people and the world around her, we can build concepts of the uses and experiences of female hostages in the Middle Ages.

---

[4] Gwen Seabourne, 'Female Hostages: Definitions and Distinctions', in *Hostage-Taking and Hostage Situations: The Medieval Precursors of a Modern Phenomenon*, eds Matthew Bennett and Katherine Weikert (London: Routledge, forthcoming); Gwen Seabourne, *Imprisoning Medieval Women: The Non-Judicial Confinement and Abduction of Women in England, c. 1170–1509* (Farnham: Ashgate, 2011); Gwen Seabourne, 'Eleanor of Brittany and her Treatment by King John and Henry III', *Nottingham Medieval Studies* 51 (2007); Annette P. Parks, '"Thy Father's Valiancy Has Proven No Boon": The Fates of Helena Angelina Doukaina and Her Children', in Bennett and Weikert, *Hostage-Taking*; Annette P. Parks, 'Rescuing the Maidens from the Tower: Recovering the Stories of Female Political Hostages', in *Feud, Violence and Practice: Essays in Medieval Studies in Honor of Stephen D. White*, eds Belle S. Tuten and Tracey L. Billado (Burlington, VT: Ashgate, 2010); Annette P. Parks, 'Prisoners of Love: Medieval Wives as Hostages', *Journal of the Georgia Association of Historians* 17 (1996).

[5] Seabourne, *Imprisoning Medieval Women*; Annette P. Parks, 'Prisoners of Love'.

[6] Seabourne, 'Eleanor of Brittany;' Parks, 'Rescuing the Maidens'; Katherine Weikert, 'The Princesses Who Might Have Been Hostages: Margaret and Isabella of Scotland', in Bennett and Weikert, *Hostage-Taking*.

Alice here serves as an example of writing a life that may be an exemplar of this probably larger yet somewhat undocumented experience. Her life in the frantic months of the loss of Normandy, 1203 through to 1205, and her position as hostage and wife form the focus of this chapter, but beyond a close biography, the record allows us to view her importance in the larger political arena of the lesser baronage of England and Normandy at the time of John's loss of Normandy. Alice was not just a pawn to her father's ambition; her position and placement in the realm of the lower gentry of King John's reign can be viewed as an attempt by the king to manoeuvre and manipulate the loyalty of his barons with an exacting, calculating precision in an effort to maintain his authority over his flagging Continental lands.

There is little that can be said about Alice's early life. It is not known when she was born, although based upon her marriage we can guess that she was born no later than 1192 assuming that she was of the canonical age of consent at the time of her marriage. Her father, William de Huntingfield, was a landowner who held several knight's fees in the honours of Lancaster and Eye, where the manor of Huntingfield in Suffolk provided the family's toponym.[7] Of Alice's mother we know only her name, Isabel, and nothing more.[8]

Alice entered the historical record in 1203 at the same time her father officially entered King John's service. William was granted custodianship of Dover Castle by the king, in return for which the king took hostages of Alice and her younger brother Roger.[9] The imbalance of power between the parties was typically transparent, with the king holding two minors in return for William's faithful holding of the important castle, a crucial link between England and Normandy.[10] The choice of William's two children reflects the typical selection for a surety with a preference generally for sons or close relatives of the grantee, relying on the ties of lordship to bind the agreement;[11] or, as Sir James Holt ably put it, King John 'did not want second cousins twice removed; there was no guarantee of loyalty in that'.[12] As for the king's wish for hostages in

---

[7]   Ralph V. Turner, 'Huntingfield, William of (d. in or before 1225)', *Oxford Dictionary of National Biography* (Oxford: Oxford University Press, 2004), online edition, accessed 15 January 2012, doi: 10.1093/ref:odnb/14238.

[8]   Walter Rye (ed.), *A Short Calendar of the Feet of Fines of Norfolk in the Reigns of Richard I, John, Henry III, and Edward I* (Norwich: Agas H. Goose & Co., 1885), 11.

[9]   Sir Thomas Duffus Hardy, *Rotuli litterarum patentium in Turri londinensi asservati* (G. Eyre and A. Spottiswoode, 1835), hereafter *Cal. Pat. R.* [year of reign-king, page number]; Turner, 'Huntingfield, William of (d. in or before 1225)'.

[10]   Paul Hyams, pers. comm.

[11]   Kosto, 'Hostages', 134.

[12]   J.C. Holt, 'Presidential Address: Feudal Society and the Family in Early Medieval England: III. Patronage and Politics', *Transactions of the Royal Historical Society* 34, Fifth Series (1984): 13.

exchange for the position of castellan, this too is not unknown: in 1201, John had made arrangements with Juhel of Mayenne that the castellans at Ambrieres and Coumont should provide John with hostages of their sons, and should these hostages die, their fathers would be replaced in their posts by others who were to give their sons as hostage. In such ways, John ' ... in small affairs and great ... went behind the immediate relations between himself and his tenants-in-chief';[13] we can see this detail in John's plans for Alice after her hostageship, as his meddling hands would set the course for her life in the next several years.

What strikes us as different and notable about the hostageship of the de Huntingfield children is the taking of both a son and daughter as this surety. Sons, specifically speaking heirs, were generally the hostages of choice in the Middle Ages.[14] The giving and taking of Alice along with Roger reflects both the practical point of the lack of multiple sons of William and Isabel de Huntingfield at the time of the hostageship but also the flexibility of the expectation of male hostages. It is hard to say where Alice and Roger were held at the time of their hostageships. The hostage-taking was recorded on 16 September 1203 at Falaise, with the oath given from William de Huntingfield to King John.[15] It is doubtful that Alice was there as well but we might assume that she was neither with her family in Suffolk nor her father in Falaise or, consequently, Dover.[16] One antiquarian source lists Alice as being held by the Earl Ferrers, presumably William de Ferrers, 4th Earl of Derby, while Roger was said to have gone to the Earl of Arundel, though the lack of citations to this information in this secondary text make it difficult to confirm these men as hostage-keepers.[17] However, it is interesting to note that both men were married to sisters of the Earl of Chester,[18] a firm favourite of John at this time. The circumstance

---

[13]   Sir Maurice Powicke, *The Loss of Normandy 1189–1204: Studies in the History of the Angevin Empire*, second edition. (Manchester: Manchester University Press, 1961), 146–7.

[14]   Kosto, 'Hostages', 134.

[15]   Sir Thomas Duffus Hardy, *A Description of the Patent Rolls in the Tower of London: To Which Is Added An Itinerary of King John, with Prefatory Observations* (London: G. Eyre and A. Spottiswoode, 1835), 195.

[16]   It is worth noting that the timeframe for William de Huntingfield's custodianship is difficult to pin down with precision. De Huntingfield was clearly temporarily covering for the current custodian in 1203, Hubert de Burgh, who is listed in John Philpot's *Roll of the Constables of Dover Castle and Lord Wardens of the Cinque Ports, 1627* (London: G. Bell and Sons, 1956) whilst de Huntingfield is not.

[17]   Richard Thomson, *An Historical Essay on the Magna Charta of King John* (London: J. Major and R. Jennings, 1829), 297, accessed 17 December 2012, http://archive.org/details/historicalessayo00thomuoft.

[18]   J.R. Maddicott, 'Ferrers, Robert De, Sixth Earl of Derby (c.1239–1279)', *Oxford Dictionary of National Biography* (Oxford: Oxford University Press, 2004), online edition, accessed 17 December 2012, doi:10.1093/ref:odnb/9366; Ralph V. Turner, 'Aubigny,

of entrusting a hostage to a third party would not be unlikely, as by doing so John would further the networks and the strength of the relationships between these families and himself.[19] Here too it is useful to draw a parallel to the other, better-documented royal captive of the day, Eleanor of Brittany, to surmise Alice's probable circumstances. With Eleanor being a dangerous claimant to the Duchy of Brittany as well as the throne of England, Alice's *political* situation emphatically did *not* echo that of Eleanor. Alice's hostageship to John was less a political or diplomatic hostageship than a personal surety, a literal 'living pledge'[20] taken to insure her father's continued loyalty and held to make certain her father refrained from doing anything foolish at the crucial coastal fort of Dover. Eleanor was captured at the siege of Mirabeau along with her brother; William (III) de Braose handed over Arthur to King John and others were taken away in chains,[21] though the details of Eleanor's transport to England are left unclear. Throughout her hostageship Eleanor only travelled with John during his 1214 campaign to Poitou[22] but was otherwise kept away from the king, though not in a prison. Indeed Eleanor kept suitable company for her rank including John's queen, Isabella of Angoulême, and the two princesses of Scotland, Margaret and Isabella, and was generally well-provisioned for with clothing and food.[23] In fact Eleanor's lengthy hostageship must have looked much like many noblewomen's lives except for the obvious fact that she was not free and was indeed closely guarded, particularly after the early 1220s.[24]

We might expect Alice's hostageship to be somewhat the same despite the noted difference of Alice being freely given by her father whilst Eleanor was forcibly taken through battle. Alice was more than likely held in a castle or manor suitable for her position,[25] under restrictions that may have resembled something more like a house arrest than an uncomfortable imprisonment. Alice was probably reasonably provisioned for in terms of diet and upkeep, based upon the known terms of Eleanor's captivity. She was very possibly kept in company

---

William d', Third Earl of Arundel (c.1174–1221)', *Oxford Dictionary of National Biography* (Oxford: Oxford University Press, 2004), online edition, accessed 17 December 2012, doi: 10.1093/ref:odnb/283.

[19]   Ryan Lavelle, 'The Use and Abuse of Hostages in Later Anglo-Saxon England', *Early Medieval Europe* 14, no. 3 (2006): 284.

[20]   Annette P. Parks, *Living Pledges: A Study of Hostageship in the High Middle Ages 1050–1300* (Unpublished PhD thesis, Emory University, 2000).

[21]   Hardy, *Patent Rolls*, 33–6; Powicke, *The Loss of Normandy*, 151.

[22]   Seabourne, 'Eleanor of Brittany', 79–80.

[23]   Joseph Bain, *Calendar of Documents Relating to Scotland Preserved in Her Majesty's Public Record Office, vol. 1, A.D. 1108–1272* (Edinburgh: H.M. General Register House, 1881), nos. 579, 581.

[24]   Parks, 'Rescuing the Maidens', 285; Seabourne, 'Eleanor of Brittany', passim.

[25]   Seabourne, *Imprisoning Medieval Women*, 61–4.

suitable for her age and position, and almost certainly within a cadre of women both for these reasons as well as due to her sex and her fertile age. Although there is little evidence of sexual mistreatment of female hostages in this period, there were earlier accusations against Henry II that he had allegedly seduced or raped women in his hostageship so the possibility of assault was certainly not unknown.[26] As Colleen Slater has noted, the potential of violence or abuse would almost always be present with a medieval hostage, and 'the implicit threat [to the hostage] was likely to produce results [with the hostage-giver]'.[27] Female hostages further presented the risk of possible sexual assault or other misconduct by the keepers, which would result in the woman's loss of virginity and honour. Alice was at least 11 years old at the time of her hostageship with the age of canonical consent for marriage at hand, and so this concern for the possible loss of her virginity, as well as her future career as wife and mother, would have been a real one and an eventuality to be protected against.

An interesting aspect of Alice's hostageship at this time, in late 1203, is the increasing unease of the baronage with John's ability to honourably hold hostages due to the death of Arthur of Brittany, the brother of Eleanor and a potential claimant to both Brittany and England through his father Geoffrey, John's elder brother. Arthur was captured at Mirabeau in August of 1202 and turned over to the king, but it was thought that Arthur was dead by Easter of 1203 with the popular tale circulating that John himself had struck Arthur dead with a stone and tossed his body into the Seine.[28] Rumours were rife about John's hand in Arthur's disappearance by late 1203, following a sinister turn of phrase about Arthur written by John in a letter to the barons of Brittany in August.[29] By October Philip Augustus had expressed his scepticism of Arthur's being alive, explicitly qualifying a charter reference to Arthur with the ominous 'if he still lives'.[30] It was at this time in late 1203 that many of John's important barons began falling away from him, probably due less to the fate of Arthur than to their own interest in their Norman holdings; the death of the Duke of Brittany simply provided an easy catalyst for the defections.[31] But in this we can see that John's actions in regard to his nephew had a major effect within his baronage

---

[26]   Ibid., 74.

[27]   Colleen Slater, '"So Hard was it to Release Princes whom Fortuna had put in her Chains": Queens and Female Rulers as Hostage- and Captive-Takers and Holders', *Medieval Feminist Forum* 45, no. 2 (2009): 14–15.

[28]   Michael Jones, 'Arthur, Duke of Brittany (1187–1203)', *Oxford Dictionary of National Biography* (Oxford: Oxford University Press, 2004), online edition, accessed 31 January 2012, doi:10.1093/ref:odnb/704.

[29]   Powicke, *The Loss of Normandy*, 156.

[30]   Delisle, *Catalogue des Actes de Phillippe-Augustus*, no. 783, cited Powicke, *The Loss of Normandy*, 311.

[31]   Powicke, *The Loss of Normandy*, 157–67.

and ultimately with the baronage's willingness to hand over their sons – and daughters – as hostage.[32]

These suspicions of John's harsh treatment of his hostages were only in their infancy but well-founded as John unintentionally fostered a 'reputation as an untrustworthy custodian of important guests'[33] over the next decade. When Maud de Braose, wife of William (III), and her son William (IV) were taken hostage by King John, they were transported to the king in cages and allegedly starved to death at Windsor Castle.[34] William (III)'s and Maud's daughter Annora, who had been taken prisoner at the same time as Maud and William (IV), was only released after papal interference in 1214, whilst William (IV)'s wife and four sons remained imprisoned at Corfe Castle until 1218.[35] In 1202 some of the hostages from the siege at Mirabeau were starved to death at Corfe Castle.[36] In 1205 John demanded and received William Marshal's oldest son but in 1207 was refused the hostageship of his second son after a public warning against it by Isabella, the Marshal's wife.[37] In 1210, Cathal Crobderg, king of Connacht and high king of Ireland, refused to hand his heir over to John in fear for his son's safety after consultation with his wife.[38] However, on a different occasion he gave a younger son who died years later still in English captivity.[39] The year 1211 saw the well-known hanging of 28 Welsh hostages, all sons of princes, the youngest just seven years old.[40] In an interesting parallel to Eleanor of Brittany and Alice de Huntingfield, in 1209 John took as hostage two daughters of King William of Scotland.[41] John promised to marry the older daughter to

[32]   Ralph V. Turner, *King John* (London: Longman, 1994), 17, 121.

[33]   Seán Duffy, 'King John's Expedition to Ireland, 1210: The Evidence Reconsidered', *Irish Historical Studies* 30, no. 117 (1996): 17.

[34]   Kate Norgate, *John Lackland* (London: Macmillan, 1902), 287–8.

[35]   Ralph V. Turner, 'Briouze, William (III) de (d. 1211)', *Oxford Dictionary of National Biography* (Oxford: Oxford University Press, October 2006), online edition, accessed 28 November 2012, doi: 10.1093/ref:odnb/3283.

[36]   Thomson, *Historical Essay*, 475–6; Walter de Gray Birch, *A history of Margam Abbey: Derived from the original documents in the British Museum, H.M. Record Office, the Margam muniments, etc.* (London: Bedford Press, 1897), 175, accessed 17 December 2012, http://archive.org/details/historyofmargama00bircuoft.

[37]   Brock W. Holden, 'King John, the Braoses, and the Celtic Fringe, 1207–1216', *Albion* 33, no. 1 (2001): 18.

[38]   Helen Perros (Walton), 'Ó Conchobhair, Cathal (1152–1224)', *Oxford Dictionary of National Biography* (Oxford: Oxford University Press, 2004), online edition, accessed 2 February 2012, doi: 10.1093/ref:odnb/20513.

[39]   Duffy, 'King John's Expedition to Ireland', 17.

[40]   Holden, 'King John, the Braoses, and the Celtic Fringe', 20.

[41]   A.A.M. Duncan, 'John King of England and the Kings of Scots', in *King John: New Interpretations*, ed. S.D. Church (Woodbridge: Boydell, 1999), 260. E.L.G Stones has done the most complete work in restructuring the documents surrounding the princesses' hostage-

his own son and heir and the younger to his younger son; however, years later the princesses were still unmarried and were eventually pawned off to English barons below their rank.[42] Whilst some of these hostages may be more properly considered captives according to Adam Kosto's definition of the terms,[43] they have in common the concept of the person or persons as surety, whether seen in the dire warning issued by John to the barons of Brittany or in the taking of Maud, William (IV) and Annora de Braose ostensibly on account of William (III)'s debt.[44]

The circumstances of the daughters of King William are of particular interest in regard to Alice's hostageship. Margaret and Isabella were given to King John with the promise of release into high-ranking marriages.[45] Although the custody of the Scottish princesses began in 1209, a few years after Alice's hostageship in 1203, it is interesting to note that Alice too probably went directly from her hostageship to her marriage to Richard de Solers. Adam Kosto opined that the situation of many hostageships runs 'parallel to that of individuals involved in marriage alliances',[46] while Annette Parks has deftly noted the similarities in 'the practices and ambiguities which governed both marriages and hostageships'.[47] Indeed, Parks has illuminated that the detention of females in the Middle Ages is often hard to spot as the circumstances could have been hidden within political marriages, betrothals or wardships, and further that political marriages of women could serve the same purpose as the custody of a male hostage.[48] Control of the distribution and detention of women would affect the political activities of those involved in the process of detaining and marrying the women in question.[49] In light of these ideas, it becomes possible to view the record of Alice's marriage in 1204 as an altered version of her initial hostageship to King John, a symbolic second detention stemming from the first, but at the very least as a marriage arranged with the king's authority and to the king's benefit.

Definitions of marriage within the Middle Ages have been well elucidated in the past and need not be repeated in depth here. Christopher Brooke has

---

ship: *Anglo-Scottish Relations 1174–1328: Some Selected Documents* (Oxford: Clarendon Press, 1965, reprinted 1970), xlv–xlviii.

[42]   G.W.S Barrow, *Kingship and Unity: Scotland, 1000–1306*, New History of Scotland 2 (Toronto: University of Toronto Press, 1981), 63; Weikert, 'Princesses'.

[43]   Kosto, 'Hostages', 128.

[44]   Holden, 'King John, the Braoses, and the Celtic Fringe', 8.

[45]   David Carpenter, *Magna Carta* (London: Penguin, 2015), 474–5.

[46]   Kosto, 'Hostages', 146.

[47]   Parks, 'Prisoners of Love', 72.

[48]   Parks, 'Rescuing the Maidens', passim; 'Prisoners of Love', 61.

[49]   Parks, 'Prisoners of Love', 61–2.

convincingly outlined the importance of the consensus between parties in a twelfth-century marriage,[50] while Georges Duby wrote that

> [the] order [of marriage] also implied peace, because *the institution of marriage was the very opposite of abduction* ... It was founded on an agreement, a treaty, known as the marriage pact (*pactum conjugale*), that was concluded between the two houses. Under such a pact, one of the houses would give up, the other receive or acquire, a woman. The exchange, then, involved a woman, or, more precisely, her anticipated motherhood, her 'blood' and all that it brought to the new family in terms of both ancestral force (*virtus*) and claims to inheritance.[51]

This definition is somewhat reliant on contract law wherein both parties are bound by an exchange or promise; a marriage pact via hostageship creates a pact between the captor and the family of the marriage partner. In this case the gift of a wife in the person of Alice de Huntingfield fashioned a 'special kind of bilateral contract'[52] between King John and the de Solerses. Alice's father, William de Huntingfield, had no known connections to the de Solers family: the Huntingfields were a rising family in East Anglia with little known about them previous to William's generation,[53] while the de Solerses, with their maternal connections to the de Redvers family and links to the houses of the earls of Gloucester and Devon,[54] were in the late twelfth and early thirteenth century focused on their holdings in south-west England and their Norman properties. Alice's marriage to the younger son of Mabel and William (I) de Solers was not immediately or practically advantageous for the de Huntingfields outside of the honour of having their daughter given in marriage by the king, so we have to try to see why this match was advantageous to King John. This marriage certainly provided a connection between the de Solerses's holdings and influence in Normandy with a rising Englishman loyal to John. But more importantly, this marriage tied the de Solerses to John himself as a provider of such a gift of a wife. In viewing this marriage as a political one we can see John

---

50   Christopher Brooke, 'Marriage in Law and Practice', in *The Medieval Idea of Marriage* (Oxford: Oxford University Press, 1989), 137–41.

51   Georges Duby, *Medieval Marriage: Two Models from Twelfth-Century France*, trans. Elborg Forster, The Johns Hopkins Symposia in Comparative History 11 (Baltimore: The Johns Hopkins University Press, 1978), 4. Italics my own.

52   Paul Hyams, pers. comm.

53   Turner, 'Huntingfield, William of'.

54   Robert Bearman, *Charters of the Redvers Family and the Earldom of Devon 1090–1217*, vol. 37, Devon and Cornwall Record Society New Series (Devon and Cornwall Record Society, 1994). Matriarch Mabel de Solers's descent through the line of the earls of Gloucester also make her a descendant of King Henry I, John's great-grandfather, and thus distantly related to the King himself.

grasping at what he could in Normandy: rewarding the de Solerses's past loyalty, seeking their continued allegiance, and creating a link between the fidelity of one important castellan, William de Huntingfield, the Norman holdings and influence of the de Solerses and his own flagging authority in Normandy. At this point, in a very real way, the keys to Alice's security if not her release were now in the hands of the de Solerses's continued loyalty to John instead of William de Huntingfield's faithful holding of Dover Castle.

To embrace the idea that Alice was used to connect the de Solerses's Norman holdings to the king, we of course have to examine the de Solers family itself, and in this circumstance, hold a microscope to two generations: William (I) de Solers and his wife Mabel, and their children, particularly William (II) de Solers and Richard. In the mid-twelfth century William (I) de Solers held the manor of Ellingham, Hampshire,[55] along with property in Berkshire.[56] William was married to one Mabel, a daughter of the combined houses of Gloucester and Devon and the heir of her parents Hawise de Redvers and Robert fitzRobert.[57] William (I) and Mabel had at least four children, the eldest Phillipa, the heir William (II), second son Richard and younger daughter Johanna. William (I) died sometime in the 1190s, as Mabel begins appearing in the Pipe Rolls on behalf of one William de Solers, presumably the not-yet-of-age William (II).[58] William (II) was of age by 1199[59] and his younger brother Richard followed shortly thereafter, as he is paying fees for his own properties in England and Normandy in 1200.[60] Richard is in possession of what is probably his main

---

[55]   William Page (ed.), 'Parishes – Ellingham', in *A History of the County of Hampshire: Volume 4*, (1911), accessed 2 February, http://www.british-history.ac.uk/report.aspx?comp id=56882, 563–7.

[56]   Pipe Roll 24 Henry II, 1177/8, hereafter cited as PR [year king, page number]. All Pipe Rolls references are (London: Pipe Roll Society, [various publishers and dates]).

[57]   Bearman, *Charters*, 11.

[58]   The chronology of the death of William (I) and the majority of William (II) is difficult to unpick. The VCH lists William (I) as disseising William de Punchardon of the manor of Ellingham in 1194 and being fined for his 'intrusion' in 1199; however Pipe Rolls from various years of the 1190s lists Mabel de Solers as making payments on behalf of a William de Solers, presumably William (II) in his minority, whilst a quitclaim from 1197 is explicitly in the name of Mabel de Solers and her son William (II) (*Feet of Fines in the Public Record Office of the Seventh and Eighth Years of King Richard I* (London: Pipe Roll Society, 1896), 55–6, no. 76). The exact chronology is not entirely necessary for this research, however, and whilst the two Williams may have been conflated in the historical records at some points in the 1190s, this does not immediately affect the study of Alice de Huntingfield's hostageship.

[59]   *The Memoranda Roll for the Michaelmas Term of the First Year of the Reign of King John (1199–1200)* (London: Pipe Roll Society, 1943), 45.

[60]   PR 2 John, 206.

estate at Faccombe Netherton in Hampshire at this time,[61] and had probably married Alice de Huntingfield by 1204. By Michaelmas 1205, Richard had 'left the service of the king'[62] and fled to Normandy, his lands referred to as the classic '*terra Normannorum*' by the 1207 Close Rolls.[63] Other than outstanding fees and difficulties with the inheritance of his English properties after his death, Richard disappears from historical sight, and we know that he had shuffled off this mortal coil only by mention of William de Huntingfield's petition and payment to the king for the right for Alice's remarriage in 1211.[64]

But with little known of the de Solerses in England other than some of their land base and basic life details, judging the de Solerses in Normandy bears fruit when one wants to see their relative wealth and power in terms of the 'new men' of King John's reign.[65] As C. Warren Hollister has pointed out, the Norman families whose land base was greater in England began to take English toponyms in the mid-twelfth century,[66] so even the name 'de Solers' – based upon their Norman holdings – can give us an indication of the family's strong ties in Normandy. In viewing the de Solerses as a Norman family, several clear reasons emerge as to why Richard might leave the service of the king to risk his future – and that of his wife's – in Normandy.

We have to return to William (I) de Solers, Richard's father, to begin to see the sphere of influence of the family in Normandy. In 1160 a charter announced that William (I) had given the church at Ellingham to the abbey of Saint Sauveur le Vicomte on the Cotentin, and this for the soul of his uncle the earl Richard, probably Richard de Redvers; this document was witnessed by one Jourdan Taisson and confirmed by Henry II within the decade.[67] In 1178 William (I) witnessed a charter of the abbey at Aunay in Calvados, and in 1180/1 another

---

[61] For further details on the de Solerses's tenure at Faccombe Netherton, see Katherine Weikert, 'The Biography of a Place: Faccombe Netherton, Hampshire, ca. 900 – 1200', *Anglo-Norman Studies* 37 (2015): 257–84.

[62] Sir Thomas Duffus Hardy (ed.), *Rotuli Litterarum Clausarum in Turri Londinensi Asservati* (London: G. Ayre and A. Spottiswoode, 1833), 31b. Hereafter CR [year of reign-king, page number].

[63] CR 9 John, 93b.

[64] PR 13 John, 6.

[65] See Ralph V. Turner, *Men raised from the dust: Administrative service and upward mobility in Angevin England*, Middle Ages Series (Philadelphia: University of Pennsylvania Press, 1988).

[66] C. Warren Hollister, 'The Aristocracy', in *The Anarchy of King Stephen's Reign*, ed. Edmund King (Oxford: Clarendon Press, 1994), 44.

[67] J. Horace Round (ed.), 'Anjou: Part 2', in *Calendar of Documents Preserved in France, 918–1206*, (London: Her Majesty's Stationery Office, 1899), 395–420, accessed 28 November 2012, http://www.british-history.ac.uk/cal-state-papers/france/918-1206/, 395–420; Bearman, *Charters*, 187.

from King Henry II to the Hospital of St Jean, Angers.[68] These are all important moments displaying William (I)'s rank in Norman society leading up to his position within the political and diplomatic realm of Normandy. In the 1180s William was the castellan of Moulins and the canton of Bourguebus, fulfilling both a judicial and a military role in the region.[69] What is missing from these listings of the family's basis of authority is the de Solerses's land holdings. This, as yet, has not been discovered through documentary sources. However, the position at Bourguebus reveals an interesting geographic fact: Bourguebus is just shy of two kilometres from the commune of Soliers, itself still in the same canton as Bourguebus. It is a relatively safe bet to say that the de Solers family, called de Soliers in Normandy, probably held this land and others in this area to the immediate south-east of Caen.

So here we have the authority, and possibly the land, of the de Solers family in Normandy. As previously discussed, William (I) died sometime in the 1190s while his heir William (II) was probably in his minority, and in any case we know that in the 1190s the positions in Normandy formerly held by William (I) were held by Guerin de Glapion, a future seneschal of Normandy.[70] This, though, does not mean that the de Solers family had lost their land or potential influence in the area, as King John seemed to favour a 'policy of frequent changes' in the sorts of offices held by William (I) de Solers.[71] Indeed there is an indication that William (II) was still a desirable alliance in Normandy: in 1198, in yet another example of a diplomatic marriage, Ralph Taisson paid 60 livres angevins to King Richard I for the marriage of his sister to William (II) de Solers.[72] Ralph Taisson and his unnamed sister are the children of Jourdan Taisson who earlier witnessed the same charter as William (I) de Solers.[73] By late 1201, Ralph Taisson was the king's seneschal in Normandy,[74] which meant he was at that time an unusually

---

[68]   Round, *Calendar*.

[69]   *Pipe Rolls of the Exchequer of Normandy for the Reign of Henry II 1180 and 1184: Printed from the Originals in the National Archives: Public Record Office and the Archives Nationales, Paris*, vol. 91, ed. Vincent Moss (Publications of the Pipe Roll Society New Series v. 53, 2004); Daniel Power, *The Norman Frontier in the Twelfth and Early Thirteenth Centuries*, Cambridge Studies in Medieval Life and Thought Fourth Series (Cambridge: Cambridge University Press, 2004), 76.

[70]   Power, *The Norman Frontier*, 78.

[71]   Powicke, *The Loss of Normandy*, 173.

[72]   Thomas Stapleton, *Magni rotuli Scaccarii Normanniae sub regibus Angliae*, vol. II, 2 vols. (London: Society of Antiquaries, 1844), lv (hereafter MRSN II [page number]); Power, *The Norman Frontier*, 235.

[73]   MRSN II: lvi, note 2.

[74]   MRSN II: ccxix

close ally of the king.[75] Taisson gave hostages to the king on behalf of the Earl of Chester and acted as seneschal at least as late as the end of May 1203;[76] he vacated this post by late 1203.[77] His lands in England were partially seized by 13 June 1204 and the remainder by the end of September.[78]

Alice, in her position first as hostage to King John followed by wife to Richard de Solers, served as a link between all of these men. Assuming her marriage to de Solers took place before Taisson left the service of the king by mid-1204, Alice's connections with the seneschal of Normandy, her own loyal father at Dover and her hostage-taker the king tied these people together at this precarious time. What is astonishing is how this marriage, this essential and rather contractual transfer of Alice's person from the king to Richard de Solers, shows the political and diplomatic lengths to which John was prepared to go to in order to keep a grasp on his retainers in Normandy. The figure of Alice de Huntingfield represented a link between the faithful East Anglian de Huntingfields, the king, and the influential men of Normandy whom John was desperately trying to keep on his side.

This didn't work. As mentioned before, Taisson as well as Richard de Solers had left the king's service by sometime in 1205. Daniel Power has demonstrated that the Norman baronage of lower ranks pre-1204 had risen to leading roles in Normandy after 1204, and this included Ralph Taisson.[79] It is no surprise then if Richard de Solers's tenuous link to the king via his wife Alice seemed to him less important than his possible fortune in Normandy. His father had previously held some authority near Caen, and his kinsman the former seneschal of Normandy now saw his future there rather than in England, as did Richard's own mother.[80] Richard de Solers sensibly fled for Normandy with Alice in tow. Away from the jurisdiction of the king of England, Richard's marriage contract with its implications of loyalty to the crown was null and unenforceable. Alice may have considered herself finally freed from her hostageship, if not her marriage, by her exile from England.

---

[75]   F.M. Powicke, 'The Angevin Administration of Normandy', *The English Historical Review* 22, no. 85 (1907): 21.

[76]   MRSN II: cclvi, ccxliv

[77]   Powicke, *The Loss of Normandy*, 173.

[78]   T.K. Moore, 'The Loss of Normandy and the Invention of Terre Normannorum, 1204', *The English Historical Review* CXXV, no. 516 (2010): 1071–109.

[79]   Daniel Power, 'L'Établissement du Régime Capétien en Normandie: Structures Royales et Réactions Aristocratiques', in *1204, la Normandie entre Plantagenêts et Capétiens*, ed. Anne-Marie Flambard Héricher, Véronique Gazeau, and Roger Jouet (Caen: Publications du CRAHM, 2007); Moore, 'The Loss of Normandy', 1087.

[80]   Bearman, *Charters*, 146.

From this hurried migration to Normandy by 1205,[81] the facts of Alice's life become slim once again. Richard de Solers's fortune was not made in Normandy, or at least he had little time for that as he was dead by 1211.[82] Alice and Richard had no children, and his sister Johanna was heir to some of his English estates.[83] Without her own kin or family in Normandy, without apparently turning to her well-connected mother-in-law, or even to Ralph Taisson, in whom Richard de Solers had probably placed much hope, Alice returned to England to her father, as it seems most if not all of the de Solerses including William (II) had also fled to Normandy by that time.[84] However, by this point, Alice's father's star was on the rise as itinerant justice on the eastern circuit of the eyre in 1208–09, and sheriff of Norfolk and Suffolk in 1209–10.[85] In 1210 William also sent knights on the king's expedition to Ireland, mentioned above as another moment when the king's reputation for his treatment of hostages had preceded him. In 1211 we know Alice was back in the custody of her father, who was in marriage-making mode; William offered the king 'six beautiful Norwegian hawks' for the remarriage of his daughter and the right to hold her dower lands from Richard de Solers's former properties including Faccombe Netherton, making her a good match.[86] By 1215 Alice was remarried to one Hugh de Rus or Rufus who soon claimed in her name their right to Faccombe Netherton; however, Hugh and Alice were disseised upon the war of John and the barons.[87] This reflects the time and place of 1215: William de Huntingfield had joined the barons' rebellion and was himself disseised by the king in the same year.[88] This, however, is a different story for a different biography, for it is here, with the notice of Alice and Hugh Rufus's loss of claim to Faccombe Netherton, that Alice's historical life draws to a close. She herself is not seen in the historical record after this point.

However, there is an interesting, albeit perhaps coincidental, appendix to Alice's historical life. In March 1216, Isabella, the daughter of Hugh Rufus, was given as hostage to King John in exchange for Hugh's seisin of lands in Norfolk and Suffolk.[89] This too is a reflection of time and place; alongside William de Huntingfield, Rufus seems to have been disseised by December 1215.[90] It is

---

[81]   CR 6 John, 31b.

[82]   PR 13 John, 6.

[83]   PR 9 John, 60.

[84]   Thomas Duffus Hardy, *Rotuli de Oblatis et Finibus in Turri Londinensi asservati tempore Regis Johannis* (London: Eyre, 1835), 333; Page, 'Parishes – Ellingham'; Bearman, *Charters*, 114.

[85]   Turner, 'Huntingfield, William of '.

[86]   PR 13 John, 6.

[87]   CR 16 John.

[88]   Turner, 'Huntingfield, William of '.

[89]   Thomas Duffus Hardy, *Rotuli de Oblatis et Finibus*, 587–8.

[90]   Ibid., 568.

unclear if Isabella was Alice's daughter as well as Hugh's. If the pair were married after 1211 and Isabella was the result of this union, she would have only been four or five at the time of her hostageship in 1216. But regardless if daughter or stepdaughter, Alice saw her kin removed from her in order to once again uphold a pledge to King John. Alice's own experience would have no doubt echoed in her mind in March 1216 as Isabella went off to her own pledge-keeping. Perhaps Alice's experience in 1203–04 was not harsh enough for her to plead to keep Isabella at home; perhaps (unlike Isabella Marshal) Alice did not wield enough influence to try to prevent her husband from agreeing to the hostageship; perhaps the family's position was precarious enough in 1215–16 that there simply was no other option.

So what does this truncated life of Alice de Huntingfield's ultimately mean to us? What does it show us about life as a hostage, wife and widow at the turn of the thirteenth century? It is temptingly easy to view Alice de Solers Rufus née de Huntingfield as nothing but an unimportant pawn, and thrice-over at that: a pawn to her father's ambitions, her king's desperation and her husband's family's manoeuvres. It is impossible to even argue against Alice's consistent use as a pawn to the lower barony throughout the time of the loss of Normandy. But Alice's position as hostage and pawn does not make her life any less valuable or any less important, particularly not in terms of a social history. Alice de Huntingfield existed within the spheres of kings and seneschals and though not herself a politician, baron or royal, her crucial links between several families in the fast-paced months of 1203 and 1204 provides a unique window into the frantic diplomacy in which King John engaged to keep the Norman dukedom from slipping through his fingers. Furthermore, Alice's abbreviated life gives us the opportunity to view (even if at a distance) that rarest of beasts, a female hostage of the high Middle Ages. Alice de Huntingfield may stand for an unknown number of lost lives, women who slip past the historical record and thus the historian's view, and so in seeking to tell her life we seek to restore her life not only to her but any number of other medieval women.[91] We have no way of knowing if her experience was extraordinary or commonplace, but it was certainly real and no theorist's construct. By rescuing this forgotten life we can at least have a glimpse into the complicated existence of a hostage, wife and widow of the Middle Ages.

---

[91] Pauline Stafford, 'Women and the Norman Conquest', *Transactions of the Royal Historical Society (Sixth Series)* 4, no. 1 (1994): 249.

Chapter 2

Writing the Lives of Legal Writers: The Use of Prosopography in Medieval Legal History

Kitrina Bevan

Introduction

When putting together the history of the life of an individual person, the expected outcome of such an endeavour is a biography – but what comes of a similar study which concerns more than one person? In the study of a group of people, is it possible to write a 'group biography'? The answer to that question is a resounding 'yes' and the technical term for this approach to the study of the life, or communal experience, of a group of people is known as prosopography. As a methodology, or more specifically, as an approach to research, prosopography focuses on the links and similarities between individuals within a broader group. In this way, it differs from biography which studies the lives, personal circumstances, motivations and personalities of individuals alone. Instead, prosopographers are interested in the collective experiences of the members of a strictly defined group. Therefore it can be said that where biography is concerned with the extraordinary and unique qualities of the individual, prosopography is concerned with the ordinary and common characteristics of a group of people.

Prosopography has been described as an attempt to bring together bits of biographical data pertaining to the members of a group in order to systematically organise this data so that 'they acquire additional significance by revealing connections and patterns influencing historical processes'.[1] Consequently, this approach is especially useful for the study of medieval legal professionals, about whom we often have very little data and have only slightly more data pertaining to their professions. This chapter aims to introduce historians to the use of prosopography in medieval history in general and legal history in particular by exploring prosopography as an approach to the study of legal professionals

---

[1]   Koenraad Verboven, Myriam Carlier and Jan Dumolyn, 'A Short Manual to the Art of Prosopography', in *Prosopography Approaches and Applications*, ed. K.S.B. Keats-Rohan (Oxford: Prosopographica et Genealogica, 2007), 37.

by focusing on a small group of legal clerks who are underrepresented in the historiography of medieval law – scriveners. In order to do so, a two-pronged approach will be followed. First, this chapter will define and briefly outline the ways in which scholars have used prosopography as a method for historical investigation in the past. The second part of this chapter constitutes a practical application of the prosopographical method in order to show how it can be used as an innovative interdisciplinary research method in the present. The purpose of this is to demonstrate how prosopography can be used in legal history and to reveal some of the ways in which scriveners, or legal writers, expressed their individual and group identities through the written word. In order to tackle some of the underlying questions regarding medieval scriveners and scrivening, this investigation will consider provincial scriveners as a group and how they viewed the importance of their work and how this was reflected in their use of signatures.

Prosopography is a method by which we learn something about the group by collating the information that pertains to individuals within the group as defined by the parameters set by the researcher.[2] Perhaps the most influential definition of prosopography and explanation of the intellectual roots of the method were given by Lawrence Stone in the journal *Daedalus* in which Stone describes prosopography as:

> The investigation of the common background characteristics of a group of actors in history by means of a collective study of their lives. The method employed is to establish a universe to be studied, and then to ask a set of uniform questions – about birth and death, marriage and family, social origins and inherited economic position, place of residence, education, amount and source of personal wealth, occupation, religion, experience of office and so on. The various types of information about the individuals in the universe are then juxtaposed and combined, and are examined for significant variables.[3]

As a multi-purpose tool for tackling difficult historical questions, there are many different applications of prosopography and historians have used it for several decades to extract information about a group from both small and large amounts of data.[4] Stone saw prosopography as a way to approach the structure

---

2   These parameters for the subject population can be self-defining or set by the researcher. This research focuses primarily on a small group of town clerks from within a larger group of legal writers (scriveners) who can certainly be described as members of an identifiable group. The narrow focus of this research is ideal for applying prosopography as a method.

3   Lawrence Stone, 'Prosopography', *Daedalus* 100/1 (1971): 46.

4   In fact, collections of a prosopographical nature have been popular since well before prosopography was a recognised historical method, especially throughout the eighteenth and nineteenth centuries when antiquarians eagerly collected snippets of biographical

of society and the mobility of groups and individuals within it. Initially it was primarily used by political historians who sought to make sense of the political actions of small high-status groups. This is known as the 'elitist school' of prosopography. At the time of Stone's writing in the early 1970s, this tool was beginning to be used by social historians and adapted to suit their purposes by applying prosopographical approaches to larger low-status groups. This is known as the 'mass school' of prosopography. Both schools elicited considerable debate in the historical community throughout the 1970s, as illustrated by T.F. Carney's 1973 article, 'Prosopography: Payoffs and Pitfalls'.[5]

The two schools offer very different perspectives on what constitutes a group and the overall purpose of group biography. Proponents of the first school typically focus on small groups of politically powerful elites and their investigations involve recording meticulously detailed information on the individuals within the groups by considering their genealogy, business interests and political activities.[6] The interpretation of this data is based on a minimal amount of statistical analysis and takes an explicitly political and economical approach to understanding the past. By contrast, proponents of the mass school are more statistically minded and ask broader, less probing questions of their subjects who typically make up larger groups than those dealt with by the elitist school. The mass school takes a sociological approach grounded in a statistical analysis of 'meaningful relationships between environment and ideas, and between ideas and political or religious behaviour'.[7] Fundamentally, the mass school believes that history is determined by popular movements rather than by the great men or elite groups who held the most economic and political power within past societies.[8] No matter the school of thought or the social status of their subjects of study, all prosopographers are similarly concerned with the 'group' rather than individuals. Despite this, there is still an ongoing debate about how prosopography can be used as a 'proper' historical method in other fields of history.

Since Stone wrote his article defining these schools of thought, other scholars have relied upon his interpretation in order to situate their own work. Most recently, Katherine Keats-Rohan has described the field and the variety of

---

information found in their researches. For varieties of approaches to prosopography, see: K.S.B. Keats-Rohan, 'Introduction: Chameleon or Chimera? Understanding Prosopography', in *Prosopography Approaches and Applications*, ed. K.S.B. Keats-Rohan (Oxford: Prosopographica et Genealogica, 2007), 1–32. For the historiography of prosopography, see: Lawrence Stone, 'Prosopography', 46–79.

[5]   T.F. Carney, 'Prosopography: Payoffs and Pitfalls'. *Phoenix* 27/2 (1973): 156–79.

[6]   See: Charles A. Beard, *An Economic Interpretation of the Constitution of the United States* (New York: Macmillan, 1913).

[7]   Lawrence Stone, 'Prosopography', 48.

[8]   Ibid.

perspectives found within it, concluding that 'prosopography is in this sense a plural rather than a singular beast so attempts at definition are necessarily more descriptive than prescriptive.'[9] She focuses instead upon two points which she argues need continual emphasis:

> First, the chief value of prosopography is that it is a uniquely source-critical historical method; secondly, prosopography demands tireless attention to detail, whether in the study of the sources, the composition of databases, or the meticulous documentation of decisions made in the construction of the project and its database and in their later evolution.[10]

Not all approaches to prosopography are so strict or scientific and it can, in fact, be a considerably flexible method for historical research. In fact, prosopography can easily be adapted as one component of a mixed methodological approach to a research question and does not have to be the only method employed in an investigation. The work presented in this chapter, for example, cannot be situated wholly within either of the two main schools of prosopographic thought. Instead, prosopography will be used in order to reveal the professional identity of provincial scriveners and to begin to answer some basic questions regarding the way some individuals within this group perceived themselves as scribes and how they expressed this through the written word.[11]

---

[9]   K.S.B. Keats-Rohan, 'Introduction: Chameleon or Chimera? Understanding Prosopography', in *Prosopography Approaches and Applications*, ed. K.S.B. Keats-Rohan (Oxford: Prosopographica et Genealogica, 2007), 20.

[10]   Ibid., 26.

[11]   Other researchers have approached the study of scriveners from biographical perspectives. Scholars such as H.G. Richardson, I.D.O. Arnold, John Baker and Graham Pollard have made very valuable contributions to the literature on scriveners through their work on business teachers, town clerks, scriveners and scribes. However, these are either studies of individual scriveners (as in the case of Richardson) or 'prosopographies' loosely defined (as in the case of Pollard's article which is more a list of mini-biographies which follows the *Dictionary of National Biography* format by prioritising the collection of data over its analysis). See: H.G. Richardson, 'Business Training in Medieval Oxford', *The American Historical Review* 46/2 (1941); H.G. Richardson, 'An Oxford Teacher of the Fifteenth Century', *Bulletin of the John Rylands Library* 23/2 (1939); J.H. Baker, 'The Attorneys and Officers of the Common Law in 1480', *The Journal of Legal History* 1/2 (1980); Graham Pollard, 'The Medieval Town Clerks of Oxford', *Oxoniensia* 31 (1966).

Application

The first step in approaching a prosopography of scriveners is to define the group in question. Scriveners were a group of specialists that existed as a subsection of two different groups which often overlapped – clerks and legal professionals. Historians have called this motley group of writers by a variety of names in an attempt to categorise them, but what sets scriveners apart from clerks in general is the nature of the work they did and the specialised skills that they brought to their craft. No matter the appellation, the work that they did was scrivening – that is to say that they read and wrote and performed secretarial and administrative duties that traditionally included composing legal instruments. The history of provincial scriveners is a largely under-explored territory and prosopography is a useful tool for investigating this group of legal writers. The greatest impediment to studying the members of this group is the dearth of secondary source material available on the lower reaches of the legal profession in general and on legal writers in particular. Until relatively recently, the existing historiography on the subject of medieval English scrivening has focused overwhelmingly on the model provided by the Scriveners' Company of London, its members and the craft regulations enshrined in the guild's *Common Paper*.[12] In contrast, provincial scriveners have attracted only modest passing attention from a small number of historians whose work has positioned English notaries as the primary concern.[13] Overall, these studies reflect an inconsistent approach to the criteria applied to scriveners when attempting to define them or to identify them as a group. Consequently, it can be difficult to ascertain whether or not scriveners are in fact

---

[12]   Francis W. Steer (ed.), *Scriveners' Company Common Paper 1357–1628* (London: London Record Society, 1968).

[13]   To date, the majority of the literature available that pertains to medieval scriveners working as legal professionals has been produced by Timothy Haskett, Christopher Cheney and Nigel Ramsay. See: Timothy S. Haskett, 'Country Lawyers? The Composers of English Chancery Bills', in *The Life of the Law: Proceedings of the Tenth British Legal History Conference*, ed. P. Birks (London: Hambledon, 1993); Timothy S. Haskett, 'The Presentation of Cases in Medieval Chancery Bills', in *Legal History in the Making*, ed. William Gordon (London: Hambledon Press, 1991); C.R. Cheney, *Notaries Public in England in the Thirteenth and Fourteenth Centuries* (Oxford: Clarendon Press, 1972); Nigel Ramsay, 'The History of the Notary in England', in *Handbuch zur Geschichte des Notariats der Europäischen Traditionen*, eds Mathias Schmoeckel and Werner Schubert (Baden-Baden: Nomos, 2009); Nigel Ramsay, 'Scriveners and Notaries as Legal Intermediaries in Later Medieval England' in *Enterprise and Individuals in Fifteenth-Century England*, ed. Jennifer Kermode (Gloucester: Alan Sutton, 1991).

the subject of study since historians do not universally connect this term with the type of legal work that was characteristic of these writers.[14]

This present study will focus on one narrow aspect of scrivening – the act of scribal identification – in order to demonstrate some of the varied ways in which provincial English scriveners expressed their belonging to this group in the fourteenth and fifteenth centuries. This study redefines the term 'scrivener' in accordance with the work that they produced and the scribal activities in which they participated. This work-based perspective serves to expand rather than limit the definition of scrivener to apply equally to those individuals who self-identified as scriveners and to those who were identified as scriveners in either documentary sources or existing literature.[15] It also adds to the analysis of scriveners by including individuals who do not fit into either of the aforementioned groups of traditionally identified scriveners. According to this broader definition of scriveners based on their actions rather than on arbitrary labels, scriveners can be considered to be a larger sub-group of legal professionals that incorporates certain types of scribes working at all levels of the legal profession and in various public offices, such as the office of town clerk. Following this approach, finding evidence of the scriveners' work in the form of legal instruments is the first step in identifying them.

Despite their obvious utility as clerks fluent in the law, historically scriveners have suffered in both the estimation of their peers and that of historians. Rarely is a scrivener glorified or exalted in any work of literature that addresses the man with the quill. Instead, his mistakes are exaggerated and his skills derided and degraded. Quotes found in popular works of medieval English literature have undoubtedly contributed to the negative perception of the scrivener and his abilities as a writer. From John Lydgate's *Poems*, the reader is led to believe that a scrivener was no more than an automaton or amanuensis when the poet writes:

> As doth a skryuener
> That can no more what that he shal write
> But as his maister beside both endyte.[16]

---

[14]   As a result, the literature that exists which pertains to scrivening sometimes never mentions the word scrivener at all. Whether this has been done intentionally to avoid delving into the question of provincial scriveners when they are not the focus of the historians' studies or merely reflects an oversight in terminology on the part of non-specialists, the result is the same as scriveners continue to be overlooked.

[15]   In his article examining the increase in lawyers acting as members of parliament, S.J. Payling redefines the term 'lawyer' in order to justify the inclusion of town clerks in his study of the legal element at work in the House of Commons in the later medieval period. See: S.J. Payling, 'The Rise of Lawyers in the Lower House, 1395–1536', *Parliamentary History* 23/1 (2004), 104.

[16]   J. Norton-Smith (ed.), *John Lydgate: Poems* (Oxford: Clarendon, 1966), 52.

Even Geoffrey Chaucer highlights only his scrivener's failings in his *Wordes unto Adam, His Owne Scriveyn*:

> Under thy long lokkes thou most have the scale
> But after my making thou wryte more trewe,
> So ofte a-daye I mot thy werk renewe,
> It to correct and eek to rubbe and scrape,
> And al is thorugh thy negligence and rape.[17]

Contrary to Chaucer's chiding tone, evidence points to the opposite being true as we know that his scribe, Adam Pinkhurst, cannot by any means have been considered an incompetent clerk, or a simple copyist. Instead he was a professional scrivener and a member of the Scrivener's Company which was the official body of organised legal writers in the City of London. In fact, it was the presence of Pinkhurst's signature on the register of the Scrivener's Company (called the *Common Paper*) that made it possible for Linne Mooney to match his 'hand', or style of handwriting, to that of 'Scribe B' who not only copied Chaucer's manuscripts but Gower's as well and until Mooney's 2004 discovery had been an anonymous clerk.[18]

By coupling Mooney's palaeographic approach to scribal hands with a prosopographic approach to studying scriveners as a group, these legal writers can be identified from among the large body of lay clerks working in provincial England in the medieval period. Prosopography depends upon a solid foundation of available sources in order to guarantee success, or as Maryanne Kowaleski stated: 'the success of the prosopographical method rests largely on the quality of the sources employed to identify individuals. For the medievalist, the survival rate of documentation and the type of information offered are the most important determinants of source quality'.[19] Thus it is through a source-based biographical investigation that the accomplishments of scriveners as a whole can be understood and the documents the group produced can be interpreted.[20] Evidence found in their own written work shows us how scriveners were conscious of their place within the body of lay clerks and within the administrative offices of local government as town clerks. The clearest indication of this can be found in the instances in which the scribe of a legal instrument

---

[17]   F.N. Robinson (ed.), *The Works of Geoffrey Chaucer* (Oxford: Oxford University Press, 1957), 534 (modified punctuation).

[18]   Linne Mooney, 'Chaucer's Scribe', *Speculum* 81 (2006), 97–138; John Ezard, 'The Scrivener's Tale: How Chaucer's Sloppy Copyist Was Unmasked after 600 Years', *The Guardian*, 2004.

[19]   Maryanne Kowaleski, *Local Markets and Regional Trade in Medieval Exeter* (Cambridge: Cambridge University Press, 1995), 335–6.

[20]   Lawrence Stone, 'Prosopography', 53.

directly identifies himself as either a clerk or as the town's clerk. Signatures are a hallmark of identity and they can appear in different ways. In this chapter only the most straightforward form will be considered, that is to say only the self-reflexive signatures used as a means of identifying oneself as the writer, scribe or clerk of a document will be examined here.[21]

The most readily identifiable examples of self-reflexive signatures can be found in the closing clauses of legal documents in which the names of the witnesses and the date and place of writing were given as a matter of convention. This is also the place where the author highlights his role in the writing or composition of the text by saying that it was made by him. Examples of this are numerous and most are simple statements, such as 'this deed was made by Henry, clerk'. Other scriveners were more explicit in their use of reflexive signatures and identify themselves as writers or scribes.[22] The use of the terms 'scriveyn', 'scryvenere' or 'escrivain' as a means of both self-identification and external identification with the trade of legal writers begins to appear with some frequency in London from the end of the fourteenth century, corresponding with the establishment of the scriveners' guild, but it is very rarely used outside the city. Instead, in provincial England scriveners were much more likely to identify themselves as clerks, scribes, writers or as town clerks if they held that office.

Medieval scriveners also identified themselves through another type of signature – the autograph. The autograph signature appears in the form of initials or surnames placed outside of the body of the text and it is usually used in addition to the scribe's name as it appears in the case of attested documents like deeds. One of Bridgwater's town clerks was an early adherent of this method. John Kedwelly was active as a clerk in Bridgwater, Somerset, from October 1383 until around 1420. Between the years 1383 and 1404, a large number of local deeds were witnessed by him in his capacity as the town's clerk. Fascinatingly, from 1396 John Kedwelly's documents began to bear his surname separately from the list of witnesses in addition to his full name.[23] From this date, 'Kedwelly' began to appear as an autograph situated within the text box

---

[21]   It is perhaps worth mentioning that later medieval society did not put the same value on personal signatures as modern society does today. While signatures were not unheard of in England in this period, they appeared relatively infrequently in the years leading up to the mid-fourteenth century. The convention of signing a letter which is now a universal standard was not established until the late tenth century and even then these signatures were most often added by the scribe on behalf of the signatories rather than written in the signatories' own hands. See: Lawrence J. McCrank, 'Documenting Reconquest and Reform: The Growth of Archives in the Medieval Crown of Aragon', *The American Archivist* 56/2 (1993), 263.

[22]   For example, in a grant Godfrey de Sowy called himself 'Godfrey, clerk and scribe'. Exeter, Devon Record Office ED/M/81 [1253–54].

[23]   The earliest example of this is found in The National Archives: Public Record Office WARD 2/57A/204/5 [24 August 1396] (hereafter abbreviated as TNA: PRO).

and just touching the edge of the right margin at the bottom of his deeds, along with a series of signature flourishes placed under his autograph. This sudden tendency to sign his name to his deeds leaves little doubt that these documents were written in Kedwelly's own hand as the signed conveyances demonstrate palaeographic parallels with his earlier, non-autographed, deeds.[24] The presence of this autograph does raise the question of why Kedwelly's practices shifted at this time. Had he merely become comfortable in his position and felt like he could sign his name if he wanted to or was this part of a more general and ongoing shift towards autographs and self-identification within the community of fourteenth-century scriveners and town clerks?

The signatures of clerks can also be found among the upper echelons of government clerks from at least as early as the later thirteenth century when chancery clerks began to write their surnames in the corner of their writs. This could indicate that they were influenced by the legal text *Fleta* which instructed writers of writs to sign their instruments as a form of best practice or that *Fleta*'s instruction was a reflection of pre-existing scribal procedure in Chancery.[25] As early as 1326 the Exchequer had begun to request that the names of the auditors of its accounts be listed, without requiring that these names be written in the auditors' own hands.[26] Throughout the fourteenth century, clerks of both the Chancery and the Privy Seal regularly added their names to warrants and other legal instruments; whether this was done as a result of external influences such as treatises like *Fleta* or if this was done spontaneously and of the clerks' own accord may never be known.[27] It does seem as though there was a general movement towards scribal autograph signatures on the instruments produced by scriveners in the fourteenth century. If this is true then Kedwelly may have

---

[24] Some of Kedwelly's earlier, unsigned deeds are TNA: PRO WARD 2/57A/204/65 [6 January 1384]; TNA: PRO WARD 2/57A/204/2 [17 April 1385]; TNA: PRO WARD 2/57A/204/37 [6 November 1385]; TNA: PRO WARD 2/57A/204/14 [1 March 1390]; TNA: PRO WARD 2/57A/204/15 [29 February 1390] and TNA: PRO WARD 2/57A/204/90 [3 October 1390].

[25] M.T. Clanchy, *From Memory to Written Record: England 1066–1307* (2nd edn; Oxford: Blackwell, 1993), 306; H.G. Richardson and G.O. Sayles (eds), *Fleta*, 4 vols. (2; London: Bernard Quaritch, 1955), 126, Ch. 113.

[26] Hilary Jenkinson, 'On Autographs', *History* 8/30 (1923), 104.

[27] Ibid. Yet another example of the use of signatures at the top of the secretarial ladder can be found on the Parliament Roll for the parliament held at Westminster, 13 January 1489–27 February 1490. This roll bears the signature of parliament's clerk, John Morgan. Although the text itself was written by several scribes, Morgan's signature is accompanied by an explicit statement that it was he who had examined the roll. See *Parliament Rolls of Medieval England*, 'Introduction 1489', signature Hen VII, 1485 November, Membrane 47, see also A. Luders et al. (eds), *Statutes of the Realm (1377–1504)* (2; London: Record Commissioners, 1816), 505–6 (c. viii).

been perpetuating what he saw in documents produced by central government clerks, or perhaps he was familiar with the Scriveners' Company's ordinances and professional practices which directed its members to sign their instruments.[28]

In the fourteenth century, Bristol's town clerks began to sign their instruments with increasing regularity and from the fifteenth century we have several examples of them signing their names or otherwise identifying themselves in their work which suggests that this may have been an internal policy or convention within the city's secretariat. One of the earliest of Bristol's town clerks to engage in this practice was John Bolton who held this post from 1418 until 1432. Bolton's own unique form of signature appears in the chirographs that he made from at least as early as 1420 and continued until as late as 1439. Chirographs were used primarily for legal agreements, like deeds, that were made between two parties and became more commonly known as 'indentures' in the later medieval period. This term, 'indenture', is in reference to the indented or tooth-like appearance of the jagged, wavy or otherwise irregular cut which was a defining characteristic of this type of document. This cut was made in order to divide a single sheet of parchment containing two copies of an agreement into two separate sheets. One copy was then given to each of the two parties involved in the transaction. Another type of chirograph could be made by making a tripartite indenture. This third copy of the chirograph was made near the bottom, or the 'foot' of the parchment where the other two copies of the agreement, or 'fine', appeared and hence is the origin of the term 'feet of fines'. Before the single sheet was divided into its parts, the scrivener would write a word, phrase or a combination of letters in the blank spaces between the copies. The indenture, or cut, was then made through this lettering thus protecting against forgery and allowing for a

---

[28]   There is also another possible explanation for the increase in the sudden appearances of autographs and signatures in the fourteenth century. We know that scriveners learned their trade by being apprenticed to a master, although direct evidence of this is patchy outside of the Scriveners' Company. In cases when the same autograph is appended to documents written in different hands, it raises the possibility that this is a physical reflection and evidence of the apprentice-master relationship. It is possible that a master scrivener might have put his name to the work of a sub clerk, perhaps as a means of affixing his stamp of approval on, or indicate his verification of, the quality and accuracy of a subordinate's work. One rather curious example can be found on an award of writ of seisin and return in the Bristol Record Office which is signed quite elaborately with the name 'Caryll' – despite the fact that no one with that name appears anywhere within the content of the document. See: Bristol, Bristol Record Office P.St P & J/D/15/d [30 October 1499] (abbreviated hereafter as BRO). This could be a relatively rare indication of apprenticeship within the town clerk's office as well. John Kedwelly, for example, employed at least two apprentices during his career as town clerk.

straightforward means of identification and authentication of the constituent parts if and when they were ever brought together again.[29]

As has been demonstrated, autograph signatures were increasingly common in certain scribal circles but were still relatively rare on documents in general in this period. Autographic convention, however, was no obstacle for John Bolton of Bristol who managed to integrate his autograph into the indenture of his chirographs. Commonly, the text that was severed when chirographs were cut was often simply the word 'C I R O G R A P H U M' or letters from the alphabet, 'A B C D E' or a phrase like 'A V E M A R I A' or any other word, acronym or phrase of the scribe's choosing. Less predictably, but much more interestingly, John Bolton used his own surname for the text in the space between the chirographs, writing 'B O L T O N' in large block letters which he then cut with a wavy indent. The majority of the examples of this date from the 1420s and there are two complete sets of Bolton's chirographs that still survive in the Bristol Record Office. The first is the lease and counterpart of an agreement made between Thomas Stamford and Thomas and Agnes Filour in 1422; the second is also a lease and a counterpart detailing the terms of payment and renovation of a High Street messuage and cellar in 1425.[30] Other examples of Bolton's signed chirographs exist, however they are missing their counterparts, which is unfortunate, but is also to be expected from the traditional two-part chirograph as each party kept a hold of their copy, and without good reason the two parts would never again be reunited.[31] Somewhat curiously, Bolton does not sign any of his other instruments. Despite his apparent preference for leaving his mark on chirographs, there can be no mistaking that it is his holograph hand that appears in both his 'signed' chirographs and his unsigned works.[32]

---

[29] Along with oral testimony of the witnesses to the agreement and the seals affixed to each chirograph, it was possible to test the validity of this type of document in three ways. First, there was the oral evidence of the witnesses who were present when the chirograph was made (or were present when they heard the agreement read aloud); second, the presence of at least two visual cues to test the validity of the document in the form of the shape of the indented cut and the accuracy of the seals. These visual cues were made by legally and linguistically literate scribes in a way that could easily be interpreted by illiterate people without the immediate need for intermediaries or interpreters to read the contents of the chirograph.

[30] BRO P. AS/D/NA/40 a & b [1422]; BRO P. AS/D/NA/42 a & b [1425]

[31] These are BRO P. St J/F/28/24 [1420]; P. St J/F/28/26 [1420]; AC/D/6/48 [1439]. Of these, the letters used in the latter two are more difficult to discern; however the shape and number of the letters do seem to match the examples above and positively indicate that Bolton has used his signature in the indentures.

[32] See for example, BRO P. St MP/D/8 [9 May 1422] and BRO P.AS/D/BS/B/3 [1437]

As Bristol's town clerk, John Bolton's name and hand were not only recognisable, and therefore traceable and verifiable, but they also carried an additional element of authority by virtue of Bolton's position. This is demonstrated in a memorandum found in one of the city's custumals, called *The Little Red Book of Bristol.* It is a brief note recording the date of the death and burial of Enmota Chilcombe, written by John Bolton himself. This fact is recorded by John Bolton as he tells us (in the third person) that he wrote the note in his own hand, (*'manu sua propria scripsit'*) at the prayer and request (*'ad instanciam et rogatum'*) of the Prioress and sisters of St Mary Magdalen and of John Haddon, vintner.[33] This note tells us at least one of two things: either the interested parties listed in the memorandum believed in the authorial power and significance of Bolton's hand which is why they asked him to write it, or it tells us that John Bolton believed in his own hand so much that he felt it was appropriate to promote it in this way. Evidence suggests that there is an element of truth in each of these possibilities. Judging by Bolton's use of his surname in his chirographs, it is clear that he was adept at self-identification and self-promotion, however this does not mean that Bolton was undeserving of the plaudits. References to Bolton in the wills of prominent burgesses show that he oversaw the execution of the wills of Thomas Pappeworth (proved in 1425) and James Cokkes (proved in 1427).[34] Overseers of wills were people who were especially trusted by the testator and who were given the task of overseeing the performance of the executors and checking that they did their jobs with due diligence. As a reward for fulfilling this role, Bolton was given 20s from Pappeworth's estate and Cokkes left Bolton a legacy.

The autograph of another of Bristol's town clerks frequently appears on several mid-fifteenth-century manuscripts in the Bristol Record Office. While Thomas Oseney was town clerk (fl. 1458–c. 1478), he not only wrote wills (like that of John Brown, baker and burgess) and witnessed the making of wills,[35] but also proved them in the borough court and granted them probate.[36] Like John Kedwelly and John Bolton, Oseney signed some but not all of the instruments that he wrote.[37]

---

[33]   Francis B. Bickley (ed.), *The Little Red Book of Bristol,* 2 vols. (1; Bristol: W. Crofton Hemmons, 1900), 2.

[34]   T.P. Wadley, *Notes or Abstracts of the Wills Contained in the Volume Entitled the Great Orphan Book and Book of Wills* (Bristol: Bristol and Gloucestershire Society, 1886), 111–12, 112–14.

[35]   Ibid., 161.

[36]   Ibid., 148–9, 153, 161. Like Bolton, Oseney was also a man whom testators remembered in their wills: in 1474 he received 'three yards of scarlet cloth, and forty shillings in ready money' from William Coder, burgess and merchant of Bristol and in the following year a merchant named William Hoton left Oseney a legacy of an unknown amount. Ibid., 149–50, 155–6.

[37]   Such as: BRO P. St T/D/311, 312, 313 and BRO 5163/161 [all written in 1456].

However, he began to do so with regularity from January 1457, perhaps in an effort to distinguish himself from his predecessor, John Joce (fl. *c.* 1449–1457), who may have trained Oseney in his clerical office. It is possible that Oseney acquired his habit of adding his name to his instruments from Joce who can also be found occasionally signing his instruments in precisely the same place where Oseney left his mark.[38] Oseney's signature is always found on the right hand side of the document and is almost always hidden under the fold of the seal flap along the bottom of the parchment, with few exceptions.[39] This indicates that the signature was placed there before the parchment was folded and the seals were attached, thus suggesting that the mark was not meant to be immediately noticeable but that much like Bolton's name in a chirograph cut it could be used as an authoritative mark to validate the authorship of the document if necessary.[40]

At first glance this may seem to be a stylistic device or perhaps a purely practical one; a means by which the seal tag could be more securely attached through reinforcing the parchment to reduce the likelihood of the seal(s) being

---

[38] An example of this can be found in a deed appointing the first chaplain of Halleway's chantry in the parish of All Saints in Bristol, which Joce signs with his surname in a similar style to Oseney's: BRO P. AS/D/CS/A/24 [1453]

[39] Examples where the signature is not hidden: BRO 5163/222 [28 October 1471]; BRO 5163/170 [28 December 1461]; BRO 5163/164 [20 February 1457]

[40] The placement of this signature tells us something else. The conventions for the formalisation of legal documents and their authentication (through the use of seals) flourished in the twelfth and thirteenth centuries as increasing amounts of information were recorded in writing, making sealed deeds more common and widespread. Affixing one's seal to a deed was as punctilious and ceremonious a gesture as the act of adding one's signature to a legal document is today. Furthermore, it is a physical marker of a perceivable shift in society from relying on parties to honour oral agreements to a move towards a greater dependence upon the physical presence of a written record, sealed by the parties' own matrices for evidence. From the presence of signatures on documents, it seems that seals were not the only means by which the makers of deeds ensured the security of their work; the position of the text on the parchment could also prevent tampering. By using stock phrases such as '*Sciant presentes et futuri quod me AB dedi, concessi et hac presenti carta mea confirmavi CD ...* ' (in gifts) and distinguishing the first line from subsequent lines (say by elongating the ascenders) scribes could protect their deeds from other unscrupulous clerks who might try to insert additional information into the beginning clauses. Furthermore, the content of deeds almost invariably ends with the list of witnesses (sometimes with '*et multi aliis*' added after the last name) and a dating clause as an indication that the text of the instrument was complete. Sometimes the scribe stretched out the text so that it reached the right margin, sometimes the scribe added a flourish after the phrase in order to reach the margin, thus ensuring the justification of the text in a solid block format and preventing anything from being added to the end of the deed and its closing clauses. The scribe's last act before sealing the document was to fold the bottom of the parchment up and make horizontal knife cuts through the two layers of parchment, into which the seal tags would be inserted.

accidentally torn off and thus invalidating the deed. This fold served another purpose as well. By folding the bottom of the sheet up to the last line of the text, the scribe added another guarantee that no addenda could be added to his instrument. Chirographs were yet another way of preventing tampering when multiple copies of the same deed were made, as the uniqueness of each cut was very difficult to copy. And of course, the scrivener's writing itself prevented against forgery. Whereas the parties to an agreement relied upon their seals to act as the authentication and identification, the individuality of the scribe's own hand was his signature and it was present on every line in every word and in each and every letter that appeared on the page. As a person's handwriting is unique to the individual, explicitly identifying the owner of the hand on the instrument itself must have acted as a further precaution against counterfeiting. Taken together with these other fail-safes, the use of scribal autograph signatures indicates that the fifteenth century witnessed the arrival of a period of additional security measures for the authentication of legal instruments composed by English scriveners.

An individual's autograph signature, much like an individual's handwriting, can be seen to have evolved over time. This can be demonstrated in examples of Thomas Oseney's signature which appear on various types of witnessed legal instruments between 1457 and 1471. His signature first appears in January 1457 and from the following month Oseney's signature is applied universally to his writings. In its earliest incarnation, Oseney's name is spelled 'Oseney', however by November 1457 Oseney's name is spelled with a double 's', resulting in 'Osseney'.[41] This change in spelling occurs despite the continuity in the spelling of 'Thomas Oseney', as a witness, made with a single 's'. These two spellings are used interchangeably between 1454 and 1471 in deeds that appear to all have been written in a single scribe's hand. Notably, the mark, or flourish, found beneath the signature remains consistent no matter the variation in spelling.[42] The fact that Oseney varied the way he wrote his own name does not indicate that it was not actually written by him. To the contrary, the variation in Oseney's spelling of his own name was not unusual as a plethora of alternate spellings of various words could be found written by the same person. Michael Clanchy identifies Louis, clerk of Rockingham, as an example of a scribe who varied the way he wrote his own name in order to argue that, in opposition to the authoritative act of using seals and witnesses to authenticate documents, 'the idea of a distinctive signature was unfamiliar in England'.[43]

---

[41]   In the beginning of the year only one 's' is used: BRO 5163/162 [20 January 1457], BRO 5163/164 [20 February 1457] and BRO 5163/165 [20 February 1457]. The earliest surviving record of an 'ss' spelling is found in BRO 5163/166 [25 November 1457].

[42]   In comparing the signatures found on BRO 5163/165, 5163/166, 5163/167, 5163/169 and 5163/222, there is continuity in the wavy flourish mark present beneath the autograph which is not present in either 5163/170 or 5163/162.

[43]   M.T. Clanchy, *From Memory to Written Record: England 1066–1307*, 128.

While this statement is true to an extent, by the end of the fourteenth century signatures appear with greater frequency and seem to carry greater currency than they did in King John's time when Louis the clerk was adding the phrase 'who wrote this charter' to his signature. Nonetheless, it is true that unlike modern orthographers, uniformity in style and spelling was not the aim of the medieval clerk. However, as a skilled scribe, Oseney had a range of scripts at his disposal and as a result a wide variety of styles could be written by the same man which could be easily mistaken for a multiplicity of hands. Writing masters' books which survive from the medieval period display the range of scripts that could be employed by a single scribe, so we cannot rely upon the discrepancies present within the variety of scripts as evidence of the presence of a variety of hands in a body of documents, especially when they have more points in common than they have points of difference.[44] His expertise in writing using a wide range of scripts might explain why it appears as though Oseney spelled his autograph signature in two different ways, when in reality what this reflects is the variations in Oseney's own writing style. Consequently, a single scribe could easily be responsible for writing in more than one 'hand'.

Thomas Oseney is only one scrivener, however even the relatively small corpus of his surviving instruments is able to raise questions regarding authorship, apprenticeship and scribal practice that are intriguing and worthy of further study. While it is true that only a small number of documents were signed by their authors, it is wrong to conclude from this that manuscript cultures were anonymous and lacking the hallmarks of individuality.[45] In the thirteenth century, the unique quality of clerks' hands was officially recognised in English law. The Statute of Acton Burnell (1283) provided for the protection of creditors

---

[44] S.J.P. Van Dijk, 'An Advertisement Sheet of an Early 14th-Century Writing Master at Oxford', *Scriptorium* 10 (1956). See also the commonplace book put together by Humphrey Newton: Deborah Youngs, *Humphrey Newton (1466–1536) an Early Tudor Gentleman* (Woodbridge: Boydell, 2008).

[45] This statement was made by Hodson in his 1974 article: J.H. Hodson, 'Medieval Charters: The Last Witness', *Journal of the Society of Archivists* 5/2 (1974), 71. It is repeated by Clanchy who supports Hodson's conviction that only a small minority of the scribes of English charters identified themselves through either the use of signatures or by identifying themselves as the writers of their instruments in the closing clauses of their documents. This thesis needs updating in order to take the scribal practices of the later medieval period into account. Clanchy's book is undoubtedly a seminal work in the field of early medieval English literacy, however we must remember that it covered only the first 241 years following the Norman Conquest. As of yet, no one has continued where Clanchy left off, despite the fact that the latter years in the later medieval period deserve equally detailed attention. At page 89, Hodson ends his article with the hope that by identifying the hands and names of local scribes we might 'reach a fuller and richer knowledge and understanding of [their] varied activities'. See also: M.T. Clanchy, *From Memory to Written Record: England 1066–1307*, 304–8.

by the enrolment of debts in London, York, Bristol, Lincoln, Winchester and Shrewsbury.[46] The statute considered the individuality of clerk's hands to be an essential element for validating the authenticity of the debts enrolled which in turn gave these documents greater authority and validity. In order to recover a merchant's debt, the statute specifically required the debtor to appear before the mayor of the statute merchant and his clerk to acknowledge the debt and the terms of its repayment. It was the clerk who was responsible for entering the recognisance onto a roll in his own hand, 'which shall be known', and likewise for making 'with his own hand a bill obligatory'.[47] Evidence of a fairly literal interpretation of the statute's instruction can be found in the dating clauses of some recognisances which give not only the name of the staple town and the date of the agreement but also clearly state that the document was written in the hand of the clerk of the staple.[48] Therefore, it was the recognisability of the clerk's hand alongside the debtor's seal and the seal of the statute merchant or staple that authenticated the debt and facilitated its speedy recovery in case of default. In this way, the writers of these instruments used their handwriting as their signatures.

This limited study of scriveners' writing has demonstrated the willingness of some scriveners to identify themselves as the authors of deeds, wills and other legal instruments. To what extent does this challenge the notion of provincial scriveners as an anonymous group of scribes? Evidence found in their own written work demonstrates a tendency towards self-expressions of scribal identity that suggests more than a simple practical desire to reflect authorship. It would be remiss to discuss signatures without addressing a statement made by Michael Clanchy in which he posited that 'English scribes were not required to identify themselves, [and] not [required] to put their *signa* on the documents they wrote, because writers were of little significance'.[49] Whether or not Clanchy said this in order to be controversial is not going to be debated here. What is

---

[46] The New Ordinances, 5 Edw. II (1311), *c.* 33 expanded the number of staple towns to include Newcastle-upon-Tyne, Nottingham, Exeter, Southampton, Northampton and Canterbury. See: A. Luders et al. (eds), *Statutes of the Realm (1235–1377)* (1; London: Record Commissioners, 1810), 53–4, 98–100, 165.

[47] ' ... enroulee de la main le avaundit clerk qi serra conue. E estre ceo lavaundit clerk face de sa main le escrit de obligation ... ' Owen Ruffhead (ed.), *The Statutes at Large: From Magna Charta to the End of the Last Parliament, 1761* 8 vols. (1; London: Mark Baskett, 1763), 76.

[48] A typical example of this is found in the dating clause of BRO P. AS/D/NA/11 which states that the recognisance was made in 'Bristoll', by the hand of John Bathe, Mayor, and John Woderoue, Clerk, 8 April 44 Edward III' [1370]. Another example is BRO 5163/111 which was made 'by the hand of William Derby, mayor, and John Woderoue, clerk' [21 Feb 1381].

[49] M.T. Clanchy, *From Memory to Written Record: England 1066–1307*, 308.

clear, however, is that based on the evidence gathered above, writers, the ability to write and the uniqueness of an individual scribe's hand all mattered as they carried a certain currency within the sphere of legal documentary production in medieval England.

Conclusions

The goal of this chapter was first to provide insight into how prosopography can fruitfully be used as a method of approaching a group biography of scriveners and second, in conjunction with the other studies offered in this collection, to demonstrate how relevant and insightful interdisciplinary biographical studies can truly be. The purpose of taking a brief look at the instances of self-identification of a small number of clerks in their written work has been to challenge the myth of the humble clerk through an examination of some of their legal instruments. Turning to the legal and administrative products of provincial scriveners and asking these sources to reveal something about their authors' professional identities and sense of self is clearly an effective methodology and from a biographical, social history viewpoint, it is clear that there is much for us to learn about legal writers from the very documents that they produced.

In fact, scriveners may very well have told us more about themselves through the writing that they did for others than we ever could have hoped to learn from what was written about them by third parties. These individuals exercised their voices through the medium with which they identified themselves – as writers, they spoke through their writings and the written word represented their presence and authority. In doing so, these individuals consciously, and perhaps subconsciously, chose to present themselves as individuals, as practitioners of a skilled craft and as invaluable members of their local government administrations through the indelible personal marks they left in their written work. As individuals with their own personalities, drivers, motivations and ambitions, all the clerks examined in this study were absolutely conscious that what they wrote would be around for a long time, conceivably forever. Consequently, one can never be too critical of these sources, who wrote them and what they said. The fact that we have more and more evidence of their self-reflections and an increasing number of signatures as the medieval period progressed also suggests that as town clerks, scriveners gained confidence in their positions over time and therefore readily asserted their authority through their association with this role.

As part of a combined methodology, prosopography is a useful and practical approach. However there is also something profoundly symbolic about reading between the lines of a manuscript that cannot fail to resonate with historians who are not only writers themselves but as medievalists rely upon these documentary records to write their own histories. In this chapter, textual interpretation has gone beyond what the documents say in order to examine what they mean on another level by considering who wrote them and why, thus giving us reason to reconsider how we use legal instruments as historical sources and what we can learn about the group of men who wrote them. By turning our focus to the relationship between documents and their creators we can learn something more about this group of legal writers than what would otherwise be gleaned from the content of a legal instrument on its own.

Chapter 3

The Scandalous Life of a Puritan Divine: John Harmar at Winchester College, 1569–1613[1]

Robert F.W. Smith

Introduction

The career of John Harmar, doctor of divinity and master of humane letters, was a glittering one, characterised by scholarly achievement and favour from the highest quarters. Harmar was, in the words of Eleanor Rosenberg, 'one of those young men of humble birth whose distinguished scholarship won them the encouragement of the Elizabethan authorities'.[2] He was born in the 1550s and evidently showed promise from an early age. He was educated at Winchester College and New College, Oxford, apparently gaining his places thanks to the support of the Earl of Leicester: in 1579 he published his first major work, a translation of Calvin's sermons on the Decalogue, complete with a dedication in which he expressed his gratitude for Leicester's 'good procurement of her Maiesties gratious fauour' in preferring him first to Winchester and then to New.[3] While still a fellow of New College, in the mid-1580s, he 'travayled 3 yeares & 3 monthes in the partes beyond the seas', undertaking a scholarly grand tour of the republic of letters, during which he won the 'love and esteem of the learnedest of Argentyne [Strasbourg], Basle, Lausanna, Augsburge, Leipzig,

---

[1] The research for this chapter was undertaken during the preparation of my doctoral thesis, 'John Trussell: A Life (1575–1648)' (University of Southampton, 2014). I must acknowledge the generous financial support of the Arts and Humanities Research Council which allowed me to undertake this research. I also wish to acknowledge The Warden and Scholars of Winchester College by whose kind permission I have been able to cite documents in the archive at Winchester College; and the assistance of the archivist, Suzanne Foster. I must also acknowledge Vicki Perry of Hatfield House, and the staffs of Hampshire Record Office and Lambeth Palace Library.

[2] Eleanor Rosenberg, *Leicester, Patron of Letters* (New York: Columbia University Press, 1955), 219.

[3] John Calvin, *Sermons ... on the x. commandments of the Law ...* trans. John Harmar (London, 1579), 3.

Heydelberg, Geneva, Padua, Lyons, Orleance, Paris'. His finest hour during this time was at Strasbourg, where, by his own account, he 'was intreated' to dispute the anti-Calvinist doctrine of the ubiquity of Christ's body 'against the chief of the Lutherans there', Jean Pappus; 'whiche howe I performed Jo: Sturmius ... hathe reported in his booke, intitled Antipappus quartus, printed Anno 79'.[4] At Geneva he studied divinity under Theodore de Bèze, later translating the master's sermons on the Song of Songs into English.[5]

On his return from Europe in 1585 he printed a selection of homilies by his favourite patristic writer, St John Chrysostom, and was granted the Regius Professorship of Greek at Oxford by the queen; the full text of Chrysostom's homilies followed in 1590.[6] He gained the Wardenship of Winchester College, one of England's most prestigious schools, by royal appointment in 1596. Nor did his star fade after the deaths of Leicester and Elizabeth: on the contrary, his standing as a classical scholar, and reputation as a devout and orthodox Christian, was such that in 1604 he was appointed to the cohort of scholars responsible for the translations of the Gospels, the Acts and Revelation for the King James Bible, which stands today as the most enduring literary triumph of the English Renaissance.[7] Until his death in 1613, he lived at the centre of a network of Hampshire's most scholarly puritans, among them the dean of the Winchester cathedral chapter, Dr Thomas Morton; the Master of St Cross, Dr Arthur Lake; 'and other worthy Divines'.[8]

But there was another John Harmar, whose existence the readers of his printed works need never have suspected; a second life which has remained submerged in the archival details, yet was nevertheless as real as his public persona. During his time at Winchester, Harmar was at the centre of a succession of major scandals. The most extraordinary of these saw him cast in the role of innocent victim, the others in a more complicated part. Between them they demonstrate the complexity and many-sidedness of Renaissance lives. This chapter seeks to describe this other, less visible life of John Harmar, not only because it is interesting in itself but because it illuminates the institutional life of a scholarly community in early modern England.

---

⁴   Hatfield House, Cecil Papers: 48/28a.

⁵   Theodore de Bèze, *Master Bezaes sermons vpon the three first chapters of the Canticle of Canticles* ... trans. John Harmar (Oxford, 1587).

⁶   J.W. Binns, *Intellectual Culture in Elizabethan and Jacobean England: The Latin Writings of the Age* (Leeds: Francis Cairns, 1990), 223–4.

⁷   Paul Quarrie, *Winchester College and the King James Bible* (The Warden and Fellows of Winchester College, 2011), 19–21.

⁸   R.B., J. Naylor and J. Nelson, *The life of Dr. Thomas Morton, late Bishop of Duresme, begun by R. B. secretary to his Lordship; and finished by J. N., D. D., his Lordship's chaplain* (York, 1669), 48–9.

From Schoolboy to Warden

The life of Harmar, the individual, is scarcely divisible from the life of Winchester College, the institution. Much of his life was spent there, and much of the rest was spent as a Fellow of William of Wykeham's other foundation, New College, Oxford, which Winchester was established to provide with well-educated undergraduates. T.F. Kirby, following the admission registers, states that John Harmar was admitted to Winchester College in 1569, at the unusual age of 14 – an early indication of his remarkable intelligence and facility in Latin, since the Statutes of the College state that no boy shall be admitted 'who has exceeded his twelfth year, unless being less than seventeen he has been so educated in grammar that in the judgement of the electors he will be able to show sufficient facility in grammar before his eighteenth year is completed'.[9] Harmar himself recalled in a letter written in 1596 that he had been admitted to Winchester '29 yeres since', which would make the date 1567 and (assuming he was in fact born in 1555) his age of admission a more normal 12 years old.[10] However this may be, it is certain that he matriculated at New College in 1575, taking his MA in 1582.[11] As we have seen, he then travelled abroad, and returned to a professorship. In 1588, he was appointed headmaster of Winchester College and remained in that post almost nine years.[12]

The next step came in 1596. In April that year, Thomas Bilson, the Warden of the College, succeeded in securing a bishopric for himself (Worcester), thus rendering the Wardenship vacant.[13] The Wardenship was the most senior and lucrative position in the College, the government of which was conducted by the Warden presiding over a council of ten Fellows. When a vacancy arose a new Warden was chosen by an electoral college made up of Fellows of Winchester's sister foundation, New College, Oxford. During the summer of 1596, disregarding the normal process, Elizabeth I attempted to impose her favoured candidate for the Wardenship on Winchester College, namely Henry Cotton, a man who had never been a Fellow of either of William of Wykeham's foundations. It was strictly against the statutes – which the Fellows had all sworn

9   T.F. Kirby, *Winchester Scholars: A list of the Wardens, Fellows, and Scholars of Saint Mary College of Winchester, near Winchester, commonly called Winchester College* (London: Henry Frowde, 1888), 142; *Winchester College Statutes*, 001–059: Winchester College Muniments, Reference A5/102, Rubric 2.

10   Hatfield House: Cecil Papers, 48/28a.

11   Leslie Stephen and Sidney Lee (eds), *Dictionary of National Biography*, vol. 24 (London: Smith, Elder and Co., 1890), 412–13.

12   Sheila Himsworth (ed.), *Winchester College Muniments*, vol. 1, xxxvii.

13   William Richardson, 'Bilson, Thomas (1546/7–1616)', *Oxford Dictionary of National Biography*, Oxford University Press, 2004 [http://www.oxforddnb.com/view/article/2401, accessed 2 Aug 2014].

oaths to uphold – that any such person should be admitted to the Wardenship. Evidently the queen felt that her prerogative enabled such details to be overlooked; but the majority of the Fellows disagreed, refusing to admit Cotton to the College despite his royal warrant.[14] Indeed, when he arrived there to be confirmed in his place by the Bishop of Winchester, Thomas Day, the Fellows shut the gates against them both.[15] Bilson, who was awkwardly positioned between his beloved *alma mater* and the queen upon whose patronage he relied for present and future advancement, wrote a stream of letters to the Secretary of State, Robert Cecil, attempting to smooth everything over.

One of these letters, written from Winchester on 3 May 1596, shortly after Bilson's formal election as Bishop of Worcester, contains the only direct evidence we possess of a remarkable scandal which took place at Winchester College during John Harmar's schooldays. The letter is a unique document and worth quoting at length:

> Right Honorable: Mr Harmar the Schoolemaster of our howse advertiseth me that he is touched in credite before your Honor for certain things donne here in Winchester Colledg when he was a Scholer under mee being then his Master; I must needes ghesse at their meaning that so traduce him, because my self was the man that desired the then Busshop of Winchester to enter into that Action. The trewth of the cause I protest before God and your Honor I will not conceal or dissemble. The then usshur, being one that might commaund him and correct him, had made him the child of his chamber and sought by some meanes to abuse him; whereat the youth, I terme him as he then was, repyning, made meanes by one Mr Shingleton yet lyving, then a Fellowe of our Colledg, to give mee to understande of his thraldome and miserie; I forthwith acquainted Busshop Horne therewith, who, taking present occasion to come hither, removed the usshur, and recommended the Scholer being verie towardly to the then Warden Dr. Stempe, and to my self. And when some of the fellowes not knowing the case because it was kept close to cover the usshurs shame, envyed the Scholer as a false accuser of his master, and laboured to stopp his going to Oxford, I did the second tyme report to Busshop Horne the malice of those men, that sought with authoritie to abuse boyes, or els to deprive them of all preferment. The honest inclination of the Scholer being otherwise verie religious, I so well liked, that I did not only hasten his advauncement to Oxford, but afterward made choyce of him to be Schoolemaster synce I was Warden, which I assure your Honor no earthly meanes should have wonne me to doe, but that I lyked from the begynning his disposition and hatred of that vyce wherewith now some so perversely slander him, and trewly, synce his being Schoolemaster, I have fownd him not only

---

14   Hatfield House, Cecil Papers 43/16, 41/108.
15   Hatfield House, Cecil Papers 43/16.

learned sober and religious, but pursuing all suspitions of any such offence with severe correction.[16]

Bilson goes on to say that the episode was kept a secret, known by only three people other than Harmar and his abuser (and now Cecil): Bilson, Warden Stempe and Bishop Horne. The guilty usher (otherwise known as 'undermaster' – an educational role subordinate to the headmaster) was probably one William Miller. Harmar left Winchester College and was admitted to his probationary period at New College on 18 March 1573, the year he would have turned eighteen; Miller was replaced as usher after nine years of service in January that year.[17]

The 'abuse' referred to can be taken to be sexual in nature, for several reasons. Firstly, the reference to Harmar being 'the child of his chamber' implies it. Secondly, it is doubtful whether a case of excessively beating or railing at a boy would have caused the usher such 'shame' that it was kept a close secret known to only three people. Most especially, Bilson refers to a 'vice', a perceived *moral* crime, which Harmar was accused of as a result of having been abused in this way; this seems likely to refer to buggery. A.F. Leach evidently came to the same conclusion about the nature of the abuse when researching the election of 1596 for his *History of Winchester College* (1899). Leach had seen Bilson's letter to Cecil and was suitably impressed by Harmar's triumph over adversity, but, presumably in order to shield the delicate sensibilities of his Victorian readership (which could easily have included Winchester schoolboys), he was studiedly vague about the precise detail of the allegations levelled against Harmar, saying only that 'discreditable tactics were resorted to against Harmar, by secret attacks on his character, which Bilson disposed of in a letter to Burleigh, bearing very remarkable testimony to the strength of character Harmar had shown'.[18] Although he allowed his readers to assume that Harmar had demonstrated this 'strength of character' by overcoming the wagging of malicious tongues, Leach clearly knew that Harmar's resilience was of a different and 'very remarkable' kind.

It is true, however, that Harmar's strength of character lay not only in forging a successful career in spite of the emotional and perhaps physical trauma which had been inflicted on him at a vulnerable age, but in defying the malicious whispering about him which Bilson's letter makes clear was taking place as a result of the abuse he had suffered. Harmar rose to great heights, even though what had happened could easily have left him paralysed by fear of what might ensue should he come to any kind of public attention. The Tudor sodomy law –

---

[16] Hatfield House, Cecil Papers, 40/49.

[17] New College 9749 (Registrum Protocollorum vol. iv); Sheila Himsworth (ed.), *Winchester College Muniments*, vol. 1, xl.

[18] Note that Bilson's letter was in fact to Robert Cecil, not to his father Lord Burleigh.

the Buggery Act of 1533 as re-enacted in 1563[19] – was unclear about whether being anally penetrated was itself a crime or whether only the act of penetrating another person constituted the offence of sodomy; in practice a clearly unwilling victim of rape may have been unlikely to be prosecuted, but if Harmar had been a consensual participant in homosexual intercourse, as his accusers were presumably insinuating, he had committed an offence for which the statutory penalty was death. Neither prestige, nor high position, nor influential supporters were a guarantee of safety; a bishop and a nobleman were among those executed for this crime during the early modern period.[20] Harmar's danger was not acute: the scarcity of witnesses and (by 1596) the length of time that had elapsed were in his favour. As Cynthia Herrup remarks, 'most prominent men against whom there were public complaints of sodomy were never indicted'.[21] But Harmar was nevertheless undeniably fortunate to have, in Thomas Bilson, an influential patron and advocate, someone who could intercede on his behalf when scandalous gossip came to the Secretary of State's ear. Such suspicions could have broken his career, even if they did not send him to the gallows.

It seems clear that the reason why insinuations were being made about Harmar at precisely this time is because of the vacancy that had arisen upon Bilson's preferment to the bishopric. On 2 February 1596, two months before Bilson's official election to Worcester, Harmar wrote a letter, now preserved among the Cecil Papers, to a 'Mr. Beeston' in London, who is clearly associated with an unnamed member of the nobility referred to by Harmar as 'that honorable'. This lord would appear to be a senior clergyman, since Harmar refers to him coming 'to preach'; arguably the most plausible identification of him, then, is William Day, the then Bishop of Winchester. In the letter Harmar states that, having been told by Bilson that he had now received a promise of the bishopric from the queen as a result of the Earl of Essex's intervention, he (Harmar) 'would not slacke to putt you in minde of my sute which hath now on ye expectaunce of his remove so long depended'. This can only refer to the Wardenship. Harmar refers to this 'sute' as having been being advanced for some time under Mr Beeston's 'continual care'. Harmar assures him that 'notwithstanding when now everie competitioner will worke his mayne, I would have you to see yt my zeale is not quenshed with ye length of time, but rather inflamed with ye opportunitie now offerd'.

---

[19] *Statutes of the Realm*, vol. 3 (1817), 25 Henry VIII 6, 441; vol. 4 (1819), 5 Elizabeth I 17, 447.

[20] On the trial of Mervyn Tuchet, 2nd Earl of Castlehaven, see Cynthia Herrup, *A House in Gross Disorder: Sex, Law and the 2nd Earl of Castlehaven* (New York: Oxford University Press, 1999). On the life, death and afterlife of Bishop John Atherton, see Peter Marshall, *Mother Leakey and the Bishop: A Ghost Story* (Oxford: Oxford University Press, 2008).

[21] Herrup, *A House in Gross Disorder*, 36.

In return for Beeston's support, Harmar assures him of the performance of unspecified 'promises', and openly offers Beeston's 'honourable' master 'a farther complement': 'to take order for ye deriving' to him of the College manor of 'Piddle' in Dorset, 'one of ye principallest we have, 300[ll] fayerlie better than ye rent ... I have so delt with Dr Warden therein'.[22] That Harmar and Bilson appear to have colluded together to give away a valuable College manor as a bribe is somewhat scandalous in itself; although in fact, the manor in question does not appear to have been permanently alienated. There is also another, undated note by Harmar advertising his qualifications and entitlement, also among the Cecil Papers and evidently dating from the early months of 1596, in which he recalls that at his last meeting with Queen Elizabeth, during her most recent visit to Hampshire, 'she vouchsafed to take notice of my beinge her Scholler, of my travells, of my beinge skyled in the tonges, her professor, of publishinge many things in print, and said she would haue me in remembrance for my preferment'.[23]

Harmar was therefore ambitious for the Wardenship and this would surely have been generally known in college. His taking of holy orders in early 1595 in order to become first a prebendary of Winchester Cathedral and soon afterwards rector of Compton, near Winchester, and in July 1596 the further living of Droxford (Hampshire) can be seen as a tactical move preparing the way for the Wardenship – it was necessary for the Warden and Fellows alike to be priests and Harmar had never been beneficed before.[24] This was perhaps seen as an opportunist and discreditable move; in a petition to the queen asking for the wardenship, Henry Cotton, referring to Harmar as a competitor for the post, attacked him for entering holy orders only recently.[25] The Fellows' preference was for the subwarden, George Ryves, who appears to have marshalled the resistance to Cotton; petitions asking to have Ryves were sent to the chancellor of Oxford University, Lord Buckhurst, from both New College and Winchester.[26] After a summer of determined resistance by the Fellows, Elizabeth had to accept that getting Cotton put in was more trouble than it was worth; but she did not therefore have to accept Ryves. The queen turned instead to Harmar, whom the Fellows had no colour to refuse. By July, orders had been issued to install Harmar as Warden.[27] Harmar was undoubtedly well qualified for the post, but it is tempting to think that Elizabeth's eventual choice must have been calculated

---

[22]   Hatfield House, Cecil Papers, 30/86a.

[23]   Hatfield House, Cecil Papers, 48/28a.

[24]   Lambeth Palace Library, Reg. Whitgift 2, fol. 139 [prebend, 8 January 1595; Compton, 18 August 1595]; Hampshire Record Office, 21M65/A1/28, fol. 6 [Droxford, 31 July 1596].

[25]   Hatfield House, Cecil Papers 136/59.

[26]   *Calendar of State Papers Domestic*, (London: Longmans, Green, Reader and Dyer, 1869), vol. 4, 227–31.

[27]   Hatfield House, Cecil Papers 43/16.

to put the obstinate Fellows in their place by forcing in a candidate whom she knew they did not like.

The Visitation

If Harmar was not unpopular already, he certainly became so afterwards. It would seem that the manner of his election permanently soured his relations with the College and it surely played a part in motivating a scandal which broke in 1607/8. A document in the Winchester College archives illustrates the depths of corruption to which Harmar had sunk – or, alternatively, the depth of the Fellows' malice and vindictiveness towards their Warden; or, of course, both. It takes the form of a list of accusations against Harmar, charging him with misconduct of all kinds. It is undated, but since it is clearly associated with the metropolitical visitation of Archbishop Richard Bancroft it can be presumed to date from the period October 1607 to August 1608 when the visitation was taking place.[28] The sheet is unsigned, but is written from the perspective of a cabal of outraged Fellows. There are 20 items in the list, mostly to the effect that Harmar was living beyond his means and pillaging the College's resources and revenues, both money and kind, for his own selfish ends:

> 1. Ffines of divers copyholds to the sum of 40^{li} 60^{li} and 80^{li} apece taken to the wardens private use, when the College hath but 30^s or 40^s fyne for the same.

> 2. The woods of Allington that were exceding fayer and greate and ever kept to the Colledges peculiar use, utterly spoyled by him … for his private & sumptuous buildings and by his private sales.

> 3. Arthur Harmar the wardens brother is made woodward and selleth both tymber & woode at his plesure without consent or knowledge of the fellowes.[29]

Harmar's 'private and sumptuous buildings' were a cause of particular resentment:

> 4. Leade & stone of the Colleges taken thence, & namely owt of the church, & carried to his new howse, there to build porches & places of pleasure.

> 5. He buildeth, altereth, & changeth his rooms in the Colledge, to the greate & excessive charge of the College without any consent or allowance of the fellowes, expresly against the tenor of the Statute, and spareth neither the tymber, leade nor

---

28   Hampshire Record Office: 21M65/A1/29, f. 25.
29   Winchester College, 23262.

any other store of the Colledge to his private, superfluous & glorious buildings of thre houses in the City & Soke, wherof the building of one (as he saith) cost him 1000 marks.[30]

The party ultimately responsible for settling any internal discord of this kind was ordinarily the Visitor, the Bishop of Winchester. In 1608 this was none other than Harmar's old friend and partner in crime Thomas Bilson, who, after a brief incumbency at Worcester, had translated gratefully back to his hometown of Winchester as soon as the opportunity presented itself. However, during the metropolitical visitation the diocesan bishop's authority was suspended, which is why the allegations were answered officially by 24 orders enjoined by the Archbishop of Canterbury, Richard Bancroft.

Bilson may still have been the prime mover. T.F. Kirby claims that

> the Commissioners were Bishop Bilson, Dr. Thomas Ridley, and Dr. Lake, afterwards Bishop of Bath and Wells; and they visited the College on January 11, 1607–8. The Warden and Fellows protested at first, but ultimately submitted to the Archbishop's jurisdiction. The occasion of this visitation was the case of Richard Borne, a Fellow, in whose election in the preceding year there had been an irregularity; and the Archbishop removed him.[31]

A.F. Leach makes some similar assertions, perhaps following Kirby. The source for this information is obscure (it does not appear to be the *Concilia* of David Wilkins which Kirby and Leach both cite).[32] But the register of Archbishop Bancroft contains a commission of 27 July 1607 nominating five men, including Bilson, Ridley and Lake, to preside over an enquiry, sitting not at Winchester College but in the Lady Chapel at Winchester Cathedral, into 'discords' which had arisen between the Warden and Fellows of Winchester College [*discordias inter Custodem et Socios*] over the nomination, election and admission of one Richard Bourne into the society of same College.[33] It is not unlikely that their findings prompted Bancroft to initiate a full-scale visitation, appointing the three of them as his commissioners once more. In the eighteenth century, the Fellows under Warden Nicholas also believed that an improperly elected Fellow had been removed by Bilson acting with Bancroft's authority, which lends credence to this account.[34]

---

[30]　Winchester College, 23262.

[31]　T.F. Kirby, *Annals of Winchester College from its Foundation in 1382 to the present time* ... (Winchester: P. and G. Wells, 1892), 301–2.

[32]　[David Wilkins], *Concilia Magnae Britanniae et Hiberniae ab Anno MDXLVI ad Annum MDCCXVII*, vol. iv (London, 1727), 434–6.

[33]　Lambeth Palace Library, Reg. Bancroft, fol. 218.

[34]　Winchester College, 23302Aa.

In any case, in 1608 Bancroft issued a series of injunctions answering most of the points raised by the charge-sheet, starting with the most substantial: those pertaining to the revenues and fabric of the College.

[1.] That no timber trees growinge in the woodds, or uppon the lands of the Colledge be given to any whosoever uppon any occasion, nor that any of the saide tymber trees be soulde but uppon verie extraordinary and urgent occasions, and then not without the consent of the more part of the fellowes, unles it be for the necessary reparations of the Colledge howses to be allowed by the Warden, at the motion of the rider, or one of the boursers.

[2.] That the fellowe which rideth the progresse with the warden be not only made privy to all the fynes raysed uppon the graunts of Coppyhoulds, but give his consent for the tyme that he is rider to the pitchinge of the fynes assessed either by the Warden or the steward: And that neither the steward, nor he that occupieth that place shall by any meanes without the warden and the rider of the progresse rate or appoynte any fynes for Coppyhould lands to the use of the Colledge or any other …

[6.] That the store of the Colledge in lead, glass, stone, tymber and such like necessaries for buildinge be not taken or ymploied by the Warden or any other member of that house without the consent of the three Officers or the most part of the fellowes, and that by no meanes they be ymploied to any private use out of the said Colledge, except they be first bought and payde for by the party that will so use them.[35]

Other allegations in the charge-sheet ranged from the very specific, for example that Harmar took a bribe of £100 to install the then headmaster, Benjamin Heyden, to the lurid, for example that 'a kinsman of his being in his house begat two basterds, and a man of his verie lewdely abusing a woman in his buttry at Drocksford went untouched, and all these matters by him husshed'.[36] Not all these can necessarily be taken at face value. Certainly Bancroft did not answer or otherwise acknowledge them in his visitation injunctions.

Nepotism was undeniably a feature of Harmar's wardenship, however, and the Fellows complained about it, albeit obviously with some exaggeration:

9. He hath brought 30 kinsmen & kinswomen of his & his wives to the City & Soke of Winchester since he was Warden, and all did or doe lye upon his allowance from the Colledge, making one of them Steward, another Woodward, and all the

---

35 Winchester College, 251.
36 Winchester College, 23262.

services of the howse of any charge, as Baker, Brewer & suchlike, he disposeth to some of his owne or his wives kyn or alliance, & into any fellows place voyde since his coming, he hath sought to bring in a kinsman of his owne.

According to them, the feeding and watering of these ravening hordes was breaking the back of the College finances:

> 11. His allowances of breade, beare, & all commons are most unreasonable, and taken by him withowt consent of Officers or fellowes, contrary to the Statute, aswell in his absence for his wife & kinsfolkes, as in his presence, and amownt to the fourth parte of the whole revenews of the Colledge.[37]

The only near relations brought in by Harmar who can be directly identified are his brother (the aforementioned Arthur Harmar the woodward) and his brother in law, Henry Trussell, who became steward of the manor of Titley in 1598 and is later found keeping court in other manors such as Sydling and Hamble-le-Rice.[38] Harmar's patronage was probably also influential in the election of Trussell's younger son William as a scholar at Winchester in the same year that his uncle was made Warden and his employment as usher (after a spell at New College) from 1608.[39] Henry Trussell came in for further criticism from the Fellows who accused him of facilitating Harmar's arbitrary rule and that incompetently: as they cattily remarked, Harmar 'doth begin, pursue & ende very grete & waighty matters of the Colledge withowt consent or knowledge of the fellows directly against the Statute, & by his wives brother taking upon him to be skillfull in the law, though it be farr otherwise.'[40]

In answer to these complaints, Bancroft's fifth item was 'that no three of consanguinitie or affinity with the Warden or any other of the fellowes shall hereafter be permitted to be fellowes of that house together, and that no two of any such consanguinitie or affinity be chosen or suffered to be officers in any one yeere.'[41] The archbishop passed no official comment on Henry Trussell's legal skills, but his seventeenth injunction stipulated that 'the common servants of the Colledge, as the baker, brewers, and butlers be not entertayned with the Wardens liveries or wages, but that they be obedient and subiect to the Subwardens and boursers checke and correction when they do amisse, as other the Colledge servants should be and are', which appears to confirm that

---

[37] Winchester College, 23262.

[38] Sheila Himsworth (ed.), *Winchester College Muniments*, vol. 1, liii; see also, for example, Winchester College 18309 [Sydling]; Winchester College 10785c [Hamble-le-Rice].

[39] Sheila Himsworth (ed.), *Winchester College Muniments*, vol. 1, xl.

[40] Winchester College, 23262.

[41] Winchester College, 251.

a baker and a brewer were members of Harmar's affinity, as the Fellows' ninth allegation states. As for the question of food and drink, it seems that by the time the visitation concluded, Harmar and the Fellows had come to an agreement about the dietary allowance for the Warden and his kinsfolk; Bancroft's third order stipulates that all parties should accept

> the rate lately agreed uppon in writinge by the Warden, subwarden and fellowes …
> this to be allowed to the Warden as well in his absence as in his presence because
> he is contented with a lesser rate then formerly he hath had, and nowe requireth
> no allowance for festivall and gaudy daies.[42]

Overall, it is difficult to say whether Bancroft's orders were a confirmation of the truth of the allegations of corruption that were made against Harmar, or whether they were more preventative and peace-keeping, designed to affirm principles which would satisfy both parties and draw a line under the dispute. Bilson's previous patronage of Harmar tells us nothing as to this question, since, as a Wykehamist himself, he was bound by affection as well as duty to ensure the health of the institution as a whole.

It is interesting to note the points of similarity between the accusations made against Harmar and those made a century later against the master of another learned community, whose relations with his Fellows had likewise broken down: Richard Bentley, the Master of Trinity College, Cambridge. In 1710 the high-handed and domineering Bentley – like Harmar one of the most learned men of his age – was accused of self-enrichment, waste of College provender, misuse of College money to glorify his sumptuous lodgings and abusing his statutory powers of discipline to force Fellows who questioned him into conformity with his will. It is tempting, but not wholly convincing, to imagine Harmar as a Bentleian figure. In fact, these seem to be the types of accusations which it was easy to make, standard currency in situations when the usual personality clashes within college chapters were blown up by some trigger into something more serious and sustained. At Winchester, too, in the first decade of the eighteenth century, Warden Nicholas was accused by his Fellows of excessive living costs, wasting College resources on his family and building overly expensive new lodgings, as well as various other offences.[43] The anti-Nicholas party even produced a pamphlet 'Narrative of Proceedings' in which Nicholas was denounced as another John Harmar, who was taken by them to be the very exemplar of a tyrannical Warden. The pamphlet commended the action taken by

---

[42] Ibid.
[43] Roger Custance, 'Warden Nicholas and the Mutiny at Winchester College', *Winchester College: Sixth Centenary Essays* (Oxford: Oxford University Press, 1982), 313–50.

Bilson and Bancroft to restrain Harmar and, as they saw it, secure the rights of the Fellows; a thinly veiled appeal to contemporary authorities to do likewise.[44] The godly Harmar would scarcely have been pleased, could he have known that he would survive in the institutional memory of Winchester College as a notorious ogre and wastrel.

The 'Cash-for-Resignations' Scandal

Harmar was also involved in a third scandal at about this time, one which was probably the most serious of all in the eyes of contemporaries; certainly it provoked the most official activity. This was the ineradicable scandal of corrupt resignations. New College was statutorily limited to a membership of 70 fellows. Each year, six electors – The Warden of New College, two senior fellows of New known as the 'opposers', the Warden and Subwarden of Winchester, and the headmaster – met at Winchester College to elect scholars to New College. Each year an indenture would be drawn up by these electors. As Penry Williams confirms, they were 'in practice drawing up a waiting list, and there was no guarantee that its members might actually gain admission to New College'.[45] The scholars at the top of the 'waiting list', which was made up freshly every year after each election, could expect to take their places at New College before those lower down. But it became a common practice, shortly before the annual election, for fellows of New College to resign their places on some pretence of having become ineligible, in return for a money payment from Winchester scholars who had already been elected to New, but had not yet been able to take up their places there. With the connivance of the staff doing the electing, the purchasers were thus enabled (for a price) to jump ahead of others who had been, and were about to be, elected.

In July 1619, the Bishop of Winchester, Lancelot Andrewes, wrote to the Warden and Fellows of Winchester College on the basis of 'reports of sundry persons of the better sort' that the recent elections had been marred by this corruption. As he pointed out, the problem was far from new:

> By divers records that haue ben shewed me of the Reverend Fathers my worthy predecessors, Bp Horne, Bp Cooper & Bishop Bilson (the copies whereof I haue willed the Registrar to deliuer to Mr Warden of Winchester) it should seem that heretofore things haue not ben so well carried in the eleccons either into

---

44 Winchester College, 23302Aa.

45 Penry Williams, 'Reformation to Reform, 1530–1850', in John Buxton and Penry Williams (eds), *New College Oxford 1379–1979* (Oxford: the Warden and Fellows of New College, 1979), 52.

the Colledge of Winchester, or from thence to New Colledge in Oxford, as had ben to be wished, but that corrupcion coloured by indirect courses hath formerly borne sway in them, dominatus pecunia saith Bishop Horne, turpis locoque emptio et venditio, Bp Cooper; frequent buying and selling of resignations at excessiue prices, Bp Bilson.[46]

Andrewes reconfirmed the injunctions of his predecessors, commanding that 'there should be an utter cessacion of making any place voyd either by accepting any such corrupt resignacion, or by admitting any like corrupt confession of being maried or contracted, entering into service, having more living than the Statutes beare, or (I wote not what) other fraudulent pretenses'.[47]

At no point had any of the Bishops directly accused the senior staff of Winchester College of corruption, but it is clear that there is no other way it could have worked. As Lancelot Andrewes reminded them,

> You yt are ye electors are not bound to accept of ye partie to whom such resignacion is corruptly meant nor to supply ye place according to ye will of him yt shall so resigne ... you may keepe & continue the place so void till you haue made up your full elecion, & then to supply it out of ye new Indenture which by all meanes I wish to be done.[48]

Clearly, this was so. Therefore, members of staff must have been taking a cut in return for arranging the smooth transfer of the fellowship of the Oxford scholar who had sold his place to the Winchester scholar who had bought it. Two letters by Thomas Bilson, written to Harmar and the Fellows in the summer of 1609, are reproduced in Lancelot Andrewes' register; copies of them had been sent along with Andrewes' own to underline his injunctions. Bilson places the blame on New College, and especially its subwarden, for accepting resignations, which he had no power to do, and then for sending letters to Winchester College requesting boys to be sent up to fill the vacated places: 'both which facts of the Subwarden there as well in admitting voluntarie resignacions or confessions as in sending for Scholars hither in the time of your Supervision & election heer I declare to be directly repugnant to ye Statutes'.[49] It is difficult to avoid the conclusion, however, that responsible members of staff at Winchester College would have had to be in on it as well – otherwise, the scholars who had purchased the resignations could not be sure of being the ones sent up. Harmar, as Warden, is this time placed firmly in the frame.

[46] Hampshire Record Office, M1032: Register of Lancelot Andrewes, fols 138–9.

[47] Ibid., fol. 139.

[48] Ibid., fol. 139.

[49] Ibid., fol. 142.

The suspicion is reinforced by interrogations ministered to the opposers from New College and the subwarden and headmaster of Winchester by order of Lancelot Andrewes after another corrupt election in 1620 (discussed below). In 1620, the electors seem to have thought they could circumvent the repeated episcopal injunctions against inter-elections by postponing the resignations until after the election had been carried out. In practice, what was being done was little different; in a letter addressed to both Colleges the next year, Andrewes referred to the stratagem as a 'cunning eluding of what (my hope was) had lately ben reformed touching interelecions .... I see no difference ... It is all one to make a place void beforehand to be sped by an interelecting; and beforehand to preelect into a place to be made void after'.[50] But one of the interrogatories administered to the corrupt electors states that their offence was more scandalous than in previous corrupt elections, because 'these nominacions upon the Indenture cannot be withstood by two of ye six, and it wilbe easier for foure to concurr upon these scandalous nominations then for all ye six Electors to agree upon such Inter elecions as in former times haue ben practised'.[51] If this is correct, it implies that Harmar must have been party to the corrupt resignations scandal.

Bilson warned all concerned to 'forbeare under the danger of procuring graue scandall to your house, & the paines imposed by your founder upon ye procurers of all scandall against the state & honor of your College. Which I assure you I will not fayle to lay upon ye wilfull neglecters hereof'.[52] His blunt approach did not enjoy any more success than Andrewes' more handwringing appeals to the Warden and Fellows' better natures would do later, however. In September 1620, the Warden of New College, Robert Pink, sent Andrewes a detailed description of 'some passages in our last elecion at Winchester College' which proved that the corruption was still running in much the same courses, despite the bishop's letter of the previous year. The letter is a fascinating step-by-step account of how matters were arranged by corrupt fellows and staff members. In the evening of Saturday 12 August, their examinations of the scholars completed, Pink and his fellow electors sat down to finalise the elections. They soon agreed on which boys should be admitted to Winchester College, but when it came to the 'indenture to Oxford', they were unable to agree. Pink proposed first a scholar named Barker.

> Next to him in order I moved for Rider, Miller, Wells, all superannats and all competently fit for the places. Yet here we fell at difference, four of the Electors, the two Opposers, Mr Subwarden and Mr Schoolmaster, naming Edmunds, Sadler and Booth for the three first, some of them alleging as they had done before to

---

[50] Ibid., fol. 169.
[51] Ibid., fol. 168.
[52] Ibid., fol. 142.

me more privately for them, that they should not stand long in the way to hinder any behind them, there being resignations ready provided to speed them away.[53]

Pink, a man of unusual probity, replied that he could countenance the election of Edmunds, Sadler and Booth even less if there were resignations prepared for them. The electors were unable to agree, and the election ended in farce, with Pink procuring the services of a public notary to officially record that since the electors had failed to agree the choice now devolved upon the Visitor (Andrewes), and making his escape from Winchester College on horseback before the others had a chance to declare 'that *in penam contumacis* they would proceed without me, which hath ben done sometimes'.[54]

The interrogatories ministered to the other electors show that Edmunds, Sadler and Booth had purchased the resignations of three fellows of New College named Edmund Coles, Richard Flemming and Edmund Gray.[55] Edmund Coles, then, was surely the 'partie' who offered his resignation to Pink 'straytway after my returne to the College', as he reported to Andrewes. Pink

> did not absolutely refuse it, but taking it into my hand crav'd some time to consider of it, telling ye partie that when I should accept it, which would not be yet a while, I should happilie send for Barker, & not for Edmunds ... the partie learning this, though he had in his paper profess'd to resigne pure, sponte, simpliciter, yet would not trust me with his resignacion but desird to be in statu quo prius.[56]

Subsequently Pink was threatened with action at common law to make him accept the resignation, which indicates how engrained the expectation of corruption had become in the electoral process; fellows were even prepared to make threats against their own Warden to ensure that things fell out as they wished – statute or no statute.

Given that there was no other mechanism for removing fellows of New College in a timely enough fashion to keep up with the annual elections, the sale of resignations was an almost inevitable development, a safety valve for the pressure building up in the system. But it was a far from perfect solution. By making wealth rather than ability the crucial factor, the sale of resignations produced the damaging consequences described by Lancelot Andrewes in his letter of 1619: 'ye superannuating, & so utter defeating of many of a toward witt of their preferment, and to ye sending in their places others, which well

---

53   Ibid., fol. 164.
54   Ibid., fol. 164.
55   Ibid., fol. 168.
56   Ibid., fol. 164.

might stay a longer time, being nothing so well grounded'.[57] In his 1621 letter Andrewes rehearsed the especially pernicious consequences for poor scholars: if the selling of places be once permitted, he wrote, 'ye first places shall euer go by purchace, and poore scholars unhable to contract, though of neuer so good desert, shall still be sett lower and lower in ye Roll, till there be no more contracters left' – except that, as he went on to say, there would never be an end to the cycle of corruption:

> if way be giuen to this, there will a wide dore be opened, neuer to be shutt more: for they yt compound for places now, will looke another day to be compounded with for their places; and so this mischiefe run on without end; for what they did pay when they came in they will looke to be paid when they go out.[58]

In 1620, Robert Pink succinctly illustrated the human cost of the scandal: ' ... thus your Lordship sees how resignacions yet pester our Elecions, how they wrong the poorer and ye better sort ... Barker, an hable & worthy Scholar, though the Statute was urg'd by me in his behalf, he is putt of till I know not when'.[59]

Conclusion

John Harmar's place in the history of English intellectual culture is assured. This chapter has aimed to deepen our understanding of the man who produced such learned works by showing him in a different context. It is rarely possible to pronounce authoritatively about the psychology of early modern people, but it is fascinating to wonder how John Harmar felt about Winchester College, the place which had abused him, but set him on his path to great achievements. His petition for the Wardenship makes his unhappiness as headmaster of Winchester plain enough: 'I was specially requested for the good of that place, to undertake the schole of Wynchester the paynes whereof, in hope of this preferment (for that of the 7 last wardens fower laboured before in the schole) I haue theis 9 yeres almost sustayned'.[60] It is easy to imagine how he could have felt that the place owed him nothing; it had inflicted 'paynes' of many kinds upon him, and the Wardenship was his opportunity to extract recompense. His use of his position to secure offices and scholarships for his kinsmen is unexceptionable; his participation, if such it was, in the scandal of corrupt resignations, is less so. It is still more interesting to consider his feelings towards the monarchy and

---

[57] Ibid., fol. 138.
[58] Ibid., fol. 169.
[59] Ibid., fol. 164.
[60] Hatfield House: Cecil Papers, 48/28a.

its agents, whose influence had put him into Winchester in the first place and on whose whims he had been dependent for every subsequent development. 'What part of my age hath not beene honored with the patronage of your Lordships fauor and goodwil towardes me?' he rhetorically asked Leicester in his dedication of 1587.[61] Would it be surprising if the gratitude were admixed with a certain private reservation?

Thomas Bilson, too – a man known mainly as a political theologian and for his influential work on subjection and rebellion – perhaps emerges in a fresh light. Here we find him struggling against the endemic corruption in his *alma mater*, against 'the malice of those men' – both in 1573 and in 1609 – 'that sought with authoritie to abuse boyes, or els to deprive them of all preferment'. It seems that one of the boys whom he had protected went on to be one of those men; to participate, at least, in a scandal that deprived distinguished scholars of humble birth – scholars like John Harmar had once been – of their preferment. We do not know how that affected him, or if it did. It is impossible to separate Bilson's personal reactions from the necessary, prescribed reactions of an agent of the early modern state. Even when he stepped in to protect Harmar as a schoolboy from the usher's abuse and when he sought to clear his name in the eyes of Robert Cecil, was he doing more than furthering the interest of somebody who was already in receipt of the favour of the queen and her senior ministers – and, in so doing, currying favour of his own? Bilson and Harmar alike were put into their places, and made what they were, by royal power. Its stamp is all over their lives like the imprint of the great seal on red wax. There is a view that early modern lives, like works of art, are no more than this: merely artefacts, the product of social and political pressures impacting on human material that lacks true selfhood.[62] This chapter, however, has not sought to diminish John Harmar and Thomas Bilson, or to deny their individual agency. It has sought only to bring to the fore aspects of their lives – dominated, as they were, by the gravitational pull of Winchester College – which previous scholarship has tended to occlude; and thus, hopefully, if not to understand them better, at least to let their complexity be recognised more fully than before.

---

[61]   *Master Bezaes sermons*, trans. John Harmar, 2.

[62]   See, for example, Stephen Greenblatt, *Renaissance Self-Fashioning: From More to Shakespeare* (Chicago and London: University of Chicago Press, 1985 and 2005). Cf. John Jeffries Martin, *Myths of Renaissance Individualism* (Basingstoke: Palgrave Macmillan, 2004).

PART II
The Lives of Objects and their Owners

Chapter 4

The Lives and Deaths of People and Things: Biographical Approaches to Dress in Early Anglo-Saxon England

Toby F. Martin

To an archaeologist, the thrill of excavating a grave is rarely macabre and it is certainly nothing to do with the detached process of collecting data. The exhilaration stems from uncovering a scene last experienced by a small gathering of people in the remote past. No other kind of archaeology quite equals the directness of the connection conjured between the modern excavator and the ancient gravedigger. Time may have changed the appearance of the burial tableau, but it still offers an unparalleled connection between the past and present. As the archaeologist sets about their work, they encounter an oblong of differently coloured soil, suspiciously person-sized. Scraping back the earth, the first thing they expose might not be the curve of a cranium, the convolutions of a pelvis or the disquietingly white enamel of a tooth. If the grave is from the early Anglo-Saxon period, the first thing they notice might be the unmistakable green patina of bronze, or more remarkably, the lustre of gilt, still as bright as on the day of its burial. As the archaeologist works, the brooch – for this is what the object turns out to be – is cleaned in situ and recorded prior to being carefully lifted. But before the excavator is finished they might encounter further objects: another brooch, some brightly coloured glass beads, a distorted iron buckle, knife or pin, deformed by rust. Perhaps unconsciously, perhaps not, our archaeologist has also just brushed away the long-decomposed remains of textiles: the ghost of a woollen cloak or a linen dress that the brooches pinned together. This costume clothed the cadaver for its final journey and included personal jewellery, some on display, some sandwiched between layers of textile. The inevitable question that formulates in the archaeologist's mind is 'why were the lives of this person and these particular objects coterminous?'

The links between dress, biography and identity can be very close. Identity develops over the course of an individual's life and the role that costume plays in this process can be crucial. For instance, clothing received during rites of passage can become materialisations of those important life events from which an individual formally construes their identity. Additionally, clothing accrues meaning from everyday, informal performances that gradually galvanise the links between a person and their intimate possessions. Such formal and informal events, which continuously occur between people and things, accumulate to produce human and material cultural biographies. Although biography is an important consideration for many different kinds of material culture, because of its intimate links with the body, dress illustrates the matter particularly well. The growing and anatomically developing body makes practical demands for a series of different costumes through life and consequently the dress of an individual is never static. Moreover, dress tends to underline those anatomical dimorphisms and chronological transformations from which notions of gender and age are constructed. Clothing provides a second skin that encodes specific, culturally intelligible values.

Objects, however, are not just blank slates upon which biography is inscribed and from which it can be read, but their meanings are dynamic and reflexive: 'as people and objects gather time, movement and change, they are constantly transformed, and these transformations of person and object are tied up with each other'.[1] The meaning of an object, and even its materiality, changes dramatically from its origins in raw materials, through to becoming a commodity, a gift, a possession, a votive sacrifice, an heirloom or refuse.[2] Objects also accumulate biographical meanings that run parallel to the lives of people. An item obtained in childhood, for instance, may have a different significance to its adult owner.[3] Like identity, therefore, the meaning of objects is not static, but cumulative and contingent with a biographical trajectory. The present meaning of an object is different from its meaning in the past, but ultimately depends and builds upon its historical contexts if they are known, or re-imaginings of a past use-life if they are not.[4] The idea that material culture is inseparably involved in

---

[1]   Chris Gosden and Yvonne Marshall, 'The cultural biography of objects', *World Archaeology* 31, no.2 (1999): 169. For a summary of archaeological approaches to object biography see Jody Joy, 'Reinvigorating object biography: reproducing the drama of object lives', *World Archaeology* 41, no.4 (2009): 541–3.

[2]   Igor Kopytoff, 'The cultural biography of things: commoditization as process', in *The Social Lives of Things: Commodities in Cultural Perspective*, ed. Arjun Appadurai (Cambridge: Cambridge University Press, 1986), 66–7. On heirlooms see Katina T. Lillios, 'Objects of memory: the ethnography and archaeology of heirlooms', *Journal of Archaeological Method and Theory* 6, no.3 (1999): 241–4.

[3]   On the relationship between human biography and material culture, see Roberta Gilchrist, 'Archaeological biographies: realizing human lifecycles, -course, and -histories', *World Archaeology* 31, no.3 (2000): 327.

[4]   For known biographies, see Annette B. Weiner, *Inalienable Possessions: The Paradox of Giving-While-Keeping* (Berkeley: University of California Press, 1992) and for unknown or re-imagined biographies see John Moreland, 'The world(s) of the cross', *World Archaeology*, 31, no.2 (2000): 202–5; Hella Eckardt and Howard Williams, 'Objects without a past? The

the construction and maintenance of social relationships is well established in contemporary archaeological theory.[5] Identity being caught up with the known histories of particular objects is a good illustration of the point.[6]

Early Anglo-Saxon England: History and Archaeology

The fifth- to sixth-century inhabitants of early Anglo-Saxon England have left us very little in terms of biographical literature.[7] A very small number of historical texts are concerned with this period. Only one of them, Gildas' *De Excido Britanniae*, probably composed at some point in the first half of the sixth century, was broadly contemporary with the events it describes. As Gildas' title betrays ('On the Ruin of Britain'), he was not attempting a neutral standpoint, but provides only a brief, if impassioned, condemnation of the advances of paganism in post-Roman Britain. Two major Anglo-Saxon sources from later periods describe the events of the fifth to seventh centuries. These are Bede's *Historia Ecclesiastica Gentis Anglorum* (written in the first half of the eighth century) and the *Anglo-Saxon Chronicle* (the earliest compilation of which belongs to the late ninth century), both of which also offer only highly fragmented information. Although we learn something of the character and deeds of a few named individuals, the accounts are highly abbreviated and they clearly emerge from a pseudo-historical oral tradition.[8] They offer us little in terms of biography. We learn, for instance, that in AD 449, the British tyrant Vortigern invited Hengest and Horsa to defend against Pictish incursions. In 455, these mercenaries rebelled against Vortigern, with Horsa dying in the process. During the next couple of decades, Hengest and his son Æsc went on

---

use of Roman objects in Anglo-Saxon graves', in *Archaeologies of Remembrance: Death and Memory in Past Societies*, ed. Howard Williams (London and New York: Kluwer/Plenum, 2003), 146.

[5]   E.g. Chris Gosden, 'What do objects want?' *Journal of Archaeological Method and Theory* 12, no.3 (2005): 194; John Robb, 'Beyond agency', *World Archaeology* 42, no.4 (2010): 500.

[6]   Janet Hoskins, *Biographical Objects: How Things Tell the Story of People's Lives* (London and New York: Routledge, 1998).

[7]   Archaeologists traditionally define 'early Anglo-Saxon England' as the pre-Christian fifth to seventh centuries AD. However, this chapter deals with a specific type of feminine dress that went out of use toward the end of the sixth century. Therefore, for the purposes of this chapter, I use this term to refer only to the fifth and sixth centuries, also known as the 'Migration Period'. See John Hines, *The Scandinavian Character of England in the Pre-Viking Period* (Oxford: British Archaeological Reports, 1984), 19, 30.

[8]   Barbara Yorke, 'Fact or fiction? The written evidence for the fifth and sixth centuries AD', *Anglo-Saxon Studies in Archaeology and History* 6 (1993): 46–7.

to achieve a series of victories against the British and the Welsh. This is about the maximum we know of any historical character from fifth- and sixth-century England. Even ignoring the fact that the account contains large elements of fiction, it hardly constitutes a biography. In terms of the historical literature, we are very much in the dark about the course of people's lives in early Anglo-Saxon England.

Archaeological sources of information are therefore critical to understanding biography in the fifth and sixth centuries. Not only does archaeology provide a greater quantity of information, but it also concerns a wider spectrum of individuals. That is not to say that the archaeological record for this period is without bias. Because Anglo-Saxon buildings were made of wood rather than stone, they have left only ephemeral traces in the archaeological record. Historically, the difficulties of locating and excavating such sites have limited our knowledge of early Anglo-Saxon settlements. Work in recent decades, however, has increased our knowledge of such matters considerably, including our knowledge of the life cycles of buildings.[9] Nevertheless, the vast majority of archaeological material from the fifth and sixth centuries still comes from cemeteries. As such, the picture we receive is not necessarily a representative snapshot of early Anglo-Saxon society, but a deliberately assembled mortuary tableau, depicting the body of the deceased and particular possessions or offerings intentionally selected by their mourners to accompany them in death.[10] This puts us in the unusual position of knowing far more about the way in which early Anglo-Saxons died than how they lived. A major part of the challenge for archaeologists, therefore, is reading backwards from the mortuary evidence to interpret what we can about how these people lived from the social processes that determined which items should be included in their graves. Approaching these mortuary assemblages with a methodology sensitive to biography offers a novel technique for addressing the problem.

Early Anglo-Saxon Dress

Our direct knowledge of early Anglo-Saxon dress comes from excavated graves with some reference to earlier continental sculpture featuring Germanic

---

[9]   A recent synthesis of the settlement evidence, including work on the life cycles of buildings, is provided by Helena Hamerow, *Rural Settlements and Society in Anglo-Saxon England* (Oxford: Oxford University Press, 2012). Recent work by Clifford Sofield suggests that the use-lives of some buildings may well relate to the lives and deaths of their occupants. See Clifford M. Sofield, 'Placed Deposits in Early and Middle Anglo-Saxon Rural Settlements', (University of Oxford D.Phil. thesis, 2012), 209–11.

[10]   Heinrich Härke, 'The nature of burial data', in *Burial and Society: The Chronological and Social Analysis of Archaeological Burial Data*, ed. Claus Kjeld Jensen and Karen Høilund Nielsen (Aarhus: Aarhus University Press 1997), 24.

costume. No actual garments, or even substantial fragments, survive from this very early period. Although tiny fragments of textile very occasionally survive in graves, the impression of long-decayed textiles on the corrosive products of metallic items is more common. Painstaking analysis of these fragments, mapped against their location relative to the skeleton, has revealed the range of garments worn during this period.[11] Because women frequently fastened their clothing with large, decorative brooches, we tend to know a lot more about feminine dress, which in any case seems to have been a much more elaborate affair than masculine garb. While men seem to have worn tunics and trousers, these were very rarely fastened with elaborate jewellery.[12] Only a small number of decorative buckles are known from masculine costumes, the most famous of which is probably the example from Finglesham, Kent (grave 95), which incidentally depicts a man wearing nothing but a belt and a horned helmet.[13] Whether this startlingly minimal costume was purely fictional, worn during ritual or battle, or regularly assumed, is open to question, but it presents a remarkably stark contrast to feminine dress, which screened the body behind numerous layers of textile. Women regularly wore multiple layers of cloaks and dresses, fastened by a number of brooches, pins, belts, girdles and clasps, accessorised with other items such as toilet sets, purses, pendants, keys, 'girdle-hangers' and festoons of beads.[14] The most typical feminine garment was the *peplos* dress, which took the form of a tubular gown pulled up over the body and fastened with pair of brooches on the shoulders, sometimes worn over the top of a sleeved dress fastened at the wrists with clasps (Figure 4.1, left). Some women also wore one or more cloaks on top of this, fastened on the chest or the throat with one or two additional brooches (Figure 4.1 middle and right). The numbers of these garments worn in the grave could occasionally be upwards of four and we shall encounter some of these particularly elaborate costumes below. The disparity between evidence for male and female dress is a major problem, but at present, it is intractable. Consequently, I will address only feminine dress, partial as the resultant picture will inevitably be.

Dress in early Anglo-Saxon England was obviously important when it came to constructing and displaying identity and status and this was especially the case

---

[11] Gale Owen-Crocker, *Dress in Anglo-Saxon England* (Woodbridge: Boydell Press, revised edition, 2004); Penelope Walton Rogers, *Cloth and Clothing in Early Anglo-Saxon England, AD 450–700* (York: Council for British Archaeology, 2006).

[12] Owen-Crocker, *Dress in Early Anglo-Saxon England,* 105.

[13] Sonia Chadwick Hawkes and Guy Grainger, *The Anglo-Saxon Cemetery at Finglesham, Kent* (Oxford: Oxford University School of Archaeology, 2006), 264.

[14] 'Girdle-hangers' are decorative items of an ultimately unknown function, but are likely to have been symbolic of keys, see Kathrin Felder, 'A Key to Early Anglo-Saxon Identities? Girdle-hangers in 5th and 6th Century England', (University of Cambridge D.Phil. thesis, forthcoming).

Figure 4.1   Early Anglo-Saxon feminine dress. From left to right: *peplos*,
                fastened by a brooch on each shoulder; cloak, fastened by a
                brooch at the throat; cloak, fastened by two brooches on the chest.
                Drawing by Lynne Martin, reproduced with permission.

for women. This is not only indicated by the elaborate, varied and nuanced nature
of feminine costume, but also by the fact that mourners felt the compulsion
to send these valuable garments and jewellery with the deceased into the grave.
There were probably many reasons for this practice. For instance, removing these
objects from circulation provides a means of restricting the inheritance of material
goods, hence ensuring a continuing reliance on the gift exchange relationships by
which these dress objects were obtained, perhaps through powerful individuals
and the craftspeople they patronised.[15] Depositing dress objects in graves also
creates enduring social memories that cemented the deceased, their dress, their
identity and, by association, the status of their surviving kin.[16] Overall, however,

---

[15]   *Cf.* Heinrich Härke, 'The circulation of weapons in Anglo-Saxon society', in *Rituals
of Power: From Late Antiquity to the Early Middle Ages*, ed. Frans Theuws and Janet L. Nelson
(Leiden: Brill 2000).

[16]   Howard Williams, *Death and Memory in Early Medieval Britain* (Cambridge,
2006).

the prominence of dress objects in women's graves strongly suggests that the links between identity, personhood, the body and clothing – those pervasive and biographical entanglements between people and objects mentioned above – were especially unshakeable in the early Anglo-Saxon period. These objects were fundamental to constructing and displaying a specific identity, which, as we shall see below, was an intersection of gender, age, social hierarchy and possibly even ethnicity, no doubt among other less archaeologically visible facets. These bonds between people and things formed through parallel events in the life course of the deceased individual and in the historical trajectory of the object i.e. through human and material biographical processes.

Reconstructing the Lives of Anglo-Saxon Women

While differences in sexual anatomy and physique often form the basis for gender distinctions, dissimilarities caused by the growth and physiological ageing of the body, taken together with the measured passage of time, inform understandings of age. Hence, gender and age identities tend to be interdependent.[17] As the individual ages, their gender gathers new meanings and loses old ones. Puberty, for instance, is generally attributed significance as a key biographical event in the development of an individual's sexuality and gender and it is often marked with various rites of passage that manage biological changes and make them culturally intelligible and formally sanctioned. Childbearing and the menopause represent some other key biographical events in a woman's life course, which are also often ritualised and culturally elaborated. As mentioned above, dress is especially important in this process due to its intimate associations with the body and the manner in which garments tend to accentuate, or even create bodily differences.

It is by now quite clear that gender loomed large in the orchestration of early Anglo-Saxon inhumation rituals, with more than half the adult burial population receiving gendered grave goods; most obviously weaponry for men and jewellery for women.[18] Age was also an important consideration in the mourner's choices of grave goods.[19] Both age and gender were also occasionally

---

[17]   Jean S. la Fontaine, 'Introduction', in *Sex and Age as Principles of Social Differentiation*, ed. Jean S. la Fontaine (London: Academic Press, 1978), 1.

[18]   From a sample of 3,401 burials from 45 cemeteries, Stoodley records that 60 per cent of adult female burials included jewellery, while 45 per cent of male burials included weaponry. See Nick Stoodley, *The Spindle and the Spear: A Critical Enquiry into the Construction and Meaning of Gender in the Early Anglo-Saxon Burial Rite* (Oxford: British Archaeological Reports, 1999), 75.

[19]   Heinrich Härke, 'Knives in early Anglo-Saxon burials: blade length and age at death', *Medieval Archaeology* 33 (1989); Nick Stoodley, 'From the cradle to the grave: age organization and the early Anglo-Saxon burial rite', *World Archaeology* 31, no.3 (2000);

marked in the cremation burial ritual, if to a less obvious extent. In cremation burials, the age of the deceased sometimes related to the size of the urn, while specific objects burned on the pyre and placed in the urn before its burial occasionally referenced gender.[20] It seems clear that early Anglo-Saxon society possessed relatively consistent age sets, indicated most obviously by the specific nature of the material culture included in the inhumation rite.[21] By comparing the ages of deceased individuals with their grave goods, Nick Stoodley has demonstrated that women tended to fall into about four age sets and men about three.[22] For men, age was signified by including different quantities and types of weaponry. For women, age seems to have been symbolised by a small number of standard costumes. Below about the age of four, girls received none of the standard elements of adult female garb, perhaps a single bead, but very rarely anything more than these small tokens.[23] Between the ages of four and about twelve, girls generally wore garments that, at the very most, required a single brooch or pin. However, from here onwards women started to wear the adult *peplos* dress described above, evidenced by the presence of a pair of brooches on the shoulders. At the age of about 18, women started to obtain items worn at the girdle: keys, girdle-hangers and purses. It was also generally only from about the age of 18 that a minority of women began to wear a cloak over the top of a *peplos* gown.[24]

Not only were different costumes appropriate for different feminine age groups, but the costumes themselves were pinned together by types of brooch appropriate only to certain ages. There is a multitude of early Anglo-Saxon brooch types but practically all of them can be categorised as bow, plate or ring brooches (see Figure 4.2). The major types of bow brooches include great square-headed, cruciform and small long brooches (Figures 4.2 a, b, c). Plate brooches

---

Rebecca Gowland, 'Ageing the past: examining age identity from funerary evidence', in *Social Archaeology and Funerary Remains*, ed. Rebecca Gowland and Christopher Knüsel (Oxford: Oxbow, 2006).

[20]   Julian D. Richards, *The Significance of Form and Decoration on Early Anglo-Saxon Cremation Urns*, (Oxford: British Archaeological Reports, 1987), 195–6; Kirsty E. Squires, 'Piecing together identity: a social investigation of early Anglo-Saxon cremation practices', *The Archaeological Journal* 170 (2013).

[21]   Heinrich Härke, 'Early Anglo-Saxon social structure', in *The Anglo-Saxons from the Migration Period to the Eighth Century: An Ethnographic Perspective* ed. John Hines (Woodbridge: Boydell Press, 1997), 126–30.

[22]   Stoodley, *The Spindle and the Spear*, 117.

[23]   Sally Crawford, 'Children, death and the afterlife in Anglo-Saxon England', *Anglo-Saxon Studies in Archaeology and History* 6 (1993): 85; Stoodley, 'From the cradle to the grave', 462; Gowland, 'Aging the past', 148.

[24]   Toby F. Martin, 'Women, knowledge and power: the iconography of early Anglo-Saxon cruciform brooches', *Anglo-Saxon Studies in Archaeology and History* 18 (2013): 13.

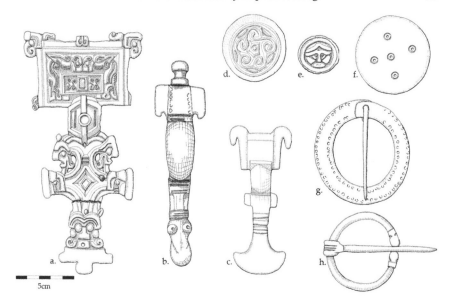

5cm

Figure 4.2   Common varieties of early Anglo-Saxon brooch. (a) Great square-headed brooch from Lakenheath, Suffolk (Cambridge University Museum of Archaeology and Anthropology, Z21357); (b) Cruciform brooch from West Stow, Suffolk (West Stow Museum, 1988.146); (c) Small long brooch from grave 37, Great Chesterford, Essex (after Evison 1994, 148 figure 28.3); (d) Saucer brooch from Welford, Berkshire (drawn from the Portable Antiquities Scheme database, BERK-A6EC93); (e) Button brooch from the Isle of Wight (drawn from the Portable Antiquities Scheme database, IOW-F0C2A5); (f) Disc brooch from grave 77, Butler's Field, Gloucestershire (after Boyle et al. 1998, 219, figure 5.66.2); (g) Annular brooch from grave 4a, Empingham II, Rutland (after Timby 1996, 171 figure 93.1); (h) Penannular brooch from grave 58, Broughton Lodge, Nottinghamshire (after Kinsley 1993, 141 figure 70.9a). All drawings by T.F. Martin.

were generally, though not always, circular. Among these, saucer brooches, button brooches and disc brooches are the most common (Figures 4.2 d, e, f). Ring brooches consisted of a hoop and a ring. They essentially functioned like a simple buckle that pinned fabric rather than a belt. Annular and penannular brooches are the most frequently encountered types among these (Figures 4.2 g, h).

The idea that each of these varieties of brooch possessed individual meanings, making them differentially popular through time and between regions, has been established among archaeologists for at least a century. Artefact chronologies based on style, alongside ideas about regional identity operate from this principal.[25] Additionally, however, a number of these types were only appropriate for women over particular ages. Cruciform brooches, for instance, are generally associated only with women over the age of about 18.[26] The restriction of these large cloak-fastening bow brooches to older women is, in fact, how we know that the cloak was an age-specific garment. Saucer brooches were also seemingly restricted to women over the age of 18,[27] although they were generally worn in pairs to fasten a *peplos* dress, not cloaks.[28] Some brooches seem to have been more appropriate for younger individuals, such as disc brooches, which apparently show a slight tendency toward being included on the clothing of children under the age of about 12.[29] Other items show less specificity according to age, such as annular brooches and small long brooches, which, perhaps because they were relatively plain items, were generically popular with women from the age of about 12 and upward.

In summary, there were standard age-appropriate feminine costumes, fastened with specific jewellery, which many women progressed through over the course of their lives. Such items helped to signify social seniority as well as create the impression of a maturing body. An important aspect of this biographical process is that the costume was cumulative. Hence, at the age of 18, some women added particular brooches, cloaks and girdle items to their existing clothing. As a result, the adult feminine costume, as items were added to it, could be read like a biographical text. Clothing referenced specific events in the life course that signified adaptations in gender and age status and hence explained, legitimated and authenticated their position in society.

Major questions remain concerning how women obtained these items: from where, from whom and through what mechanism of exchange. Answers have to be speculative, as we must rely on indirect evidence and analogy. Nevertheless, there are compelling reasons to suggest that these objects may have been gifts associated with rites of passage: biographical events in the human life course

---

[25]   Nils Åberg, *The Anglo-Saxons in England*, (Uppsala: Almqvist and Wiksells, 1926); Edward T. Leeds, 'The distribution of the Angles and Saxons archaeologically considered', *Archaeologia* 91 (1945).

[26]   Martin, 'Women, knowledge and power', 13.

[27]   Stoodley, *The Spindle and the Spear*, 115–16; Gowland, 'Aging the past', 148.

[28]   Because cruciform and saucer brooches are traditionally seen as the brooches of Anglian and Saxon women respectively, their age restriction may also have something to do with special role these women played in the construction and display of regional/ethnic identities.

[29]   Gowland, 'Aging the past', 148.

during which identity formation is especially intense. As Arnold van Gennep expressed some time ago, a rite of passage must involve the severing of an individual from one social status (e.g. childhood) and integration into the next (e.g. adulthood), always separated by an intermediary liminal phase.[30] It seems that for early Anglo-Saxon women, part of their excision from childhood was the loss of their juvenile clothing. Their integration into adult society was facilitated by their acquisition and donning of adult garb. We can only guess at what the liminal phase included, but it may well have concluded with the gifting of particular dress objects to the initiate.

Rites of passage, however, do not comprise the only events at which relationships between identity, biography and material culture are forged. The structuration of these facets of identity through relatively mundane, daily, repeated performances is an equally important factor.[31] Hence, when mourners laid the dressed body of the deceased in the grave, their mortuary garb would have also evoked general memories of daily life. Memory has recently become a key idea in the interpretation of early Anglo-Saxon mortuary rituals and it is a crucial consideration in the link between biography, identity and material culture.[32] Composing the physical body and its material accessories as a mortuary tableau provides a fitting analogy to the writing of an obituary, with the assembled mourners as a readership.

Object Biographies

Quite how the material culture deposited in graves came to be so meaningfully loaded with biographical significance may have been partly dependent on the histories of these objects themselves. To support this idea, it would be helpful to demonstrate that at least some of them were in fact the same items that the deceased had obtained at transitions in their life course. A few key grave assemblages suggest that this was at least sometimes the case. The importance of these particular assemblages is that their components are relatively datable to slightly different times. Hence, they give the impression of having been obtained at different stages of life. Of course, this is a risky endeavour, as these objects are

---

[30]   Arnold Van Gennep, *The Rites of Passage*, trans. Monika B. Vizedom and Gabrielle L. Caffee (London: Routledge, 2004).

[31]   Pierre Bourdieu, *Outline of a Theory of Practice*, trans. Richard Nice (Cambridge: Cambridge University Press, 1977); Anthony Giddens, *Central Problems in Social Theory* (London: Macmillan, 1979).

[32]   Williams, *Death and Memory in Early Medieval Britain*, 46–55; Zoë L. Devlin, 'Social memory, material culture and community identity in early medieval mortuary practices', *Anglo-Saxon Studies in Archaeology and History* 14 (2007): 41–3.

not reliably datable with such high resolution.[33] Nevertheless, for a very small number of exceptionally datable assemblages, the case has important enough implications to merit its presentation. The 10 examples to which I would like to draw particular attention all include multiple instances of cruciform brooches, some of which indicate dissimilar dates of manufacture due to their stylistic differences (see Figure 4.3). They were all excavated from secure archaeological contexts and have been published to modern standards. The sites include Bergh Apton,[34] Cleatham,[35] Morning Thorpe,[36] Sewerby,[37] Snape,[38] Spong Hill,[39] Tallington[40] and Westgarth Gardens.[41]

Cruciform brooches, thanks to their elaborate decoration, rapid stylistic development, abundance and numerous associations with other artefacts, are among the most datable of early Anglo-Saxon objects. Nonetheless, even the most datable examples are only broadly assignable to the closest half-century or so and refining their dating any further than this, in absolute terms, is extremely

---

[33]   For a critical outlook see David M. Wilson, 'Almgren and chronology: a summary and some comments', *Medieval Archaeology* 3 (1959): 115–16. More recent research is, however, more optimistic, see Kenneth Penn and Birte Brugmann, *Aspects of Anglo-Saxon Inhumation Burial: Morning Thorpe, Spong Hill, Bergh Apton and Westgarth Gardens* (Gressenhall: Norfolk Museums and Archaeology Service, 2007), 42–71; Alex Bayliss, John Hines, Karen Høilund Nielsen, Gerry McCormac and Christopher Scull, *Anglo-Saxon Graves and Grave Goods of the 6th and 7th Centuries AD: A Chronological Framework* (London: Society for Medieval Archaeology, 2013).

[34]   Barbara Green and Andrew Rogerson, *The Anglo-Saxon Cemetery at Bergh Apton, Norfolk* (Gressenhall: The Norfolk Archaeological Unit, 1978).

[35]   Elizabeth Coatsworth, Maria Fitzgerald, Kevin Leahy and Gale Owen-Crocker, 'Anglo-Saxon textiles from Cleatham, Humberside', *Textile History* 27 (1996); Kevin Leahy, *Interrupting the Pots: The Excavation of Cleatham Anglo-Saxon Cremation Cemetery* (York: Council for British Archaeology, 2007).

[36]   Barbara Green, Andrew Rogerson and Susan G. White, *The Anglo-Saxon Cemetery at Morning Thorpe, Norfolk*, volumes i and ii (Gressenhall: The Norfolk Archaeological Unit, 1987).

[37]   Susan Hirst, *An Anglo-Saxon Cemetery at Sewerby, East Yorkshire* (York: York University Archaeological Publications, 1985).

[38]   William Filmer-Sankey and Tim Pestell, *Snape Anglo-Saxon Cemetery: Excavations and Surveys 1824–1992* (Ipswich: Environment and Transport, Suffolk County Council, 2001).

[39]   Catherine Hills, Kenneth Penn and Robert Rickett, *The Anglo-Saxon Cemetery at Spong Hill, North Elmham. Part III: Catalogue of Inhumations* (Gressenhall: The Norfolk Archaeological Unit, 1984).

[40]   James Albone and Kevin Leahy, 'The Anglo-Saxon cemetery at Tallington, Lincolnshire', *Anglo-Saxon Studies in Archaeology and History* 11 (2000).

[41]   Stanley E. West, *Westgarth Gardens Anglo-Saxon Cemetery, Suffolk: Catalogue* (Bury St Edmunds: Suffolk County Planning Department, 1988).

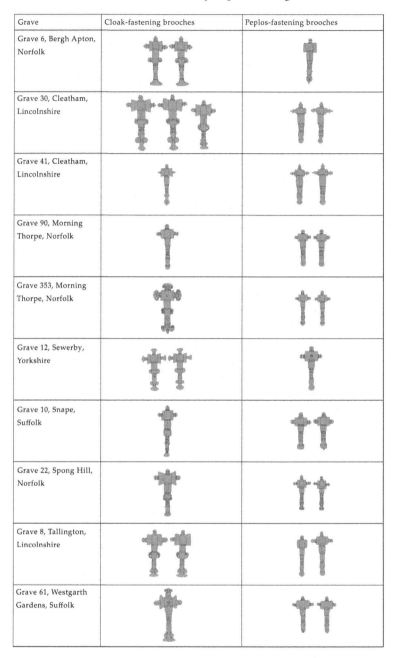

Grave	Cloak-fastening brooches	Peplos-fastening brooches
Grave 6, Bergh Apton, Norfolk		
Grave 30, Cleatham, Lincolnshire		
Grave 41, Cleatham, Lincolnshire		
Grave 90, Morning Thorpe, Norfolk		
Grave 353, Morning Thorpe, Norfolk		
Grave 12, Sewerby, Yorkshire		
Grave 10, Snape, Suffolk		
Grave 22, Spong Hill, Norfolk		
Grave 8, Tallington, Lincolnshire		
Grave 61, Westgarth Gardens, Suffolk		

Figure 4.3   The cruciform brooches from 10 grave assemblages, showing the stylistic differences between cloak- and *peplos*-fastening brooches. All drawings by T.F. Martin.

difficult.[42] The relatively strong chronological indicators that cruciform brooches provide mean that they tend to date other items found in the same grave. For example, in a grave containing two annular brooches and a cruciform brooch, the latter would generally date the former, as well as the whole assemblage, because cruciform brooches offer a higher dating resolution. As the dating of annular brooches depends almost entirely on their find-combinations with cruciform brooches, arguing for chronological disparity between any of these items would involve a circular argument. However, when several cruciform brooches of different types occur in the same grave, there is an opportunity for drawing some distinctions between their relative dates.

As mentioned above, cruciform brooches generally fastened cloaks. However, there was a short period, relatively early in their stylistic development, at some point around the third quarter of the fifth century, when pairs of small, simple, primitive cruciform brooches more commonly fastened *peplos* dresses.[43] It is often the case that *peplos* dresses fastened by cruciform brooches from this transitional phase were worn underneath cloaks fastened by one or two cruciform brooches, and in many of these cases, the *peplos*-fastening brooches are stylistically earlier than the cloak-fastening ones. In some cases, as might be expected, chronological distinctions are not feasibly demonstrable and some of the assemblages in Figure 4.3 appear to be broadly contemporary (e.g. Morning Thorpe grave 353, Snape grave 10, Spong Hill grave 22) but in no case are the outer, cloak-fastening brooches demonstrably earlier than the inner *peplos*-fastening brooches. Chronological differences between brooches within assemblages are, however, likely for a number of these graves, including Bergh Apton grave 6, Morning Thorpe grave 90, Sewerby grave 12, Tallington grave 8 and Westgarth Gardens grave 61. They are almost certain for Cleatham graves 30 and 41.

A little detail on the stylistic development of cruciform brooches is necessary. Figure 4.4 illustrates their basic development from small, simple pin-like objects into large, elaborate, flat brooches covered in complex decoration. This development is broadly measurable, with the earliest cruciform brooches originating in the first half of the fifth century and the largest, latest examples

---

[42]   Hines, *The Scandinavian Character of Anglian England*, 27–30; Toby F. Martin, 'Identity and the Cruciform Brooch in Early Anglo-Saxon England: An Investigation of Style, Mortuary Context, and Use' (University of Sheffield PhD thesis, 2011), 150–51.

[43]   Martin 'Identity and the Cruciform Brooch', 282–3. It may be the case, in fact, that all the earlier cruciform brooches dating up until about AD *c.* 475 were used to fasten *peplos* dresses, but no reliably complete grave assemblages have yet been found in Anglo-Saxon England to demonstrate this as they have in north Germany. Either way, *c.* 475 marks the approximate date at which cruciform brooches began to fasten cloaks and ceased almost entirely to fasten *peplos* dresses.

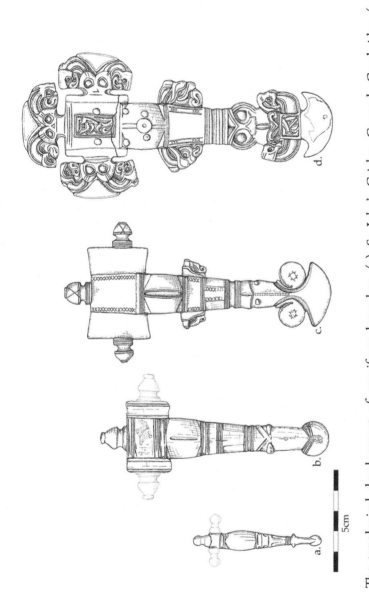

Figure 4.4   The typological development of cruciform brooches. (a) St John's Cricket Ground, Cambridge (partially reconstructed, Cambridge University Museum of Archaeology Anthropology, A 1904.534B); (b) Grave 48, Holywell Row, Suffolk (partially reconstructed, Cambridge University Museum of Archaeology and Anthropology, Z7128D); (c) Grave 9, Londesborough, Yorkshire (Hull and East Riding Museum, KINCM:2005.694.4; (d) Grave 30, Norton, Tees (Preston Park Museum and Grounds, STCMG:2006.1500.30.4). All drawings by T.F. Martin.

dating to around the second and third quarters of the sixth.[44] Certain features of these brooches are key chronological indicators. The knob at the top of the head-plate, for instance, changes from possessing a fully round cross-section to a half-round section. This feature is relatively rare, but is seen on the *peplos*-fastening brooches from Cleatham graves 30 and 41 in Figure 4.3. The animal head on the foot of the brooch gradually gains a brow and then spiral nostrils before it becomes an even more elaborate feature. Again, most of the *peplos*-fastening brooches in Figure 4.3 lack these features aside from Morning Thorpe grave 353, Snape grave 10 and Spong Hill grave 22, while the reverse is true for the cloak-fastening brooches, Cleatham grave 41 and Sewerby grave 12 excepted. Earlier brooches also typically lack the triangular or crescent-shaped termini that protrude from the foot of later brooches, as well as the lappets that sometimes project laterally from just beneath the bow. Every *peplos*-fastening brooch in Figure 4.3 lacks these features, while only the cloak-fastening brooches from Cleatham grave 41 and Morning Thorpe grave 90 possess neither. None of these stylistic details is a decisive or independently reliable indicator of an absolute or even relative date. Some craftworkers will obviously have adapted to new styles sooner, while others may have used antiquated features long after they were fashionable. Nevertheless, as a broad indicator of date, and when the whole series of brooches is taken *en masse*, these general stylistic changes seem to have occurred at some point around AD *c.* 475.[45]

To summarise this complex account, the later fifth century was when most *peplos*-fastening cruciform brooches went out of use and it marks the point at which this type of brooch began to fasten cloaks instead. The key suggestion is that the lives of at least some of the individuals buried in the graves listed in Figure 4.3 had lives that spanned this transition. Hence, the brooches fastening their *peplos* dresses appear, in most cases, to be relatively early. They are all small, squat and simple brooches. However, if this was the only distinction, one might put their differences down to function rather than chronology. This is of course partly true, as earlier brooches tended to be smaller and many had a different function fastening *peplos* dresses. Yet, those subtle stylistic details outlined above (fully round top-knobs, brows, spiral nostrils, lappets and triangular termini), which have nothing to do with size or function, provide more compelling evidence for differential dates of manufacture. The implication is that most of the individuals in Figure 4.3 obtained cruciform brooches at the age of about 12 or so, to mark their passage into adulthood by assuming adult garb, at a time

---

[44]   Hines, *The Scandinavian Character of Anglian England*, 127–30; Catherine Mortimer, 'Some Aspects of Early Medieval Copper-Alloy Technology, as Illustrated by the Anglian Cruciform Brooch' (University of Oxford D.Phil. thesis, 1990), 143; Martin, 'Identity and the Cruciform Brooch', 149.

[45]   Martin, 'Identity and the Cruciform Brooch', 135, 149.

when cruciform brooches were still used to fasten *peplos* dresses. Later in life, when the function of cruciform brooches had changed, and when they had advanced to an age when a cloak was an appropriate garment, they obtained stylistically advanced cruciform brooches and used them to fasten a cloak.

These are just 10 graves among several thousand that are known from early Anglo-Saxon England, in which the circumstances have aligned to offer a unique opportunity for relative dating. The stylistic indicators of date are subtle, but they are exceptional in the resolution they offer. As is always the case in attempts to infer chronology from style, their relative dating can only be tentative. Taken together, however, these examples may well stand for a practice that was more typical than the dating resolution in most graves allows.[46] Nevertheless, we must certainly concede that women did not necessarily always retain the jewellery they had accumulated through life for deposition in the grave. The vagaries of everyday unpredictable events intervene, including breakages and losses, or perhaps individual circumstances that led to individual items becoming heirlooms. Such events, as well as the unpredictable nature of archaeological survival, will often ensure that the picture we receive from excavated data is never neat or absolute.

In the cases of breakages, it seems that individuals made significant efforts to repair and retain these items, even when the brooch was so battered and fragmented that it could no longer sustain any practical usage.[47] In a sample of 117 cruciform brooches from secure and published archaeological contexts, more than 45 per cent displayed some form of damage upon their interment in a grave, and over 20 per cent had been repaired.[48] Owners of brooches frequently improvised repairs with yarn, which sometimes reattached the pin, or simply tied the object onto the garment, forfeiting any of its dress-fastening function (Figure 4.5a). In some cases, however, repairs were highly skilled and time-consuming affairs and craftspeople occasionally supplied custom-built components to replace missing ones. More frequently, plates of iron or copper-alloy were riveted to the severed halves of a broken brooch to make a join (Figure 4.5b). It seems that the retention of particular objects was very important, even when they were well beyond any functional use. This was perhaps due to the

---

[46] Though the relative dating must be tentative, the idea that women retained these brooches for life is nevertheless corroborated by continental research that positively correlates the extent of wear and tear on brooches and the age of the wearer. See Max Martin, 'Beobachtungen an den frühmittelalterlichen Bügelfibeln von Altenerding (Oberbayern)', *Bayerische Vorgeschichtsblätter* 52 (1987).

[47] Toby F. Martin, 'Riveting biographies: the theoretical implications of early Anglo-Saxon brooch repair, customisation and use-adaptation' in *Make Do and Mend: Archaeologies of Compromise, Repair and Reuse*, ed. Ben Jervis and Alison Kyle (Oxford: British Archaeological Reports, 2012).

[48] Ibid., 56.

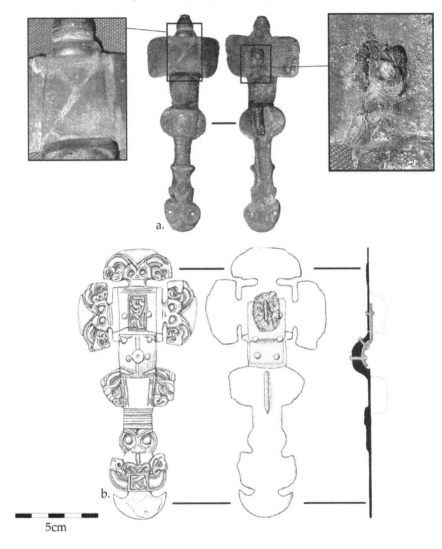

5cm

Figure 4.5   Common types of repair on early Anglo-Saxon brooches.
(a) Cruciform brooch from grave 63, Norton, Tees, repaired
with yarn (Preston Park Museum and Grounds, STCMG:
2006.1500.63.5). (b) Cruciform brooch from grave 30, Norton,
Tees, repaired with rivets and a plate (Preston Park Museum and
Grounds, STCMG:2006.1500.30.4). Drawings and photographs
by T.F. Martin. The photograph (a) is reproduced here with
permission from Preston Park Museums and Grounds.

irreplaceable biographical meanings these items had accumulated and the meaning of these items in the biographies of their wearers.

The handing-down of jewellery items as heirlooms does not seem to have been a typical practice. Of course, there is no reliable way at present of being sure, but most assemblages tend to be of broadly corresponding dates. That said, the major problem with proving the presence or absence of heirlooms is the same as that outlined above: circular argument is forever close at hand due to the methodology of dating by find-combination. A few objects possess chronologies with reliable subdivisions within the early Anglo-Saxon period (cruciform, great square-headed and saucer brooches, for instance). Accordingly, one can only really make a case for conflicting dates when these exceptionally datable objects occur in the same grave, which is a relatively rare occurrence. When they do occur in the same context, their dates tend to agree, but this is partly because the chronologies were constructed from these associations in the first place. Additionally, most types of early Anglo-Saxon dress-accessory seem to fall within a surprisingly short period, perhaps as brief as a single century (the late fifth century to the late sixth). Hence, we are talking about a relatively small number of generations. Despite all these problems, dating by find-combination has been successfully implemented and this would not be possible if objects were frequently exchanged between generations.[49]

Nevertheless, some convincingly earlier objects do occasionally occur in later graves. Roman coins (perforated for wearing as pendants) and Roman brooches, for instance, appear in Anglo-Saxon graves relatively frequently.[50] Although it is possible that these objects were handed down within families spanning the Roman to Anglo-Saxon transition, Howard Williams and Hella Eckardt make a convincing case when they suggest such items were most likely found objects, retained for their imagined rather than their known biographies.[51] A more convincing case for heirlooms is suggested by the occurrence of relatively rare post-Roman objects of the earlier part of the fifth century, turning up in graves that are most probably sixth century. For example, the 'Saxon' equal-arm brooch of type Nesse from grave 55 at Westgarth Gardens was probably considerably older than the two late fifth- or sixth-century cruciform brooches with which it

---

[49]   Claus Kjeld Jensen and Karen Høilund Nielsen, 'Burial data and correspondence analysis', in *Burial and Society: The Chronological and Social Analysis of Archaeological Burial Data*, ed. Claus Kjeld Jensen and Karen Høilund Nielsen (Aarhus: Aarhus University Press, 1997); Penn and Brugmann, *Aspects of Anglo-Saxon Inhumation Burial*, 42–58. That is, of course, unless whole assemblages were handed down, in which case the dating of their individual elements still stands.

[50]   Roger A. White, *Roman and Celtic Objects in Early Medieval Britain: a Catalogue and an Interpretation of their Use* (Oxford: British Archaeological Reports, 1988).

[51]   Eckardt and Williams, 'Objects without a past', 146.

was found.[52] A supporting-arm brooch of type Perlberg from grave 49 at Linton Heath, Cambridgeshire may also have been considerably older than the small long brooches with which it was associated.[53] Of course, heirlooms offer equally interesting aspects of object biography, as they demonstrate instances where the lives of objects transcended the lives of people. Such objects act to sustain social meanings, including privilege, claims to particular ancestries, or perhaps even associations between kin who exchanged such items as gifts in the ancestral past.[54] They do, however, appear to be the exception rather than the rule in the fifth and sixth century.

The Lives and Deaths of People and Things

In the early Anglo-Saxon period, the most personal possessions of the dead, those that described and demonstrated their passage through life, were frequently removed from the world of the living and sunk into the ground with the body they had dressed in life. The reasons for their burial and removal from circulation were undoubtedly complex and multifarious. The archaeological literature tends to emphasise the role of the mortuary ritual as structuring the identity of the deceased, and hence creating an idealised picture of gender, age and other social aspirations. By creating an aggrandised ancestor, mourners legitimated or even bolstered their own place in society and re-affirmed roles and order in a time of potential social crisis. Ideas about social memory run parallel to this interpretation, whereby the mortuary ritual represents a manufactured communal memory that does not just commemorate a socially valued individual, but recreates their persona in the collective consciousness. These are established perspectives in archaeological interpretation,[55] and if we prioritise the idea that the mortuary ritual possessed a function in the renegotiation of communal power structures, they are good conclusions at which to arrive. However, we must also accommodate the biographical meanings of the particular objects that accompanied their owner in death.

Objects involved in gift exchange, which these elaborate items of jewellery almost certainly were, have a tendency to accumulate inalienable meanings, which occasionally forbid their exchange outside a particular, generally kin-

---

52   West, 60.

53   Vera I. Evison, 'Supporting-arm and equal-arm brooches in England', *Studien zur Sachsenforschung* 1 (1977): 137.

54   Lillios, 'Objects of memory', 236–7.

55   Since Michael Parker Pearson, 'Mortuary practices, society and ideology: an ethno-archaeological study', in *Symbolic and Structural Archaeology*, ed. Ian Hodder (Cambridge: Cambridge University Press, 1982).

based, social group.[56] One can easily envisage the situation in which some objects not only become inalienable from a particular circle of kin, but also from a specific individual. In the event of their death, such personal objects might become polluting, dangerous or taboo objects to own.[57] This would seem especially logical if these items had been received under a formal protocol of gift exchange, during initiation rituals for example, and could not be simply inherited *ad hoc* from deceased or ageing kin. Considering the sheer amount of wealth deposited in cemeteries in the fifth and sixth centuries, it seems that there might have been some prohibition on the accumulation of material goods. One way of governing this would be to restrict inheritable objects, thereby simultaneously restricting the inheritance of social roles and privileges.[58] Of course, this alone cannot explain the complexities of the material aspects of early Anglo-Saxon burial customs. As is the norm for social conventions, such prohibitions on the retention of possessions, if they existed, would have been occasionally contravened. Nevertheless, thinking about these objects as biographical possessions considerably enriches our understanding of them.

So as the archaeologist excavates an Anglo-Saxon grave, gently coaxing these remarkable items of jewellery from the remote past, they should not only be affected by peeling back the centuries that intervene between us and this remote other. As the last few centimetres of soil are prised from around the skeleton, and the ghosts of those long-decayed layers of textile are consecutively removed, the excavator might also contemplate peeling back the years, months and days over which these surviving objects, now dulled by patina or rust, but once bright from the workshop, were cumulatively obtained. They might consider the circumstances under which this woman received them, how she carried them through her life, how much a part of her they eventually became, and how they told at least part of the story of her life to her contemporaries, just as they do to us.

---

[56] Annette B. Weiner, 'Inalienable wealth', *American Ethnologist* 12, no.2 (1985): 210. Among objects generally restricted from becoming commoditised, Kopytoff, 'The cultural biography of things', 73 lists the 'paraphernalia of political power', or objects which are, in general, part of the 'symbolic inventory of the society'. Early Anglo-Saxon brooches certainly fall into this category.

[57] After Mary Douglas, *Purity and Danger: An Analysis of Concepts of Pollution and Taboo* (London: Routledge and Kegan Paul, 1966).

[58] Lillios, 'Objects of memory', 236–7.

Chapter 5

Roger Machado: A Life in Objects

Gemma L. Watson

Introduction

Microhistory is the pursuit of answers to larger questions from smaller places –
individual lives, a single family or one event;[1] in this case, the life of the late
fifteenth-century herald, Roger Machado. Machado was Richmond King of
Arms for Henry VII and he lived in Southampton in the later fifteenth century.
In 1976, Machado's Southampton residence was excavated and a rich corpus
of material culture was recovered. In addition to this material, Machado's
memorandum book has survived and is housed in the archive of the College
of Arms. It includes an inventory as well as mercantile accounts, a description
of Edward IV's funeral and journals of diplomatic embassies to Europe.[2] The
survival of both archaeological and documentary evidence for Machado makes
him an ideal candidate for interdisciplinary research. This chapter, therefore,
offers the microhistory of Roger Machado to illustrate how interdisciplinary
research can be achieved within biographical writing. I will also demonstrate
how this unique methodological approach can further our understanding of the
wider world in which Machado lived when we consider him (and his objects)
within their wider social and cultural context.

A New Biographical Approach

Roger Machado was herald in both the Yorkist and early Tudor royal courts.
The medieval heralds had many responsibilities: they granted coats of arms
and adjudicated tournaments and other chivalric events, they presided in and

---

[1]   Charles Joyner, *Shared Traditions: Southern History and Folk Culture* (Urbana and
Chicago: University of Illinois Press, 1999), 1; Carlo Ginzburg, *Threads and Traces: True,
False, Fictive*, trans. Anne C. Tedeschi and John Tedeschi (Berkley and London: University
of California Press, 2012), 193–4.
[2]   London, College of Arms, MS Arundel 51, ff. 14–88.

recorded royal ceremonial and they were diplomatic envoys and messengers. Machado did all these things, but is most famous for his diplomatic work.[3]

Machado is considered to have been a close friend and special favourite of Henry Tudor after joining Henry in exile in Brittany at the end of 1483.[4] Whilst in exile, Machado was appointed Henry Tudor's personal herald and given the title of Richmond.[5] After the Battle of Bosworth Field in August 1485, Machado was swiftly promoted to Richmond King of Arms and then Norroy King of Arms in that year.[6] In 1494, Machado was promoted once again, this time to Clarenceux King of Arms, second in rank amongst the English heralds.[7] Machado's heraldic duties may also have involved espionage.[8]

Machado lived in Southampton on Simnel Street between 1486 and 1497 where he was also the King's Searcher of Customs at the port there and was made a free burgess in 1491.[9] Although Machado appears to have had a small but significant role in the early Tudor court, very little is known about his personal life. This is not surprising as he was living during a time where surviving documentary evidence is fragmentary. It is currently unknown when or where he was born, whom he married, and how many children he had. Even

---

[3]   Machado kept journals of three embassies he attended: one to Spain and Portugal in 1488–1489 and two to Brittany in 1490. London, College of Arms, MS Arundel 51, ff. 29–88. They have been edited and translated: *Memorials of King Henry VII*, ed. James Gairdner, Chronicles and Memorials of Great Britain and Ireland During the Middle Ages Series 10 (London: Longman, Brown, Green, Longmans, and Roberts, 1858), 328–89. For further information on Machado's duties as a herald see Gemma L. Watson, 'Roger Machado: A Life in Objects' (PhD diss., University of Southampton, 2013).

[4]   Anthony Richard Wagner, *Heralds of England: A History of the Office and College of Arms* (London: HMSO, 1976), 137.

[5]   Adrian Ailes, 'Machado, Roger [Ruy]', *Oxford Dictionary of National Biography* (Oxford: Oxford University Press, 2004), online edition, accessed 19 January 2010, doi: 10.1093/ref:odnb/17527.

[6]   William Campbell (ed.), *Materials for a History of the Reign of Henry VII, from Original Documents Preserved in the Public Record Office* (London: HMSO, 1965), 370.

[7]   London, College of Arms, MS Officers of Arms, vol. 3, 110; Anthony Richard Wagner, *Heralds and Heraldry in the Middle Ages: An Inquiry into the Growth of the Armorial Function of Heralds* (London: Oxford University Press, 1939), 61.

[8]   For further information see Gemma L. Watson, 'Roger Machado, Perkin Warbeck and Heraldic Espionage', *The Coat of Arms* 3rd Series 10 (2014): 51–68.

[9]   J.M. Kaye (ed.), *The Cartulary of God's House, Southampton* (Southampton: Southampton University Press, 1976), 290; *Calendar of the Fine Rolls: preserved in the Public Record Office: Henry VII* (London: HMSO, 1962), 36; Cheryl Butler (ed.), *The Book of Fines: The Annual Accounts of the Mayors of Southampton 1488–1540* (Southampton: Southampton University Press, 2008), 15.

the date of his death is currently uncertain.[10] However, analysis of his name and writing would suggest he was Portuguese; previously he was thought to have been French or Breton.[11] The excavation of Machado's Southampton residence in 1976, therefore, provided a rare opportunity to study this enigmatic figure in a uniquely different way. Not only did it provide another dimension to his life which was otherwise unknown, it offered the possibility of applying a new biographical approach – interdisciplinary microhistory.

The first person to use the word 'microhistory' as a self-defined term was the American scholar, George R. Stewart in 1959, when he minutely analysed the decisive battle of the American Civil War at Gettysburg, an event that lasted only 20 minutes.[12] He argued that by approaching the battle as a microcosm it was possible to see the American Civil War 'as clearly by looking minutely and carefully at a period of a few hours as by looking extensively and dimly throughout four years'.[13] However, the original theory of microhistory came from within Italian social and cultural history in the 1970s, being known as *microstoria*, which was a reaction to the *histoire des mentalités* of the French Annales School. Both schools of thought shared the agenda of bringing common people into history, but the Italian micro-historians were more concerned with focusing on in-depth investigations of little-known individuals, families, communities, or events than the Annales School, who were generally preoccupied with quantitative methods and historical demography.[14] Microhistory places a strong emphasis on the importance of clues as a means to gain new information.[15] Machado makes an ideal candidate for a microhistorical approach, but not for traditional biography, for this very reason. There are many gaps in the evidence

---

[10] 6 May 1510 has been given as the date of Machado's death in Walter Hindes Godfrey and Anthony Richard Wagner, *The College of Arms* (London: The London Survey Committee, 1963), 7980.

[11] According to Thomas Lant, Portcullis Pursuivant 1588–97, he was a Frenchman, and John Anstis, Garter King of Arms 1718–1744, states that Thomas Wriothesley believed that Machado was Breton: 'The common Tradition is that he was a native of Bretagne in France and came hither Richmond Herald with Henry Earl of that place'. *Cf.* Wagner, *Heralds and Heraldry*, 61.

[12] George Rippey Stewart, *Pickett's Charge: A Microhistory of the Final Charge at Gettysburg* (Boston: Houghton Mifflin, 1959). Stewart's work is discussed in Ginzburg, *Threads and Traces*, 193–4.

[13] Stewart, *Pickett's Charge*, xii.

[14] Examples include Giovanni Levi, *L'eredita immateriale. Carriere di un esorcista nel Piemonte del seicento* (Einaudi, Torino, 1985); Carlo Ginzburg, *Il formaggio e i vermi* (Einaudi: Torino, 1976). Discussed in Ginzburg, *Threads and Traces*, 193–214.

[15] Matti Peltonen, 'What is Micro in Microhistory?' in *Theoretical Discussions of Biography: Approaches from History, Microhistory and Life Writing*, ed. Hans Renders and Binne de Haan (Leiden: Koninklijke Brill, 2014), 105–18.

for his life making a biographical narrative near impossible. The evidence for his life, like clues in a mystery, can be defined as vague and ambiguous. As a result, evidence, or clues, needs to be rigorously analysed and scrutinised to be able to inform us on his life and the world in which he lived. However, it is the multiplicity of the evidence for his life that makes him particularly appropriate for microhistorical research. It means that he can be used as a lens to focus on broader themes within the period of history in which he lived.

Machado's objects (both material and textual) are the central axis on which this microhistory rests. It is therefore necessary to define and discuss the term material culture and what its study brings to this methodology. Material culture can be defined as the material manifestation of culture. It can take different forms (e.g., architecture, objects, ecofacts, ephemeral archaeological features revealed through excavation), but for the purpose of this chapter, material culture refers to the objects that Machado came into contact with throughout his life. This includes the objects excavated from Machado's Southampton residence, but also the objects described and mentioned in his extant memorandum book (the objects listed in his inventory, the objects Machado bought and traded that are documented in his mercantile accounts, and the objects he came into contact with whilst working as a herald). All these objects have something to say about Machado and the world he inhabited.

The medieval world was very visual; objects and other forms of material culture carried meanings that might surprise us today. The vast majority of the population could not read or write and therefore materiality was a significant part of everyday life. Things could express ideas and values that were both consciously and subconsciously understood, influencing people's day-to-day lives on many levels. This is explored by Tara Hamling and Catherine Richardson in their edited volume *Everyday Objects: Medieval and Early Modern Material Culture and its Meanings.* They argue that to understand people's experience of daily life, you need to know about people's possessions – their material culture.[16] Therefore, by considering Machado's objects and what they can say about him and the world in which he lived, we can understand things about both his life and his culture that the documentary sources alone cannot offer.

Materiality (the social value placed on physical things) is an integral part of culture and there are dimensions of social existence that cannot be fully understood without it.[17] The anthropologist and material culture specialist, Daniel Miller, argues in his seminal work on materiality that: 'Objects are important not because they are evident and physically constrain or enable, but

---

[16]   Tara Hamling and Catherine Richardson (eds), *Everyday Objects: Medieval and Early Modern Material Culture and its Meanings* (Farnham: Ashgate, 2010).

[17]   Christopher Tilley et al. (eds), *Handbook of Material Culture* (London: Sage, 2006), 1.

often precisely because we do not "see" them ... They determine what takes place to the extent that we are unconscious of their capacity to do so.'[18] This implies that much of what we are exists outside of our body or consciousness, in the external environment that 'habituates and prompts us.'[19] Therefore the study of the material dimension of society is fundamental to understanding culture.

In contrast to Miller, the anthropologist Alfred Gell argues that people act through objects by distributing their personhood onto things which represent an index of their agency, rather than the objects themselves influencing human agents. As a result, these things have the potential to serve as secondary agents well beyond the biological life of the individual. The person is 'a spread of biographical events and memories of events, and a dispersed category of material objects, traces, and leaving ... which may, indeed, prolong itself long after biological death.'[20] Therefore, we are able to reconstruct a person (and the life choices they made) through the material things they have left behind. Rather than seeing Gell's and Miller's interpretations of the relationship between human agent and object as distinct from one another, I consider the relationship to be reciprocal and far more complex. People do act through and consequently place a value on objects, whether intentionally or unintentionally, but they are also subconsciously influenced by the material world around them. With this in mind, this chapter will show how material culture can contribute to our understanding of Roger Machado's life and how his relationship with objects affected him.

As well as taking a microhistorical approach that uses and interprets material culture, my research also draws upon documentary evidence. The main difficulties facing biographers of the medieval and early Renaissance are how to interpret the complexities of the different sources associated with the lives of individuals, and how to fill in the missing gaps in the records. One approach is to be interdisciplinary, mobilising all available evidence. For instance, Robin Fleming's article in *Writing Medieval Biography* used the bone analysis of a seventh-century woman to gain insights into personal stresses affecting individual lives in Anglo-Saxon England.[21] However, being interdisciplinary has its own difficulties. There is always the risk in interdisciplinary research of focusing heavily on our own specialism and reducing other types of evidence to mere illustrations, rather than being considered equally dynamic and important

---

[18]   Daniel Miller (ed.), *Materiality* (Durham and London: Duke University Press, 2005), 5.

[19]   Miller, *Materiality*, 5.

[20]   Alfred Gell, *Art and Agency: An Anthropological Theory* (Oxford: Clarendon Press, 1998), 222.

[21]   Robin Fleming, 'Bones for Historians: Putting the Body back into Biography', in *Writing Medieval Biography 750–1250: Essays in Honour of Professor Frank Barlow*, ed. David Bates, Julia Crick and Sarah Hamilton (Woodbridge: Boydell, 2006), 29–48.

resources. This is due to the fact that the traditional separation of scholarship into different disciplines artificially compartmentalises textual, visual, and material evidence. This then creates the problem of how to combine different types of evidence in scholarly research.[22] This research is an example of how we can overcome these difficulties by drawing upon all available evidence for Machado's life, both documentary and archaeological. As a result, my methodology draws upon 'documentary archaeology'.

Documentary archaeology is a popular approach to history in North American scholarship. It brings together diverse source materials related to cultures and societies that peopled the recent past (within the last 500 years or so) in a way not possible through single lines of evidential analysis.[23] Documentary archaeologists tend to see their archive of source material as including written records, oral traditions (where possible), and material culture that produces overlapping, conflicting, or entirely different insights into the past.[24] Anne Yentsch's archaeological study of the eighteenth-century Calvert family of Annapolis, Maryland provides a good example of how the analysis of family papers in conjunction with archaeological remains can result in the construction of a richly detailed understanding of lived lives.[25] Yentsch states that 'the ultimate goal was to see the people through the things they left behind'.[26] This approach is similar to the one my research has adopted for the life of Roger Machado and the interpretation of his objects.

Documentary archaeology studies that have successfully combined archaeological and documentary data also include Laurie Wilkie's research on two African-American women and their families who lived in the late-nineteenth and early-twentieth centuries.[27] Wilkie's work has a microhistorical slant. For instance *The Archaeology of Mothering*, on one level, is an archaeology of Lucrecia Perryman and her life, but it is also an archaeology of Lucrecia Perryman as representative of the broader experiences of thousands of other women, and an archaeology of African-American women who were midwives. Wilkie treads the fine line between rigorous data-driven interpretation and historical fiction.

---

[22]   Hamling and Richardson, *Everyday Objects*, 9–10.

[23]   Laurie A. Wilkie, 'Documentary Archaeology', in *The Cambridge Companion to Historical Archaeology*, ed. Dan Hicks and Mary C. Beaudry (Cambridge: Cambridge University Press, 2006), 13.

[24]   Wilkie, 'Documentary Archaeology', 14.

[25]   Anne Elizabeth Yentsch, *A Chesapeake Family and their Slaves: A Study in Historical Archaeology* (Cambridge: Cambridge University Press, 1994).

[26]   Yentsch, *A Chesapeake Family*, xxii.

[27]   Laurie A. Wilkie, *Creating Freedom: Material Culture and African American Identity at Oakley Plantation, Louisiana, 1840–1950* (Baton Rouge: Louisiana State University Press, 2000); Laurie A. Wilkie, *The Archaeology of Mothering: An African-American Midwife's Tale* (New York and London: Routledge, 2003).

Wilkie punctuates her interpretations with fictitious dialogues (called narrative interludes by Wilkie) in the form of interviews between early twentieth-century women and an invented character, Hazel Neumann. Her aim is to fill some of the spaces between historical sources. She argues that the strength of using narrative in archaeological interpretations is its ability to make dry material accessible to non-professionals.[28] Wilkie is not afraid to push the evidence to its limits to produce a piece of research that best reflects the lives she is trying to understand.

By considering Machado's life as microhistory informed by material culture theory and documentary archaeology, a broader approach can be taken that considers Machado in his wider political, cultural, social, economic and historical context and offers a fresh perspective on the early Tudor period. Roger Machado was living at a time of great change in England – the time of the Wars of the Roses, the establishment of the Tudor dynasty and the beginning of the English Renaissance. As a result, Machado's life is well placed to consider wider questions surrounding these events. We are also not looking at the period from the point of view of royalty or high nobility or solely from a material culture perspective, but from the viewpoint of someone who was not high-born or even English and for whom we have a variety of still extant sources (both material and textual) for his life.

This research into the microhistory of Roger Machado through material culture is relatively unique, especially within medieval archaeological scholarship. People rarely feature in archaeological analyses, which are more concerned with the organisation of data, cataloguing, typologies, classifications and the defining of dates and chronologies, with the overall aim of understanding technology, trade and social structures of past cultures at a generalised level.[29] However, biographical and microhistorical narratives which bring people back into the archaeological study of the past have started to be employed within European post-medieval archaeology and American historical archaeology, and this study of Machado can be situated in relation to this growing body of work.[30]

---

[28]   Wilkie, *The Archaeology of Mothering*, xxv.

[29]   Harold Mytum, 'Ways of Writing in Post-Medieval and Historical Archaeology: Introducing Biography', *Post-Medieval Archaeology*, 44 Issue 2 (2010), 241.

[30]   Examples of the use of biographical and microhistorical narrative in post-medieval and historical archaeology include: Mary C. Baudry, "'Above Vulgar Economy": The Intersection of Historical Archaeology and Microhistory in Writing Archaeological Biographies of Two New England Merchants', in *Small Worlds: Method, Meaning and Narrative in Microhistory*, ed. James F. Brooks, Christopher R.N. DeCorse and John Walton (Santa Fe: School for Advanced Research Press, 2008); Annie Gray, '"The Greatest Ordeal": Using Biography to Explore the Victorian Dinner', *Post-Medieval Archaeology*, 44 Issue 2 (2010), 255–72; Wim Hupperetz, 'Microhistory, Archaeology and the Study of Housing Culture: Some Thoughts on Archaeological and Historical Data from a Cesspit in Seventeenth-Century Breda', in *Exchanging Medieval Material Culture. Studies on Archaeology and History Presented to*

Roger Machado's Inventory

Machado's extant inventory forms a small part of Machado's extant memorandum book and is written in French on paper.[31] The inventory was compiled in 1484 when Machado is thought to have been in exile in Brittany with Henry Tudor. The inventory lists valuable, movable objects: a wide selection of linen, especially for the dining table, wine, clothing, furs, books, pewter vessels and a saltcellar (See the Appendix for a full transcription and translation). The transportability of the objects is significant to the interpretation of the inventory. If Machado was indeed in exile at the time of its composition, then transportability of wealth would have been essential.[32] Alternatively, these may have been items left behind in England that Machado may have put into safe-keeping, or just simply left hoping to retrieve them when he returned. Perhaps more interesting, however, are the objects that were not listed in the inventory. What were they and why are they absent? The excavation of Machado's Southampton residence has provided some answers to this question.

The Material Evidence

From May 1976 to February 1977, a site was excavated on the corner of Upper Bugle Street and Simnel Street in the old quarter of Southampton. It was identified as tenements 423 and 424 in the Southampton Terrier of 1454.[33] From 1486 to 1497 'Rychmont' rented the property for 13s 6d per year.[34] It is without doubt that Machado was this 'Rychmont'. Roger Machado has long been identified as Richmond in the Southampton civic records: in the Book of Remembrance for 1486 Machado is referred to as 'Richemond kyng of herawds' and 'Richmond herald of arms'; he is 'Richmond' in the Steward's Book of

---

Frans Verhaeghe, ed. K. De Groote, D. Tys and M. Pieters (Brussels: Vlaams Instituut voor het Onroerend Erfgoed and the Vrije Universiteit, 2010); Harold Mytum, 'Biographies of Projects, People and Places: Archaeologists and William and Martha Harries at Henllys Farm, Pembrokeshire', *Post-Medieval Archaeology*, 44 Issue 2 (2010): 294–319.

[31]   London, College of Arms, MS Arundel 51, f. 19.

[32]   For further information regarding the reason Machado kept an inventory and the evidence for his exile see Gemma L. Watson, 'A Herald and his Objects in Exile: Roger Machado and his Memorandum Book, 1484–5', in *Travels and Mobilities in the Middle Ages: From the Atlantic to the Black Sea*, ed. Marianne O'Doherty and Felicitas Schmieder (Turnhout, Belgium: Brepols, 2015).

[33]   Kaye, *Cartulary*, 289–91.

[34]   Ibid.

1492–3; and 'Richemond' in the Book of Fines in 1491.[35] He is only referred to once by his personal name, when he was created a free burgess in 1491.[36] We also know from Machado's embassy accounts in his memorandum book that he lived in Southampton and it was also common for heralds to be known by their official title at this time.[37]

The excavation revealed the remains of two stone undercrofts fronting onto Simnel Street that dated back to the thirteenth century.[38] These would have formed the foundations of timber-framed structures that were converted into one property in the fourteenth century. A stone-lined garderobe and a cellar tunnel were found filled with artefacts dating mostly to the end of the fifteenth century when Machado inhabited the tenement.[39] This artefact assemblage largely consists of imported continental ceramics, including Italian maiolica and Raeren stoneware, as well as luxury Venetian glass vessels, much of which was *cristallo*, dating to around the time when Machado inhabited the tenements.[40] These exact or similar objects are not listed in Machado's earlier inventory compiled only a few years previously.

---

[35] Kaye, *Cartulary*, 289–91; H.W. Gidden, *The Book of Remembrance of Southampton*, 3 vols (Southampton: Southampton Record Society, 1927–30), III (1930), 40, 109; Anne Elizabeth Thick (ed.), *The Southampton Steward's Book of 1492–93 and the Terrier of 1495*, (Southampton: Southampton Records Society, 1995), 8; Butler, *The Book of Fines*, 17.

[36] Butler, *The Book of Fines*, 15.

[37] James Gairdner (ed.), *Memorials of King Henry VII* (London: Longman, Brown, Green, Longmans, and Roberts, 1858), 330; H.S. London and Anthony Richard Wagner, A. (eds), *The Life of William Bruges, the First Garter King of Arms, with a Biographical Notice of the Author and a Bibliography of his Published Writings, by Sir Anthony Wagner* (London: Harleian Society, 1970), 78.

[38] M. Shaw, 'Upper Bugle Street III Report', Southampton Archaeological Research Committee, unpublished.

[39] Duncan Brown dated the pottery to c. 1490–c. 1510 in Duncan H. Brown, *Pottery in Medieval Southampton c. 1066–1510* (York: Council for British Archaeology, 2002); Robert Charleston dated the Venetian glass to the end of the fifteenth century in R.J. Charleston, 'Glass Report UBS III', Southampton Archaeological Research Committee, unpublished.

[40] *Cristallo* glass is a high-quality clear glass that was produced on Murano in Venice. It was the only medium, other than rock crystal, that could achieve this visual effect in the later Middle Ages and was very difficult to produce, making it a very desirable commodity. *Cristallo* glass required sodium oxide usually made by burning and ashing salt marsh plants, widely available in the Venetian Lagoon, the addition of a stabiliser, usually lime, and then to get a very clear finish manganese oxide was also added. The ingredients then had to be fired to a very high temperature, preferably to over 1000 degrees Celsius.

A Life in Objects

Both the inventory and the archaeology described above offer different but complementary types of evidence. Ceramic and glass vessels were not listed in the inventory, but have survived physically. We could argue that Machado did not own these objects when he compiled the inventory since the inventory and archaeology are separated by at least two years, probably more. This may have been the case, but he would have owned similar vessels in 1484. Glass vessels and ceramics especially were invaluable receptacles for food and drink at this time and it is very unlikely that Machado favoured only pewter vessels in his kitchen and at his dining table. This then raises the question of why ceramics and glass were not listed in Machado's inventory. The answer may be due to the fragility of such objects. If the inventory was compiled as a list of objects transported with Machado whilst in exile, then ceramics and glass would not have been taken because they could break in transportation. The pewter vessels listed in Machado's inventory would have been much more resilient to hasty packing and long journeys. Alternatively, if the inventory was compiled as a list of objects left behind or in safe-keeping, then it is unlikely that glass and ceramic vessels would have been listed because they had little monetary value and were easily replaceable.

The material culture excavated from Machado's house provides another dimension not only to his life, but also to the inventory. However, it is a two-way relationship, as the inventory provides a source of evidence for other objects that Machado owned, objects that have not survived in the archaeological record. Linen, fur, leather and textiles very rarely survive in archaeological contexts, except under extreme environmental conditions such as water-logging, and metals such as pewter were often recycled rather than thrown away. Therefore, the inventory provides a source for the perishable and lost objects that Machado owned: linen tablecloths and serviettes, clothing, furs and pewter vessels. In addition to the enrichment that both sources of evidence offer one another, the inventory and material culture can also enhance our knowledge and understanding of Machado's material life in Southampton at the end of the fifteenth century, especially when compared with other excavations and similar documentary sources from the town. By using an interdisciplinary approach that draws upon archaeology and historiography, a greater understanding of the man who was Roger Machado and his lived experience of Southampton will be revealed. As Catherine Richardson and Tara Hamling put it: 'Knowing about people's possessions is crucial to understanding their experience of daily life, the way they saw themselves in relation to their peers and their responses to and interactions with the social, cultural and economic structures and processes which made up the societies in which they lived'.[41]

Machado's Southampton

Southampton was a thriving port town in the fifteenth century, so much so that Henry VI was moved to remark in 1447 that Southampton 'abounds in merchants, sailors and mariners who flock from distant parts to that town with an immense quantity of cargoes, galleys and ships plying with merchandise to the port there'.[42] The town had a substantial Italian community who were drawn there for the trade in English cloth and wool, and some rose to hold prominent positions within the town's local government.[43] Henry VII appointed Machado as his Searcher of Customs at the port of Southampton in 1485, which possibly prompted Machado's choosing to rent a property there. Perhaps one of the most revealing documents associated with Machado's life in Southampton is the 1488 description of the town's wards:

> ... and so to Mr Joh' Dawtrey and in to the litill' lane to the posternegate and vp agayn' a long by Shropshire and so on that side till' the Pylgrymesyate and (to the litill' yate of the Castell' ouer both sides vn to) the said Pilgrymes Yate and so vpward on the tother side along by Alyward' Place what Richemond inhabites ... [44]

For someone who probably did not spend a great deal of his time in Southampton, due to his heraldic commitments at court and his diplomatic obligations abroad, this short document clearly shows that he was well enough known for his home to become a landmark. Perhaps we could go as far as to say he was a local celebrity. Southampton was a good strategic location for Machado to choose as it provided good links to the Continent, which would aid his diplomatic work and also his trading adventures. Machado would have spoken with an accent and may have had exotic dark looks, but he would not have stood out in cosmopolitan Southampton. This may be another reason he chose Southampton as a base:

---

[41]   Tara Hamling and Catherine Richardson (eds), *Everyday Objects: Medieval and Early Modern Material Culture and its Meanings* (Farnham: Ashgate, 2010), 9–10.

[42]   Colin Platt, *Medieval Southampton: The Port and Trading Community, AD 1000–1600* (London: Routledge, 1973), 153.

[43]   For example, Christopher Ambrose was a Florentine by birth and was a prominent merchant in Southampton in the late fifteenth century. He rose to become bailiff in 1481–2, sheriff in 1483–4, alderman in 1488 and was mayor twice in 1486–7 and 1497–8 (Platt, *Medieval Southampton*, 153.

[44]   Description of the fourth ward in Lawrence Arthur Burgess (ed.), *The Southampton Terrier of 1454* (London: HMSO, 1976), 152.

because he could come and go without arousing much attention, something especially important when on secret business for the king.

Other excavations in the town provide a good comparison for the material culture excavated from Machado's residence and give us an indication of material life there at the end of the fifteenth century. Quilter's Vault is a medieval undercroft located on the west side of the High Street, close to its south end and the Town Quay. It has a surviving barrel vault and an adjacent stone-built cellar and garderobe that were filled in with material in the later fifteenth century.[45] The material retrieved was rich in ceramics and metalwork, and contained large quantities of imported ceramic tableware similar in range and quality to Machado's residence.[46] A Beauvais Earthenware mug decorated with the heraldic device of Henry Tudor was amongst the ceramic assemblage, being almost identical to the one found at Machado's residence.

A site known as the Woollen Hall was excavated in 1989 and revealed the remains of a twelfth-century family house with a thirteenth-century cellar below.[47] Agnes Overy lived there in the mid-fifteenth century and was one of the wealthiest landholders in Southampton.[48] The excavation unearthed a rich ceramic assemblage dating to the Overy family's occupancy. It included imported pottery from the Low Countries, Spain, Germany, France and Italy – for instance, Raeren stoneware mugs, Low Countries redware and late medieval Saintonge whiteware jugs and pitchers.[49] A small quantity of Venetian glass was also found which included *cristallo* vessels.[50] Agnes was probably born in the early 1400s. She married twice and had four children.[51] In December 1486, her husband William Overy was appointed surveyor of the customs, subsidies and other sums of money in the port of Southampton, and all of the customers, collectors and controllers there.[52] He was also in charge of supervision of all

---

[45]   Southampton City Council, SOU 128, unpublished excavation records.

[46]   The assemblage included Martincamp flasks, Normandy Stoneware, Late Saintonge pottery, Low Countries Redware, a South Netherlands Maiolica ring-handled vase, and also a yellow.

[47]   Southampton City Council, SOU 393, unpublished excavation records; it must be noted that Agnes's home was misidentified in the nineteenth century as the town's Woollen Hall by Henry Englefield and therefore, Agnes's Woollen Hall should not be confused with the actual Woollen Hall located on St Michael's Square above the Fish Market.

[48]   Southampton City Council, SOU 393, unpublished excavation records.

[49]   Sian E. Jones, 'Keeping Her in the Family: Women and Gender in Southampton, c. 1400–c. 1600' (PhD thesis, University of Southampton, 1997), 2.

[50]   Southampton City Council, SOU 393, unpublished excavation records.

[51]   Jones, *Keeping Her in the* Family, 2–3; Southampton City Council, SOU 393, unpublished excavation records.

[52]   *Calendar of Patent Rolls preserved in the Public Record Office: Henry VII* (London: HMSO), 143.

the town's port books. Machado would have known him through his position as the King's Searcher of Customs and they may have even socialised at each other's houses where their luxury imported table wares would have been used and displayed.

The extant Southampton probate inventories for the fifteenth and sixteenth centuries are also an excellent source for other items owned by inhabitants in the town, especially items that have not survived in the archaeological record. The majority of extant inventories are from probate records.[53] They are far more comprehensive than Machado's, which is no more than a brief list. They show the high level of material wellbeing of the men and women of the high and middling classes living in Southampton at that time.[54] Items are usually listed by room and their monetary value is given. Matthew Salmon was mayor of Southampton in 1494 and may have been an acquaintance of Machado's. His inventory dated 1495 lists hangings, spruce tables and cushions amongst items in the Hall totalling £3, 4s, 8d; and in the Parlour were a painted cloth, a feather bed and bolster, amongst other things, totalling £10, 8s, 4d.[55] His inventory illustrates his high status amongst the town's inhabitants. Like Machado's inventory, ceramics and glass vessels do not feature. However, the inventory of Jane Rigges, widow, dated 1559, does list a 'glas casse' in the hall.[56] Drinking glasses required their own special storage to prevent breakages, which in the sixteenth century was provided by a 'glass case', which would have been a lightly built wooden case of shelves.[57] The glass vessels themselves are however not listed. Stoneware jugs were common in the sixteenth-century inventories of Southampton, such as 'halfe a dozen of silver stones & ij stoned juggs covered' listed in the 1573 inventory of Richard Coode, a baker, and stoneware cups as in 'ij stone cupps covered with silver one parcell gilt' listed in the 1570 inventory of Thomas Edmondes, a cloth merchant.[58] Stoneware was made of a mottled or flecked brown stoneware pottery made firstly in Germany and later copied in England. There are several examples from the Machado assemblage.

The most expensive linens were imported from abroad.[59] Diaper and damask were imported from the Continent and each country had its own pattern.[60] Diaper was more valuable than similarly plain woven fabric and was therefore

---

[53] Edward Roberts and Karen Parker (eds), *Southampton Probate Inventories, 1447–1575*, 2 vols (Southampton: Southampton University Press, 1992).

[54] Platt, *Medieval Southampton*, 183.

[55] Roberts and Parker, *Southampton Probate* Inventories, 10–11.

[56] Ibid., 156.

[57] Ibid., xxiii.

[58] Ibid., xxxiii.

[59] Ibid., xxxi.

[60] Ibid.

restricted to those of a higher social status who could afford it.[61] Diaper features heavily in Machado's inventory listing seven long towels and 27 napkins of diaper amongst other items and it also features in the Southampton probate inventories. For example, the 1566 inventory of Thomas Mill, a gentleman, lists a diaper table cloth and 12 napkins of '*checker*'.[62] Table napkins appear in large numbers in the Southampton inventories, usually as multiples of 12. At this time napkins were used more frequently than today for wiping fingers and the mouth and for drying the hands after washing and therefore were invaluable at the dining table. At a time when there were no forks, spoons also played a more important role than today at meal times. Silver spoons are frequently listed in the Southampton probate inventories as they were popular items to bequeath. Spoons are not mentioned in Machado's inventory, but the remains of two bronze spoons, one of which is silver gilt, are amongst the Machado finds assemblage.[63]

This brief comparison of Machado's material culture and inventory with other sources in Southampton shows that Machado's objects were not unique for the town. Many other merchant households owned exotic imported pottery, luxury Venetian glass and expensive linens. Southampton seems to have been a prime port of entry for Venetian glass in the Middle Ages because of the numerous specimens excavated there and the fifteenth-century port records frequently mention glass coming from Italy and the Netherlands, with some later entries often referring to 'crystal', probably a term used to describe *cristallo*.[64] Ceramics were also imported into Southampton from France, the Low Countries, Iberia and Italy, forming part of ship cargoes. The port records describe Genoese carracks as carrying 'painted pots', which is probably a reference to brightly-painted maiolica made in Iberia and Italy.[65] Therefore, these commodities were readily available to the merchant class in Southampton as well as to Machado. However, even for Southampton, Machado's table was at the height of fashion and sophistication for the time. Not many other excavated sites in the town yielded the same quantities of

[61]   Kristen M. Burkholder, 'Threads Bared: Dress and Textiles in Late Medieval English Wills', in *Medieval Clothing and Textiles*, ed. Robin Netherton and Gale R. Crocker (Woodbridge: Boydell, 2005), 141.

[62]   Roberts and Parker, *Southampton Probate Inventories*, xxxi.

[63]   Southampton City Council, SOU 124, unpublished excavation records.

[64]   Robert J. Charleston, *English Glass and the Glass used in England, c. 400–1940* (London: George Allen and Unwin, 1984), 43.

[65]   Duncan H. Brown, 'The Imported Pottery of Late Medieval Southampton', *Medieval Ceramics* 17 (1993): 77.

Venetian glass and maiolica vessels as Machado's did.[66] Machado would have displayed his colourful maiolica and enamelled *cristallo* vessels on his table where they were used during the rituals of dining.

The Late Medieval and Early Renaissance Dining Table

We know from Machado's accounts of the foreign embassies he attended that he had his fellow ambassadors lodged with himself and other town members whilst on their way to the Continent from Southampton. In January 1489, Machado along with Thomas Savage, doctor of law, and Richard Nanfan, knight of the king's body, three ambassadors in an embassy of the King of Castile and a Scottish herald, set out on their embassy to Spain and Portugal. Machado documents who the ambassadors lodged with when they stayed at Southampton:

> ... the doctor of Castile at the house of John Gildon, then bailiff of the said town; and the knight of Castile at the hotel of a merchant citizen, called Vincent Tyt; and the chaplain of the Queen of Castile was lodged in the house of another citizen, called Laurence Nyenbolt. And there was lodged in the house with this chaplain and in his company a herald of the King of Scotland named Snowdon, who was sent into Castile by his sovereign lord the King of Scotland. The ambassadors of the King of England, my sovereign lord, were lodged thus: the doctor Master Thomas Savage was lodged with a citizen called Thomas Wilson. And Mr. Richard Nanfan, knight for the king's body, was lodged with Richmond King of Arms of Norroy, who was staying at the time in the said town.[67]

Machado must have known and trusted these men to let them lodge such esteemed guests. Vincent Tyt, for instance, was a prominent citizen of Southampton. He was mayor twice in 1484–85 and 1498–99, and an alderman in 1488. We can imagine that Machado would have put his colourful ceramic and glass tableware to good use when having a guest, such as Richard Nanfan, to stay. It seems logical to assume that he may have had Vincent Tyt, John Gildon, Laurence Nyenbolt and Thomas Wilson, amongst others, to dinner at his home during his residency there. Being a herald he would have been familiar with the lavish feasts at the English court and the royal courts abroad and may have incorporated his experiences at his more modest table.

---

[66] Venetian glass may have been more common than the archaeological record suggests as glass recycling was prevalent at the time. This, however, offers the question as to why Machado's glass assemblage was not recycled.

[67] Gairdner, *Memorials*, 330.

Dining was one of the most important social acts in late medieval and early Renaissance cultural life, and this was reflected in the formalisation and complexity of the affair.[68] Bridget Henisch summarises the late medieval feast:

> a ceremonial dinner was a visual demonstration of the ties of power, dependence and mutual obligation which bound the host and guests. It was politic for the host to appear generous, because the lavishness of his table gave a clue to his resources; it was wise to be both hospitable to dependents and discriminating in the choice of guests of honour, therefore the number and calibre of diners in the hall revealed his importance and his power.[69]

The dining table was also a place where business was discussed and where deals were made and broken. Therefore, it was important that one knew the correct dining etiquette, and from the fourteenth century books on dining custom were widely available to instruct one on how to do things properly.[70] We know of the great feasts of royalty and the nobility, but less scholarly attention has been given to the dining arrangements of others. This is not surprising as information has usually come from personal accounts, conduct books, illuminated manuscripts or from pieces of decorative art that usually describe or depict the grandeur of great feasts. Nevertheless, they are useful tools as it can be assumed that those lower down the social scale emulated the dining rules and customs of the elite to some extent.[71] Machado and his guests would have known the proper dining etiquette and one can imagine Machado discussing the coming embassy with Richard Nanfan. Machado may even have had all members of the embassy to dine with him.

Dining in the fifteenth century was an arena where concepts of hierarchy and status were confirmed through the seating plan and order of service, and the physical layout of the room and table and the vessels used carried hidden messages.[72] There were a few basic set-rules that were followed at the fifteenth-century dining table.

---

[68]   Hugh Willmott, 'Tudor Dining: Object and Image at the Table', in *Consuming Passions: Dining from Antiquity to the Eighteenth Century*, ed. Maureen Carroll, D. M. Hadley and Hugh Willmott (Stroud: Tempus, 2005), 121.

[69]   Bridget Ann Henisch, *Fast and Feast: Food in Medieval Society* (London: Pennsylvania State University Press, 1976), 56–7.

[70]   Roy C. Strong, *Feast: A History of Grand Eating* (London: J. Cape, 2002), 91.

[71]   Duncan H. Brown, 'Pottery and Manners', in *Consuming Passions: Dining from Antiquity to the Eighteenth Century*, ed. Maureen Carroll, D. M. Hadley and Hugh Willmott (Stroud: Tempus, 2005), 95.

[72]   Willmott, 'Tudor Dining', 126.

Before the meal started Machado's hall would have been set up with trestle tables and benches, and the tables laid.[73] The hall was not merely a room, but a hierarchical space with places for the owners of the house, for their guests and for their servants according to their status. It was a stage for one of the central events of the day, where the formal rituals of serving and consuming food could take place.[74] Once all diners were seated, trenchers of bread were cut, the saltcellar was laid on the table and salt was spooned onto each trencher.[75] Where the saltcellar was placed at the table signified that the person seated there was at the apex of the dining hierarchy.[76] A saltcellar is listed amongst the objects in Machado's inventory. It may have been placed in front of Machado, but if Machado had all members of the embassy to dine then Thomas Savage, who was leading the embassy, would perhaps have held that place. Hands were then washed and dried using linen serviettes and grace was said. After grace the meat was carved at a side table and carried to the guests, who ate in messes.[77] There were customs governing the number of diners of each rank that comprised a mess and similar rules applied to how many dishes were served to each group. Servants brought food to the table, ensured trenchers were clean or replaced if wet and kept the table tidy and free from waste and refilled cups with ale or wine as soon as they were empty.[78] The presentation of ale and wine to diners was also accompanied by much ceremony, and guests were not allowed to serve themselves.[79]

The provision of water for washing and the serving of ale would have been provided by large ceramic pitchers and jugs, whilst wine may have been served from fine imported earthenware and Venetian glass flasks. The variety of vessel types reflected a wide range of dining customs: jugs were used for serving liquids; cups, mugs, beakers and goblets were used for drinking; dishes and bowls were used for serving food or as finger bowls for washing hands; chafing dishes were used to keep food warm.[80] There were conventions that governed the sorts of materials suitable for different social ranks. For instance, servants would

---

[73]   D.M. Hadley, 'Dining in Disharmony in the Later Middle Ages', in *Consuming Passions: Dining from Antiquity to the Eighteenth Century*, ed. Maureen Carroll, D.M. Hadley and Hugh Willmott (Stroud: Tempus, 2005), 102.

[74]   Mark Gardiner, 'Buttery and Pantry and their Antecedents: Idea and Architecture in the English Medieval House', in *Medieval Domesticity: Home, Housing and Household in Medieval England*, ed. P.J.P. Goldberg and Maryanne Kowaleski (Cambridge: Cambridge University Press, 2008), 38.

[75]   Brown, 'Pottery and Manners', 95.

[76]   Strong, *Feast*, 99.

[77]   Messes were groups of diners who shared food from the same dish.

[78]   Brown, 'Pottery and Manners', 95.

[79]   P.W. Hammond, *Food and Feast in Medieval England* (Stroud: Alan Sutton, 1995), 112.

[80]   Brown, 'Pottery and Manners', 96.

not have been offered food or drink served in precious metal vessels; ceramics would have been much more suitable for the lower ranks that may have also been in attendance.[81]

Hierarchy was also determined by the order of service and the allocation of food. For instance, game birds such as pheasants, herons, swans and peacocks were strictly reserved for the high table.[82] Hierarchy even controlled the bread that was served with finer, fresh bread going to the host and his guests whilst those seated further down the hall received three-day-old bread.[83] Tablecloths may have also been layered, each layer being revealed after each course, and serviettes may have been starched and stiffened and deployed in sculpture. The material culture of dining was part of the performance that encompassed this important part of medieval and early modern life.

By the end of the Middle Ages there was the start of a movement away from the importance of sharing at the table towards the individual use of vessels, which began in Renaissance Italy.[84] A Venetian observed in c. 1496 that the English were

> very sparing of wine when they drink it at their own expense. And this, it is said, they do in order to induce their other English guests to drink wine in moderation also; not considering it any inconvenience for three or four persons to drink out of the same cup.[85]

Rachel Tyson argues that this statement suggests that the practice of sharing the cup may have been unusual in Italy and suggests that Venice was by now accustomed to providing individual diners with their own drinking vessels. The Italian Renaissance brought with it new attitudes towards the individual and an increasing concern with hygiene resulting in the disappearance of sharing vessels during dining. This is supported by many north Italian paintings which show equal numbers of glass beakers and diners by the fifteenth century.[86] The exact date when this significant shift towards the individual in the material culture of

---

[81] Brown, 'Pottery and Manners', 96.

[82] Strong, *Feast*, 104.

[83] Ibid., 106

[84] Willmott, 'Tudor Dining', 128.

[85] C.A. Sneyd (ed. and trans., *A relation, or rather a true account, of the island of England; with sundry particulars of the customs of the royal revenues under King Henry the Seventh, about the year 1500*, Camden Society 37 (London: Offices of the Royal Historical Society, 1847), 21; As quoted in Rachel Tyson, *Medieval Glass Vessels Found in England c. AD 1200–1500* (York: Council for British Archaeology, 2000), 30, and Hugh Willmott, *Early Post-Medieval Vessel Glass in England, c. 1500–1670* (York: Council for British Archaeology, 2002), 127.

[86] Tyson, *Medieval Glass*, 31.

dining occurred in England is still uncertain.[87] However, the discovery of the fragments of no fewer than 12 beakers from Machado's Southampton home may suggest that it was happening (at least in English port towns where there was frequent contact with Europe and alien residents in the town) at the end of the fifteenth century.

This new concern with the importance of the individual can also be observed in the ceramics at the dinner table. The Italian production of ceramics changed the appearance of the late medieval table, replacing the trencher with the plate as the diner's receptacle for food.[88] During the fifteenth century, the craft of faience ware was imported from Spain. The Italians were quick to learn how to produce it, and by the 1480s they had developed their own unique style.[89] The increasing availability of maiolica meant that the practice of sharing food receptacles gradually ceased.[90]

The dining table was also a place where display was important, and Machado would have displayed his fashionable Venetian glass and imported ceramics at his table for his guests to see. The fourteenth century saw the emergence in high-status residences of the *dressoirs de parement*. These were buffets purely designed for the display of plate.[91] They started life as simple cupboards serving as a place where beverages could be kept in large pitchers, where food could be deposited before it went on the table or where utensils could be usefully stacked.[92] Wine would have been decanted into glass flasks and displayed on the dresser. Machado owned many Venetian glass flasks, most of which were *cristallo*, and he also appears to have been a great lover of wine. Two barrels of wine are listed in his inventory, but he also imported it, as evidenced by his mercantile accounts and also the special licence he was granted by the king to import Gascon wine in 1494.[93] Drinking vessels, such as Machado's *cristallo* glass beakers, would also have been kept on the dresser rather than on the table. They would have been filled from there and brought to the table when required, then brought back to the dresser to be cleaned ready for the next user. This was a development away from the medieval idea of a communal cup, but diners at this time in England still did not have their own individual drinking vessel.[94]

---

[87] Rachel Tyson, 'Medieval Glass Vessels: Public and Private Wealth', *Current Archaeology*, 186 (2003): 255.

[88] Strong, *Feast*, 166.

[89] Ibid.

[90] Willmott, 'Tudor Dining', 128.

[91] Strong, *Feast*, 96.

[92] Ibid.

[93] London, College of Arms, MS Arundel 51, f. 19v and ff. 21r–22r. Noble, M. 1805 *A history of the College of Arms*, London, p. 111.

[94] Willmott, 'Tudor Dining', 125.

William Harrison talks of the display of vessels at a cupboard in his 1577 treatise, *A Description of England*:

> As for drink, it is usually filled in pots, goblets, jugs, bowls of silver in noblemen's houses; also in fine Venice glasses of all forms: all which notwithstanding are seldom set on the table, but each one as necessity urgeth, calleth for a cup of such drink as him listeth to have, so that, when he has tasted of it, he delivereth the cup again to someone of the standers by, who, making it clean by pouring out the drink that remaineth, restoreth it to the cupboard from whence he fetched the same.[95]

Luxury ceramics could also be displayed on the dresser. Ceramic production in Europe took off in the thirteenth century when *de luxe* vessels worthy for exhibition on the buffet emerged for the first time.[96] Earthenware declined in popularity as brilliantly colourful maiolica took over after c. 1450 and was the ceramic to have at one's dinner table.[97] Ceramic vessels were used by all levels of society, but it was the exotic forms and decoration of high-status imported wares that elevated their social value and not the material they were made from. They could also embody emerging Renaissance ideals, especially evident in maiolica. Decoration was evolving away from spontaneous looking effects of bold shape and incidental decoration of the medieval period to more ordered and calculated effects of contrasting pattern. The alteration of broad straight stripes and thin spirals, the deployment of contrasting colours and lines of direction are evidence of a new study of the basic principles of balance and rhythm.[98] Duncan Brown has extensively analysed the pottery from medieval Southampton and argues that pottery was clearly important to the people there and that the quantities of Continental wares present correspond to the significance of the port at that time.[99] Brown has also commented on the increasing variety of ceramic forms and range of sources represented in late medieval pottery in Southampton. He argues that this reflects the increase in sophistication of mealtime ceremony and etiquette at that time.[100] In addition, Hugh Willmott has argued that by the late sixteenth century, functional vessels were becoming elaborate decorative table

---

[95]   William Harrison, *A Description of England*, 3 vols, ed. Furnival (London: New Shakespeare Society 1877), vol. 1, 147, as quoted in Charleston, *English Glass*, 52.

[96]   Strong, *Feast*, 100.

[97]   Ibid.

[98]   Philip Holdsworth, *Luxury Goods from a Medieval Household* (Southampton: Southampton Archaeological Research Committee, 1986).

[99]   Duncan H. Brown, 'The Social Significance of Imported Medieval Pottery', in *Not So Much a Pot, More a Way of Life*, ed. C. G. Cumberpatch and P.W. Blinkhorn (Oxford: Oxbow Books, 1997), 112; Brown, *Pottery in Medieval Southampton*.

[100]   Brown, *Pottery and Manners*, 96.

centrepieces; for example, expensive silver gilt saltcellars, colourful maiolica and decorative glasses were displayed in this way.[101] However, I would argue that this was already being established at the turn of that century. Machado's tableware surely illustrates this.

The use of glass vessels was almost exclusively confined to the higher classes in this period, but this has little to do with the cost or availability of such items but a result of how vessels were used by the higher classes compared with the lower.[102] In comparison with vessels made from silver and gold, glass was significantly cheaper and a popular medium for tableware in the late medieval period and early Renaissance. William Harrison commented in 1577 that:

> our gentility, as loathing those metals of gold and silver because of the plenty do now generally choose rather the Venice glasses, both for our wine and beer, than any of those metals or stone wherein beforetime we have been accustomed to drink ... the poorest also will have glass if they may, but sith the Venetian is somewhat too dear for them, they content themselves with such as are made at home of fern and burned stone.[103]

The high demand for Venetian glass at this time was partly due to the failure of the English glass industry to supply similar vessels, although even the best glass manufacturers in England could not compete with the finest glass from Venice.[104] Imported glass tableware was intended to be seen in the public sphere and had a social importance that went beyond their practical purpose.[105] Their consciously styled form and decoration embodied the symbolic codes and values of high-status European culture.[106] For instance, glass goblets were often intentionally styled to emulate the Christian chalice.[107] Its fragility also made investment in glass a demonstration of conspicuous consumption and wealth. Those who owned it could afford to keep replacing it when it broke or when a different style became fashionable,[108] something that was also observed by Harrison:

---

[101] Willmott, 'Tudor Dining', 128.

[102] Tyson, *Medieval Glass*, 24.

[103] Hugh Willmott, 'English Sixteenth- and Early Seventeenth-Century Vessel Glass in the Context of Dining', in *Material Culture in Medieval Europe: Papers of the 'Medieval Europe Brugge 1997' Conference*, ed. Guy de Boe and Frans Verhaeghe (Zelik: Instituut voor het Archeologisch Patrimonium, 1997), 186–7.

[104] Willmott, *Early Post-Medieval Vessel Glass*, 18.

[105] Tyson, *Medieval Glass*, 24.

[106] Ibid.

[107] Ibid., 25.

[108] Willmott, 'English Sixteenth- and Early Seventeenth-Century Vessel Glass', 188.

In time, [glasses] go one way, that is to shards at the last, so that our great expences in glasses ... are worst of all bestowed in mine opinion, because their pieces do turn unto no profit.[109]

Goblets and beakers were the most visible form of glassware to be used at the table and therefore if only a limited investment was to be made in glass then it was made in this form.[110] As mentioned above, Machado owned at least 12 glass beakers and at least two goblets, and he may have bought them on an individual basis as demonstrated by the variety of beaker-types represented. Transparency may also have been a key factor in the desirability of glass at the dinner table as it was the only medium, other than rock crystal, that could achieve this visual effect. Montaigne, in his 1588 essay *On Experience*, wrote that 'earthenware and silver displease me compared with glass ... I dislike all metals compared with clear transparent materials. Let my eyes too taste it to the full'.[111] Being able to see the contents of the glass was evidently important.

Dining, therefore, acted as a place where display and communication through consumption could be expressed. It also acted as a vehicle by which meaning within society could pass on to the individual.[112] For instance, Machado used his dining table to exhibit his relationship with Henry VII. Amongst the objects excavated were the remains of a ceramic mug decorated with the heraldic device of Henry Tudor. Heraldry was a common theme in decorative art in the medieval world and was used to enhance the status of objects as symbols of power.[113] Heraldic devices visually showed identity and allegiance, and were perhaps more effective than the written word as a mark of distinction.[114] Machado may have drunk beer from this very mug during the meal with the ambassadors and Southampton men, reminding them that he was one of the king's most senior and trusted heralds. The material culture of the dining room, therefore, had messages to convey as well as being functional.[115]

By combining the evidence provided from the inventory and excavation, the late fifteenth-century dining table, and the ritual and customs that Machado would have followed, have been brought to life. The dining table was a place where concepts of hierarchy were enacted and wealth and status were displayed through conspicuous consumption. The paraphernalia of dining, that is the

---

[109] Harrison, *A Description of England*, I, 147, as quoted in Willmott, *Early Post-Medieval Vessel Glass*, 27–8.

[110] Willmott, *Early Post-Medieval Vessel Glass*, 24.

[111] Ibid., 27.

[112] Willmott, 'English Sixteenth- and Early Seventeenth-century Vessel Glass', 187.

[113] Tyson, *Medieval Glass*, 25.

[114] C.M. Woolgar, *The Senses in Late Medieval England* (New Haven and London: Yale University Press, 2006), 181–3.

[115] Hadley, 'Dining in Disharmony', 113.

drinking vessels, utensils, plates, bowls and dishes, the tablecloths, napkins and saltcellar were fundamental to this, whether it was at an informal gathering of acquaintances or at a lavish banquet. Machado's table was no different with its diaper tablecloths and napkins, and its colourful and lustrous ceramics and glass.

Conclusion

This chapter has explored interdisciplinarity in biography through the microhistory of Roger Machado. The archaeological evidence for Machado's life has provided the unique opportunity to consider his day-to-day existence, something that would not have been possible otherwise. Comparison of the material culture with his extant inventory has also provided a clear justification for interdisciplinary research: the objects excavated from Machado's Southampton residence are not listed in his inventory, and objects listed in the inventory have not survived archaeologically. This is also the case for other Southampton residents. Each type of evidence brings something different to the table and helps to build a more accurate picture of Machado's material possessions, which in turn give us an insight into his daily life in Southampton.

The majority of Machado's objects that have survived in the archaeological record and are described in his extant inventory pertain to dining and therefore offer the opportunity to study the dining practices of the up-and-coming, middling strata of society in the later fifteenth century. Feasting and social dining was an important part of late medieval and early modern life, which is reflected in the types and variety of objects used and displayed in this setting. Machado's table would have glittered and shone with the vessels he chose to use in this setting, conveying messages of luxury and good taste. He used and displayed his colourful maiolica and Venetian glass at his dining table as a way of showing-off his wealth and status through conspicuous consumption, regularly replacing these relatively inexpensive and fragile, although no-less socially valuable, objects when required. Machado also wanted to impress his guests by exhibiting his relationship to Henry VII at his dinner table. Dining was a performance that would have involved the layering of the table with expensive linen tablecloths and towels, hierarchical seating arrangements, the ritualistic washing and drying of hands, the placing of the saltcellar, the sharing of dishes, and the elaborate serving of drink. The analysis of the material culture of dining has enabled this chapter to discuss how Machado would have used objects in this arena as a way of reaffirming his social standing in hierarchical medieval society and negotiate his place within it.

Appendix

Transcription of Roger Machado's Inventory: London, College of Arms, MS Arundel 51, fol. 19.[116]

[19r] Ihus
Lestoffaigne de mon hostel anno 1484
Et in primis v doubliers de diaper
Item vij touailles longus de diaper
Item xxvij serviettes de diaper
Item xv aulles de diaper touailles
Item iij linceules fins de xpristien enfans
Item xiiij peres de linceules fins et gros
Item iiij touailles de lauer mains plaines
Item iij garnisses de vasselle destain
Item vng cilier et les repas et iij courtines de telle blanche
Item vne pieche de canevas panit tout neuf
Item iij courtines de toille partie de gris et bleu
Item vne sarge de bleu
Item vne verges de telle grosse crue
Item vng cuverlit de verdure de vertdimanges
Item iij robes de ma famme de viollet dassanoir
Vne fourrerie de minkes vne de menevier une de gris Regnes
Item ancore une aultre roube de ma femme
de moster de violles fourrureye de dagneulx
Item ancoure roube de ma femme
doubleye de toelle et les manches et coullier de veloures
Item vne roube mienne de crimorssin doubleye de sarcenet
Item ancore vne aultre noire courte fourrureye dagneulx
Item vne aultre longue de noir single vne de vert single
Item vng coffre long plain de livres et de letters
Item ij barriles de vin vng de blanc et vng de claret
[19v] Item ij petis coffres vng de spruche et laultre de estrech beurt viell
Item vng petijt coffre de qujer garny de fer blank

---

[116] Many thanks go to Dr Lena Wahlgren-Smith, Professor Anne Curry and Professor Maria Hayward for their help in the translation of Machado's inventory. I would also like to thank my PhD supervisors Professor Ros King, Professor Anne Curry, Professor Matthew Johnson, Duncan Brown and Karen Wardley for their time, encouragement and support throughout my doctoral research on Machado. Thanks also go to the archivists at the College of Arms for their help during my countless visits to the library there, and also to Gill Woolrich, Curator of Archaeology at Southampton. Any errors in this work are of course my own.

Translation:

Ihus
Inventory of my house year 1484
And in the first 5 doublets of diaper
Item 7 long towels of diaper
Item 27 serviettes of diaper
Item 15 ells of diaper towels
Item 3 fine linen cloths for christening children
Item 14 linen cloth fine and coarse
Item 4 towels for washing hands
Item 3 sets of pewter vessels
Item a salt cellar and 3 white table cloths
Item 1 piece of canvas cloth all new
Item 3 table cloths divided into grey and blue
Item a serge of blue
Item 7 rods of coarse raw cloth
Item 1 coverlet of green for Sunday
Item 3 dresses for my wife of violet *dassanoir*
1 fur of mink, 1 of miniver, 1 of grey animal
Item another dress for my wife, doublet of cloth and sleeves and collar
    of velvet
Item a robe of mine of crimson, doublet of sarcenet
Item another black lamb skin cloth
Item another long singlet of green
Item one long plain chest full of books and letters
Item 2 barrels of wine, one of white and one of red
Item 2 small chests of spruce and *estrech beurt viell*
Item one small chest of leather decorated/bound with white iron

Chapter 6

Mary Beale (1633–1699) and her Objects of Affection

Helen Draper

Until the last quarter of the twentieth century, art history was largely the study of objects arranged in groups, each of which had a person attached. The objects stood in for the person, but also for a broader intellectual and artistic continuum. Knowledge of an artist's world and inner life supplied a narrative setting in which to place the objects and could, perhaps, inform an understanding of them. In some cases – those of Artemisia Gentileschi and Vincent van Gogh being extreme examples – the painted objects are now defined, in part, by public awareness of particular aspects of the artist's personal life. Conversely, the personal reputation of some artists is largely defined by an interpretation of objects with which they are credited. While one artist will attempt to manage the development of her own reputation, another may leave it to chance and risk being redefined, in unpredictable ways, by third parties. By neglecting to sign her paintings, for example, a female painter opens the way for her best work to be re-attributed to male contemporaries. Twentieth-century artists' tendency to reject 'made' objects and the art market has, in the twenty-first century, necessitated the development of new art historical strategies for interpreting and evaluating works that may be comprised of performance, light, sound or nothingness. As a result, some contemporary installations are accompanied by written statements in which the artists, or their intermediaries, reflect on or explain their work. Paradoxically, these new textual objects take on material, autobiographical and perhaps even monetary values of their own and, who knows, could one day stand in for, or even become, *the work*.

Gazing wistfully back to the apparent simplicity of the seventeenth-century art world, I demonstrated, in 'her painting of Apricots: the invisibility of Mary Beale (1633–1699)', that during her lifetime the painter made a very good stab at manipulating her own reputation by astute promotion of herself and of the objects she created.[1] Beale was not the only female painter working in England

---

[1]   Helen Draper, 'her painting of Apricots: the invisibility of Mary Beale (1633–1699)', *Forum for Modern Language Studies*, [special issue on 'Artists' Statements'] 48:4 (2012): 389–405.

but, in the documented history of British art, hers was the earliest studio led by a woman artist. Other women earned money as painters, but only Beale is known to have established an independent commercial studio, and to have maintained it successfully for more than 20 years without the benefit of formal training, court patronage or guild affiliation.[2] Moreover, Mary is survived by scores of securely attributed 'made' objects including at least six self-portraits, five poems, a *Discourse on Friendship* and a unique description of how to paint.[3] Things are never as simple as they seem, however, and despite her valiant and tangible acts of self-definition, Mary Beale the artist has often been judged on the basis of a misleading selection of the works attributed to her. Mary's body of work as a whole, on the other hand, has frequently been perceived through a gauze of subjective, often inaccurate, biography about the woman.

Parish records tell us that 19-year old gentlewoman Mary Cradock married Charles Beale (1631–1705) in 1652 and for a time the couple became residents of Covent Garden, part of an artists' colony in what was then a fashionable but rather louche area of London.[4] Although long an artist of note, Mary was not a fully professional painter until 1670/1, and thereafter the income from her portrait studio largely supported her family. After a brief stint as a civil servant, Charles became Mary's studio assistant, preparing canvases, making and selling pigments and experimenting with materials. All this was at a time when rhetorical convention did its best to discourage women at most levels of society from openly expressing their ideas and creativity. Over a period of several years, Mary cultivated a public identity that allowed her to avoid such disparagement, to reach out to an audience beyond her own home, and eventually made her professional work acceptable. In projecting this respectable persona she leaned heavily upon the outward conventionality of her marriage and domestic

---

[2]   Gentlewoman artists included Lievine Teerlinc (b. before 1520–d. 1576), official painter at the courts of Henry VIII and Elizabeth I; some women were apprentices to the Painter-Stainers' Guild, see Richard Johns, 'The Painter-Stainers' Company and the "English School of Painters"', *Art History*, 31:3 (June 2008): 331; Susan E. James, *Feminine Dynamic in English Art, 1485–1603* (Farnham: Ashgate, 2009); Robert Tittler, *Portraits, Painters and Publics in Provincial England, 1540–1640* (Oxford: Oxford University Press, 2012).

[3]   Mary Beale, *Discourse on Friendship*, [1666], London, British Library, Harley MS 6828 fols 510–23; 'Observations by MB in her painting of Apricots in August 1663' in Charles Beale, *Experimentall Seacrets found out in the way of painting*, (1647/8–1663), Glasgow, University Library, Special Collections, MS Ferguson 134. See also Draper, 'her painting of Apricots'.

[4]   For the marriage see the Parish Register of All Saints' Church, Barrow, Suffolk, Volume 1, 8 March 1651/2; while the record of the birth of their son Bartholomew on the 12 February 1655 places the Beales in London, see *The Registers of St. Paul's Church, Covent Garden, London, Vol. 1 Christenings, 1653–1752*, ed. Rev. William H Hunt, (London: Harleian Society, 1906), 5.

circumstances, and on the prevailing culture of sociable writing, painting and gift giving within her closest circle. More than 80 surviving portraits, poems and letters exchanged by the Beales and their friends, attest to the central importance of precious objects shared, each having significance as a work of art, gift and as social currency. Mary Beale and her circle provide us with an opportunity to examine the complex entwining of the lives of people and things in the early modern period.

Later in my chapter I will discuss Beale's exploration of likeness and identity as expressed in the painted and written objects she made, and I will conclude by demonstrating how Mary used such objects to manipulate her reputation and to further her career. Along the way I will describe how Mary's intimate circle of friends worked together to promote her respectable, and commercial, public persona. In this first part of the chapter, however, I will draw on the critical concept of *influence* – one employed routinely by cultural historians – to extend my examination of 'made' objects to encompass objects 'seen'. Inevitably, Beale's artistic reputation came to be defined, at least in part, by the objects she created, but her own personal and artistic development was informed by objects she saw and the things she read.

Biographical researchers take a magnifying glass to their subject's family, social and political milieu, associates, letters and diaries, but might ignore the non-textual physical things that surrounded her. Yet some of those neglected objects are imbued with a wealth of sociological significance, and were often designed for the *very purpose* of influencing the thoughts and deeds of others. Based on rigorous research, the first section of this chapter is designed to address one side of the academic, but admittedly problematic, concept of 'influence' which can be, by its very nature, difficult to demonstrate using conventional methodologies. In the present context, influence is the power that one's presence or ideas can have over others in their thoughts or actions. Influence is also the power that an object, natural or created, can exert as a physical totem of one, or a set of ideas. A single object can act as a powerful visual catalyst whereby shapes, lines and colours can trigger a cerebral chain reaction of creativity. Objects, including portraits and funerary monuments, can also be the by-products of an intense emotional experience on the part of those who bring them into being, and can evoke similar responses in those who see them. The electricity of influence passes unceasingly yet often imperceptibly between people and objects in an ever-renewing cycle.

I am not about to embark, however, upon an exhaustive survey of all or even many of the objects that Mary Beale knew in her lifetime, although dozens still survive and may yet cast her in a new light. Instead I begin by examining a few of the most visually striking and highly charged objects which Mary saw every day as a child. Here my methodology uses objects as sources – not as repositories of evidence about the subject, but as one means of contextualising her early, undocumented experience of the world, an especially fitting approach for Beale, whose life later became inextricably bound up with objects which were complex repositories of ideas, as well as visual, tactile things of beauty.

My chapter does not ask in a literal sense whether a small group of objects seen in childhood later influenced the work Mary Beale created but, more importantly (within the remit of this book), considers whether my methodology offers another way of seeing the subjects of early modern biography. By examining a group of related objects, and analysing them in less mechanistic terms than the perception of 'cause and effect', I suggest is it possible to view the subject with reference to networks and ideologies not apparent in documentary sources. While the data gathered in this may be suggestive rather than empirical it can inform the interpretation of other sources and offer new avenues for investigation.

In the second section, using documentary evidence, I build upon these ideas to show the complex forces of influence at work in practice, inspiring in Beale's circle the exercise of virtue, art and patronage. Concluding the essay, I document a near perfect example of how a single public object came into being through the influence of human kindness, gratitude and shared ambition and, several hundred years later, inspired in a viewer another act of kindness and generosity. Combined in this way, the model of influence presented by my case-study as a whole may provide a complementary approach to exploring the views, motivations and decision-making processes of historical subjects.

Mary Cradock was baptised on the 26th of March 1633 by her father John Cradock (1595–1652), a clergyman at Barrow, near Bury St Edmunds in Suffolk. All Saints, Barrow's medieval church, has an impressive early thirteenth-century tower but modern visitors, like Pevsner before them, may not think its six-hundred-year-old stone font worthy of detailed inspection.[5]

Austere and conservative despite its decoration, the font is nevertheless a forceful pictorial declaration of socio-political hierarchy: of the parishioner's dutiful order of allegiance to God, country and county, and of the potency of noble lineage. Each face of the octagonal basin – from which Mary was probably anointed – is comprised of a rectangular recess in which sits one of eight carved shields painted with emblems of the Passion of Christ, or with the devices of St Edmund, St George, France and Canterbury. The font is a piece of gothic design, complete with quatrefoils and pointed arches. Shallow, faux-mullioned niches run the full height of its central column, echoing the traceried windows and blind arcading of a style of architecture that had prevailed in Europe since the twelfth century. According to Suffolk's local historian, John Gage, writing

---

[5]   'FONT. Perp, octagonal, with eight shields in panels'. Nikolaus Pevsner, *Suffolk* ('The Buildings of England' series), revised by Enid Radcliffe, (New Haven and London: Yale University Press, 2002), 86–7.

Figure 6.1   Fourteenth-century baptismal font, All Saints' Church, Barrow, Suffolk. Copyright Robin Stummer.

in 1838, the font dates from the 'close of the fourteenth century' and, from the inclusion of the arms of the le Despenser family, had been installed as a memorial to one of their number.[6] The le Despensers' heraldic shield bears a 'label of five points', a pictorial banner signifying that the arms were those of an eldest son whose father was still living. Genealogical research suggests that they may have belonged to Sir Philip le Dispenser (c. 1365–1424), Lord le Despenser of Nettlestead in Suffolk, before the death of his father, also Sir Philip, in 1401. The younger Lord Despenser inherited the manor of Barrow through his marriage to Elizabeth Tiptoft (c. 1370–d. by 1424) and the couple's only child, Margery le Despenser (d. 1478), was born between 1398 and 1400. On the basis of such compelling stylistic, heraldic and biographical grounds, it is beguiling to conclude that this piece of Barrow's church furniture may have been made to coincide with the arrival of a long anticipated child and heir. In 1404, in another public gesture of genealogical continuity, the infant Margery was betrothed to her kinsman, Sir John, 7th Lord Roos, in a familial transaction which required a papal dispensation for consanguinity.[7] It is more than likely that when John Cradock baptised Mary, his firstborn child, it was at a font created more than two hundred years earlier to mark the birth of another little girl. Whether the Cradocks were aware of the object's history and symbolism is not known, much less how such knowledge may have affected them. It is safe to say, perhaps, that the ritual use of so implacable an object, one so redolent of power and patronage, could not help but impress generations of Barrow's pastors and parishioners alike.

The le Despensers themselves were not quite so immovable, being replaced as lords of the manor of Barrow by the progeny of Margery's second marriage to Sir Roger Wentworth (1396–1452). In 1539 the Wentworths sold the manor to Sir Clement Heigham (1495–1570) who erected Barrow Hall, a moated house very close to All Saints' Church and Rectory. Heigham was an ardent Catholic persecutor of Suffolk's protestants and a Lincoln's Inn lawyer who won favour with Mary I and Philip of Spain, rising to become Speaker of the House of Commons and Lord Chief Barron of the Exchequer. On the accession of Queen Elizabeth I, however, Heigham retreated to Barrow where he was a justice of the peace and where his funerary monument can now be seen to the left of All Saints' altar. Under a gothic stone canopy, decorated with Tudor roses,

---

6   John Gage, *History and Antiquities of Suffolk: Thingoe Hundred* (Bury St Edmunds and London: Deck and Bentley, 1838), 21, in which the author suggested that the font may have been endowed for Elizabeth, the widow of Hugh, Lord le Despenser, but this does not appear to agree with biographical information on the family at the end of the fourteenth century.

7   Gage, *History and Antiquities of Suffolk*, 1–8; Arthur Collins, *Collins's Peerage of England, Genealogical, Biographical, and Historical, Greatly Augmented, and Continued to the Present Time*, ed. Sir Egerton Brydges, 9 vols (London: 1812), VI, 201.

a knight and his two families are depicted on three separate brasses. A tableau on the far left represents Heigham's first wife, Anne Moonings (1500–1540), who kneels before a prayer book with her five daughters standing to her left. On the far right-hand side second wife Anne Waldegrave (1506–1590) and her two daughters face armour-clad Sir Clement kneeling at prayer at the centre of the composition. On a partially damaged section of brass behind the patriarch stands a small boy, one of his four sons, the rest now missing. Above the frieze of figures are ranged three shields bearing the quartered arms of Heigham, Waldegrave and other related families. Below it is a biographical inscription, in anonymous verse, about the knight who feared God and selflessly served his county, monarch and Commons. Heigham, the unknown author of the inscription tells us, owed his professional advancement to a dedicated study of the law, to his refusal to 'be with bryberye defyled', and to his unerringly wise judgement in settling disputes encountered at all levels of society. All that the reader of this mixed-media portrait needs to know of Clement's personal life is furnished by the (possibly re-used) brass representations of his wives and children, each serving as a symbol of his potency and their combined lineal authority. Ironically, Sir Clement was succeeded by his equally ardent but Protestant son, Sir John Heigham (1540–1626), a patron of the Catholic-persecuting puritan movement in west Suffolk, and of Mary's clergyman grandfather, Richard Cradock (1562–1630), whom he appointed to the living at Barrow in 1608.

Despite the grandiose affirmation of abiding power represented by these church objects, the political and religious institutions that had prompted their creation were no more indispensable than the individuals associated with them. By the reign of Charles I, the le Despenser font and Heigham tomb had become relics of once prominent Catholic, Royalist families now surrounded by militant Presbyterian parliamentarians. For Barrow's parishioners in the 1630s and 40s, these familiar sculptures may have become primers, symbolic of the hubris of their long dead patrons. During the Civil Wars, when Mary was a child, Catholic estates became fair game, property for others to tax, take or destroy. Equally likely, then, is that the sculptures were physical reminders that the divisions within their community being stirred up by renewed conflict over faith, politics and other allegiances had their origins in earlier times. Their survival in All Saints' Church suggests, however, that the overt reiteration of the principle of socio-economic hierarchy, as implied by these monuments, was somehow less offensive to the iconoclasts than were other symbolic reminders of a discarded faith. These stolid declarations of economic and judicial control over the mass of the populace by a self-selecting elite may, perhaps, have appealed to the Presbyterian county gentry who, as it turned out, had no desire to embrace any fundamental 'levelling' of the social order in the post-Civil War era.

Did growing up with these dynastic objects, each a statement of inherited social privilege, influence young Mary? The familiar All Saints' font may have been an object of affection or of indifference, or may have represented to her a complex mixture of associations. Perhaps, for example, the stone basin and its imagery were symbols of her father's status and authority within the community, and that of her grandfather before him – a lesser dynasty of pastors mirroring that of the patron. Was this how children learned that objects can be subtle things, that they are more than they appear to be and have more uses than that for which they were specifically made? Even in church, acts of worship were inextricably linked to self-promotion. Financial acts of Christian charity were not anonymous gifts, knowledge of which was shared only by God and the giver, but public declarations of piety and of comfortably bestowed largesse. Public and private virtue went hand in hand with ambition, and expressions of love and friendship, in its broadest sense, were allied to the symbols of self-interest. Clement Heigham's tomb offered an account of the astute marrying of houses, mutually beneficial coupling of names and pooling of resources and the extent to which shrewd planning bears fruit. While undoubtedly designed to emphasise the family's ancient history and Clement's personal legacy, his monument presented Mary and other young gentlefolk with a formative example of self-fashioning within the bounds of duty, virtue and respectability. No opportunity to enhance one's reputation, and to model it to one's own ends, was to be missed – even death.[8] Perhaps it was a tomb very like Heigham's that later inspired Charles Beale and his brother Henry to commission a monument for their parents, complete with their coat of arms, dynastic epitaph and portrait likenesses, although this time in the Renaissance manner.[9]

The church objects with which young Mary Cradock grew up may have served as an early introduction to the pragmatic relationship, at all levels of society, between work and the necessary patronage of others. Even in Barrow parish church, co-dependency between the work of the artisan and the beneficence of

---

[8]   The monument may have been commissioned by Clement himself, but it is also possible that it was designed by Anne Heigham (nee Waldegrave), Clement's widow. There were many precedents for this, and could explain why his first wife's arms are not present, see Loveday Lewes Gee, *Women, Art and Patronage from Henry III to Edward III: 1216–1377,* (Woodbridge: Boydell and Brewer, 2002); Catherine King, *Renaissance Women Patrons: Wives and Widows in Italy, c. 1300–1550,* (Manchester: Manchester University Press,1998), 99–128; Cynthia Miller Lawrence (ed.), *Women and Art in Early Modern Europe: Patrons, Collectors and Connoisseurs* (Pennsylvania: Penn State University Press, 1997).

[9]   Commissioned from the sculptor Thomas Burman (1619–1674), the monument includes an attribution to the Beale brothers as patrons and thereby establishes them as their parents' biographers. Although both parents were dead by 1660, the monument in St Michael's Church at Walton, Buckinghamshire was not commissioned until 1672, costing £45 and was not paid for in full until 1674, a transaction recorded by George Vertue in his 'Note-books', transcribed and published in the *Volumes of the Walpole Society* (London: nos. 18 (1930), 20 (1932), 22 (1934), 24 (1936), 26 (1938), see number 24 (1936)).

Figure 6.2　Poppy head pew end, All Saints' Church, Barrow, Suffolk. Copyright Robin Stummer.

wealthy patrons was made explicit in brass, stone, wood and glass. Similarly, John Cradock's livelihood, like that of his father and other members of the Anglican clergy, depended upon his being appointed to livings by likeminded patrons, in his case Sir Edmund Bacon (c.1570–1649) of Redgrave, and the Heigham family. The clergyman's need to keep faith with his patron may well have resulted in a complex, uneasy compromise between intellectual independence and the need to earn money – a lesson Mary drew on later, perhaps, when negotiating a similar sort of compromise in the professional art business.

Visiting All Saints' Church one cannot help but conclude that its accomplished and endearing sixteenth-century bench-end sculptures may have provided Mary with an early and formative introduction to art in general, and to portraiture in particular. Amongst these finely executed wooden portraits, naturalistic likeness jostles playfully with caricature and grotesque, one form here and there melding into the other. This was art – although it may not have been given that description – that was accessible to all and, moreover, was artistry that one could revisit every day, and even touch. One can easily imagine Mary and other village children, bored by the sermon, each assigning the figures names and endowing them with apt personalities. There is no documentary evidence, however, to suggest when or from whom Mary learned to paint. It is likely that Mary's father had provided her general tuition and, as an amateur artist himself, may also have taught her to paint. In 1648 John Cradock was granted admittance to the London Company of Painter-Stainers, and this desire to formalise his status as a painter indicates that to him art was not an inconsequential pastime. Cradock presented the Guild with a still-life canvas depicting fruit and, from Mary's own description of 'her painting of Apricots', we can infer that she was influenced to some degree by her father's artistic practice.[10] Were Mary Beale's mature ideas about the making, sharing and selling of creative objects also influenced, in part, by this early association of religion, patronage and art – embodied, as it was, in the person of her father? Church teaching made it clear that generosity should not be restricted to the wealthy, but was the duty of all, an ethos that would surely transform the painter's production of still life and portraits into a godly act for the consolation and contemplation of others, especially when given as gifts. A virtuous Christian woman could do worse than to follow her father's example and, as we shall see, Mary did just

---

[10]   A John Cradock, generally considered to have been the 15-year-old Mary's father, was elected to the Painter-Stainers' Company on 7 June 1648 and presented them with 'a piece of painting of his owne makeinge' consisting of 'varieties of fruits, vizt. apricocks, quinces ffilberts Grapes Apl and other sortes of fruits', London, Guildhall Library, MS 5667/1. 'Observations by MB in her painting of Apricots in August 1663' in Charles Beale, *Experimentall Seacrets found out in the way of painting*, (1647/8–1663), Glasgow University Library, Special Collections, MS Ferguson 134.

PIAZZA in Coventgarden.

Figure 6.3   Wenceslaus Hollar, *Piazza in Coventgarden*, c. 1647, etching on laid paper (2nd state), 14.5 × 25.2 cm.

that, eventually extending these practices in order to embrace the Protestant enthusiasm for commerce.

After Mary Cradock married Charles Beale and left Suffolk in the early 1650s it is harder to trace objects which were known to her and have since been spared the ravages of fire, property development and war. Moving to Covent Garden the Beales probably lived for a time in King Street where their son Bartholomew (1656–1709) was registered at St Paul's, the parish church. Covent Garden piazza has not escaped alteration by any means, but its general configuration and the eastern facade of the church are still easily recognisable from Wenceslaus Hollar's etching of the 1640s, an evocative remainder of mid-seventeenth-century London.[11]

Here Sir Peter Lely (1618–1680), later court portraitist to Charles II, and other artists had their studios alongside the homes of the wealthy nobles who bestowed patronage on local painters and framemakers. For a young couple from the provinces, life in bustling Covent Garden must surely have been an urban baptism of fire, a rare and formative mixture of sociability, market forces and art. Turning, within this context, from rural Suffolk to London of the 1660s, and from objects seen to objects made, I will discuss the ways in which Mary Beale explored the nature of identity, personal and public, in her earliest surviving works.

Evidence suggests that Mary Beale was already a painter when she moved to London and by 1658 she was sufficiently well-known as an 'Artist' to be listed as such by Sir William Sanderson in his book *Graphice: Or The use of the Pen and Pensil; In the most Excellent Art of PAINTING*.[12] Around the same time Charles Beale was appointed a deputy Clerk of the Patents and the family moved to Hind Court, north of Fleet Street. There the couple's circle included Thomas Flatman, lawyer, miniaturist and poet, and his colleague Samuel Woodforde who married Alice Beale, Charles's first cousin; John Cooke who, as under secretary to successive secretaries of state, was their inside man at Whitehall; Charles's brother Bartholomew, Auditor of the Imprest, and his wife Elizabeth and the cousins Smith and Stephens. These and other alliances brought the Beales into the orbit of senior politicians and merchant bankers, clergymen, including John Tillotson the future archbishop of Canterbury, and members of the Royal Society, including its first historian, Thomas Spratt (1635–1713). Significantly, however, the Beales also moved in non-conformist circles, attended conventicles, unauthorised religious meetings held by Richard Baxter

---

[11]   Wenceslaus Hollar, 'Piazza in Coventgarden', (etching, state 2, 15 × 26 cm), 1640s.

[12]   ' ... in Oyl Colours [wrote Sanderson] we have a virtuous example in that worthy Artist Mrs. *Carlile*: and of others Mr[s]. *Beale*, Mrs. *Brooman*, and to Mrs. *Weimes*', in Sir William Sanderson, *Graphice: Or The use of the Pen and Pensil; In the most Excellent Art of PAINTING*, (London: [printed for] Robert Crofts, 1658), 20.

(1615–1691) and entertained, almost daily, the dissenting clergyman William Bates (1625–1699), whom Mary painted in 1662.[13] The extant documentary sources related to the Beales from this period confirm that many people in this diverse network were counted friends and most of them were, to some extent, collaborators in the business of getting on in life.

Although Mary did not write her own diary or memoir, the warmth of her circle's personal friendships and the close connection between deep affection and collective ambition are evident from the texts written by its other members. Portraits, letters and literary manuscripts – their objects of affection – were exchanged along with advice, help and access to influential alliances in what appears to have been a collaborative micro-economy of favours and payments in kind. The 1661–2 diary written by Samuel Woodforde when he and Alice were the Beales's lodgers at Hind Court, for example, illustrates both the pleasure and support afforded by their kindly, protective circle and the passing notes of discord between its members. The diary also provides evidence that Mary's portrait sittings at Hind Court were sociable gatherings, sometimes combined with meals or musical entertainment. On the 25 September 1662 Henry Hyde (1638–1709), then Lord Cornbury, made the family an extraordinary present that fed them for at least a week and allowed them to entertain their friends in style:

> A whole buck was this morn from Worcester house sent in to my Cosen Beale. oh lord let us use thy good creatures wth Moderation. Dr Bates. & Cosen Tillotson were with us this night & stayed till toward 10 a Clock, ye lord better us by their good Society.[14]

At the start of October the friends were still working their way through the deer, and Woodforde noted that 'Dr Bates Mr Cooke & Mrs Rogers dine with us to day invited to a boyld hanch of Venison[...]Make Our society comfortable one to another'.[15] The 'Mrs Rogers' invited to share the Beales's stew may well have been the wife of musician John Rogers (d. 1676) who previously, on 10

---

[13]   Samuel Woodforde, *Lib. primus*, [1662], New Haven, Yale, Beinecke Rare Book and Manuscript Library, MS Osborn b41, f. 26.

[14]   Woodforde [1662], MS Osborn b41, f. 107. At this time Henry Hyde (1638–1709), later 2nd Earl of Clarendon, was styled Lord Cornbury. Henry's father Edward, 1st Earl and Lord Chancellor was at this time living in Worcester House on the Strand, a property owned by Edmund Somerset (d. 1667), 2nd Marquis of Worcester. It was in 1662 that Henry was appointed private secretary to Queen Catherine of Braganza and his present of the buck to Charles Beale may, perhaps, have been in gratitude for the speedy grant of a patent. This was a connection that lasted and Mary Beale was commissioned to paint portraits of Henry and his second wife in 1672 and 1674.

[15]   Woodforde, MS Osborn b41, f. 120

September, had 'supped with us this night. I was much affected wth Mr Rogers's touching the Lute, & my soule began to launch out into several meditations of heavn'.[16]

Mary's early biographers relied, in great part, on the evocative autobiographical writings of her male circle, but in attempting to understand something of her preoccupations it is necessary to look to Beale's own paintings and texts. In 1999 Tabitha Barber presented the first detailed critique of Beale's autograph manuscript *Discourse on Friendship* (1666).[17] Although Barber did not apply the term autobiographical, she offered a semi-biographical reading of the text, which she interpreted as Mary's personal evocation of her Christian faith and stressed the primacy of that belief over all aspects of her life, including the conduct of her marriage. The author suggested that the *Discourse* provides an indication of the way in which Mary's circle actually conducted themselves from day to day. By placing the *Discourse* within the context of contemporary religious debate, and in suggesting a biographical reading of the text, Barber provided a sound base from which to broaden discussion of Beale's contribution and significance as a cultural figure. Thinking about Mary specifically as a painter, I published an overtly autobiographical reading of an earlier manuscript, dated 1663, in which Mary described the cognitive processes and material objects involved in the acts of seeing and painting – the earliest known English text of its sort by a woman artist.[18] I demonstrated that in recording 'her painting of Apricots' Beale identified herself as an artist, and one of sufficient status and authority to offer advice to others. Beale's written self-declaration is no small thing and, taken together with her surviving self-portraits of the period, is a clear indication that being a painter was as fundamental a part of her personal identity as her faith and her feelings for her family.

In her *Discourse*, Beale was mindful of the gap between the classical ideal of friendship and its imperfect practice in everyday life, but nevertheless considered it possible to achieve the 'nearest Union which distinct Souls are capable of' through mutual evaluation and constancy.[19] Mary's interest in the symbiotic nature of friendship also found expression in the most intimate of her portraits. Within a commercial contract, the artist and her sitter must establish between them a mutuality of intent and, in the process, ask each other some spoken or unspoken questions including *what do you want from me* and, *what do I expect from you* or, more bluntly, *what do you see in me, and can you be trusted to present me as I wish to be seen?* Does the sitter want to appear in a setting that denotes

---

    16   Woodforde, MS Osborn b41, f. 44

    17   Tabitha Barber, *Mary Beale (1632/3–1699) portrait of a seventeenth-century painter, her family and her studio*, exh. cat., (London: Geffrye Museum, 1999).

    18   Draper, 'her painting of Apricots'.

    19   Mary Beale, Harley MS 6828 fol 510v.

his social standing, or to have his virtuous character revealed? Is the finished portrait to be one that truthfully describes the colours and lines of his face, or is outrageous flattery required? When a portrait sitting springs from an emotional connection, however, from a starting point of friendship, the participants may be more likely to ask *how can we help one another*? This last question is also central to love, the practice of friendship itself, and – within the early modern culture of credit and obligation – to business. How, in short, do we understand ourselves and each other, and how can we benefit from this knowledge? Mary's interest in the relationship between artist, subject and viewer, the observed and the observer, remained central to all her work, but it is in her self-portraits that the tension inherent in attempting to fix human likeness and identity in paint is most obvious. *I am!* proclaims the artist, *but who am I*?

Mary's earliest surviving self-portrait includes half-length likenesses of Charles and her young son Bartholomew 'Bat' Beale. *Self-portrait of the artist with her husband and son* (c. 1660, Geffrye Museum, London) is a complex composition that clearly references Van Dyck and Italian Renaissance painters, but without literal mimicry. In this group portrait, one of the earliest by a British woman, the painter assumed her position as creator within the established male genre normally representing 'the artist' and 'his wife' or family.[20] This piece of aesthetic and intellectual temerity is the work of an expressive artist, an autodidact eager to learn from her predecessors and to experiment with new, possibly controversial forms. Viewed from a different perspective, not knowing that the female subject was also the artist, the family group may appear to depict a touching domestic scene, an epitome of social conformity. It is clear from these apparent ambiguities that Beale was experimenting as much with the expectations and visual literacy of the viewer, as with the subtleties of self-definition.

By 1665 Charles no longer held his civil service post and, with the onset of the plague, the Beales left London to spend several years on a smallholding at Allbrook, in rural Hampshire.[21] Mary's second known *Self-portrait* (1666, National Portrait Gallery) was painted at Allbrook Farmhouse and shows a woman literally surrounded by a multiplicity of implied identities as artist,

---

[20]   See, for example, Rubens's *Self-portrait with Isabella Brant*, c. 1609–10, and his *Self-portrait with Helena Fourment and Nicholas Rubens*, c. 1631, both at Munich, Alte Pinakothek; Jordaens, *The Family of the Artist*, c. 1621, Madrid, Museo Nacional del Prado; and Cornelis de Vos, *Self-Portrait of the artist with his wife Suzanne Cock and their children*, c. 1630s, St Petersburg, Hermitage.

[21]   Although in recent years 'development' has denuded it of its remaining small-holding and garden, Allbrook Farmhouse still stands, a unique, if not now unspoiled, survival as the earliest known home and studio of an artist, male or female, in the British Isles. Despite its historic significance, however, Mary Beale's place of work is not deemed to be worthy of anything other than grade II listing on a par, it would seem, with a public lavatory or two.

gentlewoman, mother, housewife. The subject maintains the faintly inquisitive expression of a painter conscious of both gazing upon, and presenting, a version of herself. Again the composition, and the woman's place within it, is complex and iconographically innovative. Mary carefully aligned a small canvas portrait of her two children alongside her stomach, while her artists' palette hangs on the wall in line with her head. The artist watches the viewer and herself, the subject, puzzling over this apparently enigmatic arrangement of painted objects. Was the painter telling us that a seventeenth-century woman could indeed 'have it all' – an intellectual life, creative self-expression and motherhood – or was she anxious that choices would have to be made? The portrait is at once contemplative and unsettling, a musing perhaps on an uncertain future in which her family's prosperity could depend on her ability to paint and that her self-expression could, as a consequence, be obliged to take on less independent forms. Later, as a commercial painter, Mary did indeed adopt conventional and often derivative templates for some of her numerous portrait commissions as did other studios including Lely's, but by the late nineteenth century this pragmatism had become the basis of one of the public reputations imposed on Beale alone, that of 'copyist'.[22]

Almost as compelling as the artist's self-portraits are the numerous surviving images of her husband, at least three of which have been interpreted as companion pieces to her self-depictions. Here again, Mary echoes her male predecessors' preoccupation with portraying the, generally female, object of their affections with this series of gradually aging likenesses, in various formats and settings. It is fair to assume that Charles was so often Mary's muse because he was a readily available sitter, but perhaps the repetition of his image also reflected Mary's fascination or frustration with the very possibility of capturing 'likeness' and pinning down identity – even that of someone whose face was as least as familiar to her as her own. As well as these deeply intimate portraits, Beale produced many other paintings of loved ones in the 1660s, although apparently not for money. Her sitters 'from the life' included Alice and Samuel Woodforde; the Smiths and other kinfolk; friends William Bates, Thomas Flatman, and Dr Robert Wild (1615/6–1679) a dissenting preacher and satirical poet. Was it, perhaps, the very look of love that Mary Beale was trying to capture as it passed, however fleetingly, between the artist, her friends and husband in these portraits? The 'not for profit' portraits that survive certainly seem to suggest that Mary was less interested in depicting a friend's social status or even virtuous character, than in

---

[22]   Ellis Waterhouse, for example, dismissed Beale as 'a drab and unoriginal follower of Lely's manner' in his highly influential and oft reprinted book, *Painting in Britain 1530–1790* (London: Penguin, 1953), 114.

collating moments of connection between two souls who are, by inclination and necessity, looking at each other and performing their friendship for all to see.[23]

In 1670/1 the Beale family returned to London and established Mary's commercial studio in a house on Pall Mall, just a stone's throw from St James's Palace, but how was this apparently instantaneous change from amateur to professional status achieved? A plethora of contemporary sermons and other rhetorical admonitions railed against women who made spectacles of themselves by voicing opinions in print, preaching in public, and acting on stage. In 'her painting of Apricots' I suggested that Mary turned her domestic studio into one based on cash commissions by flaunting her 1660s reputation as a virtuous Christian wife and mother, and amateur virtuosa, a feat of self-fashioning which depended on the collaboration of her friends.[24] Indeed, people at all levels of society relied heavily upon friends to obtain advancement, and to pull whatever strings they could to help each other into a job or out of trouble. Earlier, at Hind Court, Samuel Woodforde found that work for a jobbing lawyer was scarce and turned to his closest friends for support and to exert their influence in helping him to obtain a civil service post. In his diary entry for 13 October 1662, Samuel noted a conversation at Whitehall in which he spoke to 'Mr Cooke about getting in with him, but the Duke of Albemarle hath spoken already to ye Secretary for one of his nominacon, soe that there is like to be noe hope but hee tells me Mr Godolphin can doe what he will wth Sr Hen Bennett'.

On the day after his meeting with Cooke Samuel reported to his diary, and to God, that Godolphin had 'promised mee all the assistance hee can & that what ever lyes in his power at any time to doe for mee hee will with all his heart ... I had many expressions of love from him I thanck my God'.[25] In the absence

---

[23]   Portraiture has been interpreted as a form of performance art, see Joanna Woodall (ed.), *Portraiture: Facing the Subject*, (Manchester: Manchester University Press, 1997). In the twenty-first century, it finds its counterpart in the work 'The Artist is Present' by Marina Abramovic at the Museum of Modern Art, New York, in 2010, in which the artist and her 'viewer' sit silently before each other for an extended period of time, but without the mediation of paint and canvas, see http://www.moma.org/interactives/exhibitions/2010/marinaabramovic/.

[24]   Draper, 'her painting of Apricots'. For a definition of the 'virtuosa' see Fredrika H. Jacobs, *Defining the Renaissance Virtuosa: Women Artists and the Language of Art History and Criticism* (Cambridge: Cambridge University Press, 1997).

[25]   Woodforde [1662], MS Osborn b41, fols 154 and 156–7. John Cooke (d. 1691), the Beales's dear friend, was chief Clerk to the Secretary of State for the Northern Department, Sir William Morice (1602–1676), a kinsman of George Monck, 1st Duke of Albemarle; William Godolphin (1635–1696), Woodforde's friend at Oxford, was Secretary to Morice, but had just then been promoted to chief Clerk to the Secretary of State for the Southern Department, Sir Henry Bennet, later 1st Earl of Arlington (1618–1685). For commentary on the influential, not to say powerful, role of these chief clerks in government after the

of banks and other institutions, circles of kin and friends, the Beales included, lent and borrowed money amongst themselves and stood surety for mortgages. Woodforde struggled for many years with a complicated dispute over a family inheritance made up of both debt and valuable property. In the absence of a speedy resolution in court and lucrative employment, Samuel was forced to rob Peter to pay Paul:

> 25 March I tooke up of my good friende Mr Cooke 200^li towards paying my Uncles debts upon a Mortgage to bee paide 25th March 1663 … 27 March I paide Mr Honywoode 106^li.10. & tooke up a Mortgage hee had upon Westcourt. 28 March I paide Mr Archer 90^li more ye full of a debt due to Mr Lant.[26]

Participation in these mutual exchanges demanded that each man maintain a public reputation for trustworthiness, while a household's fortunes could depend upon the blameless moral character of its female members. Because their collective needs and reputations converged in this way, it was in the best interests of each member of the Beale circle to ensure that Mary's painterly divergence from the usual housewifely activities went unchallenged in their community. As part of Mary's concerted campaign to offset censure on grounds of immodesty, she was careful to associate her name in public with religious poetry and prose, literary genres deemed suitable for women writers. In 1667, for example, five poems written by Mary Beale were printed in Samuel Woodforde's *Paraphrase on the Psalms of David*.[27] This book was published when the Beales were at Allbrook and when Samuel, having settled part of his legal dispute, was living in an inherited house at Binsted, also in Hampshire. In the preface Woodforde hailed his co-author as a virtuous gentlewoman before praising her skill in both poetry and painting, thereby marrying her blameless moral virtue and creative virtuosity in the mind of the reader. Woodforde, following the contemporary literary convention, made it clear that Beale had only reluctantly allowed her work to be printed in the hope that her words would provide comfort and guidance to readers. In this and similar contexts, Beale's name was publicised in such a way as to highlight the altruism and seriousness of her intentions without leaving room for accusations of unwomanly ambition.

Restoration, and their evolution to the grander title of 'Under-Secretary', see Florence Evans, *Principal Secretary of State: A Survey of the Office from 1558–1680*, (Manchester: Manchester University Press, 1923).

   26   Woodforde [1662], MS Osborn b41, fols 22–3. West Court is a house in the village of Binsted, Hampshire where Samuel and Alice eventually went to live.

   27   Samuel Woodforde, *A Paraphrase upon the Psalms of David. By Sam. Woodford, printed by R. White, for Octavian Pullein, neer the Pump in Little-Brittain*, (London, 1667); and Mary Beale [1666], Harley MS 6828 fols 510–23.

The precautionary steps Mary and her friends took to avoid criticism were apparently successful, and once her Pall Mall studio opened for business Charles set to work recording a stream of portrait commissions from the gentry, aristocracy and clergy in his annual notebooks. By the end of the 1670s, the Beales's influential alliances were such that they could borrow Italian paintings and drawings to copy from Charles II's collection, through the auspices of William Chiffinch (c.1602–1688), the Keeper of the King's Pictures. Even though their social status was elevated and Mary's studio prospered, its cash-flow, in common with other businesses, was often erratic. Charles's notebook for 1677, for example, included a list of portraits finished by Mary in the previous year but still unpaid for the following January. As a stopgap it was crucial for the Beales to enjoy long-term credit with their suppliers, and cash loans from their circle of friends and kinfolk, of which Charles kept scrupulous account in the same book. The Beale circle appears to be unusual in that portraits, as well as manuscripts, remain behind as tangible relics of their socio-familial economy of credit and obligation, and of the trusting bonds of blood, marriage, friendship and love.

In January 1677 Charles Beale recorded in his studio notebook that his 'Dearest Heart' had:

> painted Sir Wm Turner's Picte from head to foote for our worthy & kind friend Mr Knollys, in consideracon of his most obligeing kindness to us upon all occasions. He gave it to be sett up in yᵉ Hall at Bridewell. Sir Wm Turnr haveing been chosen president of that House in yᵉ yeare he was Lord Mayor of London[28],

referring to a painting completed by Mary in 1676. On the same page, just above this entry Charles noted that he had 'borrowed of our kind friend Mr ffrancis Knollys in our great disappointments of money, a Guiney wch he sent me by my son Barth. I say lent me by him 01.01.06'. Later, on 14 November 1677, Charles listed an accumulated '£32–01–06' borrowed from Knollys in his 'Account of Debts owing', with a note in the margin that the whole debt had been repaid, although when and how is not made clear.[29] It is significant that these two, non-sequential incidents were coupled in the notebook and in Charles's mind. Mary's portrait *Sir William Turner* (1615–1692), for her a rare life-size, full-length image of an adult sitter, was clearly painted as a response to the loans provided by their friend Francis, and probably amounted to a similar

---

[28]   Charles Beale, *1676/7 Notebook* Oxford, Bodleian Rawlinson, 8° 572, fol 10.

[29]   Charles Beale, Rawlinson, 8° 572, f. 73. The debt of thirty-two pounds, one shilling and sixpence is equivalent to more than £2,500 in today's money according to the National Archive's historical currency converter.

financial investment, but in time and materials.[30] Thus the courtly culture of gift giving, long an important ritual of friendship for the Beales's intimate circle, was extended to their wider network and took on an implicitly commercial undertone. The story of this particular portrait exemplifies the ways in which an object was used, by several people including Mary, as the means to express deep personal affection and, simultaneously, to facilitate a variety of mutual aims.

Francis Knollys Esq. (d.1694) of York Street, Covent Garden was a warden of St Paul's Church and a close friend and correspondent of the Beales.[31] From another entry in Charles's 1677 notebook, and corroborating evidence elsewhere, it seems that Knollys was employed as private 'Secretary' to William Wentworth, the second Earl of Strafford (d.1695), acting as a London agent when his lordship was at Wentworth Woodhouse, his Yorkshire estate. Francis, conscientious in his Christian duty of philanthropy, was elected to the prestigious Court of Governors of Bridewell, the combined prison and charitable school providing education and apprenticeships for destitute children.[32] Sir William Turner (from whom both Samuel Woodforde and Samuel Pepys bought cloth in the 1660s) was a freeman of the Merchant Taylors' Company who rose to become Lord Mayor of London in 1669; the City's Member of Parliament from 1690–93; and President of Bridewell for more than 20 years.[33] Beale depicted Turner standing in his mayoral robes and chain of office, important document in hand, beside a velvet-covered chair and table in a grand interior with a fluted architectural column and tiled marble floor. For our purposes, however, the portrait's formal aspects are less revealing than the circumstances of its commissioning, and the ways in which it was used when the paint was scarcely dry and, once again, in the twenty-first century.

Mary Beale painted Turner's portrait and gave it to Francis Knollys primarily in an act of loving friendship with which she and Charles could return his

---

[30] The portrait was formerly in The Hall at Bridewell Hospital, and is now at King Edward's School, Witley, Surrey.

[31] York Street was the southernmost part of what is now Tavistock Street, Covent Garden.

[32] Bridewell was housed in a former royal palace off what is now New Bridge Street, see William G. Hinkle, *History of Bridewell Prison, 1553–1700*, (Lampeter: Edwin Mellan, 2006); Peter W Coldham, 'Bridewell Hospital apprenticeship indentures', *Genealogists Magazine* 23 (1991): 327, 376–7; Edward G. O'Donoghue, *Bridewell Hospital, Palace, Prison, Schools from the Death of Elizabeth to Modern Times*, 2 vols (London: John Lane, 1929).

[33] Turner was also involved with the Honourable Irish Society, East India Company, and the slave-running Royal African Company, see 'Turner, Sir William (1615–93), of St. Paul's Churchyard, London' in *The History of Parliament: the House of Commons 1690–1715*, ed. D. Hayton, E. Cruickshanks, S. Handley, 2 vols (Cambridge: Cambridge University Press, 2002), I, 708–9.

Figure 6.4   Mary Beale, *Sir William Turner*, 1676, oil on canvas, 231.2 × 144.7 cm. Copyright King Edward's School, Witley, Surrey.

generosity in kind, making the object itself one part of a chain reaction of friendship. Mary, for example, used the painting as an opportunity to cast her friend Francis in the lofty, public role of connoisseur and patron of the arts while he, with his gift of the portrait to Bridewell, demonstrated his friendship towards Sir William Turner and the institution. In sitting for the portrait Turner expressed his friendship to one and all by giving the gift of his likeness for others to bestow. The sociable sittings themselves undoubtedly gave rise to other companionable acts of friendship. Thus the object Mary made in response to Knollys's initial acts of 'most obligeing kindness' became an invitation to all parties in this friendly exchange to help each other, thereby bestowing virtue on one another, the institution and on the portrait.

The Beales's financial indebtedness to Knollys, however, means that the Turner portrait must also be seen as part of a commercial transaction and, if not literally repaying the debt, then certainly acknowledging it in material and symbolic terms. In exchange for his newfound prestige as patron, Knollys's beneficent gesture to Bridewell became the means by which he could further show his friendship to the Beales by commending Mary's work. Mary was afforded an opportunity to advertise her name and talent with the public exhibition of her signed and dated portrait. Through his patronage Francis cast Mary Beale in the role of civic painter by presenting her work to a new, institutional audience in a setting that was far from domestic but, being a charity, was suitably respectable. Turner's collaboration facilitated the commercial aspects of the commission and thus he became, by extension, Beale's second patron, and another influential name to add to her list of sitters. Moreover, the Beales's investment in the painted object was potentially the means by which they could repay their financial debt to Knollys, were the image to prompt new commissions. The commercial implications of the transaction also extended to the final recipients of Turner's likeness where, as well as being an aesthetic embellishment, the portrait of Bridewell's illustrious president became a totem of the institution's gravitas and its financial asset. Such objects enhanced Bridewell's appeal for potential patrons and governors attracting, in turn, gifts to enrich the institution, facilitate its charitable activities and promote the social standing of its officers.

In 1676 Sir William Turner endowed and had built a Hospital comprised of a school and almshouses at Kirkleatham in Yorkshire. Installed at Bridewell the following year, Beale's portrait therefore lent a visual stamp of authority to Turner's civic career and served as a metropolitan monument to his provincial charitable legacy. Not to be overlooked are other, less obvious acts of public and personal commemoration conveyed by the object and its use. In associating their names with Bridewell, its works and its president, Mary Beale and Knollys asserted their personal virtue and, by extension, their public commitment to the philanthropic aims of civic life. In displaying Francis's gift, Bridewell bestowed its blessing on him and Mary and commemorated its own prestige as it was reflected in the image of its president. With her signed and dated painting Mary once again proclaimed herself an artist, but this time in a public setting and as a professional painter capable of executing a life-size composition fit for the grandest setting in an important institution. Turner, for his part, collaborated in his own immortalising. In return for the painting, Bridewell's Governors immortalised Knollys's name in their minute book and subsequently in an inscription on the painting's frame.[34] Along with Charles's notebook entries, these textual references to Francis marked his very existence, leaving one of the few biographical traces of him that survive. Thus the object, Knollys's instrument of beneficence, became his chance to glory in the reflected immortality of a donor. Francis used the portrait as a physical commemoration of his association with and service for the institution and of his personal respect for its president. Indeed, by November 1677 Knollys's standing amongst the Governors was such that he was asked to negotiate with Sir Peter Lely over a commission for two royal portraits also destined for Bridewell's Hall.[35] Perhaps this responsible task was apportioned to Francis on the strength of the expertise as a patron of the arts he had already demonstrated in procuring Beale's portrait of their president.

Bridewell no longer exists, save for its gatehouse portico facing New Bridge Street in London, and Beale's portrait currently resides with its successor institution in Surrey.[36] In 2012 an ex-pupil of Turner's school in Kirkleatham visited the almshouses and was surprised to find there 'no portrait or lasting tribute to Sir William'.[37] The visitor, Philip Norris, later paid for a reproduction of the Beale likeness of Turner to be made, framed and displayed at the Kirkleatham Hospital in his own virtuous act of commemoration. Mary Beale's 336-year old portrait – which had sprung out of Francis Knollys's 'kindness' – was once again used as the vehicle of friendship, generosity and patronage. Coverage of Norris's gesture of thanks for Turner's civic gifts in the local press and by the BBC brought Beale's name to the attention of a non-art historical public once more. Here is evidence of the enduring power of one likeness to evoke the physical presence of a long dead man, and to stand in for him in commemoration of his most admirable deeds. Thus the object made by Beale and the kindness that inspired it remain, to this day, crucial elements of the ever-evolving biographies of at least five people.

---

[34] The inscription reads, 'Sir William Turner; elected 1669. Whole-length, by Mrs. Beale. Presented by Mr. Knollys in 1676–7', see J.G. Nichols, 'Portraits in Bridewell Hospital', in *Transactions of the London and Middlesex Archæological Society*, 2 vols (London: Bishopsgate Institute, 1864), II, p. 72–4.

[35] The Governors commissioned from Lely portraits of Charles II and James II, see O'Donoghue, *Bridewell*, II, 277.

[36] King Edward's School, Witley in Surrey.

[37] [uncredited], 'Sir William Turner artwork to be unveiled in Kirkleatham', [online text], BBC News Tees, 22 June 2012, http://www.bbc.co.uk/news/uk-england-tees-18533385.

The Turner portrait also raises some important questions about contemporary public attitudes towards women's activities and the fora available for their self-expression. If the well-documented rhetorical restrictions on women held full force in social practice, Francis's gift and Bridewell's acceptance of it must have been acts of some daring. Did the Governors' reception of the signed portrait impart a public blessing on Mary Beale's commercial activities or were they not told in advance that the artist was a woman? Perhaps the institution would never have dreamed of *seeking* a commission from a female painter, but as the portrait was a *fait accompli*, a gift and, moreover, a likeness of their president, they simply could not refuse it. If that was the case, Knollys, Beale and even Turner (a canny businessman) appear to have been acting on the premise that mild subterfuge was acceptable in order to project the public identities they desired. Alternatively, the Governors saw nothing amiss in a woman painting for a living and were happy to capitalise on the renown of a prominent society portraitist. However the object of affection worked its way into Bridewell's grand Hall, its setting bestowed a new measure of legitimacy on Beale's career and projected another of her identities – that of the artist of historical record, the chronicler of an institution and of a Lord Mayor's likeness.

The Beales's rented house on Pall Mall, part of a Restoration building boom in London, placed Mary's professional painting studio within the orbit of some of the wealthiest, and most decadent, of London's art-buying public. The house, 'next the Golden Ball', no longer exists but its plot is still clearly defined just around the corner from St James's Square. The then brand new parish church, St James's on Piccadilly, was designed by Sir Christopher Wren and consecrated in 1684. Although severely damaged at the start of the Blitz, the church still stands complete with some original features that Mary would certainly have seen, including the elaborate font and Baroque carvings commissioned from Grinling Gibbons (1648–1721). The extent to which an examination of these 'seen' objects informs our understanding of the latter part of Beale's life is debatable, but the objects in and of themselves, and by virtue of their association with Mary, can still provoke a powerful response from the viewer. I was surprised to come across St James's richly decorated communion cup one day, on display at the Victoria and Albert Museum. Along with its matching gilt church plate, the cup was made in 1683 by silversmith Ralph Leake (active 1664–1714).[38] Somehow,

---

[38] According to Evelyn, writing in November 1684, St James's chalice and paten, or 'most noble plate', used during Holy Communion to serve the consecrated wine and bread, were given to the church 'by Sir R. Geere [Sir Richard Gayre (d.1702)], to the value (as was said) of £200. There was no altar anywhere in England, nor has there been any abroad, more handsomely adorned', see William Bray (ed.), *Diary and Correspondence of John Evelyn*, new edition, 4 vols, (London: Henry Colburn, 1852), II, 201. At the time of writing the cup and plate were on loan to the V&A in the Sacred Silver & Stained Glass Gallery, room 83, case 2B.

seeing these grand public objects – even imprisoned in a glass case – suddenly brought history to life. Similarly, seeing and touching Beale's manuscript letter to her friend Elizabeth was much more affecting than reading the text reproduced in a book.[39] The power of such objects to affect us deeply is mysterious, and seems to relate to the level of intimacy implied by the object itself. Looking upon Mary's face as defined in her self-portraits, or upon Charles's face as she defined him for us, imparts a profound, probably illusory sense of familiarity and insight, especially when we know that these images sprang out of love rather than money. Gazing upon a cup to which a person's lips have been pressed can, in a similar way, be even more affecting than moving through the house in which she once lived. And the cup in question carries a special resonance having sat, as it once did, atop St James's communion table, the very spot beneath which Mary Beale the painter is said to have been buried on the 8th of October 1699.

This then, is our cabinet of curiosities containing just a few of Mary Beale's objects of affection, from baptism to grave. What do these apparently disparate things tell us about Mary, and how does this brief biography of the woman help us to understand a group of objects which we can still experience for ourselves? In writing this chapter I have learned a great deal about the ways in which objects become enmeshed in biography, and are imbued with significance far beyond their apparent utility, or evident beauty. Much has been revealed about the ways in which people use objects in attempting to set their own stamp on posterity, their reasons for doing so, and the possibly unforeseen consequences of their actions. I have learned about the vagaries of identity as it is expressed, manipulated and distorted in diaries, tomb inscriptions, letters, statues, institutions, friendships, poetry and prose – but particularly in portraits. The objects of affection made by Mary and her circle have taken on lives of their own, crossed the globe, and accumulated resonances about which their makers could never have dreamed. Most surprising of all, perhaps, is that objects made by the circle became the lasting incarnations of their friendship, and of the various obligations – mundane and transcendent – that went with it. It is clear, for example, that a portrait born out of self-expression, or of the exchange of even the most abstracted form of friendship, was quite different to one that shuffled its way into being out of mere financial necessity. When a commissioned artist and a paying sitter look at each other across a studio what happens? They think either about each other, or themselves, or about whether the curtains need a wash. When born of love, however, the same encounter has the potential to coax or force each participant to ask – *what are we to each other, and to ourselves?*

Like Philip le Despenser, Sir Clement Heigham, the unknown sculptor of the Barrow church pew-end portraits, John Cradock, Francis Knollys, Sir William Turner and Philip Norris, Mary Beale grasped the opportunities presented to

---

her to proclaim *I am!* and to define herself in words and paint.[40] The problem for artists is that identity and 'influence' are tricky customers, and posterity can take you to the cleaners, literally. Many seventeenth-century British portraits were either left unsigned, or the signatures have since been unwittingly or wittingly removed. Amidst the resulting confusion, a creative woman's over-modest failure to stake a claim on her intellectual property may result in her best work being attributed to male painters, even in her own lifetime. Eventually a female artist, like Beale, comes to be remembered by an unrepresentative, even erroneous collection of attributed objects on which disputing art historians draw when discussing her legacy and influence as an artist.[41] Mary does not appear to have signed any of her works before about 1675, and even then not uniformly, creating a frustrating mismatch with the long list of sitters mentioned by Samuel Woodforde and Charles Beale in their texts. Thus, in Mary's story, the question of attribution – and therefore artistic identity and her influence on others – is as much about the absence of known objects as it is about the physical presence of others.

Within six years of her death, Mary was praised as an artist 'little inferior to any of her cotemporaries [*sic*], either for colouring, strength, force or life' who 'worked with a wonderful body of colours'.[42] Small but seminal exhibitions devoted to Beale's work, in 1975 and 1999, introduced the world to some of her original and deeply personal portraits, but it seems that word was slow to spread.[43] In 2009, in a leading dictionary of artists, Mary was described as being responsible for 'mostly bland derivations from Lely'.[44] Since then, thanks to some keen-eyed art historians, Mary's 'style' – that indefinable something that separates

---

[40] All of an artist's paintings can thus be considered as self-portraits, as emblematic or literal statements of existence and immortality, see, for example, Colin McCahon's *Victory over death 2*, (1970, synthetic polymer paint on unstretched canvas, National Gallery of Australia), http://nga.gov.au/mccahon/1.cfm.

[41] In Mieke Bal (ed.), *The Artemisia Files, Artemisia Gentileschi for Feminists and Other Thinking People* (Chicago: University of Chicago Press, 2005), Gentileschi scholars deal at length with the complex and singular problems that arise from the disputed attribution of paintings to a female painter.

[42] Bainbrigg Buckeridge, *The Art of Painting* [...]*To which is added, An ESSAY towards an English School* [3rd ed., 1754; reproduced in facsimile], (London: Cornmarket Press, 1969), 358.

[43] Elizabeth Walsh and Richard Jeffree, '*The Excellent Mrs Mary Beale*', exh. cat. (London: ILEA, 1975); Tabitha Barber, *Mary Beale Portrait of a Seventeenth-Century Painter, Her Family and Her Studio*, exh. cat. [with an essay by Mary Bustin], (London: Geffrye Museum, 1999).

[44] 'Beale, Mary' in *Oxford Dictionary of Art and Artists*, ed. Ian Chilvers (Oxford: Oxford University Press, 2009), 48. To add insult to injury, in the same dictionary Artemisia Gentileschi's career is recorded within the entry dealing with her father Orazio [240].

her most distinctive work from that of her contemporaries – has reasserted itself, leading to important new attributions to her oeuvre. In 2013 three paintings by Beale were added to the permanent display of seventeenth-century British art at Tate Britain in London, resulting in an accompanying flurry of related press coverage.[45] The wheat is gradually being sifted from the chaff, and the breadth of Mary Beale's authentic body of work is slowly beginning to emerge in all its complexity and contradictions.

---

[45] Mary Beale's portraits are *Sketch of the Artist's Son, Bartholomew Beale, Facing Left* (c. 1660); *Sketch of the Artist's Son, Bartholomew Beale, in Profile* (c. 1660); and *Portrait of a Young Girl* (c. 1681).

Chapter 7

'Look here upon this picture': How Hamlet reads Portraits as Biographical Texts

Yolana Wassersug

Hamlet shows his mother portraits of her first and second husbands and asks her to compare the two (3.1. 56).[1] The request seems to be rhetorical, however, because he gives her no chance to speak before he launches into a speech about his own impressions of the two images. For Hamlet, the different faces of his father and uncle indicate two contrasting personalities. This chapter will consider what it means for Hamlet to put such credence in these portraits, when he uses them as interpretive tools. How can he learn about a person simply by looking at their face, particularly a painted face, unable to speak and static in one expression forever? How much biography can Hamlet glean from a two-dimensional image? This chapter will begin with the task of situating this scene within the context of Reformation visual culture, demonstrating that in sixteenth- and seventeenth-century England it was not uncommon to use portraits as interpretive tools rather than mere decoration. I will then consider what Hamlet learns by looking at portraits, and what he hopes to teach Gertrude by showing them to her. Finally, I will consider how the portraits provide a hermeneutic framework for Hamlet's understanding of his father that even the father's ghost fails to provide.

For many years, art historians touted a standard account of English Reformation visual culture that suggested that the period was defined by religious art superseding secular art and the notion that the period was visually austere at best and iconophobic at worst. Ellis Waterhouse's standard work *Painting in Britain: 1530–1790* provides an example of this critical viewpoint. Waterhouse writes that 'By 1535, at any rate, the old religious themes in painting

---

[1]   S. Wells and G. Taylor (eds), *Shakespeare, The Complete Works* (Oxford: Oxford University Press, 1988).

(All quotations in this essay are presented as they are found in the source text. Quotes from early modern texts have not been modernised, except where the letters 'I', 'j', 'u' and 'v' have been made consistent with modern usage.)

were proscribed', leaving painters with limited options about the subjects that they could depict and what impact they could expect these images to have on viewers.[2] Furthermore, his analysis is confined to courtly painting and he flatly denies that art in domestic spaces had any meaning or value; he assumes that domestic art is secular, 'mainly decorative and the work of local house-painters'. He says no more about the subject, because 'It will be sufficient to have mentioned the existence of this kind of work'.[3]

This type of criticism persisted as standard until the late 1980s when revisionist models of English Reformation history started to make their way into the forefront, bringing with them the seedlings of a revised art history. The process of coming to understand the visual diversity of the Reformation has been gradual. Even Patrick Collinson, in an influential revisionist study, argues that Protestant theology is at odds with the production of artwork, writing that 'the primary thrust of Protestantism which came to fruition around 1550 was hostile to false art, images were vehicles for false belief'.[4] He divides story of art in the Reformation into two waves: first, an iconoclastic period, during which any artwork that was not directly connected to 'good' religion was purged from English culture; secondly (post-1580) an iconophobic period, where all visual culture was rejected.[5] His diagnosis for the Reformation is a case of 'severe visual anorexia'.[6]

This view is changing. Recent scholarship has re-envisioned the Reformation as a visually meaningful time and been more open to discussing art in a domestic context. This new scholarship has put material culture at the forefront, demonstrating that the Reformation was incurably visual and that images were not in conflict with Protestant theology.[7]

It is hardly surprising that our critical understanding of the visual world of Reformation England has undergone so many changes considering that, during the Reformation itself, opinions about the credibility of visual imagery were in constant flux. Tarnya Cooper notes that the act of 'interpreting the visual culture of the English Reformation requires an acceptance of paradoxes,

---

[2]   Ellis Waterhouse, *Painting in Britain, 1530–1790*, Pelican History of Art Series (Connecticut: Yale University Press, 1994), 13.

[3]   Waterhouse, *Painting in Britain*, 49.

[4]   Patrick Collinson, *From Iconoclasm to Iconophobia: The Cultural Impact of the Second English Reformation* (Reading: University of Reading Press 1986), 297.

[5]   Patrick Collinson, *The Birthpangs of Protestant England*, (Basingstoke: Palgrave, 1988), 116–17.

[6]   Collinson, *Birthpangs*, 119.

[7]   See, for instance Tara Hamling and Richard L. Williams (eds), *Art Re-formed: Re-assessing the Impact of the Reformation on the Visual Arts* (Newcastle: Cambridge Scholars Publishing, 2007).

compromises and contested meanings.[8] While Collinson feels that Protestant scepticism towards the visual derived from a 'radical application of the Second Commandment,'[9] there are other scriptural sources that also lend themselves to the interpretation that the pious should avoid visual stimuli. Take, for instance, this verse from the First Book of Samuel 'But the LORD said unto Samuel, Look not on his countenance, or on the height of his stature; because I have refused him: for *the LORD seeth* not as man seeth; for man looketh on the outward appearance, but the LORD looketh on the heart'.[10]

This biblical instruction appears to suggest that pious Protestants would have avoided portraiture and may have felt it inappropriate to use artwork that depicts people superficially as a means to gain an understanding of the inner, spiritual life. However, as the scene from *Hamlet* demonstrates, the popularity of portraiture did not waver in England, nor did people cease to contemplate and interpret the imagery in portraiture. While the Second Commandment injunction against 'any graven image, or any likeness *of any thing*'[11] seems like a clearly anti-visual dictum, evidence that Protestant theologians did interpret the commandment as a rejection of all imagery is difficult to find. Protestant theologians were not as staunchly anti-visual as scholars once thought; they rejected a strict interpretation of these biblical passages in favour of a more lenient attitude towards the visual, often specifying that artwork was acceptable outside of sacred spaces. William Perkins's treatise, *Reformed Catholike* (1598), contains mixed messages about the inherent dangers of the visual image. While he cautions against images in churches and public places, he also writes that painting and engraving are acceptable in 'civill use': 'the common societies of men, out of the appointed places of the solemne worshippe of God. And this to be lawfull, it appereth: because the arts of painting and graving are the ordinance of God: and to be skilful in them is the gift of God'.[12]

Perkins goes on to specify that there is no sin in owning images that commemorate deceased friends.[13] Evidently, from a theological standpoint, the

---

[8]	Tarnya Cooper, 'Predestined Lives? Portraiture and Religious Belief if England and Wales, 1560–1620', in *Art Re-Formed: Re-assessing the Impact of the Reformation of the Visual Arts*, ed. Tara Hamling and Richard L. Williams (Newcastle: Cambridge Scholars Publishing, 2007), 49.

[9]	Collinson, *Birthpangs*, 117.

[10]	R. Carroll and S. Prickett (eds), *The Bible: Authorized King James Version* (Oxford: Oxford University Press, 1997) 1 Sam. 16:7.

[11]	*King James Bible*, Exod. 21:4.

[12]	W. Perkins, *A Reformed Catholike: Or, A Declaration shewing how neere we may come to the present Church of Rome in sundrie points of Religion: and wherein we must for ever depart from them* (Cambridge, 1598), 170–71.

[13]	Perkins, *A Reformed Catholike,* 172.

Reformation was a period where imagery in domestic spaces was meaningful, and could be used to inspire contemplative thought.

How then does Hamlet fit into this complex, visual world? The scene in the play shows him not only looking at portraits in a private and domestic context, but also learning from them. He uses the images to re-affirm his belief in his father's goodness. He also uses the images didactically – his interaction with the objects is not for himself alone, but an opportunity to teach Gertrude to understand her choices in a new way. In Hamlet's world, portraiture is not fearful or ungodly, but an educational opportunity for his mother and himself. The portraits, for Hamlet, are a biographical text.

It is an established fact that Tudor and Stuart portraits often contain biographical details that communicate facts about the sitter. Extant portraits from the period feature details such as Latin mottos, heraldic crests, additional symbolic imagery in the background, and clothing on the sitter's body that indicate station or status.[14] Tarnya Cooper notes that these details present a challenge for modern viewers:

> Many of these symbols are difficult to interpret fully and their meanings, perhaps connected to specific contemporary events and personal relationships are now lost to the modern viewer. ... These types of features point to the private use of portraiture as a tool for communication and sharing personal illusions between friends, lovers and groups of intellectuals or associates.[15]

The portrait of Sir Henry Lee that now hangs in the National Portrait Gallery, London,[16] painted in 1568 by Antonis Mor, depicts the subject wearing three gold rings that are tied onto red cord around his wrist, neck and upper arm. Though the meaning of these rings is unknown today, the symbolism of these distinctive accessories must have been clear to at least some contemporary viewers. Despite the interpretive problems that modern biographers face when they encounter these cryptic details, using portraits as a means to gain insight into the lives of their sitters is a strategy that biographers regularly employ. Charles Nicholl uses this approach to biography in his book for the National Portrait Gallery Insights Series, *Shakespeare and His Contemporaries*, in which he outlines biographies of a variety of individuals who lived in the second half of the sixteenth century using their extant portraits as the centrepiece and groundwork for his analysis.

---

[14] Ann Rosalind Jones and Peter Stallybrass argue in particular for the dominant signifying role that costume had in portraiture, arguing that the clothing that the sitter wears might be more significant than their face, in Jones and Stallybrass, *Renaissance Clothing and the Materials of Memory* (Cambridge: Cambridge University Press), 35.

[15] Tarnya Cooper, *A Guide to Tudor and Jacobean Portraits* (London: National Portrait Gallery Publications, 2008), 20.

[16] National Portrait Gallery Accession Number 2095.

In his introduction, he writes that these images are 'full of physical presence and detail', giving examples such as 'John Donne's raffishly tilted hat; the thin-lipped smile of the wit John Harington; the pamphleteer Thomas Nashe in leg-irons; Sir Walter Ralegh beside his eight-year-old son, who will later die in search of gold in South America'.[17]

Nicholl's career as a historian and biographer is characterised by sound and objective scholarship, but he shows a soft side in this passage. A well-made portrait is evocative; it affects the viewer, making them feel that they 'know' the sitter. Nicholl shows his readers that he has gotten to know the individuals that he writes about in this book; he sees beyond the facts, and into their personalities. Portraits, when they are viewed with a careful and discerning eye, can give a biographer insight into the interior life of their subject. Hamlet, acting as his father's biographer and advocate, uses the same strategy when he interprets the portraits.

It is important to remember, of course, that the paintings on stage in *Hamlet* are not the same as the extant Tudor and Stuart works that hang in the National Portrait Gallery. Reading biographical information out of a fictional account of portraits of fictional people is a rather more complex matter than trying to glean the biography of a real person from an extant portrait. We cannot definitely know what the portraits of Claudius and Old King Hamlet would have looked like on stage in the play's early performances, or how a contemporary viewer would have interpreted those visual details. It is not just our chronological distance from the objects that makes interpretation so challenging; understanding these portraits was likely just as much of a challenge for Shakespeare's first spectators as it is for us today. The portraits that were used as props when this play was originally staged would have been miniatures; they would not have been visible to the audience at all.[18] As readers or spectators of this play we are unable to rely on our eyes to interpret these portraits. The only tool available to us, for interpretive purposes, is not the appearance of the portraits, but the language that Hamlet uses to describe them.

---

[17] Charles Nicholl, *Shakespeare and His Contemporaries*, National Portrait Gallery Insights (London: National Portrait Gallery, 2005), 7.

[18] Much ink has been spilled debating if the portraits used in the original staging of the play would have indeed been miniature or if they were large enough to be seen by the audience. I am convinced of the smallness of the images and my argument is comprehensively outlined in my doctoral thesis (University of Birmingham, 2014): '"My picture, I enjoin thee to keep": The Function of Portraits in English Drama, 1558–1642'. Another compelling argument for the prevalence of miniature portraits in Shakespeare's plays can be found in K. Elam, 'Looking at Pictures in Shakespeare', in *Speaking Pictures: The Visual/Verbal Nexus of Dramatic Performance*, ed. V.M. Vaughn, F. Cioni and J. Bessell (New Jersey: Madison Fairleigh Dickinson University Press, 2010), 63–89.

Understanding this scene, therefore, requires us to take Hamlet's description and interpretation of the images at face value (pardon the pun). While we cannot be the biographers of Old Hamlet and Claudius, we can watch Hamlet be a biographer for these men. This is what Hamlet tells us he sees in the image of his father:

> See what grace was seated on this brow –
> Hyperion's curls, the front of Jove himself,
> An eye like Mars, to threaten or command
> A station like the herald Mercury
> New lighted on a heaven-kissing hill;
> A combination and a form indeed
> Where every god did seem to set his seal
> To give the world assurance of a man. (3.4. 57–64)

In his description of the portrait, Hamlet uses a series of similes that liken the late king's features to those of classical deities. In doing so, he equates his father's personality traits with the virtues and skills that these deities represent. It is not the first time in the play that Hamlet uses imagery from mythology to contrast the two kings. In one soliloquy, he remembers his father as 'So excellent a king, that was, to this, Hyperion to a satyr' (1.2. 139–140). Hamlet is not an objective or neutral biographer. Comparing his father to Hyperion, Jove, Mars and Mercury all within a space of eight lines could be interpreted as hyperbolic, but it is worth noting that in this scene, Hamlet is not alone on stage, delivering a soliloquy. He is speaking to Gertrude and he is motivated by the desire to urge her assent; the language he uses needs to be persuasive.

While Protestant theology supported use of images outside of sacred spaces, using those pictures devotionally would still be deemed idolatrous. This raises the uncomfortable question: can Hamlet's behaviour in this scene be interpreted as worshipping his father's image? Tara Hamling's definition of a devotional image is one that 'evoked the presence of the represented figure and thus prompted the focus of prayer.'[19] She goes on to say that the distinction between devotional images and secular images is less a matter of appearance than of use: 'particular attention bestowed on the devotional image was manifested by the actions performed before it, such as the setting up of lights, the presentation of gifts or the prolonged gazing associated with directed prayer.'[20]

Hamlet obviously does not offer gifts or kindle lights at his father's image, but his speech about the image might be interpreted as a kind of prayer.

---

[19]   Tara Hamling, *Decorating the 'Godly' Household: Religious Art in Post-Reformation Britain* (London: Yale University Press, 2010), 34.

[20]   Hamling, *Decorating*, 34.

The imagery that evokes classical deities and heroes, therefore, serves a double purpose. Hamlet's language evokes the late king's strength, leadership and moral authority and it accomplishes this without comparing Old Hamlet to religious imagery at all. The scene *could* be idolatrous, but it avoids this through self-censorship.

The dramatic conflict of the scene hinges on the fact that Gertrude has not yet been convinced to see the two kings as he does. He incredulously asks: 'have you eyes? Could you on this fair mountain leave to feed, and batten on this moor? Ha? Have you eyes?' (3.4. 66–68). Hamlet is shocked at Gertrude's inability to see traits that appear self-evident to him. His passionate and emotional behaviour in this scene, and indeed in this play as a whole, is often ascribed to feigned (or actual) madness. However, it is not clear if his desire to use portraits as interpretive objects is a symptom of this madness. Gertrude does not question Hamlet's sanity in this scene until 'alas, he's mad' (1.2. 98), which she says after the Ghost enters and Hamlet appears to be conversing with an invisible person. Hamlet's insistence that portraits are a meaningful and accurate way to understand personality, is not madness at all, but in fact a fairly commonplace belief of the sixteenth and seventeenth centuries. Portraits, at the time *Hamlet* was written, were valued not only as decorative objects, but as a means to visually represent the qualities of the sitter. As discussed above, the visual culture of Protestant England was not visually austere, but rather encouraged the use of art as an interpretive tool. Portraits were indeed supposed to provoke contemplation and to be an honest representation of the true nature of the depicted individual. This becomes clear when we consider what English Renaissance portrait artists believed was the purpose of their work.

Two of the most revealing sources on the subject of Renaissance painting are the treatises written by Nicholas Hilliard and Sir Henry Peacham, both texts that describe the necessary technical skills when drawing people. Both artists write about the challenges that come with drawing faces properly and emphasise the importance of depicting the face so that it is both accurate *and* indicative of the sitter's personality. Hilliard's treatise *The Arte of Limning* (c. 1600) explains that:

> the perfection is to imitate the face of mankind ... so near and so well after the life as that not only the party in all likeness for favour and complexion is, or may be, very well resembled, but even his best graces and countenance notably expressed; for there is no person but hath variety of looks and countenance, as well ill-becoming as pleasing or delighting.[21]

---

[21]   Nicholas Hilliard, *The Arte of Limning*, ed. R.K.R Thornton and T.G.S. Cain (Manchester: Mid Northumberland Arts Group in Association with Carcanet New Press, 1981), 75.

Similarly, in *The Art of Drawing With the Pen* (1606) Peacham specifies that faces are challenging to reproduce and that the artist must strive to capture the best possible expression of the sitter. Peacham takes his reader through facial features one by one, explaining how to adjust the painting method in order to achieve the effect of certain types of expressions on the sitter. When he describes how to draw the eyes, he comments that the features of the surface of the face can give insight into the quality of the mind within:

> A great conceit is required in making the eye which either by the dulnes or lively quicknes there-of giveth a great taste of the spirit & disposition of the mind, (which manie times I will not denie mai be as well perceived by the mouth, & motion of the body).[22]

Artists like Hilliard and Peacham agree that their task when drawing faces is to capture the 'spirit' of the individual when they are at their best, which is precisely what Hamlet expects to see in the portraits.

Not only did artists strive to create portraits that could be used to gain insight into a sitter's personality, portraits were regularly displayed in the home among objects that would have been used for didactic and contemplative purposes, suggesting that the portrait would have also been used in that manner as well. Susan Foister's study of the 'Paintings and Other Works of Art in Sixteenth-Century Inventories', reveals that portraits would have also been typically present in the homes of middling class English families, but that they were not the most popular kind of artwork. While most people who could afford art objects were more likely to own narrative or allegorical paintings, they would also hang portraits that were 'not present to the exclusion of other types of pictures'.[23] Drawing on Foister's work, Tarnya Cooper wrote that 'it is curious to note that family portraits were regularly outnumbered by allegorical figures and narrative pictures'.[24]

Indeed, inventories do show that portraits were hung amongst these other, more common, types of paintings but it is not particularly curious that they would all be grouped together. I believe that Cooper's distinction between portraits, allegories and narrative paintings is in fact an unnecessary compartmentalisation. These three forms of painting are not as different as

---

[22] Henry Peacham *The Art of Drawing with the Pen* (Amsterdam: Da Capo Press, 1970), D1ᵛ.

[23] Susan Foister, 'Paintings and Other Works of Art in Sixteenth-Century English Inventories', *The Burlington Magazine* 123 (May 1981): 277.

[24] Tarnya Cooper, 'The Enchantment of the Familiar Face: Portraits as Domestic Objects in Elizabethan and Jacobean England', in *Everyday Objects: Medieval and Early Modern Material Culture and its Meanings*, ed. Tara Hamling and Catherine Richardson (England: Ashgate, 2010), 173.

we often assume and slippages between these genres were common. In the sixteenth-century home, portraits were hung alongside allegories and narrative images because they, also, were understood to be allegorical and narrative. And like allegorical or narrative images, their purpose was didactic and instructive, encouraging the viewer to engage with the object interpretively.

To illustrate this point, consider the paintings of Sir Henry Unton (unknown artist, c. 1596) and the portrait of Sir John Luttrell (after Hans Eworth, 1591).[25] The first painting depicts Henry Unton in the centre of a large, rectangular panel. Around the figure, various scenes from his life are depicted, including his birth, his studies in Oxford, his wedding, and his funeral. The painting conflates time and space into one image, holding the story of the man's life within one frame. The portrait is inherently a narrative. In order to understand its meaning, the viewer must take the time to 'read' the image and recognise that it tells a story. Similarly, the portrait of John Luttrell requires the viewer to invest their time in the interpretive contemplation of the image. Luttrell is depicted naked from the waist up, wading into the sea. On the right-hand side of the image a wrecked ship is tossed by stormy weather, and on the upper left-hand side, Luttrell gazes up at the figure of Peace, who holds an olive branch in her hand. The portrait's symbolic content alludes to Luttrell's bravery and military service. This image is inherently allegorical. The Unton and Luttrell paintings are both typical of their period, and demonstrate the ways in which portraiture was used as an instructive object – an item with a narrative or allegorical meaning that the reader was required to interpret. While Foister's analysis of inventories downplays the importance of portraiture, these images were not unimportant simply because they were less common. These forms of painting require the viewer to connect on an emotional level with the image and to tease out hidden meanings that are locked in the visual details. This type of detail-oriented examination is how Hamlet looks at paintings. He 'reads' the image as if he was reading a narrative or an allegory. He dwells on his father's facial features one by one, blazoning him, commenting on each part individually and finding meaning therein. Hamlet's attempt to 'read' portraits as if they are biographical documents is not atypical, but rather, the avatar of how portraits were ideally used.

Hamlet's interpretive rhetoric has the desired effect. In showing the portraits to his mother, he convinces her to see her first and second husbands differently. Until this point in the play, Gertrude shows no indication that she feels guilt for her remarriage, or even recognises her new husband's flaws. As soon as Hamlet finishes his speech comparing the images, Gertrude implores him to

---

[25] The portrait of Unton now hangs in the National Portrait Gallery, London (Accession Number 710). The portrait of Luttrell is in the collection of the Courtauld Institute, London.

... speak no more.
Thou turn'st mine eyes into my very soul
And there I see such black and grained spots
As will not leave their tinct (3.4. 80–83).

This is the third repetition of the word 'eyes' in a span of only 17 lines; a repetition that drives home the point that this passage is about the transformative role that the visual world has on Gertrude. Before she saw the portraits of Old King Hamlet and Claudius compared to each other, she was blind to the differences between the men. Seeing the portraits, however, awakened her, and she experiences a significant turning point: interpreting the faces of her husbands becomes an exercise in understanding herself. The language she uses – 'black and grained', discoloured and flawed – has Gertrude characterising herself as if she is also a painted object. She is so fully immersed in the visual world that she sees herself as part of it.

Hamlet's portraits make him a biographer, an interpreter and (through showing them to his mother) a teacher. The portrait of Old Hamlet also serves one other significant function: providing comfort and soothing grief. As William Perkins wrote in his theological treatise, one of the godly purposes of images is to commemorate the deceased. Hamlet's grief at the loss of his father is central to this play; the portrait of the late king is, at least theoretically, supposed to ease that grief. Nigel Llewellyn's *The Art of Death* explains that 'in the process of dying the death of the natural body was followed by efforts to preserve the social body as an element in collective memory. Today this function is usually undertaken by photographs, but the visual culture of post-Reformation England also established and preserved the social body'.[26]

Llewellyn's distinction between the natural body and the social body draws on the 'Two Bodies' theory that Ernst H. Kantorowicz put forward in his book *The King's Two Bodies: A Study in Mediaeval Political Theology*. But as Llewellyn demonstrates, the separation between natural body and social body (or body politic) is not only relevant when applied to monarchs. English families of the middling classes would also strive to preserve the social body of their loved ones through visual art. For example, consider the painting of *Sir Thomas Aston at the Deathbed of his Wife*, painted by John Souch (1635).[27] The painting depicts Thomas Aston, with his son, standing beside the bed in which his wife died during childbirth. The corpse of his wife's (natural) body lies in the bed, and at the foot of the bed, her living (social) body sits and gazes out towards the viewer. As Souch's painting demonstrates, death has a different effect on the two bodies. 'Death has command over the natural body, in contrast with the survival of the

---

26   Nigel Llewellyn, *The Art of Death* (London: Reaktion Books, 1991), 47.
27   It now hangs at the Manchester Art Gallery.

soul and the way that the body at death can manifest virtue'.[28] Hamlet's use of the portraits as interpretive tools is neither in conflict with Protestant ideology or out of step with cultural practices; rather, it re-confirms the status of Old Hamlet as both a rightful king and a role-model and father.

However, the two-bodies theory is not entirely that simple, when considered in the context of this scene. While the natural body and social body are usually separate from each other, Shakespeare complicates this distinction with the entrance of the Ghost on stage. One might consider which of Old Hamlet's 'bodies' are on stage at this moment. His natural body, somewhere off-stage, is decomposing in a grave. His social body is preserved forever in the idyllic perfection of a commemorative portrait. The Ghost, therefore, stands in for a third, spiritual body. After death, this spiritual body should be able to rest eternally, but as we learn from the Ghost in 1.5. 10–13 he is instead doomed to walk the night until his sins are purged. In contrast to the static permanence of the painted social body, the Ghost is transient. His purgatorial existence points to Catholic theology that might have struck Shakespeare's audience as off-putting or unsafe.[29] And, as Horatio wonders in 1.4. 69–78, the Ghost may be an evil satanic trick that has come to lure Hamlet to his death. Therefore, in the 'chamber scene', the appearance of both the portrait and the Ghost on stage draws our attention to the contrasts between these two shadows of the king. The portrait is a trustworthy representation of Old Hamlet's virtues that can still be meaningful after his death, while the spectral king is otherworldly and potentially dangerous. The portrait ought to be in the household, while the Ghost should not be there at all. The portrait is visible to anyone, while the Ghost is invisible to most eyes (particularly Gertrude's). The portrait, in short, is a functional object that allows onlookers to reflect on the permanent qualities of the sitter, while the Ghost, who brings no comfort to those that see him, is out of place in Gertrude's chamber.

At the beginning of this essay, I outlined the fluctuating stances that modern critics have taken when trying to evaluate just how visual the culture of the Reformation would have been. While this scene from *Hamlet* affirms the significance of portraiture as an interpretive tool, one that provokes contemplation and insight, I do not want to overstate the importance of this scene as an indicator of what Shakespeare's works reveal about Reformation visual culture. While critics have argued that the visual world of the Reformation was iconophobic, there has been increasing awareness that art in domestic spaces played a part in making Reformation culture more visually based than previously thought. Similarly, Shakespeare's canon provides protean viewpoints

---

28 Llewellyn, *Art of Death*, 47.
29 For a detailed analysis of the dramatic impact of the Ghost's purgatorial existence see Stephen Greenblatt, *Hamlet in Purgatory* (New Jersey: Princeton University Press, 2001).

about the value and reliability of visual stimuli in our world. Only a few years after Hamlet uses portraits as a tool to understand his father's personality, Shakespeare's *Macbeth* questions how trustworthy and informative a person's face can be. At the beginning of the play, Duncan is distraught to learn that the Thane of Cawdor, whom he had trusted, is a traitor, saying 'there's no art to find the mind's construction in the face' (1.4. 12–13). Later in the play, Duncan's concern that facial expressions can be deceptive is re-affirmed by Lady Macbeth's unsettling advice to her husband:

> To beguile the time,
> Look like the time; bear welcome in your eye,
> Your hand, your tongue; look like the innocent flower,
> But be the serpent under it. (1.5. 60–64)

Macbeth takes her advice to heart and agrees: 'False face must hide what the false heart doth know' (1.7. 82). Throughout the canon, Shakespeare regularly introduces his audience to false faces; characters who appear trustworthy but whose inner motivations are hidden behind a trusted exterior. Richard III, Iago and Brutus are just a few examples of Shakespeare's fascination with the human ability to deceive. Even in comic plays, characters with good intentions and without a malicious objective will still fool other characters by disguising their outward appearance, as Viola does in *Twelfth Night*. She eventually realises the complex series of deceptions that her disguising has caused and calls the disguise 'a wickedness, wherein the pregnant enemy does much' (2.2. 27–28). In all these plays, Shakespeare concerns himself with the power that humans have to deceive one another by changing their expression. After all, as Hamlet knows, 'one may smile, and smile, and be a villain' (1.5. 109).

Portraits, while they depict faces, do not have the power to change or to deceive. While so many of Shakespeare's references to human facial features suggest changeability and the possibility for deception, his references to portraiture and sculpture do the opposite. Shakespeare affirms the stability, reliability and inherent honesty, of static artworks. In *Twelfth Night* when Olivia gives her portrait to Cesario she particularly notes 'it hath no tongue to vex you' (3.4. 203–4), pointing out that the image's silence is among its positive attributes. Even when images appear life-like in Shakespeare's works, there is often an acknowledgement of the fact that they do not have the power to move or speak like people do.[30] When Bassanio finds Portia's portrait in the gold casket, he initially praises the image and the painter who created it because it is

---

[30]   There is one notable instance of Shakespeare experimenting with the division between static artifice and changeable reality: the 'statue' of Hermione that becomes animate in *The Winter's Tale* (5.3).

so life-like that the eyes seem to move and the mouth appears to breathe (3.2. 115–20). But he is quick to note that it is only an image and that the 'shadow doth limp behind the substance' (3.2. 129).

Other scholars have considered Hamlet's attitude towards theatre, and Hamlet's opinion about how actors should perform is well-trodden ground.[31] Some of the play's best-loved quotes relate to Hamlet's attitude about the power of performance; theatre can unlock hidden truths by holding 'the mirror up to nature' (3.2. 22) and that is why 'the play's the thing wherein I'll catch the conscience of the king' (2.2. 607). But theatre is clearly not the only form of artwork that Hamlet uses as a touchstone for insight. Portraits, another kind of mimetic art, are also instructive. Unlike theatre, however, the instructive value of portraiture lies in its stasis rather than its variability. In the 'rotten' and unstable state of Denmark where he lives it makes perfect sense that the unchanging image of his father would be a source of stability and consolation for the melancholy prince. Portraits cannot change their appearance, tell lies or hide behind false expressions. It is precisely because the image is static that it is a reliable source for meaningful insights. As long as the artist has done their job correctly, as Hilliard and Peacham explain, the portrait should be representative of an individual at their best. A portrait can preserve the social body of its sitter as a reference point for viewers. In spite of any perceived theological concerns about the morality of finding moral guidance in art, the pervading visual culture of the period encouraged individuals to keep portraits in domestic spaces and refer to them for insight and comfort, just as Hamlet does.

---

[31]   See, for instance, Peter Hall, *Shakespeare's Advice to the Players* (New York: Theatre Communications Group, 2003).

PART III
The Life of the Book

Chapter 8

Textual Criticism, Biography and the Case of William White, Printer

Natalie C. Aldred

Introduction

The London printing houses of the sixteenth and seventeenth centuries produced some of the most significant and cherished texts printed in English to date. From these houses came the work of Thomas More, Isaac Newton, Francis Bacon and William Shakespeare; the King James Bible, which, in a slightly edited form, remains one of the standard versions of the Bible translated into English, was also produced within this time period. These works were disseminated to the public following a process of typesetting and presswork that, after some likely technological experimentation at the time of incunabula (pre-1501 printed texts), appears to have been remarkably unchallenged until Friedrich Koenig's functioning steam-powered press, which was used by *The Times* in 1814.[1]

Yet surprisingly little is known about the printers and the working practices that underpin these – and lesser – books and authors of the period in question. One of the earliest collections of printing house documentation to have survived is that of the Cambridge University press in the 1690s, but even then, the extent to which the workings of a large academic printing house can be used to augment our knowledge of smaller and earlier London businesses remains relatively untested.[2] Nonetheless, even in the absence of documentation, some near-Herculean efforts have been made to shed light on the work of London printers: to cite three of them, Peter Blayney in 1982 produced volume one of textual scholarship that positioned the printing of the 1608 edition of Shakespeare's *King Lear* in relation to the printer, Nicolas Okes, and Okes's printing practices

---

[1] For a description of the development of the automated press see Philip Gaskell, *A New Introduction to Bibliography* (Winchester: Saint Paul's Bibliographies; New Castle, Delaware: Oak Knoll Press, 1972; repr. 1995), 251.

[2] So far, the most comprehensive study of the early Cambridge University Press was produced by D.F. McKenzie in his *The Cambridge University Press 1696–1712: A Bibliographical Study*, 2 vols (Cambridge: Cambridge University Press, 1966).

and schedule.[3] More recently, in 2009, Graham Rees and Maria Wakely published their archive-based research into King James I's printers; and Lukas Erne in 2013 published various quantitative studies on Shakespeare and the book trade.[4] But the majority of English printers and printing house production from the sixteenth and seventeenth centuries have not been investigated, despite what such studies can tell us: through textual research it is possible to edit the printed texts of More, Newton and Shakespeare (because the number and type of perceived textual deficiencies made in a printed text can be traced); it is also possible to identify the printers for books where printers are unnamed; to identify the impact of a printing house on cultural practices and the public consumption of generic literature; and, as a concomitant of textual work, it is possible to contribute to discussions of printed morphological changes to the English language. In short, textual studies promote sixteenth- and seventeenth-century printers in terms of their cultural and intellectual contributions and the collaborative enterprise of printing.

Our lack of knowledge about printers in part stems from the nature of the documents that are extant, such as the Stationers' Register, which was essentially rescinded by the author-centred Statute of Anne in 1710. This register functioned as an early form of copyright that protected the interests of publishers, but it contained the sort of untruths that people might tell their bosses in order to skirt around what they are really doing. Other resources that might be called upon by researchers include parish registers, wills and probate records, although references to and by historical figures might be found in print, or, occasionally, manuscript sources such as diaries, archival letters and marginalia found in almanacs, bibles and account books: Adam Smyth in 2010 detailed the uses of a number of such sources, but they provide little information about how printers went about their job.[5]

The most meaningful way of identifying an early modern printer's practices is to organise and categorise the extant texts that they printed, and then to look specifically at copies of an edition (or, time permitting, more than one edition) that went through their business. The strength of this argument can be demonstrated by the case study of William White (d. 1618) and the extant output of his printing house, 1598 to 1617. White is a printer largely neglected by the scholarly community, but he made a significant contribution to the publication of plays written by Shakespeare and Thomas Kyd, as well as the poems

---

[3]   Peter M. Blayney, *The Texts of King Lear and their Origins*, 2 vols (Cambridge: Cambridge University, 1982). Perhaps tellingly, Volume 2 is to date unpublished.

[4]   Graham Rees and Maria Wakely, *Publishing, Politics and Culture: The King's Printers in the Reign of James I and VI* (Oxford: Oxford University Press, 2009); Lukas Erne, *Shakespeare and the Book Trade* (Cambridge: Cambridge University Press, 2013).

[5]   Adam Smyth, *Autobiography in Early Modern England* (Cambridge: Cambridge University Press, 2010).

of Samuel Daniel. After a brief description of White's personal life through 'standard' records such of those of the Church, I wish to show how general textual enquiries stimulate discussion about White's investment interests. Most of this chapter, however, is committed to a summary textual analysis of copies of a text – looking at differences in running titles, type shortages and press variants in William Haughton's *Englishmen for My Money; or, A Woman Will Have Her Will*, printed by White in 1616 – in order to demonstrate the 'life' of an edition as it went through typesetting and presswork.[6] Haughton's *Englishmen*, despite being the first known English city comedy, is also understudied; the first extant edition provides a useful gateway into White's printing house practices and size of business. Throughout, my study is linked to how object (book) history informs and enriches our understanding of early modern printers; as such, this chapter feeds into a wider discussion on the value and usefulness of non-traditional primary material in the reconstruction of historical lives.

Tracing White in Traditional Sources

Before I enter into such a discussion, however, I wish to begin by summarising the biographical details of White that can be gleaned from traditional sources. Parish records seemingly have not survived for his birth or christening. Nonetheless, from these records we know that in 1590 White resided in St Giles Cripplegate, where on 6 May a daughter, Margaret, was christened.[7]

As a printer, many of White's business activities were documented in the company registers of the Stationers, a surviving collection of formal registers that scrutinised and recorded the activities of London printers – an early modern form of copyright, but with its own laws that had to be honoured if the printer wished to avoid imprisonment, his books burned or his type melted down. We know from the Stationers' Registers that White was indentured to the Queen's printer, Richard Jugge and, following Jugge's death in 1577, he was presented to the Stationers to be made free of his apprenticeship (i.e. became a full member of the Company) by Jugge's widow, Joan, on 10 April 1583.[8]

It is unknown for whom White worked until the last few months of 1588, when he set up a bookshop with fellow printer Gabriel Simson in The White Horse, Fleet Lane, a shop infrequently identified on imprints as 'over-against'

---

⁶ William Haughton, *English-men For my Money: or, A pleasant Comedy, called, A Woman will haue her Will* (London: W[illiam] White, 1616; STC 12931).

⁷ William E. Miller, 'Printers and Stationers in St. Giles Cripplegate, 1561–1640', *Studies in Bibliography* 19 (1966), 38.

⁸ Edward Arber (ed.), *A Transcript of the Registers of the Company of Stationers of London, 1554–1640*, 3 vols, (London: Stationers' Company, 1875; repr. New York: Peter Smith, 1950), II, 688.

(i.e. opposite) Seacoal Lane.[9] The two printers were ambitious and expanded their business in 1594 when, for 40 shillings per annum, White acquired from Saint Bartholomew's Hospital the leasehold of a property in Cow Lane; presumably, this was for ease of location because it was only a few streets to the north (about 0.6 miles or a brisk ten-minute walk) of his and Simson's first business.[10] Quite possibly the intention was to use the Cow Lane premises as a shop for titles that they print-published, for Simson and White had acquired a press for their Fleet Lane business in or by 1595.[11]

For some reason the partners went their separate ways in 1597 when Simson kept the Fleet Lane business and White, by himself, acquired the printing press and associated paraphernalia (such as type pieces) formerly belonging to William Hill and Richard Jones, which he moved into his Cow Lane premises.[12] White on occasion provided on imprints the information that his dwelling was over-against the White Lion and so his business location in Cow Lane can be identified; however, the internal layout of his printing house is unknown.[13] If he printed anything in 1597 then it seems to have not survived: quite possibly he moved into his Cow Lane premises late in the year. White was active by 1598, when he printed *A Hedgerow of Bushes, Brambles and Briars* for the publisher John Brown.[14]

Very little can be gleaned from traditional sources about White's Cow Lane printing house and his practices. An extant imprint from 1598 suggests that the premises doubled as printing house and shop.[15] Stationers' records indicate that White had only one press: the previous owners of the business were recorded as

---

⁹   Simson and White entered their first title into the Stationers' Register on 13 December 1588 (Arber, 2: 511).

¹⁰   Saint Bartholomew Hospital, SBHB/HB/1/3, f. 90 Treasurer's Ledgers of Saint Bartholomew's Hospital, 1589–1614 [Entries detailing leasehold charges from 1594, William White].

¹¹   Extant imprints first give White and Simson as printing in 1595: one such text is Richard Greenham's *Two Learned and Godly Sermons*, 'Printed by Gabriel Simson and William White, for [the publisher] William Iones' (London: 1595; STC 12325), sig. A1r.

¹²   Arber, *A Transcript of the Registers of the Company of Stationers of London*, III, 702–5.

¹³   An example of White providing his location on imprints is the title-page to Henoch Clapham's *A Chronological Discourse Touching, 1. The Church, 2. Christ, 3. Anti_Christ, 4. Gog & Magog*, printed 'By William White, dwelling in Cow-lane ouer against the signe of the white Lion' (London: 1609; STC 5336), sig. A1r.

¹⁴   Anon., *A Hedgerow of Bushes, Brambles and Briars* (London: William White for John Brown, 1598; STC 6170).

¹⁵   Partick Hamilton's *Most excellent and Fruitful Treatise, called, Patrick's Places*, printed in 1598 (STC 12734), provides on the imprint (sig. A1r) the information that the book was 'Printed by William White dwelling in Cow-lane neare Holborne Condite, and are there to be solde'.

having one press in 1586,[16] an amount re-confirmed when White was assessed on 19 June 1612.[17] Like most printers of the time, his business consisted partly of that of printers before him: in 1598 he augmented his printing equipment after Richard Watkins presented him his stock, following Watkins's reduction to poor circumstances and, consequently, ceasing to print,[18] and on 13 August 1599 White added to this a number of titles owned by Abel Jeffes.[19] At about this time White was warned away from reprinting a number of banned satires, and in 1600 he escaped prison after printing a 'Disorderly ballad' of *The Wife of Bath*.[20] He had a number of apprentices – who would have assisted at the press – including three whose fathers were butcher, yeoman and gentleman: an interesting glimpse into the social composition of White's printing house.[21] Like many printers, White struggled to make ends meet: he is mentioned in the Stationers' Poor Book and Loan Book, and was assigned the printing of almanacs, ballads and Golding's translation of Ovid's *Metamorphoses*: material that, according to the Stationers' historian Cyprian Blagden, printers were only given if in need of poor relief.[22] White stayed at his Cow Lane premises until 1617, although as of 1615 he appears to have started handing over the business to his son, John, who went on to rent the premises for some years.[23]

White died in 1618, probably a few days after making his will of 19 March, which mentions children (Margaret and John) as well as grandchildren, but no wife; in his will, White left his son 'All my printynge house and printinge stuffe

---

[16]   Peter W.M. Blayney and Ian Gadd (eds), *Liber A* (London: The Bibliographical Society, forthcoming), f. 51.

[17]   Arber, *A Transcript of the Registers of the Company of Stationers of London*, III, 703–5; William A. Jackson (ed.), *Records of the Stationers' Company, 1602–1640* (London: The Bibliographical Society, 1957), 75.

[18]   R.B. McKerrow (ed.), *Printers' and Publishers' Devices in England and Scotland 1485–1640*, 2nd edn (London: Chiswick Press, 1913; London, The Bibliographical Society, 1949), 184.

[19]   Arber, *A Transcript of the Registers of the Company of Stationers of London*, III, 146.

[20]   N.C. Aldred, 'White, William (b. in or before 1559, d. 1618)', *Oxford Dictionary of National Biography* (Oxford: Oxford University Press, online edn, September 2011).

[21]   D.F. McKenzie, *Stationers' Company Apprentices 1605–1640* (Bibliographical Society of the University of Virginia: Charlottesville, Va., 1961), 28.

[22]   W. Craig Ferguson, 'The Stationers' Company Poor Book, 1608–1700', *The Library*, 5th ser., 31.1 (1974), 37, 50; W. Craig Ferguson, *The Loan Book of the Stationers' Company With a List of Transactions, 1592–1692* (London: Bibliographical Society, 1989), 34; W.W. Greg, *A Companion to Arber* (Oxford: Clarendon Press, 1967), 50; Jackson, *Records*, 53–4, 133; Arber, *A Transcript of the Registers of the Company of Stationers of London*, III, 157; Cyprian Blagden, *The Stationers' Company: A History, 1403–1959* (London: Allen and Unwin, 1960), 66.

[23]   Saint Bartholomew Hospital, SBHB/HA/1/4 f. 101, Saint Bartholomew's Hospital Journal, 1607–1647 [Lease of Cow Lane premises to John White].

whatsoeuer & all my estate of printing'.[24] White's children proved the will on March 30; his inventory was valued at £39, 13s, 4d.[25]

General Textual Study of White's Printing House Practices

With these facts in mind, how might bibliographical studies flesh out what we know about White? Although such studies cannot help us identify additional personal details about his family life, they can help us to uncover his general printing house practices.

From my own studies I have identified that White largely survived by acting as a trade printer (printing for others) with almost 70 per cent of the 200 extant texts produced by him being of this kind.[26] Of those edition sheets printed and published by White, a large percentage, some 49 per cent, were religious. This is typical for the time and is confirmed by H.S. Bennett who argued that from 1580 to 1603 '40 per cent of all works published fell into the category of religious;' further, David L. Gants's study of mid-Jacobean printing places the genre 'religion' as the highest proportion of extant edition sheets at 52 per cent, which would imply that White was a typical Elizabethan and Jacobean printer-publisher.[27] Although White did print and publish plays, such as Haughton's *Englishmen*, it was a smaller business venture: of the 425 or so extant edition sheets that he printed and published from 1598 to 1617, only 40.5 sheets (under 10 per cent) were printed plays.

'Economy' seems to have been a buzzword at White's business. The last page is printed upon in over half of the twenty extant playbooks printed by White

---

[24] London Metropolitan Archives, DL/C/B/001/MS01968/016 [Original will of William White].

[25] London Metropolitan Archives, DL/C/B/001/MS01968/016, f. 296r [Probate Record for William White].

[26] Printing and publishing were different ventures at the time of White. While a printer would merely be paid for their time in typesetting and printing the material, a publisher, if he wished to protect his rights to copy, would pay to enter the text into the Stationers' Register; he would also pay for the text being licensed to go through the press and pay for materials such as paper. The publisher would therefore make the costly and risky investment, but he would also, if he invested wisely, gain the financial returns. Sometimes a printer would act as both publisher and printer for a text, but this carried obvious financial risks.

[27] H.S. Bennett, *English Books and Readers 1558 to 1603: Being a Study in the History of the Book Trade in the Reign of Elizabeth I* (Cambridge: Cambridge University Press, 1989), 269; David L. Gants, 'A Quantitative Analysis of the London Book Trade 1614–1618', *Studies in Bibliography* 55 (2002): 192.

and in all four of those that he published or part-published.[28] The practice appears to have been atypical from 1565 to 1640, for a blank page offered the playbook some protection from dirt and damage.[29] White's printing on the last page suggests economy both in the amount of paper used and, if typesetters were paid by the edition sheet or forme, in the amount of labour expected from a typesetter before he was paid.[30]

White's printing house was underproductive, probably to the point of impoverishment. Gants has established that the printing house of White and (from 1615) his son, John, had the lowest output of all (22) London printing houses from 1614 to 1618 at 253 extant edition sheets. The next highest printing house – that of Thomas Dawson – almost doubled the sum at 430 sheets. At the top end, Adam Islip printed 3,751 edition sheets and the King's Printing House printed 6,069 extant edition sheets.[31] To this can be added the results from my own investigation, which establishes that White printed about 1,274 edition sheets over 19 years from 1598 to 1617, an average per annum of 67 edition sheets. In 1601, when White entered *Englishmen* into the Stationers' Register, only 64 edition sheets – averaging fewer than 3 formes per six-day week – are extant. Very few bibliographical studies of other printing houses have been done, as I have already mentioned, but my findings might be compared to the printing house of John Windet and William Stansby, which, according to Mark Bland, produced 840 sheets per annum in 1609, or more than 33 formes per six-day week.[32] Given that an experienced typesetter appears to have set half a sheet or one forme per day, the implication is that White print-published, or

---

[28]   White printed, part-printed or printed and published 20 extant playbooks. The final verso pages in playbooks printed by White (based upon W.W. Greg's *A Bibliography of the English Printed Drama to the Restoration*, 4 vols (Oxford: Oxford University Press, 1939), I are: Greg nos. 150a, 110d, 110e, 145f, 191d, 234b; those printed and published by White are 112b, 110c, 110g and 336a. Final verso page blank are 138b, 151b, 141d/d(*), 151c, 151d, 249b. White shared the printing (in which he did not print the final sheet) for 163c, 284a, 284b and 110f.

[29]   Although publishers and booksellers did on occasion sell their books with covers, most books were simply sold as sheets folded in the correct order. Blank pages at the end of a text therefore acted as part of a provisional 'cover'.

[30]   The use of blank pages in playbooks is discussed by Henry R. Woudhuysen in his 'Early Play Texts: Forms and Formes', in *In Arden: Editing Shakespeare*, ed. Ann Thompson and Gordon McMullan (London: Thomson Learning, 2003), 57.

[31]   Gants, 'Quantitative', 195.

[32]   Mark Bland, 'William Stansby and the Production of the *Workes of Beniamin Jonson*, 1615–16', *The Library*, 6th ser., 20.1 (1998): 4.

was commissioned to print, considerably fewer edition sheets per annum than other printers.[33]

My investigation does not consider the fact that various titles might be extant while not naming him on the title-pages or colophons, or that a lower rate of edition sheets per annum might indicate that White relied on higher-volume print runs.[34] Nor have I identified White's loss rate or the number of texts, entered by White in the Stationers' Register or other documents, that have not survived. White's printing of ephemeral literature is certainly higher than surviving records indicate as he was one of five printers granted a monopoly over the printing of ballads from 6 April 1612. A few studies, such as that of John Barnard as well as Alan B. Farmer and Zachary Lesser, have demonstrated the high loss rate of ephemeral material.[35] Nonetheless, my analysis suggests that White often 'scraped the bottom of the barrel' and worked just to survive. My research helps to explain why the Stationers' Company provided White with so many different forms of poor relief, as detailed earlier.

Partial Textual Study of the First Extant Edition of *Englishmen*

With some of White's general printing house practices identified, I wish to move on to the specifics of a particular book: the playtext *Englishmen for My Money; or, A Woman Will Have Her Will.*[36] Although the text was published without

---

[33]   Mark Bland, *A Guide to Early Printed Books and Manuscripts* (London: Wiley-Blackwell, 2010), 108.

[34]   Peter W.M. Blayney, 'The Publication of Playbooks', in *A New History of Early English Drama*, ed. John D. Cox and David Scott Kastan (New York: Columbia University Press, 1997), 383.

[35]   This monopoly is detailed in Jackson, *Records*, 53–4, 133. For loss rates, see John Barnard, 'The Survival and Loss Rates of Psalms, ABCs, Psalters and Primers from the Stationers' Stock, 1660–1700', *The Library*, 6th ser., 21.2 (1999), 148–50; Alan B. Farmer and Zachary Lesser, 'Structures of Popularity in the Early Modern Book Trade', *Shakespeare Quarterly* 56.2 (2005): 206–13.

[36]   Three early modern editions of the play are extant: the first was printed by White in 1616; the second was printed by John Norton in 1626 (*English-men for my money: or A pleasant comedy called, a Woman will haue her Will. As it hath beene diuers times acted with great applause* (London: J[ohn] N[orton], 1626; STC 12932)), and the third was printed by Augustine Mathewes in 1631 (*A pleasant comedie called, A woman will haue her will. As it hath beene diverse times acted with great applause* (London: A[ugustine] M[athews], 1631; STC 12933)). Transmission between editions is linear. There is some conjecture (such as by Greg in his *Bibliography*, I, 482) of a lost 'Q0' printed by White sometime between 1601 and 1616, but it is a detailed argument that will shift the focus of this chapter. I outline the principal strengths and weaknesses of the argument in my forthcoming critical edition of Haughton's *Englishmen* for *Digital Renaissance Editions*.

mention of an author, the surviving accounts of Philip Henslowe, proprietor of the Rose Theatre, identify the play as written in 1598 by William Haughton (d. 1605).[37] Haughton wrote the play for the Lord Admirals' Men, an acting troupe that, at the time based in the Rose Theatre, borrowed money regularly off Henslowe – including for *Englishmen* – to pay for props and authors' fees.[38] Presumably the play was performed in 1598, but no concrete documentation of its performance appears to have survived. At the time of composition the play was titled '*A Woman Will Have Her Will*'; the first part of the title as it was printed was probably White's idea.

White entered a manuscript of the play into the Stationers' Register on 3 August 1601.[39] It is unknown whether White acquired his copy from Haughton or a representative of the Admiral's Men. Harold Love, in his discussion of the playwright Thomas Middleton's manuscripts in print, argues that the absence of a dedication or an acknowledgement (such as in *Englishmen*) may be more typical of a play manuscript sold by the acting company. But as Love also points out, an author might deliberately leave a play unacknowledged and undedicated.[40]

The manuscript that lies behind the first edition of *Englishmen* (hereafter shortened to 'Q1') has not survived. Among others, Blayney and Grace Ioppolo have argued that manuscript copy – excluding the page on which authority to publish and licence to print were recorded – may have been discarded after the edition was printed.[41] Nonetheless, two of the play's previous editors, A.C. Baugh and L.E. Kermode, have argued that a theatrical manuscript (i.e. marked up for performance by the acting company) served as printer's copy for Q1.[42] Such

---

[37] Dulwich College, MS VII, fols 44v, 45v [Diary and account book of Philip Henslowe, 1592–1609]. Transcriptions of Henslowe's entries for *Englishmen* can be found in Philip Henslowe, *Henslowe's Diary*, ed. R.A. Foakes, 2nd edn (Cambridge: Cambridge University Press, 1961 (with R. T. Rickert), 2002), 87, 89; for digitised copies see Grace Ioppolo (ed.), *The Henslowe-Alleyn Digitization Project* (2005) http://www.henslowe-alleyn.org.uk/index.html.

[38] Payments by Henslowe to the Lord Admiral's Men have been analysed and tabulated by Neil Carson in his *A Companion to Henslowe's Diary* (Cambridge: Cambridge University Press, 1988).

[39] Robin Myers (ed.), *Records of the Worshipful Company of Stationers 1554–1920*, 115 reels of microfilm (Cambridge; Teaneck, NJ: Chadwyck-Healey, 1987), reel position 0115.

[40] Harold Love, 'Thomas Middleton: Oral Culture and the Manuscript Economy', in *Thomas Middleton and Early Modern Textual Culture: A Companion to the Collected Works*, ed. Gary Taylor and John Lavagnino (Oxford: Clarendon Press, 2007), 108.

[41] Blayney, 'Publication', 392; Grace Ioppolo, *Dramatists and Their Manuscripts in the Age of Shakespeare, Jonson, Middleton and Heywood: Authorship, Authority and the Playhouse* (London: Routledge, 2006), 93.

[42] William Haughton, *William Haughton's 'Englishmen for my money; or, A Woman will have her will'*, ed. A.C. Baugh (Philadelphia: The University of Pennsylvania Press, 1917), 91; Lloyd Edward Kermode (ed.), *Three Renaissance Usury Plays*, Revels Plays

conclusions, like my own, can only be reached by identifying certain textual clues in copies of the extant text, and comparing these clues to previous studies into printing house practices. The danger of drawing rigid conclusions is emphasised by bibliographers such as Paul Werstine, who in his *Early Modern Playhouse Manuscripts* seeks to deconstruct the bibliographical grand narrative that play manuscripts fall into discrete categories.[43] However, my provisional study into Q1 shows evidence of authorial practice in the underlying manuscript, but no evidence of theatrical use or concern for theatrical convenience. The details of such a study, even in summative form, would double the length of this chapter, but I can provide a condensed version. In a theatrical manuscript, one might expect the marking-off of entrances and exits, yet these are often inaccurate in Q1 (necessary exits are omitted, such as those for Mathea and Marina opposite G3r, 8 lines down, Frisco opposite E4r, 29 and K1v, 23, Pisaro opposite I3v, 31 and Anthony opposite I4r, 19; an entrance stage direction in B3v, 12 for Al Varo brings the character onto the stage over 230 lines too early, and in H3r, 29 Q1's version has Van Dal enter with his companions, despite at the time being suspended above the stage), while other entry directions are missing (such as an entry direction for Mathea, Maria and Mathea at F1r, 15).

An authorial hand is in evidence in Q1 where it is demonstrable that the typesetter misinterpreted authorial revisions. For example, In A3v, 5, 'young' is placed four lines into a speech of Marina's (the second line in the extract below):

> Thy euer louing *Haruie* I delight it:
> *Marina* euer louing shall requite it young.
> Teach vs *Philosophy*? Ile be no *Nunne*;
> Age scornes delight; I loue it being:

However, the apparent end-rhyme ('it'/'it') and the iambic pentameter otherwise present in Marina's speech would suggest that 'young' has been incorrectly placed. The word has by consensus (starting with Q2) since been placed a further two lines down, after 'I love it being', thus continuing the end-rhyme. The most sensible interpretation of the textual crux is that Haughton wrote a word that rhymed with 'nun' (perhaps 'sung', or 'done'), changed his mind, crossed it out (or marked the cut with a vertical line in the margin next to the text) and then wrote 'young' above it and on the same line as 'Marina … it'; the typesetter then

---

Companion Library (Manchester: Manchester University Press, 2009), 64. The first edition of *Englishmen* was printed as a quarto: a most usual format for playbooks at the time. After the customer had trimmed the edges to their satisfaction, a quarto roughly corresponded to the size of a modern paperback. 'Quarto' comes from the fact that each sheet of paper that made up a text was folded twice after printing, to make four leaves or eight pages.

[43]   Paul Werstine, *Early Modern Playhouse Manuscripts and the Editing of Shakespeare* (Cambridge: Cambridge University Press, 2013).

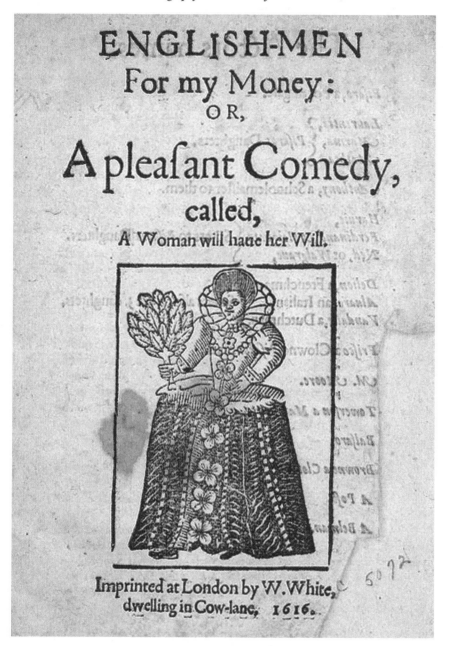

ENGLISH-MEN
For my Money:
OR,

A pleafant Comedy,
called,
A Woman will haue her Will.

Imprinted at London by W.White,
dwelling in Cow-lane, 1616.

Figure 8.1   Title-page from the first edition (Q1) of *Englishmen*. Courtesy of
the Trustees of the Boston Public Library/Rare Books.

misread 'young' as the terminal word for the line and set it as such. The fact that the typesetter did not perceive the error may suggest that this was one of many revisions that he had to negotiate.

Q1 also has a number of textual inconsistencies that indicate an unrevised manuscript. The elaborate direction in B3v, 13 is permissive,[44] giving '*other Marchants*'; later (in C4r, 8) an exit stage direction gives '*Exit … Strangers, & Marchant*'. This introduces inconsistency in both the title(s) of the extras (are they strangers, merchants or merchant-strangers?) and in the specification of supernumeraries ('*other Marchants*' in the entry stage direction, yet '*Marchant*' and '*Strangers*' in the exit). Further, the number of respondents and the assignment of speeches is left vague in '*Strang*'., B3v, 15, '*Stra*'., C2v, 17 and '*March*'., C2v, 20; and in B4v, 32 Brown enters with 'God save you, gentlemen', while the corresponding speech prefix gives '*Gent*'. (B4v, 33), thus complicating both whom Brown addresses, and who responds.

Altogether, such clues might indicate that the manuscript acquired by White consisted of authorial 'foul papers', i.e. a first draft, although without the manuscript used to hand, such conclusions should always be cautious and provisional. Whatever the nature of the underlying manuscript, *Englishmen* was apparently first printed by White in 1616 (although see n. 36). Seven copies are known to have survived.[45] A facsimile of the title-page is provided below, and a descriptive bibliography, which outlines the textual details of the play, is found in Appendix 1. For an image of the title-page, see Figure 8.1.

Running Titles

Earlier I mentioned that White was recorded as owning a single press. Yet it might be possible to demonstrate from running title analysis that White had at least two presses. Running title analysis is the identification of distinct running titles used by the typesetters.[46] These are the titles found along the top of each

---

[44]   As W.W. Greg (*The Shakespeare First Folio: Its Bibliographical and Textual History* (Oxford: Clarendon Press, 1955), 142) explains, 'permissive' phrasing is typical of an author's stage direction, in that it leaves the determination of exact numbers or speakers to be resolved later by the theatre company.

[45]   The locations of the seven copies, with abbreviations, are as follows (the order is UK, then internationally): British Library, London (BL); Bodleian Library, Oxford (Bod.); Worcester College Library, Oxford (WOR); Boston Public Library, Boston (B); The Folger Shakespeare Library, Washington D.C. (F); Houghton Library, Harvard (H); and Huntington Library, San Mario (HL).

[46]   The methods used in this study to determine the order of running titles follow those described by Fredson Bowers in his *Essays in Bibliography, Text and Editing* (Charlottesville: University Press of Virginia, 1975), 201, who argues that the bibliographer should look for 'Variations in spelling, or punctuation, or capitalization; [as well as] variation in the fount,

page. They would be set up by the typesetters and used again and again, forme after forme.[47] Changes to running titles used can tell textual scholars a number of things, depending on how they relate to other studies of the text: it might indicate a change of typesetters, a change of printers or the speed of press work.

The running titles used throughout the first edition of *Englishmen* read '*English-men for my Money; or*', on the verso pages and '*A Woman will haue her will*'. on the recto pages. One exception runs across three pages: the spelling '*Monoy*' on G3v, G4v and I1v. An examination of the running titles established eight sets. Between them, the sets exist in 15 different states. The first edition of *Englishmen* is printed on 10 sheets running from sheet A to sheet K. In the printer's alphabet 'J' was unused.

The findings have been summarised in the attached table, in a style reminiscent of Blayney in his *Texts*.[48] The table's first column is organised into the order of sheets (A through K) and each sheet is divided in the table into its outer (o) and inner (i) formes. The second to fifth columns present the running titles as they appear in the type-page, running counter-clockwise from the bottom-left quartile (outer forme: 1r, 2v, 3r, 4v; inner forme: 4r, 3v, 2r, 1v). The occurrence of a particular running title is signified by its designated group number: the numbers (1–4.2) represent verso pages, whereas the letters (a.1–d) represent recto pages (see Figure 8.2 for facsimiles of each running title). Three signatures in the forme mates that made up sheet A – one a title-page, one with a printer's device and one with the actor's names – do not have running titles and so have been left blank. Facsimiles of the running titles follow the table; their descriptions can be found in Appendix 2.

From this table a few preliminary observations can be made. Forme mates A through F, H and K use identical running titles, or a single skeleton forme; this indicates that one forme was stripped of type before the setting of the

---

such as swash forms; [and] actual broken or bent letters (and I say 'actual' because bad inking can be very deceptive)'. G. Thomas Tanselle ('The Treatment and Typesetting of Presswork in Bibliographical Description', *Studies in Bibliography* 52 (1999): 19), writes that skeleton formes may further be identified by distinctive spacing within the title, between its ends and the left and right type-page margins, as well as impressions from materials not meant to print.

[47]   So that the pages appeared in order for the customer, the type was set in metal 'formes'. Each sheet would need two formes – one for either side of the sheet. The forme that contained the first page as the customer saw it – signature 1r, with 'r' meaning 'recto', or right – was called the outer forme. The forme that was used in the printing of the other side of the sheet was called the inner forme. When setting by formes, the typesetters would typically fill with type one forme at a time. In a quarto forme, each of the four sections was called a 'quartile'.

[48]   Blayney, *Texts*, 540–41.

Table 8.1   A breakdown of running titles per forme for *Englishmen*, Q1
(where 'i' = inner forme and 'o' = outer forme)

	1r/v	2v/r	3r/v	4v/r
A(o)		1	a.1	2
A(i)			1	a.2
B(o)	a.3	3.1	b.1	2
B(i)	3.1	a.3	2	b.1
C(o)	a.3	3.1	b.1	2
C(i)	3.2	a.3	2	b.1
D(o)	a.3	3.2	b.1	2
D(i)	3.2	a.3	2	b.2
E(o)	a.3	3.2	b.1	2
E(i)	3.2	a.3	2	b.1
F(o)	a.3	3.2	b.1	2
F(i)	3.2	a.3	2	b.1
G(o)	c	1	d	4.1
G(i)	1	c	4.1	D
H(o)	a.4/a.5	1	b.1	2
H(i)	3.2	a.5	2	b.1
I(o)	c	4.2	d	3.1
I(i)	4.1	c	3.1	D
K(o)	b.1	1	a.2	2
K(i)	1	b.1	2	a.2

next.[49] The implication of identical running titles is that White had a single case of the typeface used in the setting of *Englishmen* – pica roman – and that the typesetter could only set one forme of Q1 at a time before type needed to be redistributed; this appears to have been typical in smaller printing houses, although large-scale and interconnected studies, for example into the damaged types in White's printing house, need to be conducted before apparent patterns can be confirmed.[50] Potentially, the typesetter was therefore idle as each forme was being printed, but he spent time correcting literal errors in the text of Q1

---

[49]   Similarly, Gaskell talks of the likelihood of single-skeleton formes being used when printers had a shortage of type in his *Introduction*, 110.

[50]   The immediate redistribution of type in smaller printing houses is disccused by A. Slavin in his 'Printing and Publishing in the Tudor Age', in *William Shakespeare: His World, His Work, His Influence*, ed. John F. Andrews (New York: Scribner, 1985), 132.

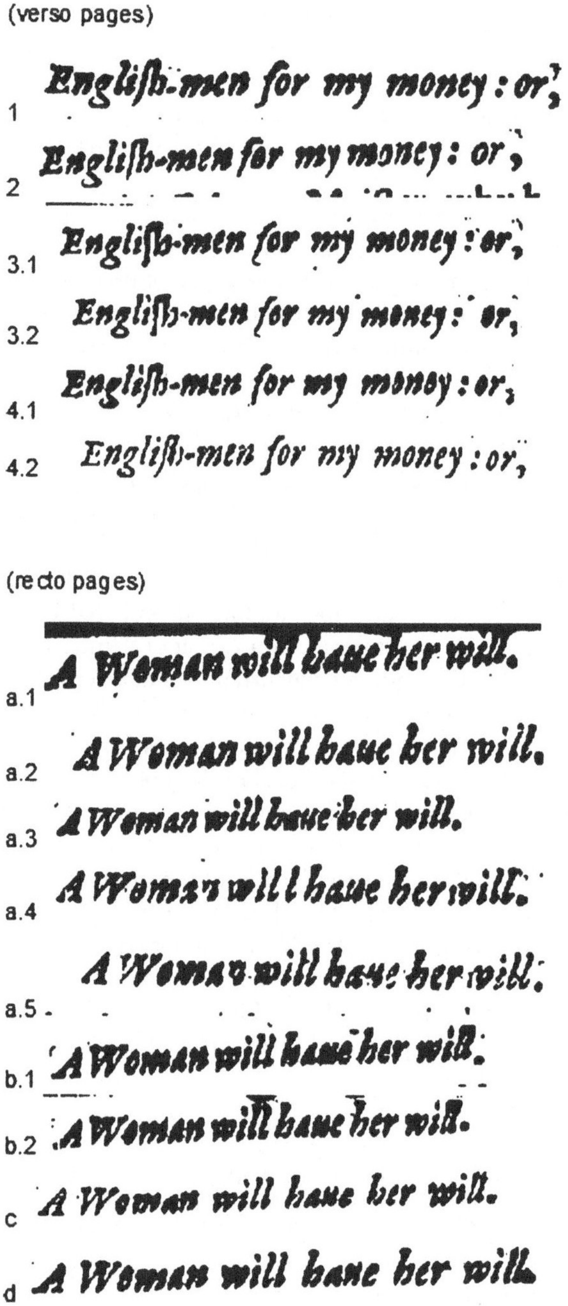

(verso pages)

1   *English-men for my money : or,*

2   *English-men for my money : or,*

3.1 *English-men for my money : or,*

3.2 *English-men for my money : or,*

4.1 *English-men for my money : or,*

4.2 *English-men for my money : or,*

(recto pages)

a.1 *A Woman will haue her will.*

a.2 *A Woman will haue her will.*

a.3 *A Woman will haue her will.*

a.4 *A Woman will haue her will.*

a.5 *A Woman will haue her will.*

b.1 *A Woman will haue her will.*

b.2 *A Woman will haue her will.*

c   *A Woman will haue her will.*

d   *A Woman will haue her will.*

Figure 8.2   Q1 running titles. Courtesy of the Trustees of the Boston Public Library/Rare Books.

and he doubtless concurrently set other texts that required a different typeface to *Englishmen*.[51]

An incomplete reconstruction of events is as follows: the typesetter began by setting the forme mates for sheets B to F. These were set with few hitches: some minor readjustments to the running titles, but not many. Sheet G, however, presents a fresh set of running titles. This is unexpected, given the reoccurrence of the same running titles in the previous 10 formes. The implication is that the typesetter had to create a new set of running titles to continue with his task, which would only occur if typesetting were ahead of presswork and the formes for sheet F were still waiting to be stripped. Two possible theories are linked to the creation of new running titles: the first, which can be rejected, is that the typesetting and presswork of sheet G was assigned to another printer. The problem with this theory is that three of the running titles in the outer and inner formes of sheet G were also used in the outer and inner formes of sheet I; the one running title not used in the forme mates of sheet I, running title 1, was replaced by running title 3, which was also used in the forme mates of sheet B and the outer forme of sheet C, as 3.1 and the inner forme of sheet C to the forme mates of sheet F as 3.2. In other words, sheet I can be linked to the printing of most of the preceding sheets. In turn, the running titles shared by sheets G and I doubtless came from the same printing house: that of White. The second theory is that sheets F and G were printed concurrently and, by extension, that White was using two presses to print the sheets. Were presswork behind, then at least two formes were waiting to be printed. In turn, this would have an impact on the amount of available type, which probably explains a shortage of type (where two capital Vs were frequently used to represent a capital W) in the inner and outer formes of sheet G.

In terms of the headlines in sheet I, three of the running titles used in I(o/i) had been transferred from G(o/i). Headline 1, also used in G(o/i), was replaced in I(o/i) with 3.1. This may indicate that running title 1 was still locked up in forme H(o). One possible implication – both of the re-use of the running title set and of the apparent printing of forme H(o) – is that composition was again (or perhaps still) ahead of presswork. I(o/i) may therefore have been printed concurrently with H(o/i).[52]

---

[51]   D.F. McKenzie discusses typesetters setting type for two or three books concurrently in his 'Printers of the Mind: Some Notes on Bibliographical Theories and Printing House Practices', *Studies in Bibliography* 22 (1969): 18.

[52]   Using running titles as evidence, a suggested order of formes is as follows (where (o/i) = unknown internal order): B(o/i), C(o), C(i), D(o/i), E(o/i), F(o/i), G(o/i), H(o), H(i), I(i), I(o), K(o/i), A(i), A(o). This would mean that the last forme to be set contained the title-page. From type shortage analysis (see below), the forme for G might have been set in the order G(o), G(i).

The implication of this micro study of *Englishmen*'s running titles is that, contrary to White's claimed number of presses as one, he in fact had at least two. His typesetters also had to strip one forme before another one was set indicating that he lacked the type to set up more than one complete forme at a time and that, by extension, White's printing house was small. Bland argues that many London printing houses had more presses than their prescribed or given amount.[53] Thus, White's second press is unsurprising. But while Bland suggests that additional presses 'served for proofing and small jobs', sheets G and I in Q1 *Englishmen* indicate that White also regarded his second press as a means to accommodate an excess of prepared formes.

Type Shortages

However, if White had barely enough type to make up one forme at a time, then how could he print concurrently – and therefore have two formes set up before stripping them – without running out of type pieces? The answer, simply, is that he *did* run out of pieces. Type shortages in the letter 'W' occurred in G(o/i) and H(i), meaning that the letter had to be substituted with 'VV' (see Figure 8.3).[54] The following table presents type shortages and the use of 'W' around the four formes for sheets G and H. The corresponding symbols show where 'VV' is used on relevant pages.

I have already argued that the forme mates for sheet G were printed concurrently with the forme mates for sheet F. The type shortage in sheet G acts as additional confirmation: with the final forme of sheet F waiting to be stripped, the typesetter would have been compelled to improvise by using the double 'V'. Part of the letter 'W' was still in his case, however, and so he could afford to choose where he used the 'VV' and where he used the 'W'. Sheet G was probably printed concurrently with sheet F, and so the typesetter would have been aware that a type shortage was imminent in sheet H. He may have therefore begun to introduce the 'VV' before there was a pressing need. This explains the unusual use of 'VV' across the signatures of sheet G, for the two signatures are not conjugate. Perhaps the outer forme of sheet G was set first; the typesetter anticipated the need for 'VV' based on the number of the letter 'W' that he had set in that forme. He may have begun the first quartile for the next forme (i.e. 1v) under the same impression, but then scouted ahead in his copy and found significantly less need for the use of 'W' in that forme.

---

[53]   Bland, *Guide*, 107.

[54]   For a discussion on the letter 'W'/'VV' in an analysis of setting by formes see George Walton Williams, 'Setting by Formes in Quarto Printing', *Studies in Bibliography* 11 (1957): 39–53.

Table 8.2 Type shortages in Q1

Sheet G	1r	2v	3r	4v	1v	2r	3v	4r
No. of 'W'	7	5	4	4	3	3	2	1
No. of 'VV'	–	–	–	4*	1#	–	–	–
Sheet H								
No. of 'W'	2	2	7	4	6	3	4	1
No. of 'VV'	–	–	–	–	–	–	4+	7†

Key to symbols:

* = 'W' and 'VV' are interspersed; however, 'VV' is used only if the first letter of the first word in a line.

= 'W' and 'VV' are interspersed; both 'VV' and 'W' are used as the first letter of the first word in a line.

+ = 'W' used up to and including the 21st line; from line 22 'VV' is used.

† = 'VV' used on all bar one occasions, both as first letter in first word and internally. Single instance of 'W' is also the last occasion for a capital w on the page.

The issue of type shortage in sheet H is unsurprising, given the need of the typesetter to improvise in sheet G. The typesetter had no need to improvise in the outer forme of sheet H, yet did in the inner forme. Because the outer forme to sheet H had been set first, this may suggest that the typesetter's case had been restocked by the time that he set H(o). By the time that he set H(i) he presumably knew that sheet I was to be printed concurrently and so thought ahead by conserving 'W'. He might also have known that the problem would have partially been relieved by the redistribution of type from the outer forme of sheet H.

Press Variants

It is a commonly held belief among both scholars and students that the printed early modern text was, at best, a perfected, finalised piece of work, and at worst, a poorly proofread text with errors replicated in every copy. Nothing could be further from the truth. Printing house staff saw the process of typesetting and printing as an ongoing opportunity to stop the press and correct the text, meaning that copies of the same edition, when compared side by side, often demonstrate a number of textual variants.

Stop-press corrections are found in six of the ten sheets of Q1 and eight of the twenty formes (in B(o), C(o), F(o), F(i), G(i), H(o), K(o) and K(i)). Greg identified variants in three formes of the British Library copy (F(o), K(o) and K(i)) and in one forme of the Bodleian copy (B(o)); Baugh identified

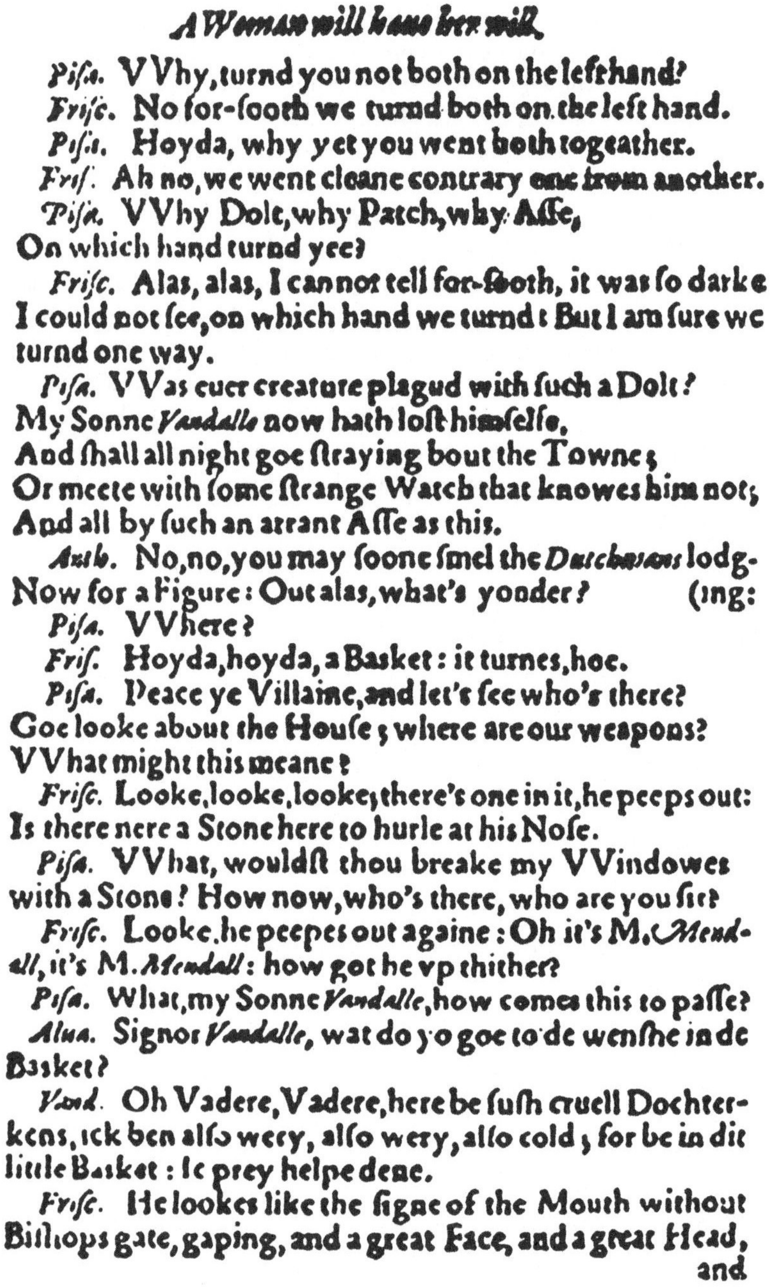

A Woman will haue her will.

Pisa. VVhy, turnd you not both on the lefthand?
Frisc. No for-sooth we turnd both on the left hand.
Pisa. Hoyda, why yet you went both togeather.
Frisc. Ah no, we went cleane contrary one from another.
Pisa. VVhy Dolt, why Patch, why Asse,
On which hand turnd yee?
Frisc. Alas, alas, I cannot tell for-sooth, it was so darke
I could not see, on which hand we turnd: But I am sure we
turnd one way.
Pisa. VVas euer creature plagud with such a Dolt?
My Sonne *Vandalle* now hath lost himselfe,
And shall all night goe straying bout the Towne;
Or meete with some strange Watch that knowes him not;
And all by such an arrant Asse as this.
Anth. No, no, you may soone smel the *Dutchmans* lodg-
Now for a Figure: Out alas, what's yonder?   (ing:
Pisa. VVhere?
Frisc. Hoyda, hoyda, a Basket: it turnes, hoe.
Pisa. Peace ye Villaine, and let's see who's there?
Goe looke about the Houfe; where are our weapons?
VVhat might this meane?
Frisc. Looke, looke, looke; there's one in it, he peeps out:
Is there nere a Stone here to hurle at his Nofe.
Pisa. VVhat, wouldst thou breake my VVindowes
with a Stone? How now, who's there, who are you sir?
Frisc. Looke, he peepes out againe: Oh it's M. *Mend-
all*, it's M. *Mendall*: how got he vp thither?
Pisa. What, my Sonne *Vandalle*, how comes this to passe?
Alua. Signor *Vandalle*, wat do yo goe to de wenfhe in de
Basket?
Vand. Oh Vadere, Vadere, here be sush cruell Dochter-
kens, ick ben also weery, also weery, allo cold; for be in dit
little Basket: Ic prey helpe dene.
Frisc. He lookes like the figne of the Mouth without
Bishops gate, gaping, and a great Face, and a great Head,
and

Figure 8.3   The use of 'W' and 'VV' in Q1, sig. H4r. Courtesy of the Trustees
of the Boston Public Library/Rare Books.

corrections in three formes of the Houghton Library copy (B(o), F(o) and K(o)) and two formes of the Boston copy (F(i) and G(i)). My own investigation, which examined all known copies, identified a much higher rate. I provide these, together with those of Greg and Baugh, in my list of variants (see below).

Because sheets were bound out of the order of printing, the number of corrected and uncorrected sheets in a copy is random. The proportion of corrected sheets in copies is 62 per cent of the known sample or more, except for the copy held at Houghton Library, which is largely made up from uncorrected sheets. A high number of corrected sheets implies that press corrections were made early in the press-run for each forme, although the slightly higher number of uncorrected formes in B(o) and H(o) might indicate that these two formes were corrected at a later stage in the press-run. The results for variants have been recorded using a system adapted from Millard T. Jones.[55] In the list, the reading before the bracket is that of the corrected state of the forme; 's' implies the long 's' in every position in a word except finally. For abbreviations see n. 45.

SHEET B(o)
Corrected: Bod., H, HL
Uncorrected: B, BL, F, WOR
Sig. B2v
> *French-man* ?] ~:
Sig. B3r
> obey.] ~,
Sig. B4v
> *Heighan*] *Heighun*
> *Walg.*] *Walsg.*

SHEET C(o)
Corrected: B, BL, Bod., WOR
Uncorrected: F, H, HL,
Sig. C3r
> North,] ~.

SHEET F(o)
First corrected state: F
Sig. F1r
> obscure] buscure
Sig. F2v
> tho u] thost

---

[55]   Millard T. Jones, 'Press-Variants and Proofreading in the First Quarto of *Othello* (1622)', *SB* 27 (1974), 178–81.

I] [I] (i.e. turned 'I']
Second corrected state: B, BL, H, HL, WOR
Uncorrected: Bod.
Sig. F1r

      obscure] buscure

      you] yo

      sir ?] ~,

Sig. F2v

      tho u] thost

Sig. F4v

      I] [I] [i.e. turned 'I']

SHEET F(i)
Corrected: B, BL, Bod., H, WOR
Uncorrected: F, HL
Sig. F4r

      soft] sost

SHEET G(i)
Corrected: B, BL, Bod., F, H, WOR
Uncorrected: HL
Sig. G1v

      Soft] Sost

Sig. G3v

      light,] ~.

Sheet H(o)
Corrected: H, HL
Uncorrected: B, BL, Bod., F, WOR
Sig. H1r

      A Woman will haue her will.] *A Woman wil l haue her will.*

SHEET K(o)
Corrected: B, BL, F, H, HL, WOR
Uncorrected: Bod.
Sig. K3r

      sing] fing

SHEET K(i)
[WOR *lacks* sig. K4; K3v is corrected]
First corrected state: BL, Bod., F

Sig. K3v
    before] defore
Second corrected state: B, ?WOR
Uncorrected: H, HL
Sig. K3v
    before] defore
Sig. K4r
    here?] ~:

From this list, it is possible to determine that the Q1 typesetter made two types of correction: (1) the correction of literal errors, such as foul case ligature 'ft' (G(i)), foul case ligature 'si' (K(o)) and turned letter 'I' (F(o)); and (2) the correction of punctuation. This second type of correction is more frequent and might indicate that punctuation was up to the typesetter. Press correction in extant sheets occurred only once in each corrected forme, except in two sheets, both corrected twice. In F(o), the sheet was first printed with the errors 'buscure', 'yo', a comma, 'thost' and a turned 'I' (Bodleian). The erroneous 'buscure' (for 'obscure'), 'thost' (for 'thou'), and turned 'I' were then corrected in one extant copy (Folger) before the press was again stopped to correct 'yo' (for 'you') and an erroneous comma for a question mark (Boston, British Library, Houghton Library, Huntington Library, Worcester). The blank type piece ('thost' > 'tho u') suggests that a typesetter identified the error, but preferred to replace the 's' with a spacing quad and the 't' with a 'u' instead of resetting the second half of the line. In K(i), the sheet was first printed with the errors 'defore' for 'before' and 'here:' for 'here?' (Houghton Library, Huntington Library). In a few copies 'defore' has been corrected (Bodleian, British Library, Folger) before the printing of one further extant copy (the error 'here:') was noticed and corrected (Boston, ?WOR).

In comparison to the limited evidence of typesetter correction, the number of literals that remain uncorrected in all extant copies is high. My list of typesetter errors, while not exhaustive, identifies error on every forme (note: 'SP' = speech prefix; [ ] = turned type):

This table indicates a regular incidence of typesetter error, uncorrected in the extant copies. The implication is that the typesetter cast a cursory glance over the formes while they were at the press, correcting blatant errors.

Conclusion

In conclusion, although bibliographical studies are limited to the printers and typesetters involved, the results that they yield are rewarding biographically. As in the case of White, such studies can be used to identify their role as trade

Table 8.3   Forms of literal typesetter error in Q1

Error	Specific error	Q1 spelling	Signature
Foul Case	Foul case full-stop	*Frisco,*	B3r, 2
	Foul case 'f'	sinde	C2r, 9
	Foul case full-stop	*Walgr,* (SP)	C2v, 7
	Foul case full-stop	*Haru,* (SP)	D1v, 5
	Foul case ligature 'fl'	sloutes	F2v, 30
	Foul case 'E'	*Fnter*	F4r, 13
	Foul case 'a'	*Laurnetios*	F4r, 34
	Foul case full-stop	*Heigh,* (SP)	H2r, 19
	Foul case 'i'	*Pesa.* (SP)	I4v, 17
Dropped type	Dropped 'o'	*Philosphy*	A3v, 6
	Dropped full-stop	*Tower* (SP)	C1v, 5
	Dropped full-stop	*Delio* (SP)	D1r, 4
	Dropped 'i'	*Frsc.* (SP)	D3v, 3
	Dropped full-stop	*Antho* (SP)	E4r, 8
	Dropped spacing	itmade	E4r, 24
	Dropped 'e'	hers	F2r, 22
	Dropped full-stop	*Laur* (SP)	G3r, 28
	Dropped full-stop	*Har u* (SP)	H1v, 28
	Dropped full-stop	*Haru* (SP)	K2r, 31
Turned type	Turned 'u'	*Danghters*	A1v, 4
	Turned 'm'	*Dutch-wan*	A4v, 16–17
	Turned full-stop	againe[.]	C3v, 34
	Turned question mark	you[?]	D1v, 7
	Turned 'n'	*Euter*	D2v, 29
	Turned full-stop	*Frisc*[.] (SP)	E1r, 35
	Turned question mark	talke[?]	E2r, 27
	Turned full-stop	*Vand*[.]	G3r, 12
	Turned question mark	ye[?]	G3v, 21
	Turned 's'	*Diogene*[*s*]	H4v, 30
Wrong Case	Wrong case 'i'	*Extt*	C4r, 3
	Wrong case 'i'	*Pesa.* (SP)	I4v, 17
Transposed letter	Transposed 'g' and 'u'	Rouge	G4r, 32
	Transposed space and 't'	Bu tas	E1r, 10

printer or publisher, their economy of page setting and the productivity of their printing house. Bibliographical studies of the texts that they printed can identify the size of the printing house and a minimum number of presses that they used.

My own studies into White's printing house helps flesh out the few details known: he was largely a trade printer, printing for others, although he did occasionally take financial risks by acting as publisher. His printing house was underproductive, which led frequently to the Stationers' Company helping him by sending business his way. As publisher, his printing on the last page of a text, exposing the page to dirt and damage, suggests that he could not afford to 'waste' paper. White had at least two presses, but really only enough type to set up and print one forme before the type had to be redistributed. The second press was used for occasional concurrent printing – thus stretching the capacity of his type – as well as proofing. Press variants between copies of Q1 *Englishmen* demonstrate that White's typesetters, when idle, did correct the text, but correcting was not done in earnest, or at least not in Q1 where uncorrected errors in extant copies are frequent. The recording of a single press, as well as the small amount of type in typesetters' boxes, would indicate that White had a small printing house. Such houses, according to Bland, would have employed between eight and ten people, including the Master (White), typesetters, pressmen, journeymen and apprentices.[56]

As a result of constraints of space I chose to limit my book study to an analysis of running titles, type shortages and press variants, but the analysis of the book as a physical object has other uses. An assessment of damaged types as they are used in formes helps identify the number of cases a printer used; spelling preferences can be used to identify the number of typesetters setting a book; type impressions on the page determines the order in which a sheet was printed; watermarks on the paper can identify the paper mill; larger bibliographical studies, such as Blayney's, might go so far as to identify the order in which a printer printed a series of texts. In order for a comprehensive discussion of a printer's output and printing practices, each extant text printed and/or published by a printer would need to be analysed, but through my limited evaluation, above, it can be seen how it is possible to pick holes in, or greatly supplement, information provided in the official records of the time. Such textual studies are therefore invaluable in identifying the businesses and business practices of printers, the unsung heroes who contributed overwhelmingly, sometimes under impoverished conditions, to our knowledge of authors, books and readers.

---

[56]   Bland, *Guide*, 107.

Appendix 1

A descriptive bibliography of Q1 is as follows:[57]

Catalogue References

STC 12931
Greg I, 336(a)

Typography

Body 82. Face 80 x 1.8: 2.9 (Pica roman). The normal type page consists of 35 lines. A drop-cap 'H' appears on A2r, to the depth of two-and-a-half type lines; the first four type lines on A2r are indented to accommodate it.

Collation

A–K4v, [80] pp; 4°.

Contents

A1r title-page; A1v 'The Actors names'.; A2r headpiece of a cherub's face with various ornaments [91 x 16mm];[58] A2r–K4v text in verse and prose; K4v 'FINIS'. Speech prefixes and stage directions are italicised and indented; proper nouns are also italicised. K4v is printed on.

Title-page

ENGLISH-MEN | For my Money : | OR, | A pleasant Comedy, | called, | A Woman will haue her Will. | [Woodcut, 80 x 60mm, woman holding a fan][59] | Imprinted at London by W. White, | dwelling in Cow-lane. 1616.

Running Titles

English-men for my Money: or, / *A Woman will haue her will.* (With numerous variations.)

---

[57] This descriptive bibliography expands the outline provided by Greg in his *Bibliography*, vol. 1, 355. Underlined letters mark the place of typographic ligatures.

[58] Not identified in McKerrow, *Printers*, or J.A. Lavin's 'Additions to McKerrow's Devices', *The Library*, 5th ser., 23.5 (1968), 191–205.

[59] Not identified in McKerrow, *Printers*, or Lavin's 'Additions'; it is, however, discussed in R.A. Foakes's *Illustrations of the English Stage 1580–1642* (London: Scolar Press, 1985), 166.

Catchwords

A2r: *Laur*] ~.
A4r: ges,] ~?
A4v: *Hntho.*] *Antho.*
C1r: Roring] Roaring
C2r: *Haruie*] *Haru.*
C4r: *Aluar.*] *Alua.*
E4r: *Marin.*] *Mari.*
H1r: New-] Newgate
K4r: *Moore.*] *Moor.*

Appendix 2

Table 8.4   Running Title (Rt) Descriptions, Q1

RT no.	r/v	No. of states	Desig- nation	RT description	Signatures
1	v	1	1	48mm. Italic '*sh*' ligature, low hyphen, swash italic '*fo*'	A2–3, G1–2, H2, K1–2
2	v	1	2	46mm. Italic '*sh*' ligature, ascending hyphen, broken swash italic '*f*'	A4, B3–4, C3–4, D3–4, E3–4, F3–4, H3–4, K3–4
3	v	1	3.1	48mm. Roman '*sh*' ligature, normal hyphen, malformed 'f', spacing around colon is 2mm : 1.5mm	B1–2, C2, I3–4
		2	3.2	As 3.1, except spacing around colon is 2mm : 3mm	C1, D1–2, E1–2, F1–2, H1
4	v	1	4.1	48.5mm. Italic '*sh*' ligature, normal hyphen, sharp flick to the bottom of the descender, '*monoy*'	G3–4, I1
		2	4.2	As 4.1, except '*money*'	I2
a	r	5	a.1	44.5 mm. 5mm between '*A*' and '*W*' in '*Woman*', 1mm between '*ll*' in first and second '*will*',3mm between '*r*' and '*w*' in '*her will*', full-stop level with text	A3
			a.2	43mm. As a.1, except 3.5mm between '*A*' and '*W*' in '*Woman*'	A4, K3–4

			a.3	43mm. As a.5, with the addition of more balanced spacing from second '*l*' in first '*will*' to the '*w*' in second '*will*', leading to 2mm between '*r*' and '*w*' in '*her will*'.	B1–2, C1–2, D1–2, E1–2, F1–2
			a.4	43mm. As a.2, except 2mm between '*ll*' in first '*will*' and 1mm between '*r*' and '*w*' in '*her will*'	H1 (B, BL, Bod., F, WOR)*
			a.5	43mm. As a.4, except 1mm between '*ll*' in first '*will*'	H1 (H, HL)*; H2
b	r	2	b.1	43mm. 0.5mm between '*ll*' in second '*will*', full-stop below the x-line	B3–4, C3–4, D3, E3–4, F3–4, H3–4, K1–2
			b.2	43mm. As b.1, except the full-stop is towards the centre of the x-line	D4
c	r	1	c	41.5mm. The '*n*' is raised higher than the '*a*' in '*Woman*'	G1–2, I1–2
d	r	1	d	42mm. The '*o*' is raised above the '*m*' in '*Woman*', the '*a*' is below the '*u*' in '*haue*', full-stop is set close to the final '*l*' in the last '*will*'	G3–4, I3–4

* Abbreviations for institutions are listed in n. 45.

Chapter 9

Scriptural Truths? Calvinist Internationalism and Military Professionalism in the Bible of Philip Skippon

Ismini Pells

In her contribution to a roundtable discussion on 'Historians and Biography' for the *American Historical Review*, Lois Banner observed that

> Historians in general, however, often rank biography as an inferior type of history. They see it as inherently limited because it involves only one life, derives from a belles-lettres tradition rather than a scientific or sociological one, and is often written by non-academic historians who attract a lot of readers but lack the rigor of PhD-trained scholars.[1]

However, since the 1990s, historians have turned to producing what Banner refers to as the 'new biography', the history that emphasises the power of culture in shaping the self but at the same time the ability of individuals to internalise cultural roles and rebel against them, thus also influencing their culture and historical development.[2] This 'new biography' interweaves a multitude of disciplines and reflects current historiographical concerns.[3] It is in this tradition that I have been endeavouring to embark upon the biography of Philip Skippon, sergeant-major-general of the New Model Army, which (surprisingly) has not been attempted to date. Recently, historians such as Barbara Donagan have emphasised the importance of England's pre-war experience in shaping ideological attitudes towards civil war in England. She argues that the actions and capabilities of armies in the English Civil War of 1642–1649 were shaped by the pre-existing mental and moral formation of soldiers, which was part of a wider European military culture.[4]

---

[1]   Lois W. Banner, 'Biography as History', *The American Historical Review* 114: 3 (2009): 580.

[2]   Ibid., 581–2.

[3]   Ibid., 580.

[4]   Barbara Donagan, *War in England 1642–1649* (Oxford: Oxford University Press, 2008), 10–11; Barbara Donagan, 'The Web of Honour: Soldiers, Christians and Gentlemen in the English Civil War', *The Historical Journal* 44:2 (2001): 367.

Born to a Norfolk minor gentry family around 1598, Philip Skippon began his military career on the Continent at a young age around 1615, serving in the English regiments in the Netherlands and in the English forces sent from the Netherlands to the service of the elector of the Palatinate and possibly also the king of Denmark.[5] On his return to England he was appointed captain-leader of London's Artillery Company in 1639, before going on to be appointed sergeant-major-general of the earl of Essex's parliamentarian army and later of the New Model Army during the Civil War.[6] As such, Skippon makes an ideal case study to engage with many of the themes current in the historiography of the Civil Wars.

Like many contemporaries, Skippon left no written record of how the mental and moral formation he developed during his time on the Continent went on to shape his military conduct in, and ideological attitude towards, the Civil War. However, his 'Breeches Bible', heavily underlined and annotated throughout, provides a fascinating insight into his personal religious ideology and some crucial clues as to how this influenced his military conduct both on the Continent and in the Civil War. Yet, it goes without saying that Skippon's Bible must only be used as a source to determine his military codes and conduct cautiously. The relationship between an individual's ideology and its application to the assortment of situations faced by that individual is not always a straightforward one. Moreover, it is impossible to be certain which annotations in the Bible were made at which time and thus chart the evolution of Skippon's ideology, as well ascertaining the political context in which each annotation was made, if the political context was indeed ever relevant.[7]

Therefore, I will attempt to compare and complement each claim made from Skippon's Bible with other surviving sources for his life and career, not least his

---

[5]   In his dedication to Philip Skippon in *A short Method for the Easie Resolving of any Militarie Question propounded* (Cambridge, 1639), John Cruso refers to Skippon's 'foure and twentie years' of military experience in 'Denmark, Germanie, the low countries and elsewhere'. This would put the start of Skippon's military career around 1615, when he would have been about 16 to 17 years old.

[6]   For a more detailed outline of Skippon's life and career see Ian J. Gentles, 'Skippon, Philip, appointed Lord Skippon under the protectorate (*d.* 1660)', *Oxford Dictionary of National Biography* (Oxford: Oxford University Press, 2004), online edition, January 2008, http://www.oxforddnb.com/view/article/25693, accessed 2 September 2011; However, note that this dates the start of Skippon's military career to Sir Horace Vere's expedition to the Palatinate in 1620 and misses the fact that Skippon may have fought in Denmark.

[7]   Indeed, it must also be noted that Skippon bequeathed his Bible to his son, also called Philip, who made his own biographical notations inside the back leaf. The ink used and slight variation in handwriting styles suggests that the annotations in the main body of the Bible belong to Philip senior but here the importance of verifying any assertions against other sources is particularly apparent.

four published books. These were written by Skippon during the Civil War as devotional works for the men under his command on the ideal religious and moral conduct of soldiers. Designed to be used in the field and dedicated to all soldiers 'of what degree soever', these books were largely comprised of Biblical quotations, which Skippon had grouped under headings into different themes and linked by his own comments and observations.[8] Much of the material for these books, published in the 1640s, was based on material Skippon wrote during his time in the Netherlands. Skippon informs the reader that his first book, *A Salve For Every Sore*, was based on a larger text, originally written for his family during his time in the Netherlands, from which he had extracted the core messages 'for more brevity, and better portage' and highlighted passages that were particularly pertinent for soldiers.[9] The second book, *True Treasure*, was also based on the same material and in his third book, *The Christian Centurians Observations, Advices and Resolutions*, Skippon specifically indicates which sections were written 'when he was a Captain in the Nether-lands'.[10] The final book, *A Pearle of Price*, was simply a second enlarged edition of *A Salve For Every Sore*.[11] Thus, whilst again it is necessary to be mindful of the fact that that ideas can evolve over time, it would not seem inappropriate to suggest that evidence from Skippon's books can be used to complement the claims made from his Bible about the influence of his religious thought upon his military conduct during the period c.1615–38, as well as that of the 1640s.

It is the aim of this chapter to use Skippon's Bible to help reconstruct his personal religious ideology, before moving on to examine how this religious ideology present in his Bible may have influenced Skippon's decision to pursue a military career on the Continent and his personal worship and military conduct once he was there. In turn, I will also examine how Skippon's Bible can elucidate how his military experiences impacted upon his ideological development. Throughout, following the best principles of 'new biography', I will endeavour to place Skippon's ideology and conduct in the context of his fellow soldiers in the English regiments in European service, in order to examine how far the individual can be used to elucidate the community. Finally, by way of conclusion, I will draw all my hypotheses together to investigate how the

[8]   Philip Skippon, *A Salve For Every Sore, or, A Collection of Promises out of the whole Book of God, and is The Christian Centurion's Infallible ground of Confidence* (London, 1643), iii.

[9]   Ibid., title page and xviii.

[10]   Philip Skippon, *True Treasure, or Thirtie holy Vowes, Containing The brief sum of all that concerns the Christian Centurion's conscionable walking with God* (London, 1644), i–ii; See, for example: Philip Skippon, *The Christian Centurians Observations, Advices and Resolutions: Containing Matters Divine and Morall* (London, 1645), 233.

[11]   Philip Skippon, *A Pearle of Price In A Collection of Promises out of the whole Book of God* (London, 1649).

evidence from Skippon's Bible might be used to reveal the stimuli behind his thoughts and actions in the Civil Wars and what this might tell the historian about the ideological attitudes of the Wars' participants in general.

Skippon's taste in Bible translation is for the Geneva Version, which is indicative of a preference for Calvinist theology – the doctrine which held that the sins of man make it impossible to achieve eternal salvation, so he must have faith in the grace of God, who has already pre-destined who will be saved and who will be condemned to everlasting damnation, without regard to virtue or merit. The Geneva Bible was the translation produced by a group of English exiles who had fled the Marian persecutions of the Counter-Reformation, which was finally published in Geneva in 1560 after the succession of Elizabeth I.[12] It was the Bible of choice for English Calvinists but it was disliked by many conservative clerics who conformed to the rites of the Church of England.[13] James I branded the Geneva translation 'the worst, and many of the notes very partial, untrue, seditious, and savouring too much of dangerous and traitorous conceits'.[14] The attraction and the anxiety that the notes provided lay in their usefulness in private study but this also allowed understanding without official Church interpretation.[15]

Skippon's attachment to the most fundamental Calvinist principles is shown by his singling out of passages, such as Ephesians 1.7 ('By whome we haue redemption through his blood, euen the forgiuenesse of sinnes according to his rich grace') and Romans 9.32 (which explained how Israel could not obtaine the law of righteousness because ' ... they sought it not by faith, but as it were by the works of the Law.'). Moreover, the suggestion that Skippon was a committed Calvinist given by his Bible can be verified by evidence from his own published works. For example, *A Salve for Every Sore* proclaims that its purpose is to show that 'notwithstanding our unmeasurable great unworthinesse', God has given man a set of infallible promises that are evident in the Scriptures and 'by faith of Jesus Christ might be given to them that believe'.[16]

Calvinists were particularly preoccupied by the contemporary belief in special providences and a concern for evidence of their sanctification.[17] Skippon's own attachment to this belief is verified by his highlighting passages such as 1

---

[12]   Tom Furniss, 'Reading the Geneva Bible: Notes Toward An English Revolution?' *Prose Studies* 31:1 (2009): 3.

[13]   Christopher Durston and Jacqueline Eales, 'Introduction: The Puritan Ethos, 1560–1700', in *The Culture of English Puritanism, 1560–1700*, ed. Christopher Durston and Jacqueline Eales (Basingstoke: Palgrave Macmillan, 1996), 16.

[14]   Furniss, 'Reading the Geneva Bible', 7.

[15]   Ibid., 5–6.

[16]   Skippon, *Salve For Every Sore*, 1.

[17]   Felicity Heal and Clive Holmes, *The Gentry in England and Wales, 1500–1700* (Basingstoke: Palgrave Macmillan, 1994), 366.

Kings 6.12 (' ... if thou wilt walke in mine ordinances, & execute my iudgements, & keep all my commandements, to walke in them, then I will performe vnto thee my promise.') and 1 Kings 8.5 (' ... there hath not failed one word of all his good promise which he promised by the hand of Moses his seruant') and the annotation 'pro'. (that is, 'promise') appears in the margin throughout his Bible, for example, at Leviticus 22.9. Indeed, the whole purpose of Skippon's *A Salve For Every Sore* was to produce '*A Collection of Promises out of the whole Book of God*' which were '*The Christian Centurion's Infallible ground of Confidence*'. As far as Skippon was concerned, those that can find 'Divers choyse and infallible markes of uprightnesse of heart' in themselves 'may safely conclude he is in the favour of God'.[18] A Calvinist's own religious conduct was the most visible way of demonstrating their sanctification and Skippon's guidelines for personal worship form almost a checklist of Calvinist piety: the importance of preaching; the use of the sacraments as outward tokens to confirm faith; the outward confession of sins (along with a hearty dose of self-mortification); the sanctification of the Sabbath; the importance of listening to Scripture; and the observance of fast days.[19]

Of course, to determine if Skippon's adherence to ardent Calvinism was a cause or a consequence of his time on the Continent may be something of a chicken-and-egg conundrum. The publication date of Skippon's Bible being 1610, it is perfectly possible that Skippon's attachment to Calvinism was already established before he departed for the Continent. The importance of establishing this lies in the fact that it may help explain why Skippon chose to take up the military profession in the first place. The most heralded justification for Elizabeth's original intervention in the Netherlands was for 'the maintenance of the Gospel, and peaceable state of the true reformed Church'.[20] It is worth noting that a large proportion of those who went to fight for the Protestant cause on the Continent were from the 'puritan' heartland of East Anglia.[21] In *The Christian Centurians Observations, Advices and Resolutions*, Skippon cited 'His God, his Conscience, his Country, his owne honour' as the crucial reasons for pursuing the military profession.[22] He was to later implore soldiers to 'avoyd and strive against rash adventures without a warrantable calling' and referred to himself as a 'Souldier of Christ Jesus', suggesting that his pursuit of the military

---

[18] Skippon, *Salve For Every Sore*, 21.

[19] Ibid., 4, 7, 23–4 and 252; Skippon, *True Treasure*, 31.

[20] Henry Hexham, *A Tongue-Combat Lately Happening Betvveene tvvo English Souldiers in the Tilt-boat of Grauesend, the one going to serue the King of Spaine, the other to serue the States Generall of the Vnited Provinces* (The Hague, 1623), 5.

[21] Blair Worden, *The English Civil Wars 1640–1660* (London: Weidenfeld & Nicolson, 2009), 25.

[22] Skippon, *Christian Centurians Observations*, 108.

profession was motivated by religious zeal.[23] Little is known about young Skippon's religious upbringing, and in reality, there may have been many reasons why Skippon took up arms, such as lack of occupation, economic opportunity or even compulsion by his parents as an exercise in character building or punishment for teenage misdemeanour. However, the pertinent point here is that Skippon at least *explained* his motivation for pursuing a military career in terms of defence of the international Calvinist cause, an explanation that his reading of the Calvinist Bible of choice probably helped to formulate.

Skippon's Calvinist preferences made him typical of those who went to fight in the Netherlands. David Trim has shown that at least for the officer corps, when the religious beliefs of the English who fought on the Continent for Protestant princes can be identified, they are almost always zealous Calvinists.[24] The Geneva Bible's explanatory notes encouraged English Calvinists to 'make direct connections between what they read about the Old Testament Jews or early Christians and their own contemporary situation in England.'[25] Christians had always viewed the Church as the spiritual Israel but English Calvinists went further and believed that not only were they the equivalent of Israel but the 'chosen' Israel, that is Judah, the kingdom comprised of the two tribes of Israel that remained faithful.[26] This did not mean that the English viewed other Calvinist nations as corrupt like Israel, as the spiritual Israel could avoid the historical Israel's unfaithfulness. It was just 'Englishmen, with their insular vanity, simply thought that England was *especially* dear to God.'[27] Yet being especially elect meant that Judah had responsibilities to Israel.[28] As other Calvinist nations were the equivalents of the other tribes of Israel, they were therefore family and this led to an obligation for England to aid them with troops or money.[29]

It is not unlikely that Skippon subscribed to this interpretation when reading his Bible, as passages such as those from 1 Samuel 12.21 ('For the Lord will not forsake his people for his great Names sake: because it hath pleased the Lord to make you his people') and 1 Peter 10 ('Which in time past were not a people, yet are now the people of God: which in time past were not vnder mercie, but now haue obtained mercy') are highlighted, which suggests Skippon drew analogies between the historical Israel and England as a chosen people. Skippon's use of 'Jacob' and 'Israel' in his quotation of Numbers 23:21 in *A Salve For Every Sore* ('He hath not beheld iniquity in Jacob, neither hath hee seene perversenesse

---

23 Ibid., 312; Skippon, *True Treasure*, title page.
24 David Trim, 'Calvinist Internationalism and the English Officer Corps, 1562–1642', *History Compass* 4/6 (2006): 1034–5.
25 Furniss, 'Reading the Geneva Bible', 8.
26 Trim, 'Calvinist Internationalism', 1028.
27 Ibid., 1029.
28 Ibid., 1030.
29 Ibid., 1035.

in Israel'), is perhaps demonstrative of a belief in England as the 'chosen' Israel, typical of English Calvinists.[30] Furthermore, in his Bible, Skippon drew attention to Obadiah's prophesy for the downfall of Edom (Esau's descendents and thus Israel's kin) for invading Judah, rather than coming to Judah's aid, whilst Jerusalem was being sacked by the Babylonians (Obadiah 12–15) and he noted in *The Christian Centurians Observations* that 'it were an unnaturall, cowardly and shamefull part, to stand still and look on, when other of our Christian brethren are abused, smitten and slaine'.[31]

Skippon's Bible can not only provide clues as to why he chose to join the armies of the Protestant Princes of Europe but how he conducted his own personal worship once he arrived there. The publication of the Geneva Bible in quarto, rather than folio, meant that it was much better adapted for home learning than the church lectern.[32] The portability of Skippon's Bible, combined with the peripatetic nature of his military lifestyle, makes it probable that Skippon carried his Bible around with him and his annotations and heavy underlining of significant verses in red ink indicates that it was well used in personal meditation. Skippon's highlighting of the passages eulogising Daniel for praying and praising God in his room three times a day (Daniel 6.10) and Abraham and Cornelius the centurion for acting 'as preachers to their families' (marginal note to Genesis 17.23) and labouring 'to haue all his household and familiar friends and acquaintance to be religious and godly' (marginal note to Acts 10.2) implies that he was encouraging of personal meditation and family worship.

Indeed, Skippon's *A Salve For Every Sore* was based on material that he had originally written for his family's use whilst in the Netherlands and much of *The Christian Centurians Observations* was based on his private meditations of the same time period.[33] Skippon would appear to be, at heart, a family man. Inside the front cover of his Bible, Skippon has dutifully recorded the events of his marriage to Maria Comes at the Dutch Church in Frankenthal on 14 May 1622 and the births of each of his eight children.[34] Skippon's Bible would have us believe that he took the sanctity of marriage very seriously, as he underlined the marginal note on the duties of husbands towards their wives accompanying Genesis 2.24 and the criticisms of Abraham's unfaithfulness to Sarah (Genesis 20.2–3). Indeed, there is no surviving evidence of antagonism between the couple and his marriage to Maria, to whom he referred to in *A Salve For Every Sore* as his 'most dearly beloved', appears to have been a happy one.[35] Moreover,

---

[30]   Skippon, *Salve For Every Sore*, 68.

[31]   Skippon, *Christian Centurians Observations*, 323.

[32]   Furniss, 'Reading the Geneva Bible', 5.

[33]   Skippon, *Salve For Every Sore*, vi; Skippon, *Christian Centurians Observations*, 233.

[34]   Suffolk Record Office, Barnardiston Papers, 613/773 (Printed Bible [Breeches Edition] of 1610 belonging to Philip Skippon), annotations inside Front Cover.

[35]   Skippon, *Salve For Every Sore*, vi.

Skippon's stoic quotation of Job in his recording of the deaths of the three children that did not survive to adulthood belies his grief at his losses and an emotional attachment to his children.[36]

The extent to which Skippon's fellow soldiers were as fastidious as he in their personal piety undoubtedly varied between them but the English regiments in the Netherlands certainly seem to have shared his desire for 'the conscionable worshipping of God', as public worship amongst these men can certainly be classified as reformed.[37] Horace Vere's regiment abandoned the Prayer Book around 1620 and even when the Prayer Book had been used, chaplains often only read selected parts and omitted the ceremonies of kneeling and adoration.[38] The English garrisons were provided with their church building by the local government, who also assisted them with the maintenance of their chaplain. Therefore, local magistrates expected to have some say in the form of worship and choice of chaplain, both of which the magistrates would want in line with the practices of their own Dutch Reformed Church.[39] The choice of reformed chaplains would have been welcomed by at least the captains and lower officers, who often expressed their preference for ministers non-conformable to the Church of England.[40] Like the Dutch magistrates, the officers would have expected some say in the choice of their chaplain, because captains were expected to pay two guilders a week towards the maintenance of the garrison chaplain.[41] However, following Charles I's succession to the English throne, the English churches in the Netherlands were ordered to confine themselves to the doctrine of the English Church, which caused much resentment.[42] The situation worsened with the appointment of William Laud as Archbishop of Canterbury in 1633.[43] Preachers to the English regiments who were not conformable to the Church of England were deprived of their charges.[44] Consequently, many chaplains to the English regiments in the Netherlands omitted the customary

---

[36]   Suffolk, Record Office, Barnardiston Papers, 613/773 (Printed Bible [Breeches Edition] of 1610 belonging to Philip Skippon), annotations inside Front Cover.

[37]   Skippon, *Salve For Every Sore*, xviii.

[38]   Keith L. Sprunger, *Dutch Puritanism: A History of English and Scottish Churches of the Netherlands in the Sixteenth and Seventeenth centuries* (Leiden: Brill, 1982), 352.

[39]   Charles B. Jewson, 'The English Church at Rotterdam and its Norfolk Connections', *Norfolk Archaeology* 30:4 (1952): 324; Sprunger, *Dutch Puritanism*, 368.

[40]   Sprunger, *Dutch Puritanism*, 353.

[41]   Ibid., 262.

[42]   John Bruce (ed.), *Calendar of State Papers Domestic Series of the Reign of Charles I, 1631–1633* (London: F Longman, Green, Longman and Roberts, 1862), 530; Sprunger, *Dutch Puritanism*, 283.

[43]   Jewson, 'English Church at Rotterdam', 326.

[44]   Christiaan de Jong, 'John Forbes (c.1568–1634), Scottish Minister and Exile in the Netherlands', *Nederlands Archief voor Kerkgeschiedenis*, 69 (1989): 47.

prayers for the king and the congregations of those who did not, including such a high-profile figure as Colonel Charles Morgan, were known to walk out during these prayers.[45]

Skippon's Bible also helps to elucidate how his private meditations impacted upon his military conduct. Throughout the so-called 'law-giving' books of the Pentateuch, that is, the first five books of the Bible (Genesis, Exodus, Leviticus, Numbers and Deuteronomy), Skippon has underlined many moral directives but prohibitions against drinking, sexual licence, keeping bad company and threatening the weak of society are singled out for particular attention. The moral misdemeanours Skippon identified were those that particularly affected the military lifestyle. Military historians often concentrate on major sieges and battles but these were only the tip of the iceberg of the military lifestyle.[46] For example, the service of the English troops in the Netherlands was dominated by garrison duty in strategically important towns.[47] The majority of the time, soldiers' lives were, if anything, mind-numbingly boring.[48] Traditionally, soldiers with nothing to do resorted to drinking, gambling, whoring and marauding amongst the local population. These vices were distractions from military discipline and their adverse side-effects could impact negatively upon military effectiveness. Armies depended on the goodwill of the local population to keep them accommodated and supplied and so could not afford to lose their support.

Consequently, the States-General of the Netherlands had issued a series of laws and ordinances in 1590 governing the moral lives of their soldiers, which, like all those in Dutch service, Skippon would have had to swear to but also upon his promotion to being an officer, he would have been expected to enforce.[49] It is noticeable that whilst many of the directives concerned purely military offences, such as mutiny, corresponding with the enemy, sleeping on watch and refusing orders, these only came after the majority of the commands regulating civilian interactions, such as murder, rape, adultery, setting fire to houses, thieving, violence, and threatening women, which were themselves only secondary to the decrees concerned with the grave offences of blasphemy and

---

[45] Thomas Cogswell, *The Blessed Revolution: English Politics and the Coming of War, 1621–1624* (Cambridge: Cambridge University Press, 1989), 318.

[46] Geoffrey Parker, *The Army of Flanders and the Spanish Road* (Cambridge: Cambridge University Press, 2004), 9–10.

[47] Matthew Glozier, 'Scots in the French and Dutch Armies during the Thirty Years' War', in *Scotland and the Thirty Years' War, 1618–1648*, ed. Steve Murdoch (Leiden: Brill, 2001), 128.

[48] Charles Carlton, *Going to the Wars: The Experience of the British Civil Wars 1638–51* (London: Routledge, 1992), 150.

[49] United Provinces of the Netherlands Staten Generaal, *Lawes and Ordinances touching military discipline* (The Hague, 1631), 1.

deriding God's word or the ministers of His Church.[50] The punishments for breaking these ordinances were severe. They included boring through the tongue, whipping and, in many instances, death.[51] Moral misdemeanours undoubtedly occurred, as after all, the Dutch laws and ordinances were instituted for a reason. Nevertheless, the attempts at enforcing moral discipline must have been at least reasonably successful, as the Venetian Ambassador noted with surprise that Dutch citizens thought nothing of leaving their wives and daughters alone with troops and some towns even applied to have troops quartered on them because they were so well behaved and brought economic benefits with them.[52]

Finally, no discussion of Skippon's religious ideology discernible in the evidence provided by his Bible would be complete without a discussion of how his experiences of war on the Continent in turn affected his religious ideology. Skippon's Bible leaves the historian in no doubt that Skippon was fully aware of the horrors of war. For Skippon, war was God's punishment for sin. At both 2 Kings 24.3 and 2 Chronicles 36.16–17, Skippon highlighted the verses that proclaimed that the attacks on Judah were a response from God to the sins that the people of Judah had learnt under King Manasseh. As a result, war was something to be feared, as Skippon noted at Ezekiel 11.8. The consequences of war were nothing short of disastrous for the whole land: 'Hee that is farre off, shall die of the pestilence, and he that is neere shall fall by the sword, and he that remaineth and is besieged, shall die by the famine' (Ezekiel 6.12); 'Destruction vpon destruction is cried, for the whole land is wasted'(Jeremiah 4.20); The enemy will ' ... eate thine haruest and they bread: they shal deuoure they sonnes & thy daughters: they shall eate vp thy sheep and thy bullocks: they shall eate thy vines and thy figge trees: they shall destroy with the sword thy fenced cities, wherein thou did trust' (Jeremiah 5.17). Much of his painful awareness of the brutalities of war would have been learnt in his tender years during his time on the Continent. It is true that the traditional view of the Thirty Years' War, in which central Europe was prey to marauding armies that laid waste to whole regions and devastated economic growth for generations, has been revised in the past twenty years to reveal a more complex picture of regional variation in terms of the social and economic impact of the war.[53] All the same, there is no doubt that the Thirty Years' War stood out to contemporaries for its atrocity, barbarity and lawlessness.[54] The people who actually had to live through the wars did not know or care if the half century before 1618 was a period of economic decline

---

[50]   Ibid., 1–6.

[51]   Ibid., 1.

[52]   Gerhard Oestreich, *Neostoicism and the Early Modern State* (Cambridge: Cambridge University Press, 1982), 79.

[53]   Ian Roy, 'England Turned Germany? The Aftermath of the Civil War in its European Context', *Transactions of the Royal Historical Society*, 5th Series, 28 (1978): 129.

[54]   Donagan, *War in England*, 29.

or that the post-war period would bring the opportunity for reconstruction and economic renewal.[55]

Nevertheless, in general, Skippon's God was not the God of fire and brimstone. His Bible reveals that he reconciled himself to the atrocities he faced by a steadfast attachment to the belief in God's promises that He will not forsake His own. The passages underlined in the book of Joshua in Skippon's Bible all display a common theme: that ' ... the Lord your God he fighteth for you, as hee hath promised you' (Joshua 23.10) and so He ' ... will not leaue thee, nor forsajke thee'. (Joshua 1.5). This belief was undoubtedly helped by the fact that Skippon personally survived many sticky situations, such as when he was shot at the siege of Breda in 1625 and when he received a dangerous wound to the neck, again at Breda in 1637.[56] It is noticeable that he underlined Joshua 14.10: 'Therefore behold now, the Lord hath kept me aliue, as he promised'. The effect of Skippon's European military experiences was to create a simple and sincere faith that took comfort in the promises of God. In fact, Skippon himself revealed in *The Christian Centurians Observations* that it was when he was 'in most extreame perplexity of spirit, and in great outward distresse, all threatening uttermost misery, even without appearance of remedy; knowing no other way to comfort and settle himselfe' that he remembered God's promises and 'choyce places of Scripture', which 'upheld him, he had else fainted utterly'.[57] It is a very positive faith in contrast to that of many of his contemporaries.[58] Even if the worst were to happen, the comfort that Skippon took in the fact that he was fighting for God's cause led him to proclaim that 'If he [God] please I end my dayes in fight against his foes, I dye a Martyr, and the very instrument of my death is a meanes to send me Heaven [*sic*]'.[59]

As Machiavelli argued in his *Discourses*, the strongest incitement to courage and enthusiasm derives from feelings of personal involvement and moral obligation, so soldiers would fight more valiantly when the war was considered

---

[55] Geoffrey Parker, 'The war for Bohemia', in *The Thirty Years*, ed. Geoffrey Parker (London: Routledge, 1984), 215.

[56] National Archives, State Papers, SP 84: State Papers Foreign Holland c.1560–1780, CXXVII, 25 and 26v (Sir Jacob Astley's sketch of work at Terheijden with list of officers engaged and losses: two copies, 5 May 1625); Henry Hexham, *A True and Briefe Relation of the Famous Siege of Breda* (Delft, 1637), vi and 22–3. Hexham precedes his account of the siege of Breda in 1637 with a relation of the 1624–1625 siege of Breda.

[57] Skippon, *Christian Centurians Observations*, 8.

[58] Wilfred Emberton, *Skippon's Brave Boys: The Origins, Development and Civil War Service of London's Trained Bands* (Buckingham: Barracuda, 1984), 40; Cecil E. Lucas Phillips, *Cromwell's Captains* (London: Heinemann, 1938), 92.

[59] Skippon, *Christian Centurians Observations*, 319–20.

a fulfilment of religious duty.[60] The Venetian Ambassador in England observed in 1616 that whilst the English disliked hardship and were susceptible to hunger and disease, they had 'always displayed great valour' and were 'certainly not afraid of death'.[61] Indeed, 'one of the core values of English martial culture was there was no hero quite as admirable as a dead hero' and many stories of valour grew up around those who had lost their lives in the Protestant cause, such as Sir Philip Sidney.[62] However, the disregard for death amongst the English did not automatically lead to an increased efficiency. A commander's desire to prove his valour could lead him to favour individual ambition over public interest and result in bad strategic decision-making and the loss of many men's lives.[63] Yet Mark Fissel made the point that praise of the feats of the English on the Continent was 'too ubiquitous to be discounted lightly'.[64] The simple fact was the Dutch relied heavily on English soldiers, who, along with the Scottish soldiers, made up nearly half of Prince Maurice's field armies.[65] It seems unlikely that someone of Maurice's military calibre would rely on men of questionable ability.[66] In fact, the Venetian Ambassador to England – a neutral observer – remarked that 'Count Maurice speaks highly of the English. He says they have been with him in a large number of his most honourable undertakings' and the Dutch artist Jacon de Gheyn admitted that 'it can not be denied but that the Provinces haue received verye acceptable services at theyr handes'.[67]

So how might the conclusions about Skippon's mental and moral formation during his time on the Continent drawn here from his Bible have related to his ideological attitude towards civil war in England and military conduct during those wars? The heavy use Skippon made of his Bible clearly shows that personal piety was extremely important to him and the implications in the Bible are that

---

[60]   Felix Gilbert, 'Machiavelli: The Renaissance of the Art of War', in *Makers of Modern Strategy from Machiavelli to the Nuclear Age*, ed. Peter Paret (Princeton: Princeton University Press, 1986), 26.

[61]   Allen B. Hinds (ed.), *Calendar of State Papers and Manuscripts Relating to English Affairs, Existing in the Archives and Collections of Venice and in Other Libraries of Northern Italy, 1615–1617* (London: Longman, Green, Longman, Roberts and Green, 1908), 137.

[62]   Roger B. Manning, *Swordsmen: The Martial Ethos in the Three Kingdoms* (Oxford: Oxford University Press, 2003), 64.

[63]   Ibid., 54 and 67; William Lithgrow, *A True and Experimentall Discourse, upon the beginning, proceeding, and Victorious event of this last siege Of Breda* (London, 1637), 36.

[64]   Mark C. Fissel, *English Warfare, 1511–1642* (London: Routledge, 2001), 167.

[65]   Manning, *Swordsmen*, vii.

[66]   Fissel, *English Warfare*, 155.

[67]   Allen B. Hinds (ed.), *Calendar of State Papers and Manuscripts Relating to English Affairs, Existing in the Archives and Collections of Venice and in Other Libraries of Northern Italy, 1615–1617* (London: Longman, Green, Longman, Roberts and Green, 1909), 396; Jacob de Gheyn, *The Exercise of Arms* (The Hague, 1608), i.

his particular religious preference was for a somewhat conventional strain of Calvinism. If the desire to defend the cause of international Calvinism was indeed amongst Skippon's motivations for pursuing a military career on the Continent, or even if this merely developed throughout his time there, it is not unlikely that the desire to defend the cause of true, reformed Calvinism against the High Church policies of Charles I was amongst Skippon's motivations for joining the parliamentarian side in the Civil War. Indeed, since John Morrill famously made the case for the Civil War being the 'last of the Wars of Religion' historians have returned to placing religion back at the heart of Civil War ideologies.[68]

However, as George Yule observed, 'most historians of the English Civil War pay lip service to Puritanism as one of its main ingredients, as a matter of fact, the analysis of religious conviction is rarely undertaken'. Religious convictions are often treated as a rationalisation of deeper economic, social or political concerns.[69] Yet the religious arguments of the politicians of the period were 'theologically sophisticated' and Biblical allusions 'subtle' and sometimes 'encyclopedic'.[70] In fact, Biblical precedent was the most important characteristic of Calvinist theology and its effect on the laity was profound for, in contrast to Lutherans, Calvinists viewed the Bible not just as Gospel but as a book of precedents.[71] This would suggest that it would be a more than worthwhile exercise to investigate exactly how Skippon might have applied the theology of Calvinist Internationalism to the peculiarities of the British context in much greater detail than there is space to do so here. It is only through such an investigation that historians will fully begin to realise the importance of the impact of European affairs on the Civil War in England, a phenomenon which was patently apparent to S.R. Gardiner and C.V. Wedgwood but one which historians have only recently begun to rediscover.[72]

The fact that Skippon's Bible placed a great importance on family worship and household religion only adds strength to this interpretation. This distinctive Calvinist piety – the sanctification of the Sabbath, the listening to and reading of the Scriptures and meditating on the Gospel – was all based on the belief in the Bible as a book of precedents to be applied to one's own time.[73] Furthermore,

---

[68]   John S. Morrill, 'The Religious Context of the English Civil War', *Transactions of the Royal Historical Society* 34 (1984): 178.

[69]   George Yule, 'The Puritan Piety of Members of the Long Parliament', *Studies in Church History* 8 (1972): 187.

[70]   Ibid., 188.

[71]   Ibid.

[72]   Marvin A. Breslow, *A Mirror of England: English Puritan Views of Foreign Nations, 1618–1640* (Cambridge, Massachusetts: Harvard University Press, 1970), 2; Cicely V. Wedgwood, 'King Charles I and the Protestant Cause', *Proceedings of the Huguenot Society of London* 19:2 (1954): 19–20.

[73]   Yule, 'Puritan Piety', 190.

family worship and household religion were especially important for those of reforming tendencies as a remedy for the shortcomings of the state church.[74] Clarendon claimed that Skippon 'having been bred always in Holland he brought disaffection enough with him from thence against the Church of England'.[75] Although from a hostile source, this suggests that Skippon felt at home amongst the reformed practices that he experienced on the Continent and disliked the 'Anglicanisation' Charles and Laud tried to impose upon the English churches in the Netherlands.

The royalist pamphlet *Persecutio Undecima* went one stage further and claimed that Skippon had been head-hunted whilst he was still in the Netherlands to become captain of London's Artillery Company because his 'sectary' religious preferences were in keeping with those of the Artillery Company, who were already preparing for civil war in the mid-1630s.[76] However, according to *True Treasure*, Skippon was deeply against 'Sectaries' and 'Schismaticks' and his later career was to demonstrate this to be true.[77] As Conrad Russell argued, the majority in England in 1642 did not want civil war and so both sides blamed the other for starting it in order to justify their subsequent actions.[78] It was very convenient for *Persecutio Undecima*, attributed to the Anglican clergyman Robert Chestlin, to portray the parliamentarians as schismatic extremists responsible for starting the Civil War and the royalists as the moderate, reasonable side. Thus whilst Skippon may have been 'disaffected' with the Established Church, this does not mean he was sectarian in religion or part of a movement to deliberately incite civil war but more that he wished for further reform within the Church of England and to defend it from Charles and Laud's High Church encroachments.

Throughout the Civil Wars, Skippon was certainly to herald the parliamentarian cause as God's cause, such as in his famous speech to his men before the confrontation at Turnham Green in November 1642:

> Come my Boys, my brave Boys, let us pray heartily and fight heartily, I will run the
> same fortunes and hazards with you, remember the Cause is for God; and for the

---

[74]   Christopher Hill, *Society and Puritanism in Pre-Revolutionary England* (London: Pimlico, 2003), 392 and 434.

[75]   Edward Hyde, Earl of Clarendon, *The History of the Rebellion and Civil Wars in England begun in the year 1641*, ed. William D. Macray (Oxford: Clarendon Press, 1888), I, 509.

[76]   Robert Chestlin, *Persecutio Undecima: Or, The Churches Eleventh Persecution* (London, 1648), 56.

[77]   Skippon, *True Treasure*, 65; See, for example, Skippon's reaction to the James Nayler case: Thomas Burton, *Diary, of Thomas Burton, Esq. Member in the Parliaments of Oliver and Richard Cromwell from 1656–59*, ed. John T. Rutt (London: H. Colburn, 1828), I, 24–5.

[78]   Conrad S. R. Russell, 'Why did People Choose Sides in the English Civil War?' *The Historian* 63 (1999): 4.

defence of your selves, your wives and children: Come my honest brave Boys, pray
heartily and fight heartily, and God will bless us.[79]

His anxiety that all men who fought for God's cause should share in the
comfort he had discovered on the Continent in God's promises never to abandon
his own, whatever the horrors faced in war, that Skippon demonstrated most
poignantly in his Bible in the book of Joshua, led to the production in 1643 of *A
Salve For Every Sore*. The publication of *True Treasure* a year later aimed to instil
the military effectiveness of the Dutch army into the men of Parliament under
his command by prescribing strict codes of conduct based on the moral maxims
he had identified in his Bible.

Nevertheless, support for the Calvinist cause on the Continent did not
automatically lead to support for the parliamentarian cause in England. There are
enough examples of committed Calvinists, for example, Jacob Astley, who fought
in the same European armies as Skippon but went on to be resolute royalists in
the Civil Wars.[80] Therefore, it would be extremely enlightening to analyse how
royalist Calvinists reconciled the theology of Calvinist Internationalism with
their defence of the royalist cause and compare this with the Biblical precedents
preferred by parliamentarians. Of course, as with his decision to pursue a
military career on the Continent, there must have also been other social and
economic reasons too amongst Skippon's motivations in siding with Parliament.
As Yule argued, to stress the religious outlook of the participants in the Civil
War, is not to argue that political or social aspirations did not play a part in
side-taking but simply that historians must understand the problems faced
by seventeenth-century Englishmen in 'their terms and not ours'.[81] Whilst in
reality there must have been many reasons behind Skippon's decision to side
with Parliament, it has been shown that he at least *explained* his decision to take
up arms in any circumstance in terms of 'His God, his Conscience, his Country,
his owne honour'.[82]

The challenge facing historians is to not stop short at simply explaining
away such statements as a rationalisation of deeper economic, social or political
concerns but to engage in the 'Biblical exposition and theological disquisition'
that 'can seem tedious to twenty-first century scholars partly because modern
minds see religion as a separate compartment of life, something done on one

[79] Bulstrode Whitelocke, *Memorials of the English affairs* (London, 1682), 62.

[80] Emberton, *Skippon's Brave Boys*, 44; Ian Roy, 'Astley, Jacob, first Baron Astley of
Reading (1579–1652)', *Oxford Dictionary of National Biography* (Oxford: Oxford University
Press, 2004), online edn, http://www.oxforddnb.com/view/article/817, accessed 25 May
2010.

[81] Yule, 'Puritan Piety', 193–4.

[82] Skippon, *Christian Centurians Observations*, 108.

day of the week and forgotten the rest of it'.[83] Yet, in the seventeenth century, when ups and downs of both public and private life were interpreted as signs of divine providence that were to be reflected upon to direct everyday actions, this approach must be taken or else historians will only have an incomplete understanding of not only what induced men to fight but to keep on fighting. It is my aim in the future to tackle some of these problems through my researches into Skippon's religious and political thought and military career, which just goes to show that, as Lois Banner argued, far from being the second-rate type of history written by non-academic historians who attract a lot of readers but lack the rigor of trained scholars, 'No less than other types of history, biography raises issues of revisionism and historiography key to the historical enterprise'.[84]

---

[83] Trim, 'Calvinist Internationalism', 1036.
[84] Banner, 'Biography as History', 580 and 583.

Chapter 10
Books and their Lives:
The Petworth House Plays

Maria Kirk

.... That place that does containe
My Bookes (the best Companions) is to me
A glorious Court, where howerly I converse
With the old Sages and Philosophers

(John Fletcher, The Elder Brother
Act 1, scene 2, 171–5.)[1]

Charles, the hero of Fletcher's 1637 comedy *The Elder Brother*, speaks of his books as 'companions', regarding them as friends, courtiers and living entities with whom he can actively engage. He does not simply speak to or listen to the 'old Sages and Philosophers', but rather converses with them in what is clearly a two-way exchange. Books have many ways of communicating with us: in the same way that Charles looks for intellectual stimulation from long-dead philosophers we can analyse Fletcher's play itself in the hope of discovering some insight into seventeenth-century attitudes to books. In this chapter I am concerned with what books as material objects have to say – one collection of books in particular.

The study of material culture teaches us that things themselves have meanings, and that these meanings are produced and developed by the interaction of those things with other things, with their owners and with the world in general. A book collection is an interesting thing, or group of things, for two key reasons: firstly, because it is a collection of culturally produced consumption goods, and secondly because it is a partially enclosed system of relationships, that is, it is a set of objects which relate to each other in a formally defined system. A commodity, according to Igor Kopytoff, 'is a thing that has a use value and that can be exchanged in a discrete transaction for a counterpart, the very fact of exchange indicating that the counterpart has, in the immediate context, an equivalent value'.[2] Commodities must 'not only be produced materially as things

---

[1]   John Fletcher, *The Elder Brother* (London: Imprinted by F.K. for J.W. and J.B., 1637).

[2]   Igor Kopytoff, 'The cultural biography of things: commoditization as process', in *The Social Life of Things: Commodities in Cultural Perspective*, ed. Arjun Appadurai. (Cambridge: Cambridge University Press, 1988), 68.

but also culturally marked as being a certain kind of thing'.[3] The way in which the Petworth collection was purchased does in fact mark it as a particular kind of thing – during the process of collecting it has been reframed from a gathering of individual objects into a new, discrete and interconnected web of things.

As Mary Douglas and Baron Isherwood have shown, 'consumption goods are most definitely not mere messages; they constitute the very system itself'.[4] We must ensure in any study of the biography of things that we are not simply looking for the signs of other lives which have interacted with the thing, but that we also consider the biography of the thing itself. The individual traces of life examined in the first part of this chapter are fascinating not only because of what they indicate about the past lives of these quartos, but also because of what they reveal about the way in which they relate to each other. Susan M. Pearce points out that collection objects, like all objects 'hold meaning only in so far as they relate to other meaningful objects ... all objects are parts of sets, often more than one set at a time, but collections are sets in a particular sense, which marks them off from other kinds of object sets'.[5]

This chapter examines what can be understood from the books themselves about the way they interacted with the world around them at the time of their printing and purchase (predominantly the early seventeenth century), what scars and signs they bear of the varied and multiple pasts and what we can learn about how and why these pasts converged to form the current collection. I will begin by briefly describing the nature of the collection and then give a detailed account of some of the various different kinds of annotations found within.[6] I will then draw some conclusions about what these annotations can tell us, particularly with regard to the collection as a whole: its provenance, acquisition and relationship to its owner. This study focuses on the traces of 'past lives' found on the Petworth plays. As I shall demonstrate, not only can much be learned about their histories as individual plays from these marks, but some of the annotations on the quartos and volumes can offer clues about their purchase, assembly and life together as a collection.

---

    3   Ibid., 64.

    4   Mary Douglas and Baron Isherwood, *The World of Goods* (New York: Routledge, 1996), 49.

    5   Susan Pearce, *On Collecting* (New York: Routledge, 1995), 20.

    6   There are, of course, many more marks and annotations on the volumes than I have space to discuss here. I have given selected examples from most of the common and relevant categories.

The Petworth Plays

The set of books in question is the Petworth play collection, a group of late sixteenth- and early seventeenth-century printed play quartos currently residing at Petworth House in West Sussex. The collection has been kept there since at least the late seventeenth century, and probably earlier.[7] It consists of 16 bound volumes each containing between 6 and 11 plays.[8] A gilt stamp on the front of each volume shows the crest of Algernon Percy, the 10th Earl of Northumberland (1602–1668).

Archival evidence concerning the purchase of books, and particularly plays, is relatively scarce in the 10th Earl's accounts. There is, however, one record of particular significance dating from 1638. This record has been previously documented and identified by Robert J. Alexander, who conducted an extensive investigation into the records contained in a microfilm of the Alnwick MSS.[9] This refers to money paid 'for playbookes vj li iiijs vjd'. The dates of the plays in the collection support this date as there are no plays in the collection published after 1638. The amount paid for the 1638 'playbookes' is a rather large sum of money: £6, 4s and 6p. There are no other purchases of 'playbooks' or 'plays', and this amount seems to have been a feasible, if a somewhat high, price to pay for the number of plays in the collection, and their bindings, in the late 1630s.[10]

In total, the volumes contain around 148 quarto plays (including *The Elder Brother*, from which this chapter's epigraph is taken). I have given the number of quartos as *around* 148 because the cataloguing is complicated somewhat by the presence of some two-part quartos which were printed together but presented separately in the collection – either by being bound in the wrong order, or simply listed as two plays rather than one in the handwritten contents list at the beginning of all but one of the volumes. These contents lists appear to be slightly later than the bindings, possibly added at the time the 1690 catalogue was written.

---

[7]   The plays are listed in the earliest extant catalogue of the Petworth library, named *Catalogus Librorum Bibliothecae Petworthianae*, which dates from 1690 (West Sussex Records Office, Petworth House Archives, MS. PHA 5377).

[8]   The 1690 catalogue reveals that there were initially 20 volumes, but the missing four appear to have disappeared at some point during the eighteenth century.

[9]   Robert J. Alexander, 'Some dramatic records from Percy household accounts on microfilm', *Records of Early English Drama* 12, No. 2 (1987), 10–17.

[10]   My calculations and estimates are based on Francis R. Johnson, *Notes on English Retail Book-prices, 1550–1640* in *The Library* volume S5-V, issue 2, p 91; p 93, and an anonymous 1619 list of book binding prices entitled *A Generall note of the prises for binding of all sorts of books*. This calculation includes the four lost volumes.

Individual Biographies: Past Lives and Different Kinds of Annotations

While the play list annotations were likely added later, the individual quartos reveal a multitude of marks and annotations which were added before the volumes were bound; some typical, some unusual but all intriguing. Of the 148 quartos, 41 of them bear a mark of some kind, ranging from ink blots and scribbles to copied passages and amendments to the text. Although many of the quartos are annotated – some quite heavily – none of these annotations appear to be in the hand of the 10th Earl of Northumberland. In fact, they are in a number of different hands, and consequently these marks suggest much about the individual histories of the quartos. The marks and annotations on the volumes can be divided into categories, each revealing a different kind of engagement with the text, and in some cases, engagement with other people involved in the history of the individual quartos.

Marks Unconnected to the Text

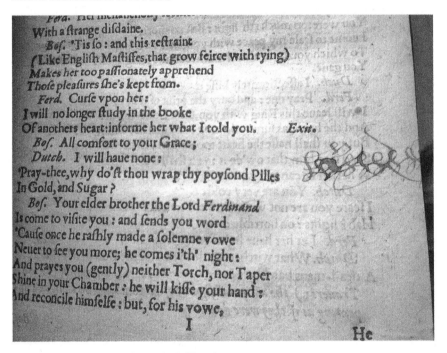

Figure 10.1   *The Duchess of Malfi*, volume 9.
By permission of The National Trust.

Sometimes, the terms 'annotation' and 'marginalia' do not seem appropriate to describe the marks on books. Such cases include ink spots and scribbles which apparently bear no relation to the printed text. Figure 10.1 shows an example of such a mark on *The Duchess of Malfi* in volume 2 of the collection.[11] These scribbles or doodles may have served a purpose beyond the alleviation of boredom; a possible explanation for their existence is that they are pen trials. As Jason Scott-Warren has pointed out, early modern pens were often 'hard to use; ink was sometimes homemade, with more or less success; and paper was expensive. Before writing anything it made sense to test out the materials on the nearest available paper, which in many cases would have been in a book'.[12] Scott-Warren considers the pen trial as a possible explanation for names appearing in early modern books as well as these 'other seemingly random and inexplicable marks'.[13] He also suggests that such names might be writing practice, or an assertion of literacy.[14] These illegible scribbles cannot be considered 'writing' as such but they, like the ink blots that appear on some other quartos, do reveal something about early modern readers and book owners. The paper in books like the Petworth plays was considered an available space by at least some of their owners when it came to writing. It was another surface on which to write. Readers obviously spent time with their books and their pens at the same time.

An interesting example of book pages used as available paper is found in *The Love of King David and Fair Bethsabe* in volume 12 of the collection (see Figure 10.2).[15]

These marks indicate that the paper has been used to design an embroidery pattern, predominately featuring the initials CK. This is evidence of a book being utilised in what appears to us to be a thoroughly unconventional way. Given that embroidery was predominantly a pursuit for women, it also suggests that either a woman was the previous owner of the book, or at least that a woman had access to the book and used the paper within it. Indeed, Heidi Brayman Hackel has shown that, far from being an exclusive area for men as we might expect, 'book closets served also as rooms for women'.[16] This quarto, it seems, was once part of a household and was utilised for activities beyond just reading.

---

[11]　John Webster, *The Duchesse of Malfy* (London: Printed by Nicholas Okes for John Waterson, 1623).

[12]　Jason Scott-Warren, 'Reading graffiti in the Early Modern Book', in *Huntington Library Quarterly* 73, issue 3 (2010) 363–81, 368.

[13]　Ibid.

[14]　Ibid. 371.

[15]　George Peele, *The Love of King David and Fair Bethsabe* (London: Printed by Adam Islip, 1599).

[16]　Heidi Brayman Hackel, '"Rowme" of Its Own: Printed Drama in Early Libraries', in *A New History of English Drama*, eds. John D. Cox and David Scott Kastan (New York: Columbia, 1997), 113–30, 119. For an in-depth study of the reading and collecting habits of an early-modern woman, see also Brayman Hackel's work on 'The Countess of Bridgewater's

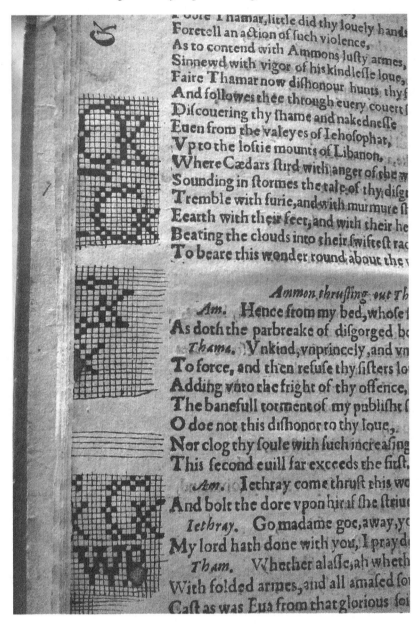

... ҃ole Thamar, little did thy louely hand
Foretell an action of such violence,
As to contend with Ammons lusty armes,
Sinnewd with vigor of his kindlesse loue,
Faire Thamar now dishonour hunts thy
And followes thee through euery couert
Discouering thy shame and nakednesse
Euen from the valeyes of Iehosophat,
Vp to the loftie mounts of Libanon,
Where Cædars stird with anger of the w
Sounding in stormes the tale of thy disg
Tremble with furie, and with murmure sh
Earth with their feet, and with their he
Beating the clouds into their swiftest rac
To beare this wonder round about the

Ammon thrusting out Th
Am. Hence from my bed, whose
As doth the parbreake of disgorged b
Tham. Vnkind, vnprincely, and vn
To force, and then refuse thy sisters lo
Adding vnto the fright of thy offence,
The banefull torment of my publisht
O doe not this dishonor to thy loue,
Nor clog thy soule with such increasing
This second euill far exceeds the first.
Am. Iethray come thrust this wo
And bolt the dore vpon hir if she striu
Iethray. Go madame goe, away, y
My lord hath done with you, I pray d
Tham. Whether alasse, ah wheth
With folded armes, and all amased fo
Cast as was Eua from that glorious fo

Figure 10.2 *The Love of King David and Fair Bethsabe*, volume 12.
By permission of The National Trust.

London Library', in *Books and Readers in Early Modern England*, eds. Jennifer Andersen and Elizabeth Sauer (Pennsylvania: University of Pennsylvania Press, 2011), 138–59.

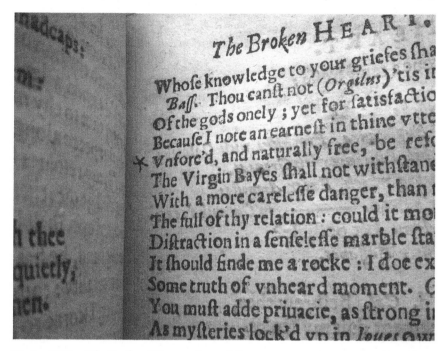

Figure 10.3   *The Broken Heart*, volume 16.
By permission of The National Trust.

Signposts

While many marks are apparently unrelated to the plays themselves, a number of annotations do directly relate to the text on the page. One such kind of annotation is the signpost.

Figure 10.3 shows an asterisk used as a signpost. Some of the asterisks, which appear throughout this quarto but not in any others, have been cut in half by cropping, and are therefore certainly the work of a previous owner. This kind of signpost shows real engagement with the text by a reader who has seen fit to mark certain lines or passages. William H. Sherman describes the manuscript manicule on the printed page as 'some of our most graphic evidence that after the printing press begins to give readers books that are relatively uniform, accurate and easy to navigate, readers continue to customise them according to their needs and tastes'.[17] The idea of annotation as customisation is an intriguing one – the reader is drawing attention to particular lines and thereby emphasising

---

[17]   William H. Sherman, *Used Books* (Pennsylvania: University of Pennsylvania Press, 2008).

them as particularly important, but without any accompanying commentary it is difficult to establish exactly why these lines are important. In any case, what we are seeing here is a very physical interaction between the reader and the text.

Copying

Copied text is a relatively common annotation on the quartos; there are nine separate incidences of it. Indeed, copying was a common kind of annotation on playbooks in general. Zachery Lesser suggests that it indicates a reader's 'desire to *extract* lines from their surrounding context for use in other, sometimes contradictory, situations', but there may be some additional motivations for this kind of annotation.[18]

In some instances, the copied lines are found directly adjacent to or underneath the line in print, as seen in Figure 10.4.[19]

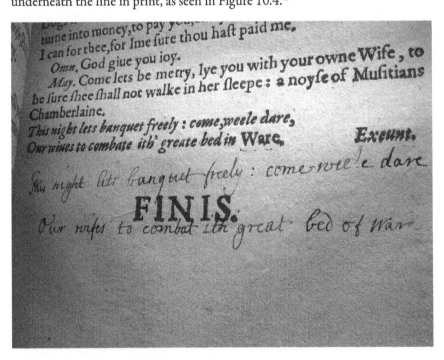

Figure 10.4   *Northward Hoe*, volume 10.
By permission of The National Trust.

_____

[18]   Zachary Lesser, 'Playbooks', in *The Oxford History of Popular Print Culture*, ed. Joad Raymond (Oxford: Oxford University Press, 2011) 520–32, 532.

[19]   Thomas Dekker and John Webster, *Northward Hoe* (Imprinted at London: By G. Eld, 1607).

At other times, the copied lines appear separated from the original line in the text. This is the case in *Hamlet* as seen in Figure 10.5.[20]

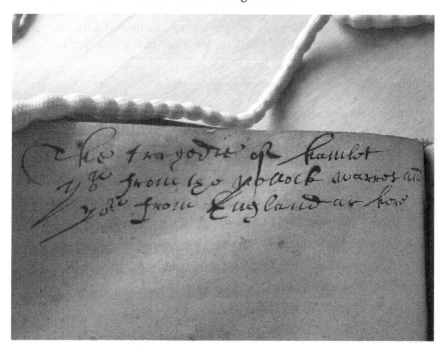

Figure 10.5   *The Tragedie of Hamlet*, volume 7.
By permission of The National Trust.

The copied lines are the only annotation to the play and are found on the verso side of the final, entirely blank, leaf – N4v. The annotator has reproduced the title and first line, plus two words from the second line, from the verso side of the previous leaf at the top of the page, N3v. The annotator may have been trying to memorise the first few lines of the previous page.

Amendments and Additions to the Text

Like the copying annotations, amendments and additions are directly relevant to the text. One annotation of particular interest in the Petworth collection is on the 1630 quarto of *Othello* which has a handwritten *dramatis personae* (not

---

[20]   William Shakespeare, *The Tragedie of Hamlet* (London: Printed by W.S. for Iohn Smethwicke, 1625).

matching any printed version) on the verso side of the last page.[21] However, on closer inspection, there appears to be two hands here, the original dramatis personae, and another which is annotating the annotation. The second annotator seems to have used a thinner pen, and some letters are formed differently: there is a defined loop on the lower case L in 'prodigal' and 'fellow' but not in the original 'Othello' or 'Generall', for example.

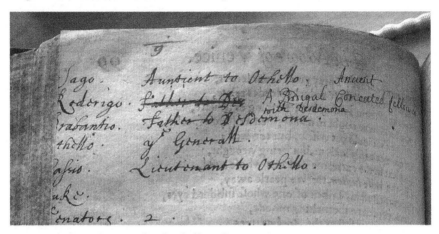

Figure 10.6   *The Tragœdy of Othello*, volume 10.
By permission of The National Trust.

The cropping on the left side of the image makes it clear that the first annotation is pre-binding. The original annotator has written 'Auntient to Othello', this has been altered by a second annotator who has corrected or updated the spelling to 'Ancient'. They have also deemed Roderigo to be 'A Prodigal Conceited fellow'. It is unclear whether the original annotator crossed out his obvious mistake of naming Roderigo as 'Father to Des' or whether it was the second annotator, though it was most likely the first as he did not finish writing Desdemona's name. Rather than correcting the mistake further, he simply left Roderigo without a description, as he has done for some other characters. Further down the page, the second annotator appears to agree with the first about Bianca's profession and role.

This kind of interaction between two owners demonstrates that handwritten annotations were not simply either ignored or preserved by new owners of the books; in some cases they became part of the text in their own right; to be read, considered and even improved upon.

---

    [21]   William Shakespeare, *The Tragœdy of Othello* (London: Printed by N.O. for Thomas Walkley, 1622).

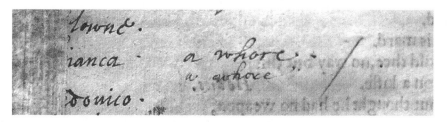

Figure 10.7   *The Tragœdy of Othello*, volume 10.
By permission of The National Trust.

Lesser cites correction as another common kind of annotation on playbooks.[22] There are several examples in the Petworth collection, although they are not found in great abundance. As with the copying annotations, we can see real engagement with the text here, as the annotator must have been reading the text and paying attention in order to spot the error. In a sense, the annotator is engaging not only with text, and so the work of the author, but also with the work of the printer.

In the first, the annotator has removed 'from a taverne' from the end of a line in Massinger's *The Picture* (Figure 10.8), and in the second the annotator has added 'in desgrace' to the end of a line in *Parasitaster* (Figure 10.9), presumably feeling that the internal rhyme with 'face' was too tempting an opportunity to ignore.[23] Someone seems to have disagreed and later crossed out 'in desgrace', or perhaps the original writer thought better of his or her addition.

The annotation on *The Picture* differs from that on *Parasitaster* in a significant way. In at least some other copies of *The Picture* the line ends with 'wine' and 'from a taverne' is not present.[24] This indicates that the loop-like mark at the end of the line may be a proofer's mark. Printed proofs marked with corrections have been identified in a number of other quartos from the period.[25] This too, is engagement with the text, although in this case for professional rather than personal reasons.

22   Lesser, 'Playbooks', 532.

23   Philip Massinger, *The Picture* (London: Printed by I.N. for Thomas Walkley, 1630)

24   There were two editions of *The Picture* published in 1630. Facsimile images from copies of both editions are available through Early English Books Online, and neither have the 'from a taverne' text. The physical copies are kept at the Huntington Library and the British Library, with the British Library copy being the same edition as the Petworth copy.

25   For specific examples see Tucker Brooke, 'Elizabethan Proof Corrections in a Copy of *The First Part of the Contention* 1600', in *The Huntington Library Bulletin* 2 (1931), 87–9, and John Russell Brown, 'A Proof-Sheet from Nicholas Okes' Printing-Shop', *Studies in Bibliography* 11 (1958) 228–31.

Figure 10.8   *The Picture*, volume 11.
By permission of The National Trust.

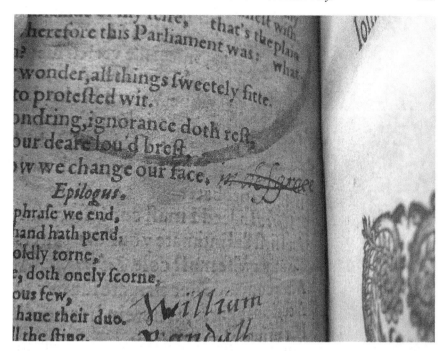

Figure 10.9   *Parasitaster*, volume 12.
By permission of The National Trust

Perhaps the most interesting example of amendments to the text is in volume 1, which contains two separate plays with matching amendments.[26] The plays, *Love's Metamorphosis* and *The Woman in the Moon* are by John Lyly. They are the only plays by the playwright in the collection and seem to have both been previously owned by someone who thought it necessary to blot out the author's name, as seen on *Love's Metamorphosis* in Figure 10.10.

It cannot be definitively proven that these annotations are definitely pre-binding, and hence made by the same previous owner rather than the 10th Earl himself, since they are in the centre of the page and therefore not cropped by the binder. They are also not ownership marks, although *Loves Metamorphosis* at least has certainly been owned before by a Jonathan Tubbe. However, there are no other examples in the collection of an author's name being removed, and it seems significant that these very similar annotations are on two plays by the same author, both of which were certainly previously owned, as evidenced by their age and also the aforementioned ownership mark on *Loves Metamorphosis*.

---

[26]   John Lyly, *Loves Metamorphosis* (London: Printed for William Wood, 1601) and *The Woman in the Moone* (London: Imprinted for William Jones, 1597).

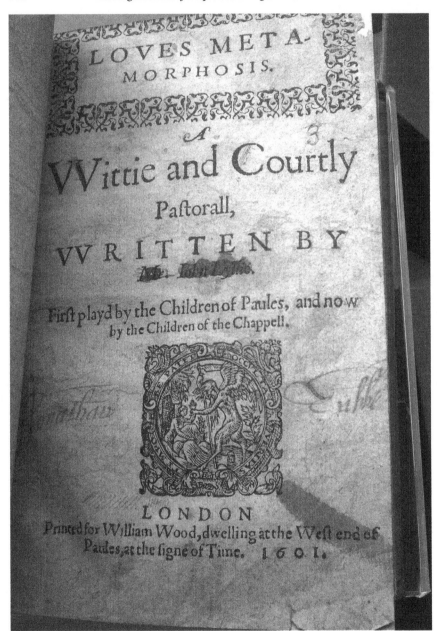

Figure 10.10 *Loves Metamorphosis*, volume 1.
By permission of The National Trust.

This raises the intriguing possibility that some of the plays in the collection did not arrive at it individually, and indeed came by the same previous owner.

Names and Ownership Marks

As with the name on *Loves Metamorphosis*, when names appear on the title page of a play framing the title, they can be assumed to be ownership inscriptions, put there to establish that Jonathan Tubbe, or whomever they refer to, is or has been in possession of the book. While there are a number of name inscriptions on the Petworth plays, the majority of them do not in fact take this form.

Figure 10.11 shows a name written twice on the quarto. Ownership marks are often found on the title page of a book, but this is not always the case, as Figure 10.11 shows. This name, found on *The Bond Man*, is written twice by the previous owner.[27] It is interesting that Robert Waterhouse has chosen an entirely blank page, A4v. This comes after the dedication from Massinger and on the blank verso side of a poem addressed 'To the reader' from 'The author's friend'. On the recto side of the next leaf, so facing the annotation, the play proper begins. Elsewhere in the collection, names are found on the title in a variety of places other than the title page. The name of a previous owner, William Randall, is found on the final page of *Parasitaster* written in the margin, despite the presence of a blank page on the verso side of the title page. These names are likely examples of what Scott-Warren terms 'dry runs of people learning to write their names' rather than simply an assertion of ownership, though of course there is an element of the latter.[28] These practice names are expressions of both literacy and ownership, and the writers are, according to Scott-Warren, '[making] a statement about the intermingling of their technical command – of writing, of the plume – and their identity'.[29] The Robert Waterhouse inscription is particularly interesting from this point of view – as the name is on a blank page but not at the very beginning or end of the quarto it shows an engagement with it, but avoids interference with the text of the play itself, maintaining a respectful distance. Coming directly after text addressed to the reader, this is certainly a particularly pertinent place for a writer to choose to place such a mark, asserting not only the writer's ownership, but also his identity as a reader.

Two plays in volume 12, *The Love of King David and Fair Bethsabe* and *A Woman Never Vext*, bear the same ownership mark, seen in Figure 10.12. This volume also contains several other heavily annotated quartos, including *Parasitaster*. Both quartos appear to have belonged to a Richard Croshaw or

---

[27]   Philip Massinger, *The Bond Man* (London: Printed by Edw: Alde for Iohn Harison and Edward Blackmore, 1624).

[28]   Scott-Warren, 'Reading graffiti', 368.

[29]   Ibid.

Figure 10.11 *The Bond Man*, volume 14.
By permission of The National Trust.

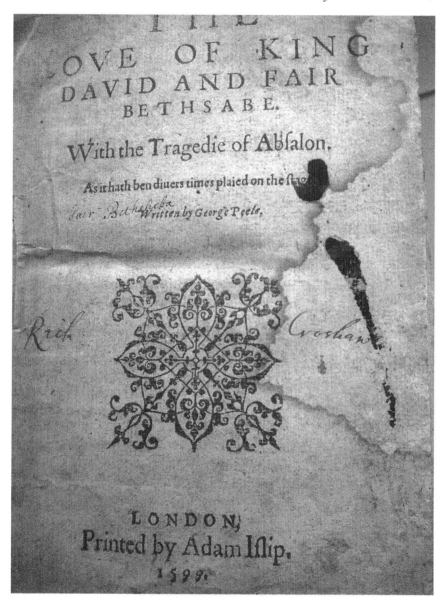

Figure 10.12 *The Love of King David and Fair Bethsabe*, volume 12.
By permission of The National Trust.

Crashaw before they made their way into the Petworth collection. It is possible that this is the poet Richard Crashaw (1612–1648).[30] While not known for collecting plays himself, Crashaw's father William was certainly a collector of books, and the Peele play, published in 1599, could have been inherited from him (the edition of *A Woman Never Vext* was published after the elder Crashaw's death, however).[31] The important point in terms of this study, however, is that these two plays evidently came from the same previous collection, and found their way into the same volume of the Petworth collection.

The Biography of a Collection

As discussed at the beginning of this chapter, the payment made in 1638 indicates that collection was acquired by Northumberland not one play at a time, but as a bulk purchase. The payment was made to a 'Mr Buroughes', who is most likely to be Sir John Borough or Burrowes, an antiquarian who, like Northumberland, was a member of the Order of the Garter. While no evidence exists of Northumberland corresponding with Borough regarding the plays or anything else, there is archival evidence of him asking others to buy books for him around the same time. In a letter to his brother-in-law Robert Leicester, Northumberland makes the following request 'There is a French booke that I have seene, but can not gett in England; your Lordship shall do me a favor to appoint me of your servants to buy it for me, the title of it I send here in this little paper.'[32] Likewise, Borough is known to have purchased this kind of material for others before – specifically he purchased manuscripts for his cousin Sir Robert Cotton in the early 1620s.[33]

The marks and annotations discussed point to two important facts: firstly that many early modern readers engaged with their texts in a variety of ways, and secondly that a person assembling a play collection in the late 1630s would

---

[30]   Thomas Healy, 'Crashaw, Richard (1612/13–1648)', *Oxford Dictionary of National Biography*, Oxford University Press, 2004 [http://www.oxforddnb.com/view/article/6622, accessed 31 Jan 2014].

[31]   W.H. Kelliher, 'Crashawe, William (*bap.* 1572, *d.* 1625/6)', *Oxford Dictionary of National Biography*, Oxford University Press, 2004; online edn, Oct 2009 [http://www.oxforddnb.com/view/article/6623, accessed 31 Jan 2014].

[32]   The Archives of the Duke of Northumberland at Alnwick Castle (subsequently 'Alnwick Castle'), DNP:MS 14, f. 257v. Letter from Algernon Earl of Northumberland to Robert Earl of Leicester, London Dec. 19. 1639. Available on microfilm at the British Library. Northumberland Archives, Microfilm 285.

[33]   S.A. Baron, 'Borough, Sir John (*d.* 1643)', *Oxford Dictionary of National Biography*, Oxford University Press, 2004; online edn, May 2011 [http://www.oxforddnb.com/view/article/2913, accessed 28 May 2013].

have been as comfortable with second-hand and evidently 'used' quartos as they would be with brand new playbooks. What these two plays previously owned by Richard Crashaw and the two Lyly plays with matching amendments point towards is that at least some of the quartos in the collection arrived in it in groups. As the other very varied annotations reveal, they seem to have come from a variety of backgrounds, and these particular quartos show that some evidently came from the same place. It seems reasonable to suggest that these two sets of plays came from the same libraries. Second-hand booksellers were certainly operating at this time, so Borough would not have had to seek out individual quartos or groups of quartos directly from other collectors and/or readers.[34]

The range of publishing dates in the collection supports this theory as well. While a number of plays have evidently been previously owned, there are also some which almost certainly have not. The collection contains five plays printed in 1638, the probable year of purchase, and 11 printed in 1637. These plays at least are very unlikely to have been through a previous owner, and were probably purchased as new. The quartos show plenty of evidence of previous bindings, but not of being bound together before being put into their current binding. If we are to consider 1638 the date of collection, then the presence of 'new' plays published the same year, or in the previous year, makes it very unlikely that the collection was assembled by Borough or another collector for his own purposes, and then subsequently sold to Northumberland. More likely, given the late date of some of the plays and the size of the collection, Borough was asked to assemble the collection for Northumberland, just as Northumberland asked his brother-in-law to find him a certain book, or as Borough sought out manuscripts for his cousin in Venice.

Many aspects of the collection do not look like the work of a discerning collector – the presence of several duplicate plays, for example, or incomplete 'sets' – such as Heywood's 'Ages' plays, of which there are only three out of four in the collection.[35] The duplicate plays and the plays from the same previous collections can be explained if Borough purchased at least some of the plays in bundles from second-hand booksellers without giving too much thought to what was contained within. The only general rule that seems to have been

---

[34] Matthew Yeo, *The Acquisition of Chetham's Library* (Leiden: BRILL, 2011). Yeo's study is focused on a slightly later period, predominately on the mid-seventeenth century, but he cites a 1628 list compiled by the Warden on the Stationers' Company of 38 booksellers dealing in '"old libraries", second-hand books and books from the continent' (84). The second hand book trade was no doubt operating well before this list was compiled.

[35] *The Iron Age* (1632), *The Brazen Age* (1613) and *The Silver Age* (1613) are all present; *The Golden Age* is not, nor was it present in the lost volumes.

imposed on the collection is that all of the quartos be in English (and originally written in English), and that they all be plays.[36]

Although Borough's main motivation for particular purchases seems to have been pragmatism, there is at least one group of plays in the collection that defies this assumption. A fact that seems relevant to both the intent of the collector and to the potential purchase date of the plays is that the collection contains very nearly all of James Shirley's plays written in or before 1638, excluding *The Wittie Fair One*, published in 1633, and the 1634 masque *The Triumph of Peace*. Shirley's plays make up the majority of the 'new' plays in the collection, those published in 1637 and 1638, making them most likely to have been deliberately purchased rather than being part of a job lot. For a collection of this size to contain 15 out of 17 of a particular playwright's works is certainly suggestive of an interest in that writer, and it may well be that Northumberland specifically requested that some of Shirley's plays be included in the collection. Furthermore, the 1690 catalogue reveals that a 1646 edition of Shirley's poems was later added to the library.

Shirley was a popular playwright in the 1630s, receiving patronage from Queen Henrietta Maria as well as from a number of other nobles.[37] His plays, typical of Caroline drama, are predominately comedies with a courtly setting. He also wrote several masques. The late 1630s were a particularly productive time for the playwright: five of his plays were published in 1637 and two in 1638, all of which are found in the Petworth collection. The late 1630s were also a rather significant time in the life of the 10th Earl of Northumberland. Having inherited his title on the death of his father in 1632, he was installed into the Order of the Garter in 1635, made admiral of the ship-money fleet in 1636, and eventually gained the position of Lord High Admiral in 1638, the same year he acquired the play collection.[38] Alongside his rise to prominence, the Earl had begun something of a campaign of public consumption. He began renovating and furnishing his various homes a few years earlier, collected art (particularly the work of the fashionable Anthony Van Dyck), and at the occasion of his installation into the Order of the Garter, Northumberland spent vast sums of money on a lavish feast followed by a procession through London, which was

---

[36]   There are, in fact, two exceptions to this in the collection which appear to have found their way in under the radar – Lydgate's prose tract *The Serpent of Division*, which was published with the play *The Tragedy of Gorboduc*, and *Andria* of Terence from the lost volumes, which, as it is dated 1588 in the catalogue, is presumably Maurice Kyffin's translation of Terence's *The Woman of Andros*.

[37]   Sandra A. Burner, *James Shirley: A Study of Literary Coteries and Patronage in Seventeenth Century England* (Boston: University Press of America, 1988), 89.

[38]   Richard Lomas, *A Power in the Land: The Percys* (East Linton: Tuckwell, 1999), 139.

commemorated by Martin Parker in a broadside ballad.[39] In the ballad, Parker states that the Earl's aim was 'to publish his magnificence', and his forays into the world of art collecting, his extensive remodelling of his properties – and perhaps also his book collection – would no doubt have served the same purpose.[40]

Northumberland's father, the 9th Earl, had a sizeable and significant library for which he was well known, but his interest was mainly in science and related disciplines, and he was certainly not a collector of drama.[41] The 1630s, when he was already investing time and money into 'publishing his magnificence' would have been the ideal time for Northumberland to make his own mark on the already vast library established by his father. Recorded in the same document as that listing the 'playbooks' is the purchase of 'a great ebony cabinet', a 'multiplying glass' and more unspecified 'books'. This certainly sounds like a man improving his library.[42] As motives for purchase on the part of Northumberland, we can consider fashion, a desire to develop a library and an attempt to display taste. We can speculate with some confidence that the specification for his play collection given by Northumberland to Borough was that it ought to consist of a variety of English quarto plays and include some recent works, particularly Shirley.

Book and Lives, Past and Present

The Petworth collection has much to tell us about its past, and in conversing with it, as Fletcher's hero would put it, we can learn much; about the individual quartos, the collection as a whole and about the people who have interacted with the quartos before – whether they leave their marks in pen like Richard Crashaw, in gilt stamps like the 10th Earl of Northumberland or in household accounts like Sir John Borough. The nature and history of the collection raises some very interesting questions about the nature of collection and the motives behind the construction of libraries in the period. As a case study, the 10th Earl of Northumberland's play collection offers a fascinating insight into the ways in which early modern book owners could construct a collection and the options available to them. Second-hand quartos nestle alongside fashionable new plays and all are given the same treatment in the binding. The collection methods

---

[39] Jeremy Wood, 'The Architectural Patronage of Algernon Percy, 10th Earl of Northumberland', in *English Architecture Public and Private,* ed. John Bold (London: Continuum International Publishing Group, 1993), 55–80

[40] Martin Parker, *A Briefe Description of the Triumphant Show Made by the Right Honourable Aulgernon Percie* (London: Printed for Francis Coules, 1635)

[41] Gordon Batho, 'The Library of the Wizard Earl', in *The Library* s5-XV, Issue 4, (1960) 246–61, 256.

[42] Alnwick Castle, DNP:MS 390. U.I,5: f. 49. Declaration of account for 1638–1639, Mr Heron and Mr Thornton 1638. Microfilm 351.

and motivations point to a combination of both pragmatism in buying existing collections and occasionally a more selective style of collection.

As I have shown in this chapter, the Petworth collection seems to be neither the work of a meticulously selective and careful collector, nor does it appear to have been assembled at random with no consideration of content. What is apparent is that the assembler of the collection (likely Borough) used a number of different methods when building it, but also that Northumberland himself used a method of collection – a kind of 'collection by proxy' – that seems counter-intuitive given how we tend to conceptualise the act of collection: a highly personal activity driven by a desire to engage with and pursue objects. The Petworth collection, then, shows us active readers who are physically involved with their texts, more so than perhaps a modern reader would be, and a somewhat passive collector who is precisely the opposite – less engaged than we would expect of a collector. But this kind of consumption is not one that we should consider a lesser act of consumption, and it is not one undertaken without any kind of thought. As evidenced by the Shirley plays, Northumberland likely did have some input into the kinds of plays that were purchased. Furthermore, his library does seem to have contained both other plays (though small in number) and also other works by some of the playwrights in the collection.[43] Northumberland's purchasing methods may have been different to the modern collector in that he did not seek out his objects individually, and he may not have engaged with the texts via the pen as some of the previous owners did, but he did engage with them by physically having his crest stamped on them. As Walter Benjamin puts it in his classic essay on book collection, *Unpacking my Library*:

> For [a collector], not only books but also copies of books have their fates. And in this sense, the most important fate of a copy is its encounter with him, with his own collection. I am not exaggerating when I say that to a true collector the acquisition of an old book is its rebirth.[44]

The Petworth collection may have had a "rebirth" in its encounter with the 10th Earl of Northumberland, unified from many objects into a collection, from one payment of 'playbooks' rather than many separate ones, but it retains the marks of its past lives. What is particularly evident from the study of the Petworth plays is the extent to which these lives overlap, and interact, with each other.

---

[43] It is not possible to adequately discuss the place of drama in the library in this chapter, but it is useful to note that the 10th Earl's library also apparently included collected plays of Lyly and Jonson, poetic works by Shirley and Marlowe and a handful of single quartos, mostly printed after 1638.

[44] Walter Benjamin, 'Unpacking my Library: A Talk about Collection', in *Selected writings: 1931–1934*, Volume 2, Part 2 (Harvard: Harvard University Press, 2005), 486–92, 487.

PART IV
Communities and Individuals

Chapter 11

Patrons and their Commissions: The Uses of Biography in Understanding the Construction of the Nave of Holy Trinity, Bottisham

Gabriel Byng

Introduction

Placing architectural and artistic commissions in the context of their patron's life has provided an irresistible historiographical challenge to biographers as well as art historians. Acts of artistic patronage present a particularly important opportunity for researchers of medieval history, for whom art and architecture can provide a rare insight into an individual's devotions, taste and ambitions, but with few documentary sources against which these inferences can be verified. Historians of the great commissions of well-documented figures such as kings and abbots are seemingly best placed to integrate art into their understanding of the character of their patron, shedding light on both the interpretation of the work and the biography of the individual. Nevertheless, even here the limitations of medieval source documents for accessing the personalities of medieval figures render the significance of their patronage highly ambiguous.[1]

For the majority of our medieval architectural heritage, most notably parish churches, the obstacles to making meaningful links between biography and building work are even more pronounced. The patrons are usually unknown, sometimes speculatively identified by modern scholars with the most senior local figure or 'the village' (often treated as a monolithic social unit or assumed to be under the leadership of the churchwardens). Even where individual patrons are

---

[1] The limitations on writing medieval biographies are discussed in many sources, including: Thomas Frederick Tout, *Chapters in the Administrative History of Mediaeval England* (Manchester University Press, 1937), 20; K.B. McFarlane, *The Nobility of Later Medieval England: The Ford Lectures for 1953 and Related Studies* (Oxford: Clarendon Press, 1973), ix; Janet L. Nelson, 'Writing Early Medieval Biography', *History Workshop Journal*, 2000, no. 50 (1 January 2000): 129–36; Michael Prestwich, 'Medieval Biography', *Journal of Interdisciplinary History* 40, no. 3 (2010): 325–46.

identifiable, they are most commonly members of the gentry, for many of whom only the outlines of careers or landholdings can typically be recovered at best.[2]

The first part of this chapter is concerned with the methodological challenges created by the combination of biographical information about gentry members with architectural patronage. The parish church takes a small but not infrequent role in studies of gentry families and culture of the late Middle Ages, usually relying on archaeological and antiquarian records.[3] Architectural evidence has also been employed in biographical studies, rather as gentry biographies feature in art historical approaches, as for instance in recent works by Nigel Saul.[4] Such works are usually taken to illustrate an aspect of a family's relationship with their tenants and locality, or the nature of their religious devotion. However, with little documentary evidence to compare these inferences to, deriving such conclusions is speculative. Gajewski concludes, similarly, that 'a central problem with current models of patronage is the tendency to draw straight inferences

---

[2]   E.g. my work on the construction of Bolney and Biddenham: Gabriel Byng, 'The Construction of the Tower at Bolney Church', *Sussex Archaeological Collections* 151 (2013): 101–13; Gabriel Byng, 'The Contract for the North Aisle at St James, Biddenham', *Antiquaries Journal* 95 (2015).

[3]   E.g. Andrew Brown, *Popular Piety in Late Medieval England: The Diocese of Salisbury, 1250–1550* (Oxford: Clarendon Press, 1995), 121; Eric Acheson, *A Gentry Community: Leicestershire in the Fifteenth Century, c. 1422 – c. 1485*, Cambridge Studies in Medieval Life and Thought 19 (New York: Cambridge University Press, 1992), 189; Christopher Harper-Bill, *Religious Belief and Ecclesiastical Careers in Late Medieval England: Proceedings of the Conference Held at Strawberry Hill, Easter, 1989* (Woodbridge: Boydell & Brewer, 1991), 134; Christine Carpenter, *Locality and Polity: A Study of Warwickshire Landed Society, 1401–1499* (Cambridge: Cambridge University Press, 1992), 235–6; Christine Carpenter, 'The Religion of the Gentry of Fifteenth-Century England', in *England in the Fifteenth Century*, ed. D. Williams (Woodbridge: Boydell & Brewer, 1987), 66; Malcolm Graham Allan Vale, *Piety, Charity, and Literacy among the Yorkshire Gentry, 1370–1480*, Borthwick Papers 50 (York: St Anthony's Press, 1976), 10–11; McFarlane, *The Nobility of Later Medieval England*, 95; Colin Richmond, *John Hopton: A Fifteenth Century Suffolk Gentleman* (Cambridge: Cambridge University Press, 1981), 156–7.

[4]   Nigel Saul, 'Chivalry and Art: The Camoys Family and the Wall Paintings in Trotton Church', in *Soldiers, Nobles and Gentlemen: Essays in Honour of Maurice Keen*, ed. Peter R. Coss and Christopher Tyerman (Woodbridge: The Boydell Press, 2009); Nigel Saul, 'Shottesbrooke Church: A Study in Knightly Patronage', in *Windsor: Medieval Archaeology, Art and Architecture of the Thames Valley*, ed. L. Keen and E. Scarff, British Archaeological Association Conference Transactions (Norwich: British Archaeological Association, 2002); Nigel Saul, *Scenes from Provincial Life: Knightly Families in Sussex 1280–1400* (Oxford: Clarendon Press, 1986), chap. 5.

from the visual evidence about the patron's character or social condition.[5] This chapter will use a single case study, the construction of the nave of Holy Trinity, Bottisham, in Cambridgeshire, to demonstrate how arguments regarding the dating and design of the church can generate very different interpretations of both the building's architecture and its patron.

The second part of this chapter extends this examination of patronal biographies to encompass the peasantry, whose contribution at Bottisham is possible, even likely.[6] The challenge here is slightly different: laying out biographical information about individual villagers, predominantly peasants, is rarely possible in any detail. A recent collection of essays on medieval biographies, for example, was dominated by discussions of the difficulties of capturing biographies of the religious and secular elites; only one paper, by Robin Fleming, discussed the life of a member of the peasantry, and relied on scientific analysis of her bones and grave goods to do so.[7] Rather than individuals, it has been social groupings and communities which make up the basic unit for most social historians of medieval England. The Toronto School, for example, demonstrated that by reading across entries in manor court rolls it was possible to analyse aspects of village life by accumulating details about large numbers of people, which would be all but meaningless if limited only to individuals. Poos has argued that combining these sources with others may be sufficient for writing peasant biographies, but his examples reveal the sparse details on offer.[8]

Although it will not be able to conjure up a biography where no documentation exists, this chapter will argue that details of peasant lives can be usefully found and combined to suggest which members of the community could have been responsible for parish church building, as may have been the case at Bottisham and was no doubt the case elsewhere. It will attempt to fill a

---

[5]   A. Gajewski, 'The Patronage Question under Review: Queen Blanche of Castile (1188–1252) and the Architecture of the Cistercian Abbeys at Royaumont, Maubuisson, and Le Lys', in *Reassessing the Roles of Women as 'Makers' of Medieval Art and Architecture*, ed. Therese Martin, vol. 1 (Boston, 2012), 243.

[6]   I argue that the majority of parish church construction in the later Middle Ages was carried out as corporate acts of patronage by elite peasants in: Gabriel Byng, 'Planning and Paying for Parish Church Construction in the Later Middle Ages' (Unpublished PhD Thesis, Cambridge University, 2014), chap. 6; see also: Gabriel Byng, '"Fabric Wardens" and the Organisation of Parish Church Construction in the Late Middle Ages', in *Proceedings of the First Conference of the Construction History Society*, ed. James W.P. Campbell (Exeter: Construction History Society, 2014), 25–34.

[7]   Robin Fleming, 'Bones for Historians: Putting the Body Back into Biography', in *Writing Medieval Biography, 750–1250: Essays in Honour of Professor Frank Barlow*, ed. David Bates, Julia C. Crick, and Sarah Hamilton (Woodbridge: Boydell Press, 2006), 29–48.

[8]   L.R. Poos, 'Peasant "Biographies" from Medieval England', in *Medieval Lives and the Historian*, ed. N. Bulst and J.-P. Genet (Kalamazoo, 1986).

lacuna in the evidence with a model built, as far as is possible, from empirical data gathered from different sources even if they are 'unlikely to be present in reality in a pure, uncontaminated, form'.[9] Such an approach has already proved useful when employed by medievalists in turning data from numerous sources into plausible, composite fictions. Beat Kümin was able to describe two villages, both fictional, by combining details of real life cases into collages that explained differences in late medieval administration and management.[10] John Hatcher went even further in creating fictional personalities for real life figures.[11] Such attempts are not without their critics.[12] This chapter will not be biography in its most familiar form, but will suggest a new methodology for combining information about peasant lives with the buildings for which they were responsible. Its claims as a work of biography are in many ways much less ambitious than those of an historian like Robin Fleming, attempting not to produce new information about an individual peasant but rather to create a plausible biography for a fictional peasant patron. However, it does attempt to restore the lives of individual peasants to a place of central relevance in the history of the architectural patronage of parish churches, and to propose a new application of the "fictional composite" to peasant biography.

Gentry Biography and the Nave at Holy Trinity, Bottisham, Cambridgeshire

One medieval building where architectural patronage and gentry biography can be usefully combined is the church of Holy Trinity, Bottisham, Cambridgeshire, where the nave was rebuilt in the early fourteenth century. Its construction has regularly been linked to the patronage of Elias of Beckingham, a justice of the Westminster bench until Hilary term 1307, after which he disappears from the records, presumably dead of old age, almost 50 years after his first mention as a court clerk.[13] The main evidence for his involvement is the presence of his brass in the centre of the new nave, the inscription reading '*Hic jacet Elias de Beckingham*

9   P.R. Coss, 'The Formation of the English Gentry', *Past & Present*, no. 147 (May 1995): 63; A. Macfarlane, *The Culture of Capitalism* (Oxford: Blackwell, 1987), 207.

10   Beat Kümin, 'Late Medieval Churchwardens' Accounts and Parish Government: Looking beyond London and Bristol', *The English Historical Review* 119, no. 480 (1 February 2004): 87–99.

11   John Hatcher, *The Black Death: An Intimate History* (London: Weidenfeld and Nicolson, 2008).

12   Clive Burgess, 'The Broader Church? A Rejoinder to "Looking Beyond"', *The English Historical Review* 119, no. 480 (2 January 2004): 100–116; Prestwich, 'Medieval Biography', 343.

13   Paul Brand, 'Beckingham, Elias (d. 1307?)', in *Oxford Dictionary of National Biography* (Oxford: Oxford University Press, 2004).

quondam justicarius Domini regis Anglie cuius anime propitietur Deus.[14] Arthur Hill described it as a 'raised Purbeck altar-tomb' in 1880 although no other earlier sources mention the tomb being raised or forming part of an altar.[15] Two other important arguments can be added to suggest Elias's role. First, there were few other wealthy lay parishioners in Bottisham in the early fourteenth century to whom responsibility could be granted: the main manors were owned by Anglesey and Tonbridge priories, who were unlikely to contribute to the construction of a large new nave, and there were no secular manorial lords – even Elias was only a free tenant, albeit a very wealthy one.[16] The church was appropriated to Anglesey, which appointed to the vicarage, valued at £5 in 1291. At the other end of the social scale, most of the Bottisham tenantry were impoverished, even for the area: at least three-quarters were smallholders or wage labourers. It seems impossible that they could have been responsible for building a nave as ambitious and sophisticated as that at Bottisham.

The second argument is the association between the building work at Bottisham and the work of Michael of Canterbury, or one of his circle.[17] The smooth, rich mouldings and 'drooping' quatrefoil tracery of the aisle windows matches those in the windows of the crypt of St Stephen's chapel, Westminster, now St Mary Undercroft, as does the use of keeled shafts in the hollows between the pier shafts; while the unity, quality and sophistication of the design, including precociously transomed windows with square heads at the east end of each aisle, suggest a court architect. This indicates not only that the patron had substantial capital, but also an awareness of the most recent developments in architectural design and access to their designers. Elias had been a justice of the common pleas while Michael was in charge of construction at St Stephen's chapel, adjacent to where the court sat in Westminster Hall. Among the 15 men he served with as justice were several with careers in royal administration and links to royal building work. Chief among them was Sir Ralph of Sandwich, who as manager of the king's southern and western demesnes had run several building projects, and had been involved with the acquisition of New Winchelsea.[18] Interestingly, another colleague for four terms was Harvey Stanton, builder of St Michael,

---

[14]   Edward Hailstone, *The History and Antiquities of the Parish of Bottisham and the Priory of Anglesey in Cambridgeshire*, Publications of the Cambridge Antiquarian Society. Octavo Series 14; 16 (Cambridge: Printed for the Cambridge Antiquarian Society, 1873), 34.

[15]   Arthur George Hill, *Architectural and Historical Notices of the Churches of Cambridgeshire* (W. Clowes, 1880), 151.

[16]   Although Anglesey did contribute to the repair of the chancel c. 1450.

[17]   Arthur Whittingham, 'The Ramsey Family of Norwich', *The Archaeological Journal* 132 (1980): 288.

[18]   Christopher Whittick, 'Sandwich, Sir Ralph (c.1235–1308)', in *Oxford Dictionary of National Biography* (Oxford: Oxford University Press, 2004).

Cambridge, just seven miles west of Bottisham and also with sophisticated, if very different, window tracery.[19]

To historians of more recent eras the details of Beckingham's life might appear sparse, but he has merited an entry in the *Oxford Dictionary of National Biography* and his patronage of Bottisham may help to shed further light on his tastes, ambitions, and associations. The gift of a new nave would be a fitting tribute to the climax of Elias's career, his economic success, and his bond with the village. He had risen through the ranks from being a clerk of the Eyre, to a senior clerk of the Westminster bench, assize justice, keeper of the writs and rolls, and finally justice of the Westminster bench, acquiring highly lucrative rectories, often from Peterborough Abbey, for whom he worked as an agent and money lender.[20] Like most successful officials he invested his payments as a justice in acquiring land holdings: in the Nene Valley, at Hemington and Southorp by 1288;[21] in Stoke by Newark, Nottinghamshire, by 1300;[22] and in Bottisham in 1275, shortly after becoming senior clerk of the Westminster bench.[23] As his landed estate grew it was his bond to Bottisham that dominated: over the next decade he doubled the size of his Cambridgeshire holding.[24] It was here he was buried and it was these lands that he would pass on to his heir, while those in Northamptonshire were granted to Peterborough Abbey in return for prayers for his soul and that of the late Queen Eleanor.[25] He made other gifts to the church: an archidiaconal visitation reports that Elias gave '*i pannus de serico, ... par frontalium*'.[26]

---

[19]   A.E. Stamp, *Michaelhouse* (privately printed, 1923); G.W. Keeton, *Harvey the Hasty: A Medieval Chief Justice*, 1978; Brand, 'Beckingham, Elias (d. 1307?)'.

[20]   Edmund King, *Peterborough Abbey, 1086–1310; a Study in the Land Market*, Cambridge Studies in Economic History (Cambridge: Cambridge University Press, 1973), 133; Edward Foss, *The Judges of England: With Sketches of Their Lives, and Miscellaneous Notices Connected with the Courts at Westminster, from the Time of the Conquest*, vol. III (London: Longman, Brown, Green, and Longmans, 1848), 52–3.

[21]   John Bridges, *The History and Antiquities of Northamptonshire*, vol. 2 (Oxford: Printed at the Clarendon Press and sold by T. Payne, London; D. Prince and J. Cooke, Oxford; and Mr. Lacy, Northampton, 1791), 400, 496.

[22]   Hailstone, *The History and Antiquities of the Parish of Bottisham*, 34.

[23]   King, *Peterborough Abbey*, 52.

[24]   A.F. Wareham and A.P.M. Wright (eds), *A History of the County of Cambridge and the Isle of Ely*, vol. 10, Victoria County History (London: Published for the Institute of Historical Research by Oxford University Press, 2002), 215–20.

[25]   Bridges, *The History and Antiquities of Northamptonshire*, 2:550.

[26]   C.L. Feltoe and Ellis H. Minns (eds), *Vetus Liber Archidiaconi Eliensis*, Cambridge Antiquarian Society (Cambridge: Printed for the Cambridge Antiquarian Society, 1917), 49; cf. Hailstone, *The History and Antiquities of the Parish of Bottisham*, 31; pace Wareham and Wright, *VCH Cambridgeshire*, 10:215–20.

There is, however, good reason to suspect that the building work postdates Elias's death, sometime after 1307. Stylistically the nave would appear to belong to the third or fourth decades of the fourteenth century by which point Elias would probably have been in his 70s or 80s, an exceptional age for a medieval man. The windows have flowing, bulbous ogees in the tracery, richly moulded piers and slimmed down, if highly complex, mouldings on the capitals and bases. The windows of the undercroft at St Stephen's are usually dated to the second wave of building work at the chapel in 1320–26, possibly replacing work destroyed in the 1298 fire.[27] Although John Harvey argued first that Walter of Canterbury was responsible for the tracery designs of 1292–97, he later changed his mind, giving responsibility to Michael of Canterbury during the year or two that he was still involved in building work at Westminster at the start of the 1320s. This was also the view of Howard Colvin, and is consistent with evidence from the accounts. Christopher Wilson has disputed the assumption that the Westminster work belongs to the 1320–26 wave of building work, but the use of a transomed square-headed window at Bottisham would strongly suggest that a date in the first decade of the fourteenth century, or before, is unrealistic. One church guide suggests the nave is of 1320,[28] another of 1300–1320,[29] and Tudor-Craig dates it to the 1330s, 1340s and even the 1350s.[30] Indeed, in the Calendar of Close Rolls there are records of gifts made '*ad fabric et emendat eccl[es]i.e. s[an]c[t]e Trinitatis de Bodekesham*' in 1345–46;[31] and '*ad opus eccl[es] i.e.*' in 1362–63, although these cannot be taken to prove that building work was in progress.[32] Indeed, it is important to note a gift '*ad opus eccl[es]i.e.*' in 1287–88 too.[33] A further, critical, piece of evidence for Elias's responsibility can also be discounted. Elias's tomb slab was not originally in the centre of the nave, but

---

[27] Christopher Wilson, 'Origins of the Perpendicular Style and Its Development to c. 1360' (PhD, University of London, 1979); cf. John Harvey, 'The Origins of the Perpendicular Style', in *Studies in Building History*, ed. E.M. Jope (London, 1961), 134–65; Maurice Hastings, *St. Stephen's Chapel and Its Place in the Development of Perpendicular Style in England*. (Cambridge: Cambridge University Press, 1955), 49; Howard Colvin (ed.), *The History of the King's Works*, vol. I (London: H.M.S.O., 1963), 513.

[28] *Bottisham Village & Church* (Cambridge: W. Heffer and Sons, Ltd, 1938), 5.

[29] Derek D. Billings, *Bottisham Holy Trinity: A History & Guide* (Bottisham: B.D. Threlfall, 1987), 9.

[30] Pamela Tudor-Craig, 'Fourteenth-Century Churches', in *Cambridgeshire Churches*, ed. Carola Hicks (Stamford: P. Watkins, 1997), 67.

[31] *Calendar of Close Rolls, Edward III: Volume 7 – 1343–1346*, ed. H.C. Maxwell Lyte (London: Institute of Historical Research, 1904).

[32] *Calendar of Close Rolls, Edward III: Volume 11 – 1360–1364*, ed. H.C. Maxwell Lyte (London: Institute of Historical Research, 1909).

[33] *Calendar of Close Rolls, Edward I: Volume 2 – 1279–1288*, ed. H.C. Maxwell Lyte (London: Institute of Historical Research, 1902).

was moved there, probably in the early eighteenth century, breaking it into three pieces which were fitted back together with metal pins.[34]

Significantly, another, later candidate for patron can be suggested. Elias settled his holding in Bottisham on the marriage of his ward, Robert de Vaux, to his niece Alice in 1283.[35] Explaining how Elias came to know Robert is speculation. The connection may have been regional: Beckingham is around 30 miles from Freiston, Lincolnshire, where the de Vaux family had a manor;[36] while another de Vaux manor and advowson is at Little Abington about 10 miles south of Bottisham.[37] Possibly it was through Elias's work for the courts. Little is known of Robert; he was of age in 1305[38] and dead by 1319 (were he the patron in life, the tracery design would have been an early trial for the St Stephen's windows).[39] He married Alice, daughter of Adam of Senlis and Elias's sister. All this is of interest because a second church, apparently by a member of Canterbury's circle and with characteristic drooping tracery quatrefoils, like those of St Stephen's chapel and the Bottisham aisles, if rather pared down in their detailing and richness, has been associated with patronage by the de Vaux family, specifically the sisters Maud and Petronilla. That church is Cley-next-the-Sea, Norfolk. Robert was descended from Roger de Vaux, the fourth son of Oliver, one of the barons who had compelled King John to sign Magna Carta but whose baronage passed to John de Vaux, the third, and inheriting, son. John's large estate was divided equally between his daughters Maud and Petronilla, and continued in the family of Maud's husband, William de Roos, lord of Hamlake.

It has already been noted that the Decorated work at Cley shows close similarities with work by John Ramsey and his nephew William at Norwich Cathedral, in the Ethelbert Gate, Carnary Chapel and cloisters.[40] Cley is usually assumed to be coeval with the Carnary Chapel, 1316–25, with the clerestory presumably built toward the end of that period and so roughly contemporaneously with the work in Westminster. It was not carried out in ignorance of St Stephen's: John Ramsey probably owned property in London

---

[34]   Billings, *Bottisham Holy Trinity*, 9.

[35]   TNA PRO CP 25/1/25/39; cf. G. Andrews Moriarty, 'The Origin of the Family of Vaux of Harrowden', *Miscellanea Genealogica et Heraldica*, 5th, v (n.d.): 281.

[36]   *Calendar of Inquisitions Post Mortem and Other Analogous Documents Preserved in the Public Record Office: Edward II*, vol. 5 (H.M.S.O., 1908), 47.

[37]   *Calendar of Inquisitions Post Mortem and Other Analogous Documents Preserved in the Public Record Office: Edward I*, vol. 2 (H.M.S.O., 1906), 402–4.

[38]   Andrews Moriarty, 'The Origin of the Family of Vaux of Harrowden', 283–5, 349; BL Add. MS. 5805, ff. 1v, 11v, 16v.

[39]   *Calendar of the Patent Rolls Preserved in the Public Record Office: Edward II 1317–21*, vol. III (London: H.M.S.O., 1908), 365; Nikolaus Pevsner and Bill Wilson, *Norfolk. 1, Norwich and North-East*, 2nd edn, The Buildings of England (London: Penguin, 1997), 432.

[40]   Whittingham, 'Ramsey Family'.

and William was employed on the *alura*, or passageway, at St Stephen's in 1323 and 1325.[41] Arthur Whittingham argues that Maud's brother-in-law Roger de Holebrook, a royal clerk, introduced them to the Ramseys after he had employed William Ramsey senior, who also worked at St Stephen's in the 1290s, at Little Wenham.[42] However, the family had other links to royal building work: William de Vaux ran construction of the new tower at Knaresborough castle,[43] while the sisters' husbands both had links with London and Westminster. Pamela Tudor-Craig has even argued that the Bottisham screen is linked to the Norwich cloister.[44] If dating the Bottisham nave to before Robert's death, c. 1319, is still too early then two other candidates for patron can be cited. Robert's son John inherited the Bottisham holding by 1319 but spent much of the time before his death in prison. The holding then passed to his younger brother Thomas (d. 1344) who was an absentee rector in Yorkshire.

The Bottisham and Cley sides of the de Vaux family chose from very different groups of masons, one from the Ramsey circle, looking toward Norwich, the other from the Canterbury circle, looking to Westminster – but the appearance of the 'drooping' quatrefoil at both churches and its common ancestry from Michael of Canterbury's work at St Stephen's, mirrors the kinship of their patrons. There is reason to believe the two lines of the family had remained close, perhaps mediated through their links to Pentney Priory or the manor at Little Abington. Petronilla died in 1326, two decades after Elias and less than one after Robert, and she may have known the two sons who inherited the Bottisham land.[45] In this alternative, the interpretation of the nave at Bottisham is profoundly altered. The building can be reframed as an act of self-assertion by the younger son of a grand family, demonstrating his growing prosperity under the guidance of his uncle-in-law, and creating a fitting setting for his patron's tomb, suggesting he had a strong sense of his debt to Elias and duty to the village and church with which he was associated. Tellingly, Robert would even call one of his sons after Elias – a name not formerly used by the de Vaux family. It was perhaps the link to his uncle that provided him with access to the Canterbury circle.

---

[41] John Harvey, *English Mediaeval Architects: A Biographical Dictionary down to 1550*, Revised edition (Gloucester: Alan Sutton, 1987), 214–15.

[42] Whittingham, 'Ramsey Family'.

[43] Howard Colvin (ed.), *The History of the King's Works*, vol. II (London: H.M.S.O., 1963), 689.

[44] It is probably of the mid-fifteenth century. Tudor-Craig, 'Fourteenth-Century Churches', 66.

[45] F. Blomefield, *An Essay Towards a Topographical History of the County of Norfolk*, vol. IV (Fersfield: W. Whittingham, in Lynn; and R. Baldwin, London, 1775), 662.

Peasant Patrons

So far these considerations, although useful in demonstrating the reciprocal value of setting church building in a biographical context, have not provided the burden of proof in assigning responsibility to either Elias or one of the de Vaux sons. The place of the church in the biographies of Elias de Beckingham or Robert de Vaux, despite its rather cosy fit and the interesting light it sheds on both their lives and the building itself, demonstrates how ambiguous the biographical significance of architectural commissions can be. The one building could be characterised either as the valedictory work of an elderly and satisfied self-made lawyer, or a heartfelt tribute by an ambitious heir. Similarly, to their biographers, Elias can be seen as a man whose worldly prosperity provided him with the means to express his piety, local pride, urbane good taste or self-regard (or some combination of these) in an exceptional artistic creation; while Robert could be regarded as a successful upstart (his success witnessed by the cost of the building) who did not let his ambition get in the way of his gratitude to his uncle, sense of civic responsibility or Christian devotion (or, again, some combination of these). The scant information available regarding the two men means, of course, that both of these interpretations are highly speculative and necessarily fanciful. The remainder of this chapter will suggest a third possibility, outside the local gentry families.

If we do wish to give responsibility to a de Vaux rather than Elias, this raises a new problem which returns us to the modelling of parish church patronage. The nave at Bottisham is outstanding in size, ambition and finish, and was probably well beyond the resources of Robert de Vaux. Caroe described it, not unjustly, as 'one of our purest and finest examples of the Decorated period', while 'no finer arcades than those at Bottisham exist in purely parochial architecture'.[46] Elias's holding in Bottisham was around 80 acres, the equivalent to that of a very wealthy peasant or yeoman.[47] We could postulate that it may have been worth a few pounds a year.[48] Despite being a junior member of the court,[49] Elias enjoyed a

---

[46]   *Bottisham Village & Church.*

[47]   William Illingworth and John Caley (eds), *Rotuli Hundredorum Temp. Hen. III. & Edw. I.*, vol. 2, Record Commission (London: printed by George Eyre and Andrew Strahan, 1818), 487–90.

[48]   £3–£4 using Dyer's estimates for the incomes of the upper peasantry: Christopher Dyer, *Standards of Living in the Later Middle Ages: Social Change in England, C. 1200–1520* (Cambridge: Cambridge University Press, 1989), 115–16.

[49]   Paul Brand, 'Judges and Judging', in *Judges and Judging in the History of the Common Law and Civil Law*, ed. Paul Brand and Joshua Getzler (Cambridge: Cambridge University Press, 2012), 29.

substantial income of 40 marks a year and held several benefices across England.[50] Several were very valuable, that at Warmington, for example, was worth over £35 in the 1291 *Taxatio*.[51] His holdings in Northamptonshire may have come to over £12 and those in Lincolnshire added another couple of pounds.[52] It is conceivable that, without a family to provide for, Elias could have sponsored church building alone, with an annual gross income in the region of £70 and no children or wife to support. If entry to the knighthood was often distrained at £40 a year, this puts Elias into the top few percentiles of medieval society. Even if Robert de Vaux inherited capital from his uncle, it is unlikely that he could have afforded to single-handedly patronise a church of the size and ambition of Bottisham, with only a few pounds in landed income and no revenue, at least that we know of, from work as a lawyer, official or rector.

However, a different explanation for the financing of Bottisham nave can be found within the parish. The Bottisham peasantry, although dominated by smallholders, was typical of Cambridgeshire landholdings in as much as the social structure of the parish had preserved a small but wealthy elite of free peasants even by the end of the thirteenth century. In 1279, there was a substantial group of 13 freehold yardlanders or more, as well as many half-yardlanders.[53] Using Dyer's estimations, the average annual net income of the parish's peasants can be estimated at over £31 in total. Over a building period lasting several years it is conceivable that this select group were able to afford the construction of Bottisham's nave. In 1327, the vill had the fifteenth largest number of taxpayers in the county at 79, whose total assessment was almost £6, in the top 30.[54] Indeed in the early fourteenth century there were other non-manorial lay families with larger holdings than Elias's. Thomas Bendish (fl. 1325–35) acquired 100 acres in 1329, and was succeeded by John Bendish (fl. 1335–50), who had 120 acres

---

[50]   John Sainty, *The Judges of England 1272–1990: A List of Judges of the Superior Courts*, Selden Society Supplementary Series 10 (London: Selden Society, 1993), 20–21.

[51]   Thomas Astle, Samuel Ayscough, and John Caley (eds), *Taxatio Ecclesiastica Angliae Et Walliae, Auctoritate P. Nicholai IV, circa 1291* (London: Printed by G. Eyre and A. Strahan, 1802), 39.

[52]   Bridges, *The History and Antiquities of Northamptonshire*, 2:496.

[53]   Illingworth and Caley, *Rotuli Hundredorum*, 2:487–90.

[54]   J.J. Muskett, 'Lay Subsidies, Cambridgeshire, I Edward III (1327)', *East Anglian Notes and Queries*, New Series, X–XII (August 1903); cf. Robin E. Glasscock, *The Lay Subsidy of 1334*, Records of Social and Economic History, New Series 2 (London: Published for the British Academy by Oxford University Press, 1975); Mary Hesse, 'The Lay Subsidy of 1327', in *An Atlas of Cambridgeshire and Huntingdonshire History*, ed. Tony Kirby and Susan Oosthuizen (Cambridge: Centre for Regional Studies, Anglia Polytechnic University, 2000).

by 1351.[55] There were other members of the upper peasantry, men like William, son of Richard Clici, and John de Longo, with substantial holdings and probably significant annual incomes but who could not lay claim to yeoman status. Perhaps, at Bottisham, it is their biographies which would offer the most important insights into the motivations that drove church building. There is considerable evidence for the collaborative patronage of parochial architecture in England in the later Middle Ages.[56] Perhaps the best known example is at Bodmin, Cornwall, in 1469–72, where 451 names are recorded as subscribers to the church's building fund, largely drawn from the wealthiest echelons of the parish.[57] This collection may have been the largest example for which documentary evidence survives but it is not unusual and many other instances of collaborative fundraising among wealthy peasantry or townsfolk survive elsewhere, albeit largely drawn from the fifteenth century or later.

A very small amount of 'biographical' information does survive about the wealthier male Bottisham peasants. John de Longo had two virgates and leased several other small plots; William had one virgate, other small plots, and at least one subtenant. These men were not only individually wealthy; they also exhibit a range of holdings which suggest an entrepreneurial approach to acquiring and leasing new land holdings. It is likely the small plots of land were purchased from poorer neighbours in order to grow cash crops, sub-let or pass on to non-inheriting sons.[58] Little other information about their lives survives but it is possible to illustrate the biographical details which may have enabled them to engage in architectural patronage.

Many peasants owed their large holdings of a yardland or more to ancestors who had been prevented from alienating fractions of them by strong lordship. Some, however, like Richard and William, were entrepreneurial and invested the profits of commercial farming in land.[59] As free tenants, it is revealing that

[55] Hailstone, *The History and Antiquities of the Parish of Bottisham*, 89; Wareham and Wright, *VCH Cambridgeshire*, 10:215–20.

[56] These examples are surveyed in my doctoral thesis: Byng, 'Planning and Paying for Parish Church Construction in the Later Middle Ages', chap. 6.

[57] Transcripts can be found here: A.R. Myers, *English Historical Documents 1327–1485*, vol. 4 (Oxford: Routledge, 1969), 741; J. J. Wilkinson, *Receipts and Expenses in Building Bodmin Church, 1469–1472* (London: Camden Society, 1874); Gerald Randall, *The English Parish Church* (London: Spring, 1988), 46.

[58] Bruce M.S. Campbell, 'The Agrarian Problem in the Early Fourteenth Century', *Past & Present* 188, no. 1 (8 January 2005): 46–8.

[59] Janet Williamson, 'Norfolk: Thirteenth Century', in *The Peasant Land Market in Medieval England*, ed. P.D.A. Harvey (Oxford: Oxford University Press, 1984), 70–76; John Hatcher, *Rural Economy and Society in the Duchy of Cornwall, 1300–1500* (Cambridge: Cambridge University Press, 1970), 98; Zvi Razi, 'Family, Land and the Village Community in Later Medieval England', *Past & Present*, no. 93 (1 November 1981): 5.

they were still in command of such large acreages at the end of the thirteenth century, after decades of fragmentation of peasant holdings in Cambridgeshire and across much of England. Their ability to turn their holdings to a profit depended on access to reliable regional markets, good harvests and weather, high agricultural prices, and low wages.[60] The upper peasantry enjoyed several advantages – they could employ commercial strategies to produce cash crops for market, plant high yielding crops suited to their locality, competitively market grain to sell during periods of high prices, and had access to substantial cheap wage labour.[61] This meant they could raise and hoard quantities of money, vital for paying wages and purchasing materials for building projects. The leading peasants can be found loaning money, leasing land, employing their neighbours, owning sheep and cattle, and trading in local and regional markets. Bottisham was just seven miles from Cambridge, home of a market which traded with Europe and several fairs of which one, Stourbridge, was of exceptional size. In the fifteenth century, half of the grain grown in one Bottisham manor was being sold in Cambridge and Swaffham.[62] The village had its own weekly market on Mondays, owned by the Earl of Gloucester.[63] The upland had fertile clay soils well suited to producing wheat, rye, barley and dredge, but the parish also had substantial meadow and pasture common land, although villagers complained it was being annexed to private estates and overused.[64] Several villagers set up illegal sheep folds in the 1330s.[65] Increases in the cost of living could be offset by high sales prices obtained through regional markets and pastoral husbandry.[66]

The upper peasantry, often with their own employees, would also have had the most free time and energy to devote to managing building work, a time consuming task requiring skills in accounting and administration. Those best suited would have had experience in office, as jurors, coroners, chief pledges, ale tasters, beadles and haywards or reeves, taking decisions about crop cultivation and organising common fields or the collective payment of tax and seigniorial

---

[60] R.H. Britnell, *The Commercialisation of English Society, 1000–1500*, 2nd edn, Manchester Medieval Studies (Manchester: Manchester University Press, 1996), 120–23.

[61] Joel Mokyr, *The Lever of Riches: Technological Creativity and Economic Progress: Technological Creativity and Economic Progress* (Oxford: Oxford University Press, 1992), 32.

[62] Wareham and Wright, *VCH Cambridgeshire*, 10:215–20.

[63] William Illingworth, George Eyre, and Andrew Strahan (eds), *Placita de Quo Warranto Temporibus Edw. I. II. & III* (London: Printed by George Eyre and Andrew Strahan, 1818), 100.

[64] Illingworth and Caley, *Rotuli Hundredorum*, 2:484; Hailstone, *The History and Antiquities of the Parish of Bottisham*, 248–9.

[65] Wareham and Wright, *VCH Cambridgeshire*, 10:215–20.

[66] Kathleen Biddick, 'Missing Links: Taxable Wealth, Markets, and Stratification among Medieval English Peasants', *The Journal of Interdisciplinary History* 18, no. 2 (1 October 1987): 287.

dues. The village would be familiar with them taking a leadership role in matters of finance, while they would have a good idea how much each of their contemporaries would be able to contribute based on their role in distributing the taxation burden within the vill (at least after 1334). Once they had proved themselves in these roles, and acquired the requisite skills, they would be trustworthy and competent candidates for the supervision of a major parochial project involving communal funds. It was often members of this group who had run maintenance work as churchwardens and had access to sources of materials, contractors, suppliers and local labourers. By the mid-thirteenth century the upper peasantry also had experience in commissioning high quality houses.[67]

The productive unit, and so a primary factor limiting the ability of peasants to donate to building work, was the household, including both family members and other employees and dependents. Children were a drain on household finances for the first years of their life but they were eventually able to contribute their labour to the family holdings, allowing for a saving to be made on the use of hired workers. A household's most profitable situation would be once the children had grown enough to reduce labour costs but before they wished to marry and farm their own land. Parcels of land might eventually have to be passed out to enable children to set up their own families. Parents were no doubt motivated by the desire to accumulate as much land, capital and property as possible to pass on to their heirs; conversely those without heirs had less motive to stockpile goods and may have made the most willing donors to pious works.

The substantial tenants of Bottisham provide a plausible alternative to Elias or Robert de Vaux as architectural patrons, but we can go further in suggesting the biographical details that would enable the leading peasants in the parish to contribute to building work. Primarily they were members of a small, free elite with substantial holdings, probably of at least a yardland and sometimes much more, perhaps with some small help from the remainder of the parish's tenantry, although it is unlikely that individually they could contribute more than a few pence. The leading peasants were entrepreneurial, understood how to invest and increase their profits through employing commercial strategies in farming, sub-letting land and investing in larger holdings, and owning livestock – these were activities that generated skills useful in running an efficient building operation. The wealthiest were probably in their middle age, old enough to have children able to contribute to the family's income but young enough to work their own land and not rely on waged labour. They probably held enough land to generate a substantial net surplus, perhaps of a pound or more.[68] Those with

---

[67]   Christopher Dyer, 'English Peasant Building in the Later Middle Ages', *Medieval Archaeology* 30 (1986): 19–45; Christopher Dyer, 'History and Vernacular Architecture', *Vernacular Architecture* 28, no. 1 (1 June 1997): 1–8.

[68]   Dyer, *Standards of Living*, 115–16.

the greatest expendable wealth had increased their holdings but had stopped seeking to invest profits in new land. Of this group those who would have had the greatest motivation for contributing to church construction were probably those without heirs. It is harder to generalise about the relative importance of civic pride, religiosity, piety or generosity, no doubt important motivators, but ones which do not explicitly appear in the documentary record. It might be added, tentatively, that those who gave the most were also those who looked to impress their neighbours, secure the future of their soul after death, and were naturally generous.

Even these highly speculative circumstances are of less significance for the financing of church building than the capacity of individuals to cooperate as a group. Raising the money for a major building project would have required an exceptional level of cooperation between parishioners in the higher levels of local society. Intra-group cooperation has been well studied and it is the upper peasantry who appear most often, taking on burdensome roles in village life and supporting one another in court even as they fell out over crimes and antisocial behaviour.[69] Those with the most expendable income, such as Longo and Clici in Bottisham, were also those with greatest experience in collaborating to run village affairs – skills and experience which could be transferred to financing church building. In 1389 seven gilds were recorded in the parish, several long standing, and they may have been critical in motivating individual gifts and transforming them into corporate expenditure, as well as providing experienced administrators and even managerial structures. Perhaps the most interesting example of cooperation that the Bottisham evidence suggests is between the tenants, who provided much of the funding, and Elias or Robert de Vaux, whose connections may have been necessary to find a high quality mason.

Donors to the church during the Middle Ages were varied: Elizabeth de Burgh (d. 1327) gave 50s and gold cloth (possibly a cloak)[70] while the arms of William Grey (Bishop of Ely 1454–78) and Clare, Earl of Gloucester, the

---

[69] As in the (much criticised) work of the Toronto School: DeWindt, *Land and People*, 217–20; Edward Britton, *The Community of the Vill: A Study in the History of the Family and Village Life in Fourteenth-Century England* (Toronto: Macmillan of Canada, 1977), 70–86; Anne Reiber DeWindt and Edwin Brezette DeWindt, *Ramsey: The Lives of an English Fenland Town, 1200–1600* (Washington, D.C.: Catholic University of America Press, 2006), 94; but cf. Zvi Razi, 'The Toronto School's Reconstitution of Medieval Peasant Society: A Critical View', *Past & Present*, no. 85 (1 November 1979): 147.

[70] J. Nichols (ed.), *A Collection of the Wills Now Known to Be Extant of the Kings and Queens of England*, Society of Antiquaries (London: Printed by J. Nichols, printer to the Society of Antiquaries, 1780), 33; Hailstone incorrectly gives the page reference 32: Hailstone, *The History and Antiquities of the Parish of Bottisham*, 32.

manorial overlord, were found in the chancel's windows.[71] Villagers who owned land on the Anglesey estate[72] and who were members of Corpus Christi guild in 1351 also donated money.[73] The inventory carried out by the Archdeacon of Ely lists gifts of liturgical implements by Andrew Car, William Marshal (Marescalli), William le Hert, Robert de Southham, and William Gode.[74] Brasses may include mayors of Lynn and other civilians,[75] an altar tomb has been identified as that of William Allington (d. 1479), whose eponymous ancestor endowed a chantry in the church in 1404, while the south, and probably the north, aisles both housed altars.[76] The body of a priest was found buried in one of the recesses in the wall of the south aisle.[77] This varied, but not unusual, range of donors is consistent with the impression of collaborative architectural and artistic patronage that stretches across social groupings.

Conclusion

The biographical details of Elias de Beckingham or Robert de Vaux offer interesting opportunities to integrate architectural patronage with the personality, ambitions and experience of contemporary individuals. The 'meaning' of the construction of a large-scale and sophisticated new nave at Bottisham changes substantially as the financing of the fabric and choice of design is set in the context of different potential patrons, while the light it sheds on the biography of each individual is similarly ambiguous. Even for Elias, whose career and income can be quite clearly established, any interpretation of his motivations, let alone taste, is still highly speculative.

Quite different challenges and opportunities occur when the same building is recast, plausibly, as an act of peasant patronage. Although the amount of biographical detail reduces significantly, by following the distribution of wealth, office holding and patterns of cooperation, it is possible to argue not only that the upper peasantry (probably those with a yardland or more) were deeply involved in parish church construction but also to suggest the circumstances

---

[71]   John Layer and William Cole, *Monumental Inscriptions and Coats of Arms from Cambridgeshire*, ed. William Mortlock Palmer (Cambridge: Bowes and Bowes, 1932).

[72]   Samuel Sandars, *An Annotated List of Books Printed on Vellum to Be Founded in the University and College Libraries at Cambridge* (Cambridge: Printed for the Cambridge Antiquarian Society, 1871).

[73]   Mary Bateson and William Cunningham, *Cambridge Gild Records* (Cambridge: Printed for the Cambridge antiquarian society, 1903), 37.

[74]   Feltoe and Minns, *Vetus Liber*, 49.

[75]   Hailstone, *The History and Antiquities of the Parish of Bottisham*, 36.

[76]   Ibid., 19–21.

[77]   Hailstone, *The History and Antiquities of the Parish of Bottisham*, 29–30.

in many peasants' lives which governed their ability to donate. In revealing the 'biography' of an optimal peasant patron in the early fourteenth century we can postulate a comparatively wealthy, entrepreneurial, middle-aged peasant with several holdings acquired over his life time, probably adding up to at least a yardland, and numerous sub-tenants. He may have had no heirs or at least grown children, substantial experience in holding office (perhaps including that of churchwarden) and familiarity with cooperating with other wealthy tenants to organise common fields or oppose the exactions of the manor. Depending on regional topography, he may have owned livestock, or grown cash crops for commercial sale, probably at large, regional markets where news of architectural developments would be discussed and skilled mason contractors hired. The religious, civic and personal motivations which encouraged such generosity are uncertain in gentry patronage but are even more mysterious for a conjectural peasant patron. Nevertheless, his involvement in the life of the church and its guilds may have been critical, as were his instinctive generosity, personal piety, and social aspiration. The role of his wife and household, both in providing sufficient income for the work and in motivating or consenting to the donation, would have been essential. This fictional type was not exclusively responsible for architectural patronage of course – in the vast majority of cases wealthy peasant patrons would need the assistance of others, older and younger, poorer and less experienced. Nevertheless, these circumstances are likely to have constricted their ability to donate, making them atypical but not uncommon.

Does all this make any great claim for the importance of biography in understanding parish church construction? The "biographies" of Elias and the de Vauxs facilitate interesting, if problematic, interpretations of medieval church building projects. The two men, particularly the former, provide for interesting studies in their own right and the building work might contribute to either. Any interpretation is, of necessity, highly ambiguous and speculative, however, even as it promises to add far more to our understanding of their character than the outlines of their careers and landholdings could. The more radical proposal is to place not only the peasantry as a group but also individual peasants in a position of prominence in the patronage of parish church construction. The plausibility of any fictional composite is difficult to determine, and inevitably disputable but it offers the only real way in most localities in which individual peasants can be understood as contributing to parish church construction and a useful device for asking further questions about collaborative building projects from an era with little documentary evidence.

Chapter 12

Writing Community: the Opportunities and Challenges of Group Biography in the Case of Wilton Abbey

Kathryn Maude

'*Sic apum ac formicarum studio feruebant in edificio celestis Ierusalem examina uirginum*' [Following the example of the bees and ants, the swarms of virgins were eagerly industrious in building the heavenly Jerusalem].[1]

In the quotation at the head of this chapter, taken from his *Legend of Edith*, Goscelin of St Bertin constructs the nuns of Wilton as a collective – an '*examina uirginum*' – working together towards the establishment of the heavenly city. Much history writing takes its cue from Goscelin's description and considers the nuns as a group with a collective narrative, bearing witness to the social nature of their lives. This social focus is important: treating nuns as individuals does not do justice to their communal lives, and Goscelin's descriptions of the nuns of Wilton make it clear that they did have a sense of themselves as a group. However, focusing on the nuns of Wilton as an intentional community – made up of individuals who chose to join the abbey – means omitting much of the evidence about their lives that might contest this claim. It therefore obscures many of the interactions taking place within Wilton Abbey; after all, the 'heavenly Jerusalem' at Wilton was not built by 'swarms of virgins' alone.

Reorienting this biography from a focus on the intentional community of nuns at Wilton Abbey to a focus on Wilton Abbey as a place allows us to recognise that the nuns are not the sole inhabitants of the abbey. There are also builders, clerics, saints, secular women and so on – revolving around and required by the intentional community of nuns at Wilton Abbey. The existence of this *un*intentional community is causally dependent on the existence of the nuns at Wilton. Centring our analysis on the nuns means that we come into the research with pre-conceived ideas about who has agency at the abbey. By shifting the focus to Wilton Abbey as a place, everyone who comes into contact

---

[1]   Goscelin of St Bertin, 'Legend of Edith', in *Writing the Wilton Women: Goscelin's Legend of Edith and Liber confortatorius*, ed. Stephanie Hollis (Brepols: Turnhout, 2004), 36. All following references to this text will be to this edition and cited in parentheses in the text.

with Wilton is necessarily a part of the story, which avoids making one group of people the entitled possessors of the abbey.

Focusing on interactions with Wilton c. 1050–1100, this chapter will show how thinking about Wilton as a place that is inhabited by both intentional and unintentional community members allows us to gain an understanding of the culture of the abbey. It is of course the case that different individuals and groups will have different levels of affective relationship with the abbey; I am not suggesting that all interactions with Wilton were of equal intensity. However, widening the focus of the biography to include everyone who came into contact with Wilton enables us to recognise both strong affective communal relationships and more fleeting, complex or contradictory responses.

The actions and lives of the unintentional members of the Wilton community had real and important effects on the intentional community of nuns. I will concentrate on three sets of concerns brought out by the sources on Wilton in the period 1050–1100: the efficacy and necessity of saintly intercession in aid of Wilton; Wilton's loss of land and wealth, and the attempts to mitigate these losses; and the porous nature of Wilton and the inability to control who enters the place and who leaves. This final concern – the failure to enforce the boundaries of the abbey – brings into question quite how 'intentional' the intentional community of nuns is. I will tentatively entertain the idea that, rather than an intentional and unintentional community, what we are in fact dealing with at Wilton Abbey is a community with intentional and unintentional elements. As will also become clear, underlying all of Wilton's concerns is a reality of uncertainty and impotence, which complicates the picture of a stable and continuous self-secure community of nuns at the abbey. At each point, widening the focus from the nuns of Wilton to encompass unintentional members of the Wilton community highlights a number of anxieties on the part of the nuns that would otherwise have been obscured.

Wilton Abbey and Sources

A biography of Wilton Abbey as a place, focusing on both intentional and unintentional community members, allows us to incorporate very different types of evidence into one narrative. I have chosen to focus on Wilton between 1050 and 1100 because there is a range of evidence about its inhabitants, including saints' lives commissioned by the community, and letters to its inhabitants and ex-inhabitants. Taking evidence of land grants, the dreams of nuns, and descriptions of the abbey's fabric and attempting to tell one story is, I believe, the only way we will come close to discovering what life was like at Wilton Abbey.

The early history of Wilton Abbey is somewhat obscure. The traditions of the nuns recorded in the fifteenth century *Chronicon Vilodunense* state that

Weohstan, an ealdorman, founded a chantry on the site before 800 and his widow Alburga had it converted into a house for nuns after his death. King Alfred then founded another house for women in Wilton around 890, and the two nunneries merged.[2] The period of interest for this chapter begins around 960, when Wulfthryth was elected abbess on her return to Wilton from King Edgar's court. She remained abbess for around forty years, until 1000. Her daughter Edith, who returned to Wilton with her mother, died young and after her translation came to be revered as a saint. I discuss these women for two reasons. Firstly, their lives were written in the latter half of the eleventh century and so provide extensive information on Wilton in that period. Secondly, Edith and Wulfthryth appear repeatedly at Wilton after their deaths, between 1050 and 1100. As I will show, the fact of their deaths is in some ways immaterial; as former nuns separated from Wilton in death but still very much present, they complicate the division of the community into intentional and unintentional members.

Our main source of information about Wulfthryth and Edith, and their connections with Wilton, is the *Legend of Edith*, written by Goscelin of St Bertin between 1080 and 1082 at the request of the Wilton nuns. The *Legend* tells the story of Edith from her arrival at the abbey with her mother up to her death in 984, and then describes her translation and the miracles that she performed. Although the nuns commissioned Goscelin to write the life of Edith, Stephanie Hollis suggests that her mother Wulfthryth was at least as important to Wilton, and Wulfthryth's life and miracles make up a large part of Edith's *Legend*.[3] Goscelin's narrative draws heavily on the testimony of the nuns and as such is an important source for Wilton in the second half of the eleventh century, as well as the earlier lives of Edith and Wulfthryth.

It seems that when Goscelin was asked to write the *Legend* he was already well known to the nuns, as he came to Wilton in the company of Bishop Herman of Sherborne in the 1070s. After Herman's death, Goscelin was forced to leave Wiltshire as he made an enemy of the new bishop. However, during Bishop Herman's lifetime, Goscelin met Eve, a nun at Wilton, and they formed (by his account) a close friendship. When she left Wilton to become a recluse in France he wrote the *Liber confortatorius* for her, in which he explained how much he missed her and hoped for their reunion in heaven. The *Liber confortatorius* is critical evidence for a group biography of Wilton as it includes

---

[2] See W.F. Nijenhuis, 'The Wilton Chronicle as a Historical Source', *Revue Bénédictine* 115.2 (2005): 370–99 for more information on the *Chronicon Vilodunense*.

[3] Stephanie Hollis, 'Strategies of Emplacement and Displacement: St Edith and the Wilton Community in Goscelin's Legend of Edith and Liber confortatorius', in *A Place to Believe in: Locating Medieval Landscapes*, ed. Clare Lees and Gillian R. Overing (Pennsylvania State University Press: University Park, PA., 2006), 156.

much information concerning the comings and goings at Wilton when Goscelin visited Eve at the abbey.

Another source for Wilton comes from *The Life of King Edward who Rests at Westminster*, a semi-hagiographical text commissioned by Queen Edith in praise of her deceased husband Edward the Confessor. This text includes a description of Edith's involvement with Wilton, from her education there as a young girl to her return in adulthood, when her position at court became difficult because of the conflict between her family and her husband the king. Alongside these narratives, Anselm's letters to Gunhild, a Wilton nun, and Queen Matilda, who was brought up at Wilton, add to our knowledge about the abbey in this period. In addition to these sources, Domesday Book evidence can also be used to investigate the economic position of Wilton and its inhabitants. Although there are not many charters extant from Wilton in this period, the Domesday Book evidence shows the movement of land from Wilton to Norman beneficiaries. I use all of these sources in this chapter to demonstrate how a biography focused on a community in place can be written.

Saintly Intercession

One of the main concerns at Wilton between c.1050 and 1100 was the intercessory power of the local saints, Edith and Wulfthryth. In Goscelin's *Legend of Edith*, the nuns repeatedly question Edith's ability to intercede for them, and this lack of faith in Edith is only resolved by visions of her present in the physical space of Wilton. Both St Edith and St Wulfthryth interact with Wilton corporeally – they appear in their tombs at Wilton or in specific places around the abbey, and when they are not present, items they owned are venerated and their tombs perform miracles in their stead. They intercede in the day-to-day business of the abbey, helping to choose the next abbess and appearing regularly to the nuns in dreams and visions. The nuns' insistence on Edith and Wulfthryth's physical presence at Wilton in the visions that they experience suggests that in order to have an effective relationship with Wilton – that is, to intercede effectively for the nuns and lay people in their struggles – the saints have to be available to them at Wilton rather than far from them in heaven. Writing a biography of the Wilton community through the lens of place calls attention to the fact that Edith and Wulfthryth's deaths merely alter their role in the Wilton community, and not their attachment to it or agency within it. The nuns see Edith and Wulfthryth in the abbey in physical form, and so they are still involved in the abbey's community. In this way the saints trouble the boundaries between intentional and unintentional members of the community at Wilton. As nuns who chose to live there in life, they demonstrate an intentional commitment to the abbey, but are separated from that intentional community by their deaths. This crossover provides them with an authoritative position from which to intervene in the abbey's politics.

Rather than the certainty of a community comfortable in its patron saints, the nuns have an anxious and uncertain relationship with their saintly intercessors. Nuns at Wilton repeatedly complained about Edith's intercessory capabilities, particularly in relation to physical sickness and the safeguarding of Wilton's lands. Goscelin records their complaints of 'abandonment' by their saintly patron. In the *Legend of Edith*, these complaints are resolved only through Edith's physical presence to the nuns. Goscelin notes that she appears: 'Not only in corporeal sights and external miracle working, but she is also radiantly visible to the spiritual eyes of pure minds, and is observed to pass among the sisters as if still present in her body' (87). When a group of nuns complain about Edith's inability to remove a 'debilitating epidemic' from the abbey, Edith appears to them 'exhorting them in a vision as if physically present' and promises that the nuns of Wilton are her 'special care' (89–90).

Goscelin relates one instance of the nuns' dissatisfaction with their patron saint, which he witnessed himself. While dining at Salisbury with the nun Ealdgyth of Wilton, she began complaining about the erosion of Wilton's possessions. She then 'defamed St Edith: she had no power from God since she suffered so great a wrong without retaliation, and had not defended her own cause with the deserved intervention' (90). At Wilton later that night, a nun named Thola is woken by St Edith:

> The golden chapel of the holy clay opened at her feet; inside, the royal virgin was seen lying at rest as if on a glorious bridal bed, splendid with adornments, and a spectacle of shining beauty. Then she addressed the woman who looked at her. 'Why', she said, 'did Ealdgyth say lately that I can do nothing? Look at my hands, and the services rendered by my virtues, what control I have, how efficacious, generous, energetic and strong I am; indeed, whatever I wish I can do, by divine power (90).

Edith resolves the doubts about her efficacy by appearing to Thola in her tomb, exposing her physical body and commanding Thola to 'look at my hands'. Edith's physical presence in the abbey is the proof of her miracle-working potential; the community's concerns about Edith's power, here expressed by Ealdgyth, can only be resolved by a saintly intercessor who remains with them in body as well as in spirit. When the nuns at Wilton have visions of Edith and Wulfthryth, they are seen coming out of their tombs in the abbey church. The placement of the saints in the church is described precisely by Goscelin, combining his own knowledge of the place with the description of the nun who experienced the vision. Both the timing and frequency of Edith and Wulfthryth's appearances at Wilton leave no doubt as to the importance of their presence at the abbey.

The narrative of the abbey for the historian, then, cannot be complete without Edith and Wulfthryth as post-mortem actors in place at Wilton, interacting with the nuns.

The presence of Edith and Wulfthryth at Wilton as effective intercessors also allows for their intervention in the politics of the abbey. Brought in by the *Regularis Concordia*, the new practice of choosing an abbess from within the community provoked tensions at Wilton and, as Barbara Yorke suggests, 'the idea of election of an abbess by the community was sufficiently novel as to require saintly endorsement.'[4] The position of Edith and Wulfthryth as sanctified insiders – former members of the intentional community of nuns but removed from it by death – allows them to intervene in the choice of abbess. Ælfhild, a 'worthy and famous lady of Wilton' sees Edith:

> descending the stairs from the bridal chamber of her dormition to the tomb of her mother, going on foot to a place on the right-hand side, where Ælfgifu stood in supplication; Saint Edith took the veil from her own head and put it on Ælfgifu's and also put a ring on her finger and addressed her thus: Accept the blessing of this monastery and take faithful care of all this family; for you will be the ruler of this house in prosperity, but indeed you will last only a short time; however when you die you will be buried in peace in this place which I have measured out beside my mother (88).

Edith does not appear beside Ælfhild; she has to leave her tomb ('the bridal chamber of her dormition') and walk down the stairs to the tomb of her mother. Ælfhild notes specifically that Edith travels 'on foot'; she has a bodily connection with the ground beneath her. Being physically present in the space, Edith can interact with Ælfgifu on the same plane, placing her veil onto Ælfgifu's head. This physical connection between Edith and Ælfgifu has practical as well as symbolic import: Edith passes on the symbol of her spiritual purity, the veil, to Ælfgifu and thus shows her to be her successor in piety. Ælfgifu herself has a similar vision of Edith, in which Edith puts 'her bracelets and armbands on [Ælfgifu], and her own veil' (88). Again, there is a physical translation of objects from one body to the next; the veil is conferred upon Ælfgifu to show that she is worthy to inhabit her new role as abbess.

Wulfthryth also intervenes in the choice of Ælfgifu for abbess. Goscelin reports that 'the lady Wulfthryth was seen by [Ælfgifu], lying in the Gabriel Chapel above the altar, most splendidly dressed, and she invited Ælfgifu to lie beside her; and when she cried out that she was unworthy, Wulfthryth grasped her and placed her beside her' (88). Again, Wulfthryth is in a specific place within the

---

[4]   Barbara Yorke, *Nunneries and the Anglo-Saxon Royal Houses* (Continuum: London, 2003), 88.

abbey – lying above the altar – and is physically present to Ælfgifu, to the extent that she is able to grasp her arm and pull her down beside her. Here Wulfthryth places Ælfgifu within the tradition of Wilton abbesses by pulling Ælfgifu into line with her, foreshadowing her eventual burial beside Wulfthryth. As Edith was never in fact the abbess of Wilton, visions of her would not automatically make Ælfgifu a candidate for the abbacy. However, Edith's transference of her adornments to Ælfgifu provides spiritual authority, and this combines with the spiritual and practical authority shown by Wulfthryth placing Ælfgifu in line with her as her successor.

It is clear from these passages that the nuns at Wilton were anxious about Edith's ability to intercede in their lives in a way that could only be resolved through continuous reminders of her physical presence at Wilton. What is more, the nuns believed Edith and Wulfthryth were physically present at Wilton and capable of intervening in day-to-day life at the abbey. Writing about Wilton as a place, and not solely as an intentional community of nuns, allows us to take this saintly agency at face-value and better capture both the experience of living at Wilton, and the experience of saintly intervention. Goscelin's *Legend of Edith*, as well as showing the devotion to Edith at Wilton, also betrays the anxiety surrounding the possibility of her saintly intercession.

Wilton's Land and Wealth

Land and wealth were of great concern to Wilton between 1050 and 1100. Focusing on Wilton as a place allows us to think about land loss both as economic fact and emotional affliction. The intentional community of nuns living at the abbey have little power over their own space: it is the actions of unintentional community members that determine what will happen to Wilton Abbey. Comparing narrative sources with Domesday evidence builds a picture of both land loss by the abbey and the effect of this loss of land on life at Wilton. The *Legend of Edith* shows the affective responses in visions to the worries about land retention and wealth, whereas the Domesday Book records the changing land ownership. Including evidence from *The Life of King Edward* provides an alternative view of Wilton as a focus for charitable giving by Queen Edith.

The problems Wilton had retaining its land are evident in Domesday Book evidence. Before 1066, Wilton lost around 65 hides of land and after 1066, 125 hides were lost.[5] The Domesday Book shows how between 1066 and 1086 Wilton fell foul of William the Conqueror's land seizures and Wilton lost much of its most valuable lands to Norman lords. This loss of land included two large

---

[5] W.F. Nijenhuis, 'The Wilton Chronicle as a Historical Source', 388–9. See also the table on pages 398–9 of the specifics of the land lost by Wilton to Norman lords.

estates: 21 hides of land at West Firle were lost to William de Warenne, and 48 hides of land at Falmer to Count Robert of Mortain. There were also smaller transfers, for example, 9 estates comprising 4.89 hides of land in total went to Count William d'Eu.[6] Yorke notes that in the Domesday Book Wilton, although wealthy for a house of nuns, 'was only the thirteenth wealthiest religious community when male and female houses are grouped together,'[7] suggesting that they could ill afford this loss of land.

In Goscelin's *Legend of Edith* the nuns have repeated visions of people being punished in the afterlife for stealing the abbey's land. As Goscelin was writing between 1080 and 1082, the focus on land loss is unsurprising, this being the period in which the abbey lost some of its most valuable landholdings. Goscelin relates two lurid stories of St Edith punishing men who take Wilton's land. During the reign of Queen Emma, a nobleman named Agamund occupies some of the abbey's land in a place called Ferelanda. After his death, he sits up, and tells his assembled relatives that Edith is hounding him in the afterlife – 'she has driven back my soul at its departure and will not allow me to stay in this body, nor to live, nor die' – for the return of her land (79–80). A similar event takes place while Godiva is abbess at Wilton (between c.1067 and 1090).[8] Brihtric, a brother of one of the nuns, takes some of the abbey's lands and dies without returning them. His sister then sees a vision of him in the afterlife begging her to hide him from St Edith, crying 'Alas! Where shall I flee, where shall I hide from her face? How terrible I see she is, how magnificent!' (81). Both of these narratives of saintly retribution show the concerns of the nuns regarding their own powerlessness in the face of land loss. It is only when St Edith intervenes that the land can be regained, and the main mechanism to stop outsiders taking land from the abbey appears to be fear of saintly retribution. In the *Legend of Edith*, Goscelin also curses those who steal ecclesiastical property, writing 'of those for whom no end of possessions and treasure is sufficient ... unless they mangle, tear at, devour, the house of God ... woe to them when God shall make them like a wheel and as stubble before the wind' (81). As a visitor to Wilton, Goscelin would have been party to the concerns of the nuns and it is no stretch to see this tirade against unscrupulous landowners as a veiled complaint against the incoming Norman lords. St Edith's attempts to hound those who took land from the abbey were only partly successful, and this lack of a material way to prevent the loss of their assets clearly preyed on the nuns' minds.

---

6   Domesday data for Wilton Abbey from *Prosopography of Anglo-Saxon England*, accessed 13 February 2014, http://domesday.pase.ac.uk/?Text_1=Wilton&qr=1&SearchFi eld_1=institution&col=c6.

7   Yorke, *Nunneries*, 87.

8   See Stephanie Hollis, 'Goscelin and the Wilton Women', in *Writing the Wilton Women: Goscelin's Legend of Edith and Liber confortatorius*, ed. Stephanie Hollis (Brepols: Turnhout, 2004), 220.

Anxiety about Wilton's wealth is also shown in the vision the nuns have concerning their deceased abbess Ælfgifu. After Ælfgifu's death, the sisters have a vision of St Edith in which she 'exhorted one of her sisters to implore her community of fellow sisters to pray very earnestly for her own Ælfgifu', as the Lord has forgiven all of her sins except one (89). Goscelin suggests that the one remaining sin St Edith has not been able to intercede for on behalf of Ælfgifu might have been her excessive hospitality. Although Goscelin is lenient – her 'hospitality itself excused' her excesses – Hollis argues that, given the background of monetary fears, Ælfgifu's hospitality 'might well have been regarded by some members of her community as a serious offence.'[9]

Queen Edith, wife of Edward the Confessor, saw Wilton's monetary problems as a chance to show charity to the abbey that educated her. The *Life of King Edward* explains that when Queen Edith returned to Wilton 'the church was still of wood' and she decided to build a stone church because 'nowhere did she believe alms better bestowed than where the weaker sex, less skilled in building, more deeply felt the pinch of poverty, and was less able by its own efforts to drive it away.'[10] Wilton is characterised here as an impoverished house unable to create its own wealth. Of course, the *Life of King Edward* was commissioned by Queen Edith and therefore attempts to show her in the best possible light, but it suggests that there were at least some people who saw Wilton as impoverished enough to need assistance. Catherine Karkov points out that this charitable giving was not gratefully accepted by the nuns, explaining that the *Legend of Edith*, despite being written after the building of Queen Edith's stone chapel, fails to mention its existence. Karkov argues that this lack of enthusiasm for the new chapel may have stemmed from issues with land, stating that 'it may be that Edith's retention of her lands after the Conquest did not sit well alongside the abbey's losses.'[11]

Considering all of these sources it is clear that between 1050 and 1100 Wilton was a prosperous abbey, although much less prosperous in 1100 than in 1050. Much of its valuable land was lost after the Norman Conquest, but it still retained 255 hides of land in 28 separate estates by 1086. The nuns felt the loss of this land keenly, both lamenting that their patron saint Edith had abandoned them and experiencing visions of Edith punishing landholders who

---

[9]   Stephanie Hollis, 'St Edith and the Wilton Community', in *Writing the Wilton Women: Goscelin's Legend of Edith and Liber confortatorius*, ed. Stephanie Hollis (Brepols: Turnhout, 2004), 253.

[10]   Frank Barlow (ed. and trans.), *The Life of King Edward who Rests at Westminster* (Thomas Nelson and Sons: Edinburgh and London, 1962), 47.

[11]   Catherine E. Karkov, 'Pictured in the Heart: the Ediths at Wilton', in *Intertexts: Studies in Anglo-Saxon Culture presented to Paul E. Szarmach*, ed. Virginia Blanton and Helene Scheck, Medieval and Renaissance Texts and Cultures, Vol. 334 (ACMRS: Tempe, 2008), 283.

had taken the abbey's land. Queen Edith's act of charity towards Wilton was not remembered with gratitude, possibly because she had managed to retain her lands after the Conquest and Wilton had not. Group biography of a community in place enables us to create narratives about existence in a certain place at a certain time from disparate sources and, as I have shown here, explore both the factual and affective aspects of a theme such as land and wealth. Both Saint Edith and Queen Edith were not members of the intentional community of nuns between 1050 and 1100, yet it is through concentrating on them and their interactions at Wilton that we can understand the nuns' anxieties over their land and wealth.

Enclosure

Enclosure is a site of anxiety for the nuns at Wilton between 1050 and 1100. Concentrating on both intentional and unintentional community members allows for a fuller picture of enclosure at the abbey. The letters Anselm wrote to women after they left Wilton can be compared with the evidence in Goscelin's *Legend of Edith* and *Liber confortatorius* as well as the descriptions of Edith's relationship with Wilton in the *Life of King Edward who rests at Westminster*. Reading one of these sources in isolation would suggest that the woman mentioned was an anomaly; by looking at them comparatively we begin to discern general trends about enclosure at Wilton between 1050 and 1100. Considering Wilton in this light means that the boundaries between the intentional community of nuns – stable and settled at Wilton – and the unintentional community of women and men surrounding the abbey – free to come and go as they wished – begin to break down.

One aspect of the Wilton evidence that leads us to reconsider enclosure at Wilton is the regular visits by men to the abbey. Bishop Herman came to Wilton often; Goscelin reminds Eve of how 'our bishop greeted you with his fatherly embrace',[12] suggesting he was an intimate of the nuns and visited the abbey regularly before his death in 1078. Goscelin himself visits Eve regularly before 1078, remembering how he 'used to come often to conversations with [her]', although sometimes he 'returned frustrated'.[13] This suggests that he was not always allowed to see Eve, although the reasons for this are unclear from his account; perhaps they were becoming too close. As mentioned above, Queen Edith financed a church building programme and there were male builders on site to complete this.[14] The

---

[12] Goscelin of St Bertin, 'Liber confortatorius', in *Writing the Wilton Women: Goscelin's Legend of Edith and Liber confortatorius*, ed. Stephanie Hollis (Brepols: Turnhout, 2004), 104.

[13] Goscelin, 'Liber confortatorius', 104.

[14] Barlow, *Life of King Edward*, 46.

presence of men on site while building this chapel is also evidenced in the *Legend of Edith*. Both laymen and priests, then, were a part of the unintentional community of Wilton Abbey, able to visit relatively freely and interact with the nuns and other women. The nuns are able to police the boundaries of Wilton to some extent, as they managed to prevent Goscelin from seeing Eve on at least one occasion, but in other situations men seem to visit the abbey without warning.

The intentional community of nuns does not even appear to have privileged access to its patron saint. In the *Legend of Edith*, Goscelin explains how a mute man named Sigeric, who was working on the building, has a vision of a woman 'advising him to keep vigil on the night preceding the feast of the nativity of St John the Baptist, before the sepulchre in the chapel where the body of the holy virgin Edith lay' (92). He manages to climb into Wilton and fall asleep in front of Edith's tomb, where he is cured. The boundary of the abbey is breached here, and Edith and the builder interact directly, without the involvement of the nuns themselves. Here we have two unintentional members of the Wilton community interacting without the facilitation of an intentional member of the abbey.

This freedom to enter Wilton was always potentially dangerous. In c.1093 Alan the Red arrived at the abbey and left with Gunhild, who appears to have been a professed nun.[15] Although secondary critical work predominantly suggests that Gunhild left voluntarily, Katherine O'Brien O'Keefe disputes this, arguing that Anselm's letter to Gunhild attributes agency to her that did not exist, and that Gunhild was abducted from the abbey.[16] Regardless, it is safe to say that had Gunhild wanted to resist, it probably would not have been in her power, despite Anselm's letter instructing her to 'resume the habit of monastic life', which would suggest she has the option of returning to Wilton.[17] As such,

---

[15] Stephanie Hollis, 'Wilton as a Centre of Learning', in *Writing the Wilton Women: Goscelin's Legend of Edith and Liber confortatorius*, ed. Stephanie Hollis (Brepols: Turnhout, 2004), 321.

[16] 'In order to construct Gunhild as a willing agent, Anselm draws on the master narratives of will and consent within which religious women were embedded in the early Middle Ages ... in order to imagine a Gunhild responsible for her own abduction. In doing so, he ascribes to Gunhild what I am calling a "phantom agency", an agency that has only a rhetorical existence and functions solely to indict her for collusion in her own rape', 203. See the rest of O'Keefe's article for details of the rhetorical strategies that Anselm employs. Katherine O'Brien O'Keefe, 'Leaving Wilton: Gunhild and the Phantoms of Agency', *The Journal of English and Germanic Philology* 106.2, Master Narratives of the Middle Ages (2007): 203–23.

[17] 'I advise, beg, beseech and command you by the authority which permits and obliges me to do so, to resume the habit of monastic life which you have cast off and return to the grace of God which you have spurned', in Anselm, 'Letter to Gunhilda', in *The Letters of Saint Anselm of Canterbury*, trans. Walter Fröhlich, Cistercian Studies 97, 3v (Kalamazoo: Cistercian Publications, 1990–94), 69–74.

the visions of the nuns concerning the inability of St Edith to keep them safe, discussed above, may have been well-founded, as men were able to remove women from the convent without sanction.

A similar incident involves Matilda, daughter of King Malcolm of Scotland, although in her case it is clear that she wanted to leave Wilton fervently. Matilda was only permitted to marry Henry I in 1100, after 'witnesses were found at Wilton who testified to her claim that she had never willingly worn a nun's habit but had been compelled to do so for her own protection by her aunt Christina'.[18] Queen Edith was also educated at Wilton, and regarded this as the basis of the learning that enabled her to marry Edward. The *Life of King Edward* states that at Wilton 'she had learned those virtues which deservedly made her seem suitable to become queen of the English'.[19] Throughout Edith's marriage she kept returning to Wilton for short periods. For example, in 1051 there was a conflict between King Edward and Queen Edith's brothers and Edith took refuge at Wilton. Although she returned to court after their reconciliation, she came back to Wilton in her widowhood.[20] Although Edith was not a nun, then, she had a long-term and intentional relationship with Wilton Abbey. Once again, this blurs the boundaries between nuns and other community members. It was not only highborn secular women such as Matilda and Edith who left Wilton and returned; professed nuns left too, although they tended to come back more quickly. Ealdgyth, for example, 'was a guest of Salisbury', where she sat with Bishop Herman and Goscelin at table complaining, of course, about the abbey's loss of land (Edith, 90). Goscelin does not remark on this event as unusual, so this suggests that nuns regularly left their abbey to visit others.

Eve, conversely, was a nun of Wilton who left and did not return, deciding instead to become an anchoress in Angers: 'she flees from the tumult of the world to the Lord of peace'.[21] Although this sounds like a commonplace, and indeed is repeated by Goscelin in his *Legend of Edith* when he describes Edith fleeing 'from the uproar of the world' (41) to be with her animals, it may nevertheless have been true of Eve. The trope is repeated in a poem written after Eve's death by Hilary of Orleans, who knew Eve at Angers, stating that she left the Wilton community 'abhorring that multitude like the offence of sin'.[22] Perhaps Wilton's multiple uses, as a boarding school for young ladies, as a refuge from the world of the court for queens, and as a place to put extraneous daughters until they were needed, were not entirely conducive to a close personal relationship with

---

[18]   Hollis, 'Wilton as a Centre of Learning', 322.

[19]   Barlow, *Life of King Edward*, 47. For further discussion of Queen Edith's upbringing see Hollis, 'Wilton as a Centre of Learning', 329 and Yorke, *Nunneries*, 90.

[20]   Yorke, *Nunneries*, 160.

[21]   Goscelin, 'Liber confortatorius', 99.

[22]   Hollis, 'Strategies of Emplacement and Displacement', 165.

the divine. Having chosen to be a nun at Wilton, a member of the intentional community of the abbey, Eve then changes her mind.

Bringing all of the evidence together about women who we know left the abbey in this period shows how fluid the boundaries were between the sacred and the secular, and between the intentional and unintentional members of the abbey's community. Elite women moved from one to the other, though for some this was easier than for others. Between 1050 and 1100, three women leave the convent for good, and at least two women leave the convent and return. By focusing on the unintentional elements of Wilton's community, leaving the abbey is shown to be a constant possibility; not an anomaly, but part of normal life at Wilton. This focus on the unintentional elements of community also demonstrates that the nuns at Wilton were not in control of their own space: men regularly visited seemingly without invitation, and secular women such as Queen Edith used the abbey as a bolt-hole in times of trouble.

Group Biography in Conclusion

In this group-based biography I have focused on thematic strands – saintly intercession, land and wealth, and enclosure. But how do these themes fit together, and where is each of them to be placed in the historical record? One of the main challenges of a biography that concentrates on a place, including both its intentional and unintentional community members, is the difficulty in establishing a chronology. I set out to answer the question 'what was it like to live at Wilton?' and the sketches I give are accurate, but they remain sketches rather than chronicles.

A corollary of this lack of chronology is that biography based around a place tends to be more fragmentary than a biography that focuses solely on an intentional community, whose members have chosen to be there. As every piece of information that mentions Wilton is relevant, aspects that detract from a coherent narrative remain part of the story. There is the possibility, then, that a biography with place as its primary organisational focus could descend into a series of fragments about people's lives, rather than the story of a place in time. Methodologically speaking, the process of collecting together every bit of information on Wilton from a variety of sources that refer to it can mean using a few relevant sentences from a long narrative work. For example, the short section of the *Life of King Edward* relating to Wilton is used but the rest of the text is irrelevant. Picking and choosing sections from longer works results in problems with contextualisation within texts, as the sections are only related to other works about Wilton rather than the rest of their context.

All of these problems with biographical methodology are real and require thoughtful engagement. However, the possibility of comparing very different sources and accessing both what happened and what people felt about what happened is worth the risk. I do not mean for biography focused on a community in place to replace other biographical modes, but I hope that it will complement them, allowing us to understand aspects of life in monastic settings that can be occluded by an understandable emphasis on pre-conceived groups. As I have shown, a biography that leaves space for unintentional community members as well as intentional community members highlights inconsistencies as well as the established communal narratives, allowing us to include the builder who visited Wilton once as well as the nuns who lived there all their lives. I want to finish with the words of Diane Watt: 'Rather than seeking to establish direct continuities where they do not appear to exist, we should embrace the disrupted, discontinuous, fragmentary nature of the history that has come down to us.'[23] I believe that thinking about community through the lens of people's interactions with place allows us to do just that.

---

23 Diane Watt, 'Literature in pieces: female sanctity and the relics of early women's writing', in *The Cambridge History of Early Medieval English Literature*, ed. Clare A. Lees (CUP: Cambridge, 2013), 364.

PART V
Representing Lives

Chapter 13

Hagiography as Institutional Biography: Medieval and Modern Uses of the Thirteenth-Century *Vitae* of Clare of Assisi

Kirsty Day

When Thomas Heffernan (1988) and Patrick Geary (1994) described the attitudes of their contemporary medievalists to the use of hagiography, neither of them seems to have had in mind the approaches of scholars writing in the twentieth century on the formation of the Franciscan order of nuns.[1] Heffernan asserted that hagiography had 'until recently fallen through the net of scholarly research', and that it had been 'avoided by the historians because it lacks "documentary" evidential status'.[2] Geary directly criticised Heffernan's assessment, arguing instead that '[n]ot only have hagiographic texts received frequent, close scrutiny from medievalists for years, but they have moved from the periphery to the center of the scholarly enterprise'.[3]

Had Heffernan or Geary been aware of the state of scholarship on Franciscan women, the conclusions that they reached might have been quite different. The body of primary material consulted by scholars working on Franciscan nuns throughout the twentieth century was formed largely of hagiographical texts, which such scholars seemed to have embraced as a source that they have regarded as meriting '"documentary" evidential status'. The use of hagiography in this particular field of scholarship thus evades Heffernan's appraisal. Geary's description is, however, no more fitting. Hagiography was used by scholars writing prior to, and contemporaneously with, Geary's survey – and is still used by scholars today – to create a historical narrative of the early formation of a

---

[1] Thomas Heffernan, *Sacred Biography: Saints and their Biographers in the Middle Ages* (Oxford: Oxford University Press, 1988); Patrick Geary, *Living with the Dead in the Middle Ages* (Ithaca, NY: Cornell University Press, 1994). For a more recent summary of how the relationship between hagiography and historical narrative has been understood in modern historiography see Gábor Klaniczay, 'Hagiography and Historical Narrative', in *Chronicon: Medieval Narrative Sources*, ed. János M. Bak and Ivan Jurković (Turnhout: Brepols, 2013), 111–17.

[2] Heffernan, *Sacred Biography*, 17.

[3] Geary, *Living with the Dead*, 10.

Franciscan 'second order' of nuns prior to 1218. This is a narrative for which we have no other evidence.[4] The *vitae* of Clare of Assisi (d.1253), in being treated in this way rather than according to the circumstances in which they were produced, have not received the 'close scrutiny' described by Geary. Moreover, the fact that the narratives derived from hagiographical material have become so engrained in scholarship on the Franciscan women means that hagiography does not occupy a strong position as evidence within this field by virtue of its genre. Rather, their status is derived from the fact that they have become so deeply entrenched in modern histories of the women's order, perhaps as a result of the fact that there is no other extant material that could be used to identify the origin and early development of a movement of Franciscan women.

Such histories typically begin with Clare's conversion, which took place in 1212, according, at least, to the hagiographical texts that were produced long

---

⁴ Scholars that have used Franciscan hagiography in this way include: Herbert Grundmann, *Religious Movements in the Middle Ages: The Historical Links between Heresy, the Mendicant Orders, and the Women's Religious Movement in the Twelfth and Thirteenth Century, with the Historical Foundations of German Mysticism*, trans. Stephen Rowan (Notre Dame, IN: University of Notre Dame Press, 1995), originally published as *Religiöse Bewegungen im Mittelalter: Untersuchungen über die geschichtlichen Zusammenhänge zwischen der Ketzerei, den Bettelorden und der religiösen Frauenbewegung im 12. und 13. Jahrhundert und über die geschichtlichen Grundlagen der deutschen Mystik* (Berlin: Ebering, 1935); Brenda M. Bolton, 'Mulieres Sanctae', in *Sanctity and Secularity: The Church and the World*, ed. Derek Baker, Studies in Church History 10 (Oxford: Blackwell, 1973), 77–95; Christopher N.L. Brooke and Rosalind B. Brooke, 'St. Clare', in *Medieval Women*, ed Derek Baker, Studies in Church History Subsidia 1 (Oxford: Blackwell, 1978) 275–87; Roberto Rusconi, 'The Spread of Women's Franciscanism in the Thirteenth Century', *Greyfriars Review* 12 (1998), 35–75, originally published as 'L'espansione del francescanesimo femminile nel secolo XIII', in *Movimento religioso femminile e francescanesimo nel secolo XIII: Atti del VII Convegno internazionale, Assisi, 11–13 ottobre 1979* (Assisi: Società internazionale di studi francescani, 1980), 265–313; Marco Bartoli, *Clare of Assisi*, trans. Sister Frances Teresa (Quincy, IL: Franciscan Press, 1993), originally published as *Chiara d'Assisi* (Rome: Istituto Storico dei Cappuccini, 1989); Maria Pia Alberzoni, *Clare of Assisi and the Poor Sisters in the Thirteenth Century*, ed. Jean François Godet-Calogeras, trans. Nancy Celashi and William Short (St. Bonaventure, NY: Franciscan Institute Publications, 2004), a collection of four English translations of studies published in Italian by Alberzoni between 1995 and 1998; Clara Gennaro, 'Clare, Agnes, and their Earliest Followers: From the Poor Ladies of San Damiano to the Poor Clares', in *Women and Religion in Medieval and Renaissance Italy*, ed. Daniel Bornstein and Roberto Rusconi (Chicago: University of Chicago Press, 1996), 39–55; Joan Mueller, *The Privilege of Poverty: Clare of Assisi, Agnes of Prague, and the Struggle for a Franciscan Rule for Women* (University Park: Pennsylvania State University Press, 2006); Lezlie Knox, *Creating Clare of Assisi: Female Franciscan Identities in Later Medieval Italy*, The Medieval Franciscans 5 (Leiden: Brill, 2008); Bert Roest, *Order and Disorder: The Poor Clares between Foundation and Reform* (Leiden: Brill, 2013).

after this date. It is, however, the case that the first piece of evidence for a form of penitential activity followed by groups of women who were dedicated to poverty – and, it is important to note, who were only later collectively subsumed into an order that might be described by modern scholars as 'Franciscan' – was produced in 1218. In a letter to Cardinal Hugolino of Ostia, the future Gregory IX, Honorius III instructs the cardinal to place the houses and churches built to accommodate the 'very many virgins, and other women' who wished to live without possessions under the jurisdiction of the Apostolic See.[5] However, the hagiographical material on Clare's life takes precedence as evidence for the origin of the women's order. It has wielded, and wields to this day, an extraordinary power over the scholarship that aims to reconstruct the early history of the order of Franciscan nuns.

This is not to say that this is the first study to bring this to the attention of the field. Maria Pia Alberzoni has cautioned against the interpretation of the 'delicate founding period [of the women's contingent of the order] in light of later developments.'[6] It is, then, curious that historians of the order – Alberzoni included – have continued to use, uncritically, material produced long after this period in order to substantiate the origin of the women's order. This practice is indicative not only of the power that saintly biography still possesses in a modern scholarly context, but also of the great compulsion that is felt by scholars of monasticism to find clear and definitive origin stories for the order on which they work – clear and definitive origin stories which place a saintly founder at their roots.

It should be noted, of course, that there is nothing to prove that the origin stories illustrated in the hagiographical accounts of Clare's did not 'happen', or that they were not based on source material which has since been lost. This essay is therefore not concerned with the extent to which hagiographical representations of Clare can be employed as a "reliable" source for the early chronology of the women's component of the Franciscan order, and it will not comment on the usefulness of Clare's hagiography to the search for a "historical" or "authentic" Clare.[7] Rather, it aims to cultivate an awareness of some of the problems that can

---

　　　[5]　'Litterae tuae Nobis exhibitae continebant, quod quamplures Virgines, et aliae Mulieres... desiderant fugere pompas, et divitias huius mundi, et fabricari sibi aliqua domicilia, in quibus vivant nihil possidentes sub Coelo, exceptis Domiciliis ipsis, et construendis Oratoriis in eisdem'. *Bullarium Franciscanum Romanorum pontificum constitutiones, epistolas, ac diplomata continens tribus ordinis minorum, clarissarum et poenitentium* 1, ed. Joannis Sbaralea (Rome: Sacra Congregatio de Propaganda Fide, 1759), 1.

　　　[6]　Maria Pia Alberzoni, *Clare of Assisi and the Poor Sisters in the Thirteenth Century*, 29–87 (32).

　　　[7]　Jacques Dalarun has charted the century-long quest of scholars working on Francis of Assisi's *vitae* to determine which of the *vitae* best represents the 'historical Francis', a quest known as the 'Franciscan Question'. See Jacques Dalarun, *The Misadventure of Francis*

arise when scholars write origin narratives from hagiography – origin narratives that had, in these cases, in turn been mapped by papally commissioned authors onto the saint's life for very specific purposes – into their chronologies of the nascent women's order.

In doing so, this chapter demonstrates how the authors of the *vitae* of Francis and Clare created, through their representations of Clare's life, a set of origin narratives that suited the needs of their papal commissioners, who were attempting at the time of the texts' production to carve out a uniform juridical identity for the many communities of women who desired to embrace religious poverty. Those who were responsible for shaping these women's penitential lives and finding a space for these forms of life encountered many problems in trying to do so. Using the neat narrative framework of saintly biography – and by neat, I do not mean that hagiographical narratives were not complex, but that their formulaic and episodic nature lent itself well to being shaped into clear narratives of origin – as a medium through which to create an origin story, the authors of Clare's hagiography developed a narrative that created a single point of origin for the disparate communities of women who were devoted to poverty. This was a narrative that made the development of the women's order seem more straightforward than it was. By interpreting this narrative within the contexts of its production in the thirteenth century, this chapter exposes the power that the *vitae* of saints were felt to have possessed by their thirteenth-century producers.

The two *vitae* under examination in this study are Thomas of Celano's *Life of St. Francis*, written in 1228–29, and the anonymous *vita* of Clare of Assisi, written at some point between 1253 and 1261. [8] These texts were produced during a time in which the papacy had asserted a monopoly over the canonisation

---

of Assisi: Towards a Historical Use of the Franciscan Legends, trans. Edward Hagman (St. Bonaventure, NY: Franciscan Institute Publications, 2002). This work is a translation from its original Italian, entitled *La Malavventura di Francesco d'Assisi: per un uso storico delle leggende francescane* (Milan: Edizione Biblioteca Francescana, 1996). Lezlie Knox has outlined the development in scholarship on Clare of a 'Clarian Question'. See Lezlie Knox, *Creating Clare of Assisi: Female Franciscan Identities in Later Medieval Italy*, The Medieval Franciscans, 5 (Leiden: Brill, 2008), 9–14.

[8]   There also exists a versified *legenda* of Clare's life, which was probably produced at some point before the prose *legenda*. There are great similarities in content between the two texts, and Regis J. Armstrong has suggested that the prose *legenda* was modelled on the verse *legenda*. See Regis J. Armstrong, 'The *Legenda Versificata*: Towards an Official Biography', in *Clare of Assisi: Investigations*, ed. Mary Francis Hone, Clare Centenary Series 7 (St. Bonaventure, NY: Franciscan Institute Publications, 1993), 69–93. It is thought that the text was not papally commissioned, but was instead produced as an appeal to Alexander IV for Clare's canonisation. For the purposes of this chapter, I have chosen to focus on the papally commissioned texts. This is not least because a speculative discussion of the circumstances in which the verse *legenda* was produced would exceed the spatial remit of this piece.

of saints.[9] The papacy knew the immense power that these writings possessed, as texts that dared to capture the lives of the individuals who interceded between heaven and earth. Innocent III's pontificate is often held up as a time during which the papacy's self-awareness as the sole body responsible for all mortal souls became more acute, and it is possible to see this awareness manifested in the pope's concern over the role that saintly intercession played in human salvation.[10] Canon 62 of the 1215 Fourth Lateran Council – codified in 1234 in the *Decretals* of Gregory IX – enjoined that no-one was to venerate relics that had not received papal approval.[11] Papal procedures of investigation into sanctity became increasingly formalised as the thirteenth century progressed.

---

[9]   A large body of scholarly literature exists on the development of the canonisation process and the papacy's assertion of a monopoly over canonisation during the twelfth and thirteenth centuries. See especially the following studies: Stephan Kuttner, 'La réserve papale du droit de canonisation', in *Revue historique français et étranger* 17 (1938), 172–228; Eric W. Kemp, *Canonisation and Authority in the Western Church* (Oxford: Oxford University Press, 1948); André Vauchez, *La sainteté en Occident aux derniers siècles du Moyen Age* (Rome: École française de Rome, 1981), esp. 25–37; André Vauchez, 'De la bulle *Etsi frigescente* à la décrétale *Venerabili*: L'histoire du procès de canonisation de saint Maurice de Carnoët (d. 1191) d'après les registres du Vatican', in *L'ecrit dans la société médiévale: diverse aspects de sa pratique du XIe au XVe siècle*, ed. Caroline Bourlet and Annie Dufour (Paris: Editions du Centre National de la Recherche Scientifique, 1991), 39–45; Michael Goodich, 'Vision, Dream and Canonisation Policy under Innocent III', in *Pope Innocent III and his World*, ed. J.C. Moore (Aldershot: Ashgate, 1999), 151–63; Gábor Klaniczay, 'Proving Sanctity in the Canonization Processes (Saint Elizabeth and Saint Margaret of Hungary)', in *Procès de canonisation au Moyen Age: Aspects juridiques et religieux/ Medieval Canonization Processes: Legal and Religious Aspects*, ed. Gábor Klaniczay, Collection de l'Ecole française de Rome 340 (Rome: Ecole française de Rome, 2004), 117–48; Thomas Wetzstein, *Heilige vor Gericht. Das Kanonisationserfahren im europäischen Spätmittelaltern* (Köln: Böhlau, 2004).

[10]   An equally large body of scholarship has been produced on Innocent's pontificate. See especially Michele Maccarrone, *Studi su Innocenzo III* (Padua: Antenore, 1972); Colin Morris, *The Papal Monarchy: The Western Church from 1050 to 1250* (Oxford: Oxford University Press, 1989), 417–51; Jane E. Sayers, *Innocent III: Leader of Europe 1198–1216* (London: Longman, 1994); John C. Moore, *Pope Innocent III (1160/61–1216): To Root Up and To Plant*, The Medieval Mediterranean 47 (Leiden: Brill, 2003).

[11]   X. 3.45.2, in Emil Friedberg, *Corpus Iuris Canonici* 2 (Graz: Akademische Druck-u. Verlagsanstalt, 1959), 650. Innocent was building on the efforts made by Alexander III to secure a papal monopoly over the veneration of saints. As Kuttner has explained, Alexander's 1170 bull *Audivimus*, in which the pope asserted that no-one was allowed to venerate a would-be saint without authorisation from the Roman Church, received greater attention from canonists during Innocent's pontificate than that of Alexander's. The bull was also codified in the *Decretals*. See X. 3.45.1, in *Corpus Iuris Canonici* 2, 650. See also Kuttner, 'La réserve papale du droit de canonisation', 172–228.

The papacy's investigation into the sanctity of Clare's life constituted the first formal inquisition into sanctity that required oral depositions from its witnesses.[12]

As a consequence of this increased vigilance, the *vitae* of saints as a textual genre gained a great deal of power. The power that narratives of the lives of saints were thought to possess can be felt in the decrees made in the 1260s by the general chapters of the Franciscan and Dominican orders, regarding the use and production of the *vitae* of their founders. One of the statutes from the 1260 General Chapter meeting of the Dominican order, composed by Humbert, states that 'the brothers should use the legend of St. Dominic that has been inserted in the lectionary, and [that] hereafter others should not be written.'[13] The lectionary was commissioned by the Dominican order in 1254 as part of the order's wider effort to make uniform the Dominican liturgy, as well as to consolidate the various different versions of the liturgy that were in circulation into one master copy.[14] The task of the composition of the lectionary fell to Humbert, who had also been entrusted by the order with the task of writing a new life of St Dominic, the order's founding father.[15] In the above statute, Humbert does not state explicitly the reasons why he was prescribing the use of his own legend of Dominic or why he was prohibiting the composition of future *legendae*. However, read in the context of the order's liturgical reform, it is most probable that his mandate was representative of a bid for uniformity; a way of eradicating the confusion caused by the multiple *vitae* that were in circulation.[16]

Perhaps inspired by Humbert, the 1266 Franciscan General Chapter took a more drastic approach to the control of the use of the *vitae* of Francis of

---

[12]   Clare's *vita* is modelled on the information provided in these depositions. The oral testimony exists only in a copy written in the fifteenth century in an Umbrian dialect; the thirteenth-century text has been lost. See P. Zeffirino Lazzeri, 'Il processo di canonizzazione di S. Chiara D'Assisi', *Archivum Franciscanum Historicum* 13 (1920), 403–507. The bull *Gloriosus Deus*, in which Innocent IV orders the inquisition, is, however, still extant in its Latin form. See *Bullarium Franciscanum* 1, 684. On oral traditions in the canonisation process see Gábor Klaniczay, 'Speaking about Miracles: Oral Testimony and Written Record in Medieval Canonisation Trials', in *The Development of Literate Mentalities in East-Central Europe*, ed. Anna Adamska and Marco Mostert, Utrecht Studies in Medieval Literacy 9 (Turnhout: Brepols, 2004), 365–95.

[13]   'Mandat Magister, quod fratres utantur legenda beati Dominici que inserta est in lectionario et alie deinceps non scribantur'. *Acta Capitolorum Generalium Ordinis Praedicatorum*, 1 (Rome: Ex Typographia Polyglotta Sacrae Conventae De Propaganda Fidae, 1898), 105.

[14]   Edward Brett, *Humbert of Romans: His Life and Views of Thirteenth-Century Society* (Toronto: Pontifical Institute of Mediaeval Studies, 1984), 80–102 (84).

[15]   Brett, *Humbert of Romans*, 84, 92.

[16]   Brett, *Humbert of Romans*, 80–102 (81). See also Dominic Monti, *St. Bonaventure's Writings Concerning the Franciscan Order*, Works of Saint Bonaventure 5 (St. Bonaventure, NY: Franciscan Institute Publications, 1994), 203, n. 15.

Assisi, the order's founder. In 1263, Bonaventure completed his *Legenda Maior* of Francis of Assisi. At the beginning of the text he claims that he had been instructed to write the legend by the General Chapter, although he does not state at which meeting of the Chapter that the *Legenda* was commissioned, or the reason why it had been commissioned.[17] The relevant statute of the 1266 Chapter is far more explicit:

> The general chapter likewise commands, under obedience, that all the legends of St. Francis hitherto composed shall be destroyed, and that the brothers should make every effort to remove any copies that may be found outside the Order, since the new legend written by the general minister has been compiled from what he himself gathered from the accounts of those who had almost constantly accompanied St. Francis and thus had certain knowledge of each and every thing; whatever it contains, therefore, has been carefully proven.[18]

The extent to which the existing texts were destroyed is mostly unknown, although we do know that at least some copies of existing *legendae* of Francis such as that of Thomas of Celano survived. What is more interesting is the reason why the Chapter felt that they needed to take such final action.[19] The implication behind the statement that the contents of the 'new legend' had been 'carefully proven', as the accounts on which it was based were given by companions of Francis, is that the other texts had not been so 'carefully proven'. This statute is then evidence of the influence that the lives of the saints – or, at least, the life of a saint who had such a profound impact on the way that the Franciscan order constructed their identity – had acquired during the thirteenth century: their power was such that it necessitated the elimination of any versions that did not reflect the needs of the order at that time.

---

[17] 'Ad huius tam venerabilis viri vitam omni imitatione dignissimam describendam indignum et insufficientem me sentiens, id nullatenus attentassem, nisi me fratrum fervens incitasset affectus, generalis quoque Capituli concors induxisset instantia'. *Analecta Franciscana* 10 (Quaracchi: Collegium S. Bonaventurae, 1941), 558. See also Monti, *St. Bonaventure's Writings*, 137.

[18] 'Item precipit generale capitulum per obedientam, quod omnes legende de beato Francisco olim facte deleantur, et ubi extra ordinem inveniri poterunt, ipsas fratres studeant amovere, cum illa legenda, que facta est per generalem ministrum, fuerit compilata prout ipse habuit ab ore eorum, qui cum b. Francisco quasi semper fuerunt et cuncta certitudinaliter sciverint et probata ibi sint posita diligenter'. *Archivum Franciscanum Historicum* 7 (Ad Claras Aquas: Quaracchi, 1914), 678. For the English translation see Monti, *St. Bonaventure's Writings*, 202–3.

[19] Although it is important to note that, unlike the Dominican General Chapter, this statute does not prevent the composition of future *vitae*.

The above examples are taken from contexts that existed – in theory at least – outside of the remit of the papacy's power. It should also be noted that, by the time that the papacy began to exert a monopoly over canonisation, saintly biography had long been a powerful medium through which to communicate an order's origin story.[20] However, via a detailed analysis of the *vitae* of Francis and Clare, it is possible to draw out papal influences over the production of these texts, and to chart how the papacy took a long-existing tradition and made it more powerful under their aegis.

On 19 July 1228, Gregory IX canonised Francis of Assisi.[21] At around this time, the pope commissioned Thomas of Celano, a Franciscan friar, to write the life story of the Umbrian saint. Celano's *legenda*, the *Life of St. Francis* of Assisi, was published in 1229. One of the first chapters of Celano's text narrates the origin of 'the order of poor ladies and holy virgins', and Celano's Francis plays a central role in this story as the very cause of the order's inception.[22] According to Celano, Francis's first major act after his conversion was to reconstruct the church of San Damiano of Assisi, which would become home to the Assisi community of Franciscan nuns. The reconstruction of a church gained symbolic significance in texts produced during the medieval period as a motif of reform. In the context of this story, it also serves to draw a connection between Francis and the 'order of poor ladies', by portraying Francis as the order's instigator.

Celano extends his construction metaphor into the following passage, in which he introduces Clare of Assisi and describes Francis's role in her conversion:

---

[20]   On the construction of origin narratives by the Cistercians in England, for instance, see Elizabeth Freeman, *Narratives of a New Order: Cistercian Historical Writing in England, 1150–1220*, Medieval Church Studies 2 (Turnhout: Brepols, 2002). See also Albrecht Diem's study of gender and monastic origins in the late antique and early medieval periods: 'The Gender of the Religious: Wo/Men and the Invention of Monasticism', in *The Oxford Handbook of Women and Gender in Medieval Europe*, ed. Judith M. Bennett and Ruth Mazo Karras, (Oxford: Oxford University Press 2013), 432–46.

[21]   For the bull of canonisation, *Mira circa nos*, see *Bullarium Franciscanum* 1, 42–5.

[22]   'Primum itaque opus quod beatus Franciscus aggreditur, liberatione sui de manu carnalis patris obtenta, domum construit Deo, illamque non de novo facere tentat, sed veterem reparat, vetustam resarcit; non fundamentum evellit, sed super illud aedificat, praerogativam, licet ignorans, semper reservans Christo: fundamentum enim aliud nemo potest ponere, praeter id quod positum est, quod est Christus Iesus. Cumque ad locum in quo, sicut dictum est, ecclesia Sancti Damiani antiquitus constructa fuerat, reversus foret, gratia ipsum Altissimi comitante, in brevi eam tempore studiosus reparavit. Hic est locus ille beatus et sanctus, in quo gloriosa religio et excellentissimus Ordo Pauperum Dominarum et sanctarum virginum, a conversione beati Francisci fere sex annorum spatio iam elapso, per eumdem beatum virum felix exordium sumpsit ...'. *Analecta Franciscana* 10, 16–17.

This is the place ... in which the Lady Clare, born in the city of Assisi, the most precious and strongest stone of the whole structure, stands as the foundation for all the other stones. For when after the beginning of the Order of Brothers, the said lady was converted to God, having been admonished by the holy man, she lived for the benefit of many and as an example to countless others ... A noble structure of precious pearls arose above this woman, whose praise comes not from men but from God.[23]

Using Clare as a model for the other women of the 'Order of Poor Ladies' instead of San Damiano in this instance, Celano again places Francis at the origin of the women's order by depicting him as the cause for Clare's conversion. As San Damiano is the first institution of the 'Order of Poor Ladies', Clare is the first 'poor lady'. The order, via San Damiano and Clare, derives its spiritual authority from Francis.

When Celano's text is read within the context in which it was produced, the papal agenda behind Celano's use of metaphor in relation to Clare's life becomes apparent. As Alberzoni was the first to make clear, the 1220s were a period during which the papacy was faced with the difficult task of creating a uniform religious identity for the many groups of women in northern Italy who wished to follow a religious vocation based on the relinquishment of the ownership of possessions, and ensuring that these women received adequate pastoral care from male religious.[24] There are many documents extant from the 1220s – produced both by the papacy and by more localised ecclesiastical authorities – that deal with the regulation of these women's lives. There is a certain degree of consistency across these documents in the terminology used to describe the communities of women, but there are also some telling discrepancies.

The early years of Gregory IX's pontificate witnessed a number of efforts to smooth over these inconsistencies. In 1228, Cardinal Raynaldus of Jenne – the future Pope Alexander IV – issued a document addressed to the 'abbesses and communities' of 24 'poor monasteries', all of which are listed in the *salutatio* of

---

[23] 'Hic est locus ... in quo domina Clara, civitate Assisii oriunda, lapis pretiosissimus atque fortissimus ceterorum superpositorum lapidum exstitit fundamentum. Nam, cum post initiationem ordinis fratrum, dicta domina sancti viri monitis ad Deum conversa fuisset, multis existit ad profectum et innumeris ad exemplum ... Super hanc quoque pretiosissimarum margaritarum nobilis structura surrexit, quarum laus non ex hominibus sed ex Deo est'. *Analecta Franciscana* 10, 17. My translation is based on the English translation of Celano's *Life of Saint Francis* in *Francis of Assisi Early Documents: The Saint*, ed. and trans. Regis J. Armstrong et al. (New York, NY: New City Press, 1999), 197.

[24] Alberzoni, 'Clare and the Papacy', 29–87.

the letter.[25] It is significant that these communities are grouped together as 'poor monasteries'. Prior to this letter, a group designation – however vague – had not been given to the religious vocation of these communities. Previously, different communities in different instances were referred to as 'poor nuns', 'poor enclosed nuns', 'poor enclosed', and 'poor ladies of the valley of Spoleto or Tuscany'.[26] Some of these communities were given a form of religious life drawn up by Gregory, in his former life as Cardinal Hugolino, and others were given a set of constitutions known as the 'constitutions of San Damiano'.[27] The papacy had also attempted to secure the care of the women from the Friars Minor, to which end Gregory IX issued the bull *Quoties cordis* in 1227. The bull committed the care of all *pauperes moniales reclusae* to the Friars Minor.[28]

It is important to note, here, that there is no evidence to suggest that any of the friars were opposed to looking after women at this time. There is a tendency in scholarship on the religious orders, particularly in scholarship which focuses on the women's components of these orders, to assume that male religious were always opposed to looking after the women, and that the negotiation for their care was a struggle across these orders in their entirety throughout time.[29] This

---

[25] 'Matribus, sororibus et filiabus carissimis ancillis Christi Sponsi, Filii Dei, abbatissis ac conventibus pauperum monasteriorum sancti Damiano de Assisio, Beatae Mariae Vallisgloriae, de Perusio, de Fulgineo, de Florentia, de Luca, de Senis, de Aretio, de Burgo, de Aquaviva, de Narnio, de Civitate Castelli, de Tuderto, de Sancta Seraphia de Terdona, de Faventia, de Mediolano, de Padua, de Tridento, de Verona, de Urbeveteri, de Eugubio, Sancti Pauli I[n]terampnen., Sancti Pauli Spoletan. et de Cortona, Rainaldus miseratione divina sancti Eustachii diaconus cardinalis, Domini Papae Camerarius, salutem et Sponsi regale cellarium introduci'. *Escritos de Santa Clara y Documentos Complementarios*, ed. and trans. Ignacio Omaechevarría (Madrid: Editorial Biblioteca Autores Cristianos, 2004), 365.

[26] The latter name first appears in the register of Cardinal Hugolino's 1221 legation, as part of a formula for the construction of a monastery ' ... in quo virgines Deo dicate et alie ancille Christi in paupertate Domino famulentur'. Guido Levi (ed.), *Registri dei cardinali Ugolino d'Ostia e Ottaviano degli Ubaldini* (Rome: Forzani, 1890), 153.

[27] *Bullarium Franciscanum* 1, 36.

[28] 'Propter quod attendentes, Religionem Fratrum Minorum gratam Deo inter alias, et acceptam, Tibi, et successoribus tuis curam committimus Monialium praedictarum in virtute obedientiae districte praecipiendo mandantes, quatenus de illis tamquam de ovibus custodiae vestrae committis curam, et solicitudinem habeatis'. *Bullarium Franciscanum* 1, 36–7.

[29] This is one of the unfortunate legacies of Herbert Grundmann's 'incorporation' paradigm. Although it should be noted that Grundmann was one of the first scholars to argue for the importance of women's agency in the development of female religious life, the idea that women were incorporated by the papacy into already present and fully formed male religious orders – in part in order to ensure that they were cared for spiritually – takes away a certain degree of agency from the female religious, and still forms a large part of how scholars have perceived the women's components of the religious orders. See Grundmann, *Religious Movements in the Middle Ages*.

has often resulted in the depiction of female religious by scholars as a perennial inconvenience to their orders, rather than as important constituents of these orders. Constance Hoffman Berman has criticised Cistercian scholarship for considering Cistercian women's houses as having acquired 'Cistercian' status only when the male component of the order began to regulate the administration of female houses in the early thirteenth century.[30] Berman demonstrates convincingly that these regulations were not the first put in place by the Cistercians to deal with women at all, but the first to originate from a recently 'centralised' Cistercian government, the General Chapter, which had only begun to meet on a regular basis since the 1170s.[31] She argued that if a Cistercian subject can be identified as such only when the General Chapter began to regulate them, then it is not possible to speak of male Cistercians before this time either. Aside from the fact that, as Berman argues, there is evidence for both male and female Cistercians from the start of the twelfth century, situating the women's origins in a set of decrees that regulated against their inclusion implies wrongly that they were a nuisance to the order in its entirety from the very start of their existence. Similarly to the Cistercians, there is no evidence in Franciscan sources produced prior to *Quoties cordis* that would suggest that the friars were opposed to the idea of administering pastoral care to the nuns. Even in later sources, aside from one concerted effort made by Crescentius of Jesi, the Franciscan Minister General at that time, to release the friars from the care of the women, complaints made by friars against their obligation to the *cura monialium* – the care of the nuns – were isolated. However, whilst there is no reason to believe that the *cura monialium* caused tension between the male and female contingents of the Franciscan order prior to *Quoties cordis*, it is also the case that there is nothing to suggest that Gregory had built his decree upon any form of historical or canonical basis.

Celano's origin narrative might then be read as an attempt to create such a basis and to give greater definition to the women's identity. His portrayal of the relationship between Francis and Clare creates a very specific type of symbolic link between the order of friars and the order of nuns. The order in which he places the events of Clare's conversion and the subsequent formation of the women's order serves to posit the establishment of the women's order as a phenomenon that was secondary to the formation of the men's. Clare's conversion – and that

---

[30] Constance Hoffman Berman, 'Were there Twelfth-Century Cistercian Nuns?', in *Medieval Religion: New Approaches*, ed. Constance Hoffman Berman (Abingdon, NY: Routledge, 2005), 217–47. For scholarship that argues against the existence of Cistercian nuns in the twelfth century, see Sally Thompson, 'The Problem of Cistercian Nuns in the Twelfth and Early Thirteenth Centuries', in *Studies in Church History Subsidia 1: Medieval Women*, ed. Derek Baker (Oxford: Blackwell, 1978), 227–52; and Brenda Bolton, *The Medieval Reformation* (London: Holmes and Meier, 1983), 89.

[31] Berman, 'Were there Twelfth-Century Cistercian Nuns?', 35.

of the other women who follow her – occurs 'after the beginning of the order of brothers'. Albrecht Diem, writing on the relationships between gender and the development of monasticisms in the late antique and early medieval periods, has pointed out the tradition in monasticism of the creation of a 'little sister' who would follow in the footsteps of the male monastic founder.[32] These 'big brothers', he argues, were usually depicted as having been tasked with adapting the religious life that they had created to fit within the limitations that the female gender posed to the ability of the 'little sisters' to follow the same religious life as that of their male counterparts, such as enclosure.[33] Diem's paradigm refers predominantly to – what purported to be – 'real-life' big brother/little sister relationships, such as that of Pachomius (d. 346) and Maria, and the time period that he discusses is much earlier than that of Francis and Clare. Moreover, Francis is not represented in hagiography as having shaped the San Damiano community, but solely as the community's instigator. Yet Celano's narrative still provides evidence that the big brother/little sister motif continued into thirteenth-century texts concerned with the formation of monastic identity. Even if Clare was not portrayed as Francis's 'little sister', she and her sisters occupy in Celano's *Life* the same position as the 'little sisters' of early monastic tradition: they were younger, their lives were more restricted, and they had less agency than their brothers. To borrow a phrase from Diem, the female institutions are portrayed by Celano as having grown 'like ribs from a male monastic backbone'.[34]

Celano's positioning of Clare and her followers in the 'little sister' role, combined with his placement of Francis at the origin of the women's order, functioned predominantly as a means of provoking admiration for Francis amongst the readership of the *vita* by depicting Francis as having fulfilled one of the traditional roles of the male founder. For the papal commissioner of the *vita*, however, this part of Celano's text served two specific purposes. By connecting the houses of poor women who did not share a uniform juridical identity with Francis's order of brothers – which had received formal approval as an order with a rule in 1223 – Celano strengthened the identity of the women as one that was uniform and papally approved. The relationship between Francis and Clare also creates a myth of a shared spiritual inspiration between the two orders, fabricating a sense of closeness that would have given the papacy a base from which to negotiate the friars' care of the women.

Nearly three decades passed between the dissemination of Celano's origin narrative and the canonisation of Clare in 1255. Clare died in 1253. Around 1231, Gregory IX had begun to refer to communities that had previously been given vague designations such as 'poor enclosed nuns' or 'poor ladies' as being

---

[32] Diem, 'The Gender of the Religious', 435–6.
[33] Diem, 'The Gender of the Religious', 435.
[34] Diem, 'The Gender of the Religious', 435.

of the 'Order of San Damiano'.[35] A move that was quite possibly influenced by the Monticelli community's desire to follow the same form of life as that of San Damiano, it gave the poor women's communities a collective identity which implied a degree of juridical uniformity, upon which Innocent IV built in 1247 when he issued a form of life 'to all the abbesses and enclosed nuns of the Order of San Damiano'.[36] It is important to note, however, that the papacy was only able to encourage uniformity within the order; this uniformity could not be fully enforced by them. In the 1240s and early 1250s, the papacy's endeavours to inspire consistency across the women's designations and forms of life, as well as their efforts to secure the *cura monialium* from the Franciscan friars, would be met with challenges. Throughout the 1240s, the papacy issued a number of decrees which exhorted bishops across Latin Christendom to threaten with excommunication groups of unenclosed female religious who claimed falsely to be of the Order of San Damiano.[37] In 1245 the Minister General of the Friars Minor, Crescentius of Jesi, petitioned the papacy to release the friars from their responsibilities towards the women.[38] In 1253, a few days before Clare's death, Innocent IV approved a form of life that Clare had composed herself with papal support, but not all houses across the order would adopt this form of life.[39]

The death and subsequent canonisation of Clare gave the papacy an opportunity to create a stronger link between the friars and the communities of the Order of San Damiano, and to develop Clare's image as an exemplar and a reference point around which the identities of other communities of poor women could be shaped. Alexander IV canonised Clare in 1255, and the prose *legenda* of Clare's life tells us that it was Alexander who commissioned the text.[40] Most

---

[35] The first instance in which Gregory uses such a formulation can be found in a 1231 letter addressed to the community of Faenza. See Francesco Lanzoni, 'Le antiche carte del S.Chiara in Faenza', *Archivum Franciscanum Historicum* 5 (1912), 261–76 (270).

[36] 'Dilectis in Christo filiabus universis abbatissis et monialibus inclusis Ordinis Sancti Damiani'. *Escritos*, 242. By this point in time, the order had spread far beyond Italy.

[37] The first letter in which this type of decree was made was Gregory IX's 1241 'Ad audientiam nostram', *Bullarium Franciscanum* 1, 290. It was reissued by Innocent IV in 1246, 1250 and 1251. For more information on these 'unlicensed' women's movements see Knox, *Creating Clare of Assisi*, 37–8.

[38] See Benvenuto Bughetti, 'Acta Officialia de Regimine Clarissarum durante saec. XIV', *Archivum Franciscanum Historicum* 13 (1920), 90.

[39] For the text of Clare's form of life, see *Escritos*, 271–94.

[40] 'Suscitavit propterea pius Deus virginem venerabilem Claram, atque in ea clarissimam feminis lucernam accendit; quam et tu, Papa beatissime, super candelabrum ponens, ut luceat omnibus, qui in domo sunt, virtute cogente signorum, Sanctorum catalogo adscripsisti ... Sane placuit dominationi vestrae meae parvitati iniungere, ut, recensitis actibus sanctae Clarae, legendam eius formarem'. *Escritos*, p. 133. For the bull of canonisation, *Clara Claris Praeclara*, see *Fontes Franciscani*, ed. Erico Menestò et al. (Assisi: Edizioni Porziuncola, 1995), 2331–7.

of the scholarship on the text estimates that the *legenda* was released between 1255 and 1256 to support Alexander's canonisation of Clare, although it could have been published at any point during Alexander's pontificate (1254–1261).[41]

The first few chapters of the text function in part as an origin narrative for the women's order. The author of the *legenda* describes in detail the relationship between Clare and Francis, Clare's conversion, and how Clare inspired countless other women to convert to religious life. In the text, Clare flees her family home in Assisi on Palm Sunday, after having been inspired by the preaching of Francis to embrace a religious vocation based on absolute poverty. Francis tonsures Clare himself, and then takes her to two monasteries, before finally settling on the church of San Damiano. The text mentions, unsurprisingly perhaps, that it was Francis who rebuilt the church.[42] After placing Clare in San Damiano, the author describes how her reputation spread quickly throughout Christendom, and how she inspired 'virgins', 'married women', 'noble and illustrious women' to follow her example.[43] The text also employs Isaiah 54:1 by way of positing Clare as the mother of the order of nuns: 'Many are the children of the barren one, more than her who has a husband'.[44]

The story of Clare's conversion and of the origin of the women's order in the prose *legenda* of Clare seems to serve a similar political purpose as Celano's origin narrative in the *Life of St. Francis*. Again, the nuns of the women's order derive their spiritual authority from Francis, via Clare. Francis's spirituality is

---

[41]   Regis J. Armstrong has outlined the debate over the date on which the *Legenda Sanctae Clarae* was composed, within the context of his discussion of the authorship of the text. While Armstrong settles on 1255 as the date on which the text was composed, Chiara Augusta Lainati has estimated that it was commissioned by Alexander at some point between 1255 and 1256, and a Dutch edition of the text which estimates that it was composed at some point between the canonisation of Clare and Alexander's death in 1261. See, in particular, Armstrong, 'The *Legenda Versificata*' 78 and Regis J. Armstrong, *Clare of Assisi: Early Documents* (New York: New City Press, 2006), 272–5. See also Chiara Augusta Lainati, 'Scritti e Fonti Biografiche di Chiara d'Assisi', *Fonti Francescane* 4 (Assisi: Movimento Francescano, 1977), and *Clara van Assisi: Geschriften, Leven, Documenten*, ed. Angela Holleboom et al. (Haarlem: Gottmer, 1984).

[42]   'Haec est illa ecclesia, in cuius reparatione Franciscus miro desudavit studio, cuiusque sacerdoti pecuniam obtulerat pro opere reparando. Haec est in qua, dum Franciscus oraret, vox ad eum de ligno crucis dilapsa insonuit: "Francisce, vade, repara domum meam quae, ut cernis, tota destruitur". In huius locelli ergastulo, pro caelestis amore Sponsi, virgo se Clara conclusit'. *Escritos*, 142–3.

[43]   'Festinant virgines eius exemplo Christo servare quod sunt; maritatae castius agere satagunt; nobiles et illustres, amplis contemptis palatiis, arcta sibi monasteria construunt, atque pro Christo in cinere et cilicio vivere magnam gloriam ducunt'. *Escritos*, 144.

[44]   'Tanta haec salutis germina virgo Clara suis parturiebat exemplis, ut in ea videretur impleri propheticum illud: Multi filii desertae magis quam eius quae habet virum'. *Escritos*, 144.

once again portrayed as an authoritative unifying concept. The connection between Clare and Francis undoubtedly served to reinforce the ideological basis, and to provide a model, for the friars' care of the women.

A bull of Urban IV's, issued in 1263, builds on Clare's recently acquired sainthood in order to organise the communities of women associated with the Order of San Damiano around a central figure. The bull, entitled *Beata Clara*, orders that the various groups of female religious who had previously been referred to as 'Sisters, other times Ladies, often [as] nuns, sometimes as the Poor Enclosed of the Order of San Damiano' should be referred to henceforth as the 'Order of St Clare', and follow one rule, which Urban outlines within the bull.[45] It is difficult to tell where the original impetus for this reorganisation stemmed from – whether the papacy, the nuns themselves, local ecclesiastical authorities, or the friars – and his ruling was undoubtedly adapted subsequently by individual female communities to accommodate their own distinct circumstances. What is interesting about this bull, however, is the myth of institutional uniformity that the invocation of Clare was intended to relay to its reader. Although this uniformity reflected only a juridical reality that would continue to be tested, the way in which the bull capitalises on the creation of the new saint lends an important insight into the way in which the saint was shaped into and employed as a unifying concept, and used also to denote a single point of origin for the female contingent of the Franciscan order.

Although the main goal of the hagiographer was to venerate their subject, an examination of the ways in which these authors used Clare's life to create a history of the women's order that would serve the needs of their papal commissioners provides a fascinating insight into the textual power and use of the lives of saints in the thirteenth century. The neat narrative that the origin stories imposed onto the history of the women's order were intended to have worked to support papal efforts to secure the friars' pastoral care of the women, and to encourage uniformity within the women's contingent of the order, at least on a juridical level. Yet the majority of modern scholars who have noted these differences have not recognised the papal agenda behind the origin stories, and instead they reproduce them in their studies as early narrative histories of the women's order.[46] The portrayal by Celano and the author of Clare's *vita* of

---

[45] 'In hoc autem Ordine, vos et alias ipsum profitentes sub nominationum varietate, interdum Sorores, quandoque Dominas, plerumque Moniales, nonnumquam Pauperes Inclusas Ordinis Sancti Damiani ... Nos itaque ... decrevimus *Ordinem Sanctae Clarae*, uniformiter nominandum ...' *Escritos*, 334–5.

[46] The exception to this is Alberzoni, who, when discussing Celano's *Life of Francis* does note the papal agenda behind the women's origin story. She refers in particular to the passage following Celano's description of Clare, in which Celano states that the women received their 'wondrous life and their renowned practices from the Lord Pope Gregory'. She reads the passage, however, as a papal attempt to institutionalise the women away from Francis's

the women's order as a secondary phenomenon is, consequently, also replicated. Given the complete absence of other evidence that would point to the origin of the women's component of the order, it is perhaps not surprising that the origin stories in these texts have been subsumed into modern narratives of the order in its nascent years. The reason that this is problematic is not because the events that they describe did not happen – there is no reason to suggest that Francis did not restore San Damiano or that he did not inspire Clare directly to embrace her vocation – but because their presentation of these events is so heavily endowed with symbolism and is governed predominantly by his use of extended metaphor. However, when scholars use this narrative as evidence for the order's origins without considering the hagiographical authors' use of symbolism, or the context in which the texts were produced, the women are made to appear in modern scholarly narratives as the copy derived from the male original. Unfortunately, the widespread endorsement in the field of the 'male monastic backbone' myth has resulted in a set of histories of the Franciscan order that perpetuate the homogeneous, androcentric, and artificial idea of an ideal Franciscan identity. As it was impossible for the women to perform their spiritual devotion in the same way as the men did, due to the increasing emphasis that was placed by the papacy on the enclosure of female religious, the women's religious life could never constitute an exact reproduction of the men's. Instead of recognising how a set of ideals that were shared by men and women were taken up and shaped by different types of Franciscan community – gendered, socio-economic, geographical – modern scholars have instead chosen to measure women's Franciscan status against this androcentric ideal, which causes the female organisations within the order to appear as a lesser, 'diluted' form of a male Franciscan order.

This idea is perpetuated in particular by scholarly narratives which use the hagiographical origin stories from Clare's *vitae* to argue that Clare and the San Damiano community lived a 'pure' Franciscan life before the papacy institutionalised the women away from Francis's ideals of poverty, either by forcing enclosure on the women and/or by forcing the women to accept property.[47] This understanding has led to the unfruitful scholarly debate over whether Clare or the papacy took the greatest responsibility for the spread of the

---

early ideal. Alberzoni, *Clare and the Poor Sisters*, 102–4. I discuss below the problems with this type of interpretation. Joan Mueller also notes this passage of Celano, but does not interpret it as evidence of a papal agenda: Mueller, *The Privilege of Poverty*, 34.

[47] In addition to the examples that I provide below, Lezlie Knox and Roest also make this argument. See Knox, *Creating Clare of Assisi*, 31–3; and Roest, *Order and Disorder*, pp. 39–41. See also Joan Mueller, 'Female Mendicancy: A Failed Experiment? The Case of Saint Clare of Assisi', in *The Origin, Development, and Refinement of Medieval Religious Mendicancies* (Leiden: Brill, 2001), 59–82.

Franciscan women's order in the thirteenth century.[48] Alberzoni and Roberto Rusconi, for instance, have both argued that Clare should not be seen as the founder of the women's order because Clare saw her community as unique in its connection to the primitive male order and its adherence to absolute poverty.[49] The other women's communities were formed by the papacy in response to the growing number of women who desired to live without possessions as a form of penitential life, but were not linked to Clare – and were therefore not linked to Francis – from the outset and so did not share the 'organic' Franciscan status of Clare and her community.[50]

Alberzoni's reading is particularly interesting because, as stated earlier in this chapter, she cautions against the weaving of later narratives into the chronology of the order in its nascent years. She also argues that the post-1218 evidence to which we have access suggests that the women's institutions dedicated to poverty did not necessarily grow as neat branches from San Damiano, as the hagiography suggests.[51] However, rather than using this to argue in turn that this leaves open the possibility that the women developed their own versions of a life dedicated to poverty without the direct influence of a 'big brother' figure, she instead uses the earliest part of the foundation myth – the description of Clare and Francis's early relationship and the foundation of San Damiano – to support her assertion that only San Damiano can be seen as a direct branch of the male Franciscan order, and that Clare saw herself and her community as separate from all of the other houses of women who were dedicated to poverty.[52] Clare was the first female branch of the otherwise male Franciscan order, but she was not the founding figure that her hagiography makes her out to be. So whilst Alberzoni rejects the latter half of the narrative – that the women's houses were the daughters of San Damiano – she still ascribes to the former.

Other scholars, most recently Joan Mueller, have used similar evidence to argue that Clare played an active role in shaping the religious life of the women's Franciscan order by encouraging other Franciscan women, such as Agnes of Bohemia, to adhere to Francis's original ideals.[53] Where Mueller's argument differs from Alberzoni's is that whilst Mueller's papacy is still an institution determined on taking away Clare's Franciscan identity, the fight made by

---

[48]   Knox discusses this tradition in scholarship in Lezlie Knox, 'Clare of Assisi: Foundress of an Order?', *Spirit and Life* 11 (2004), 11–29.

[49]   Rusconi, 'The Spread of Women's Franciscanism', 35–56; Alberzoni, *Clare of Assisi and the Poor Sisters*, 29–64. See also Anna Benvenuti Papi, 'La fortuna del movimento damianita in Italia (saec XIII): propositi per un censimento da fare', in *Chiara d'Assisi: Atti del XX Convegno* (Assisi: Società internazionale di studi francescani), 59–106.

[50]   See especially Alberzoni, *Clare of Assisi and the Poor Sisters*, 44–5.

[51]   Alberzoni, *Clare of Assisi and the Poor Sisters*, 29–64.

[52]   Alberzoni, *Clare of Assisi and the Poor Sisters*, 41.

[53]   Mueller, *The Privilege of Poverty*.

Mueller's Clare for the ability to live according to Francis's ideal of absolute poverty was one made for the entire order. In doing so she becomes a sort-of figurehead for the order, but in her own right rather than as a figure that was shaped by the papacy into a founder.

Both of these readings of the source material are problematic. As stated before, this chapter is not concerned with questions of source 'reliability': Clare and Francis may have been in a spiritual relationship, and Clare might have drawn her inspiration directly and wholly from Francis. However, there is simply no source material produced prior to Celano's *Life* that would point to a relationship between Francis and Clare. There is very little evidence for the San Damiano community prior to this date, and the available evidence only tells us that the community existed – it tells us nothing about the form of life to which the community was required to adhere.[54] We certainly do not have any evidence for what Clare might have been thinking at this point. Alberzoni bases her analysis of Clare's mentality on a promise allegedly made by Francis to the women of San Damiano that his brothers would always care for them.[55] The evidence for this promise is found in the Rule that Clare wrote for San Damiano, which was promulgated by Innocent IV in 1253, 25 years after the events of 1228.[56] Clare's Rule does not provide any indication as to when Francis gave her this promise. It states that Francis included it within a written form of life given to the women, but there is no evidence for this form of life produced within Francis's lifetime. Its usefulness as evidence for the early years of the order is therefore extremely limited, especially when used as evidence for Clare's mindset at this given point in time.

It is also important to note that these modern narratives tend to limit Clare's agency and diminish the importance of the communities of women that were formed outside of San Damiano to our understanding of the Franciscan order. If, for the sake of argument, there was evidence to support the idea that San Damiano was an offshoot of the male order, the idea put forward by both sets of scholarly discourse that Clare is motivated by a need to conform to the norms of the Franciscan men – the "real" Franciscans – rather than adapt the ideals of the early Franciscan order to a form of religious life for women is still

---

[54]   The earliest mention of the San Damiano community is a bull issued by Honorius III on 9 December 1219, to the nuns of the Monastery of Santa Maria of the Holy Sepulchre in Monticelli, who followed 'the regular observances of the Ladies of Santa Maria of San Damiano at Assisi'. *Bullarium Franciscanum* 1, 4.

[55]   Alberzoni, 'Clare and the Papacy', 44.

[56]   According to Clare's Rule, Francis's promise reads thus: 'Quia divina inspiratione fecistis vos filias et ancillas altissimi summi Regis Patris caelestis, et Spiritui Sancto vos disponsatis eligendo vivere secundum perfectionem sancti Evangelli,volo et promitto per me et fratres meos semper habere de vobis tamquam de ipsis curam diligentem et sollicitudinem specialem'. *Escritos de Santa Clara*, 283.

a troublesome one. The Franciscan status of the women's communities outside of San Damiano is then assessed by scholars according to how far the forms of life that they followed were similar to male forms of life, and how far they were linked to the primitive male Franciscan order. This reading serves not only to limit Clare's agency and posit the other women's communities as having been somehow less Franciscan, it also perpetuates the erroneous idea that the identity of the men's order was stable or coherent – or even well-evidenced – during the 1210s and 1220s.[57]

That the identity of the men's order was stable or coherent during this time is not only erroneous, it also contributes to an androcentric understanding of what it meant to be Franciscan in the thirteenth century. A subject's maleness has become an indicator of their Franciscan status, where the idea that women could embrace the same religious ideals as the men is made to seem unnatural.[58] In doing so, it perpetuates the very problem that the production of scholarly literature on women was, presumably, intended to solve – the exclusion from mainstream Franciscan scholarship of evidence written on and by women's communities.

The use of hagiography as institutional biography was a practice that was exercised throughout the Middle Ages, and one which became increasingly common during the twelfth and thirteenth centuries with the emergence and proliferation of the religious orders. By exploring the points at which discourses of papal power interacted with the narrative delimiters of the story of a saint's life, it is possible to gain a fascinating insight into the ideological mechanisms governing the production of hagiographical texts and, consequently, into the construction of religious identity in the thirteenth century. Through these texts, the papally commissioned authors of hagiography were able to create narratives of the past that served the needs of their present. Whether these narratives had their roots in other sources that might verify their "legitimacy" – however one might choose to define that term – or not, it is necessary that they are read within the contexts of the periods in which they were produced. The progressive chronologies and clear, singular points of origin that are presented in the hagiographical foundation narratives of the women's order are products, at least

---

[57] On comparing Robert of Arbrissel to Francis, Dalarun shares this anecdote: 'In contrast to Robert of Arbrissel, Francis has no plan for women. But, as Giovanni Miccoli has remarked to me, neither did he have a specific plan for men!' Jacques Dalarun, *Francis of Assisi and the Feminine* (Saint Bonaventure, NY: Franciscan Institute Publications, 2006), 52. Originally published as *Francesco: un passagio. Dona e donne negli scritti e nelle leggende di Francesco d'Assisi* (Rome: Edizioni Viella, 1994).

[58] Berman has examined a similar issue in Cistercian scholarship, arguing that where the Cistercian status of male Cistercian houses is assumed unquestioningly, Cistercian scholarship had traditionally sought an 'unusually high standard of proof' for the Cistercian status of women's houses. See Berman, 'Were there Twelfth-Century Cistercian Nuns?', 217–47.

in part, of an effort to create an order that placed Francis, along with a Clare that was deliberately crafted as his spiritual subordinate, at its roots in order to achieve various ends.

This chapter has demonstrated how the blindness to this practice in Franciscan scholarship has impacted negatively upon modern understandings of the history of the order's development. Such blindness has not only impaired a full understanding of how Franciscan identities were formed during the thirteenth century. In writing the subordination of women by thirteenth-century hagiographers into modern Franciscan histories, scholarship on the nuns has aided in the creation of a basis for the marginalisation of women's evidence within the field of Franciscan studies. By reassessing the ways in which we use saints' lives as evidence, scholars of the Franciscan order can begin to break apart this basis.

Chapter 14

Functions of Anchoritic Spaces and the Implications of Omission in Julian of Norwich's *Revelations of Divine Love*

Justin M. Byron-Davies

Julian of Norwich was an anchoress[1] and the author of the first Middle English book to be written by a woman. We know relatively little about her life beyond the few precise details and inferences that we can draw from her text because her writings are relatively self-effacing and anchoresses were advised to refrain from involvement with worldly affairs such as business transactions which might have left written records. However, we do know that she was born in 1342 and alive in 1416 since she is mentioned in wills up to this point. Such longevity enabled her to observe and experience several epoch-altering events. There was the terror of the Black Death of the mid-fourteenth century, the Hundred Years' War between 1337 and 1453, civil unrest (such as the 1381 Uprising) and the high perinatal mortality rate (although the latter was not confined to the fourteenth century). She would doubtless have been troubled by the Papal Schism – the dual papacy of Rome and Avignon from 1378 to 1417 – and the less than smooth transition from Richard II to Henry IV. Such turbulence and suffering inevitably inform her writing.

In order to become an anchoress a candidate was required to undergo a process which assessed her suitability, with the final decision going to the bishop. She took a vow to withdraw from everyday life in order to devote herself to meditation and intercessory prayer on behalf of the community. An early thirteenth century book which lays out rules and advice for female anchorites is the *Ancrene Riwle*,[2] or *Ancrene Wisse*. This book, which was written by an anonymous author, provides valuable insight into the life that Julian experienced. The anchoress committed to dying to the world, forsaking all material wealth and seeking a life of close communion with God under the auspices of the

---

[1] The role of the anchorite has its roots in the Desert Fathers of Egypt from the third century AD onwards. The noun *anchorite* dates back to the mid-fifteenth century.

[2] Marion Glasscoe and M.J. Swanton (eds), *The Ancrene Riwle*, trans. M.B. Salu (Exeter: University of Exeter Press, 2001).

Church. She would receive the last rites, and, thus purified and ready for death when it should take her, the newly anointed anchoress entered a cell, which was often connected to a wing of the parish church. Julian's cell was attached to St Julian's Church in Norwich but it was destroyed during the Reformation. The church survived until midway through the Second World War when it suffered a direct hit, but began to be rebuilt in the 1950s. A reconstructed cell has been built on foundations which may have been those of the original edifice.

The author of the *Ancrene Riwle*, warning of the danger of succumbing to unpleasant human tendencies such as grumbling and cursing, likens the cell to a tomb: 'They [such actions] are a mockery, then, and contrary to reason, in an anchoress, anointed and buried – for what is the anchor-house but her grave'.[3] Significantly though, the anchoritic life did not involve simply withdrawing from the world until death. An anchoress's day was highly structured with prayer and meditation comprising the greater part of her activities. She relied on others to sustain her and to perform household tasks, leaving her to devote the bulk of her time to religious duties. Julian acted as an intercessor on behalf of parishioners, and their deceased relatives who were thought to be in purgatory. She also served as an advisor to those who sought her counsel, which was made possible through a grille in the wall of the cell.

Julian's advanced theological knowledge has led scholars such as Edmund Colledge and James Walsh to claim that she was a nun prior to her enclosure.[4] Grace Jantzen speculated more plausibly that she may have received an early Benedictine education at Carrow Abbey.[5] However, for all its depth, Julian's knowledge could also be explained by a practice of listening attentively in church and of memorisation as well as participating in discussions with clerics. A fact which renders the probability of Julian having been a nun highly unlikely is that during her sickness a priest was called for, whereas if she had been in a convent there would already have been provision for this on site. Whatever Julian's status was prior to becoming an anchoress she was deemed suitable for enclosure by Bishop Henry Despenser of Norwich.

Evidence that Julian was considered to be part of a spiritual community, and that her reputation for wisdom on spiritual matters had spread, is found in the autobiography of her younger contemporary, Margery Kempe (c. 1373– c. 1440), entitled *The Book of Margery Kempe*. The autobiographical *Book*, which incorporates several genres, including hagiographical elements, numerous examples of affective piety, and pilgrimage travel literature – albeit with sparse

---

3   Glasscoe and Swanton, *Ancrene Riwle*, 47.

4   Julian of Norwich, *Showings*, trans. Edmund Colledge and James Walsh (Mahwah, New Jersey: Paulist Press, 1978).

5   Grace Jantzen, *Julian of Norwich: Mystic and Theologian* (London: Society for Promoting Christian Knowledge, 1987), 18–19.

descriptions of scenery – recounts the many struggles which Margery endured during her spiritual journey; we glean a strong sense of her character and life from the text. Such details are largely absent from Julian's writing and she is much more reticent in referring to herself. We gain an insightful glimpse into the interaction between medieval religious personages in chapter 18 of Margery's *Book* in which she recounts the visitation by the then 40-year-old Margery to the septuagenarian Julian in 1413 as she searched for advice on her own visions and the discernment of spirits. Thus Julian was paradoxically at once hidden and prominent as a religious figure. Through her death to the world by receiving the last rites, and both her spiritual and physical involvement in the community, there is a sense in which the anchorhold could have been perceived as occupying a space between earth and heaven. A further indication of the importance of the role of male and female anchorites in the medieval socio-religious context is found elsewhere in Margery's *Book*, in sections such as those in Chapter 21 in which Mary has spoken to Margery and the only person the latter will trust to share these intimate and holy words is her anchorite confessor who understands such matters, and who, like Margery, has visionary experiences.

Turning to Julian's written work, *A Revelation of Love* (or, as it has been called in more recent times, *A Revelation of Divine Love*) is the first known book in the English language to have been written by a woman. The use of Middle English provided Julian with a space from which to convey her experience of a series of visions, or showings, and their hermeneutic, with the fluency of her mother tongue, as opposed to Latin, in which she was probably not knowledgeable enough to write – if we interpret her claim to be unlettered as referring to her comprehension of Latin. She was able to further cement her position in a community with a shared language. Within the context of life-writing, visionary material can serve as a rich source of information about the author and the lives which provide her subject matter. The necessity of omitting sensitive subject matter due to political and religious constraints made the visionary genre attractive as a means of conveying messages. However, the challenge for readers of her text is to distinguish between allusions which appear as a result of Julian's conceptual framework and those which, from a twenty-first century position, may seem implicit yet which arise from a postmodern mind-set.

In Chapter 1 of *A Vision Showed to a Devout Woman* and Chapter 2 of *A Revelation of Love*,[6] Julian tells us that in seeking to draw closer to Christ in her youth she requested three graces by the gift of God. As she writes, 'The first was to have minde of Criste's passion. The seconde was bodelye syekenes. And the

---

    6   All in-text references to *A Vision* or *A Revelation* display chapter followed by line and are taken from the following text: Nicholas Watson and Jacqueline Jenkins (eds), *The Writings of Julian of Norwich: A Vision Showed to a Devout Woman and A Revelation of Love* (Pennsylvania: The Pennsylvania State University Press, 2006).

thrid was to have of Goddes gifte thre woundes' (*Vision*, 1, 1–3). Inspired by Saint Cecilia, the three wounds were those of true contrition, loving compassion and longing of her will for God. In 1373 Julian did indeed experience what she had earlier requested, suffering an illness which led her, and those close to her, to believe that she was on the verge of death. It was at this point that she received a series of 16 visions, in which Christ was the central figure.

A major feature of the *Revelations* is Julian's concept of the nature and function of the Trinity, to which she introduces the tropes of Fatherhood, Motherhood and Lordship in identifying the attributes of each person of the Trinity. Integral to her writing is the subject of the Passion which draws upon richly evocative imagery, as seen in the line 'The gret droppes of blode felle fro under the garlonde like pelottes, seming as it had comen out of the veines' (*Revelation*, 7, 10–12), and she compares these to herring scales, which were a familiar sight in fourteenth-century mercantile Norwich, which derived its status as a major trading port connected to the North Sea and the goods of northern Europe and the Low Countries by utilising the River Wensum. The showings also prompt Julian's reflections on sin and suffering which convey a sense of empathy – both hers and Christ's, as she experiences him in the showings. In the face of worldly suffering Julian's conception of God is of a loving Creator and her writing is ultimately positive.

There are two versions of Julian's text – a short text: *A Vision Showed to a Devout Woman*, and a long text: *A Revelation of Love* – which I will refer to as *A Vision* and *A Revelation* respectively. *A Vision* is often thought to have been written shortly after the revelations, although Nicholas Watson has argued a strong case for a later date.[7] We know (because Julian tells us) that there was a gap of more than 15 years between the versions. *A Revelation* is more detailed than *A Vision* and offers Julian's extended interpretations of the showings. It is a more mature work which sees her writing with greater authority and confidence. Julian's *Revelations* were not circulated during her lifetime; she may have wished to avoid coming under scrutiny – perhaps out of a sense of modesty which is in evidence in the self-effacing style of *A Vision*. It is however possible that she was anticipating the way in which certain passages could be construed, or misconstrued, as being of questionable orthodoxy. Putting aside the question of apparent self-censorship, the fact is that enclosure provided Julian with physical space, time, and a large degree of privacy without which the creative process of the longer text especially would have been inconceivable in the outside environment. In this sense, the anchoritic life was liberating rather than restrictive. Indeed, the anchorhold might be compared to the creative

---

[7]　Nicholas Watson, 'The Composition of Julian of Norwich's *Revelation of Love*', *Speculum* 68 (1993): 637–83.

space that is described by Virginia Woolf in *A Room of One's Own* (1929).[8] In utilising this position in which she is free to devote time to meditation and prayer, Julian fulfils a key hermeneutical role, not solely for herself but on behalf of her *evencristen*, or fellow Christians, by analysing and dissecting the visions and committing her interpretations to writing. Insofar as there are autobiographical sections in the text Julian swiftly and subtly deflects the focus from herself, frequently referring to herself as 'this creature', thereby displaying humility and alluding to her position as part of the fellowship of believers – her evencristen. In Middle English the word *creature* meant 'one who is created' (by God) and was a common term which we also find in Kempe's *Book* in addition to her self-references in the third person as 'she'. Despite the facts that Kempe's *Book* is autobiographical and we gain a vast amount of insight into her character compared with Julian's non-autobiographical writing, for Kempe these forms of identification serve both to dilute her personal identity, in what she experiences as a post-conversion state of renewal through Christ, and to discard her father and husband's respective names.

Similarly, for Julian the use of this preferred noun as a replacement for a personal pronoun, as used in *A Revelation*, is indicative of a broader attempt to omit personal references. Such deliberate linguistic substitution is one kind of omission. This aside, I define 'omission' as where through a conscious decision, or sub-conscious intuition, Julian upholds orthodoxy when her interpretation of visions or lack of specific showings appears to call for a more radical conclusion. We see this in *A Vision* Chapter 6, where she denies that she is a teacher and downplays her role. She writes,

> Botte God forbede that ye shulde saye or take it so that I am a techere. For I meene nought so, no I mente nevere soit. For I am a woman, lewed, febille, and freylle. Botte I wate wele, this that I saye I hafe it of the shewinge of him that es soverayne techare. (*Vision*, 6, 35–38)

Here Julian eschews any style that might lead to accusations that her writing equates to preaching. Instead she humbly presents herself as one member of the body of the Church and a fellow believer with those who comprise her audience/ readership. By ostensibly downplaying her own authority, she manages to claim authority indirectly by recounting the words which she hears Christ speaking to her. Likewise, Julian's hermeneutical approach neatly conveys a sense of authority, even as she denies she has any personal didactic authority. She is careful to cite scripture and the teaching of Holy Church repeatedly, always stressing the orthodoxy of words from the showings that are attributed to Christ. Insofar as she is successful in convincing her readership that the teaching is orthodox it

---

8   Virginia Woolf, *A Room of One's Own* (London: Penguin, 2000).

becomes conceivable to the reader, and potentially the religious authorities, that they could be Christ's words.

The visionary genre itself provided a further layer of security since it was one area in which it was believed that women were favoured by God to have visions and to intercede in a way that men could not. Consequently it was deemed to be permissible for women to write about these visions with a degree of safety. Therefore, in this area of inspiration and intuition at least women had a measure of authority – insofar as their visions accorded with the teachings of the Holy Church.

One of the most authoritative and influential female visionaries of the Middle Ages was the Benedictine Abbess Hildegard of Bingen (1098–1179) whose *Scivias* (1151)[9] is one of the greatest visionary works of the Middle Ages. It is notable that in her writing on the Fall in Book One, Vision Two of the same text, Hildegard challenges the commonplace medieval practice of blaming Eve for the Fall by instead holding Satan responsible.[10] Julian does not even mention Eve when she addresses the subject of the Fall and here we have one significant example of omission in Julian's text. From the gentle reasoning and measured argument in the subsequent lines to the previous quotation from Julian's *A Vision* we can identify an acute awareness, and possibly a degree of frustration, with the prevailing prejudices against the participation of women in matters pertaining to the divine: 'Botte for I am a woman schulde I therfore leve that I shulde nought telle yowe the goodenes of God, sine that I sawe in that same time that it is his wille that it be knawen?' (*Vision*, 6, 40–42).

Julian's concern to convey a sense of orthodoxy is understandable when we consider that in 1310 the French beguine Marguerite Porete had been burned at the stake for some similar views to those with which Julian has since been associated.[11] Nicholas Watson, who believes that *A Vision* was written no earlier than 1382, attributes Julian's caution to a deflecting of potential accusations of holding condemned views, such as those of the Lollards concerning images. Such a highly charged atmosphere necessitated the taking of precautionary measures, regardless of where one's views were situated in relation to the orthodoxy/ heterodoxy dichotomy. With this in mind, I now turn to the question of omission in Julian's writing, focusing on three examples.

The primary purpose of the anchoritic life was to seek union with God. Julian's removal of all but cursory autobiographical references may be attributed to her immersion in this life. Of the few such references, there are more in *A Vision* than in *A Revelation*. In Julian's vision of the last stage of the Passion

---

[9]　Hildegaard of Bingen, *Scivias*, trans. Mother Columba Hart and Jane Bishop (Mahwah, New Jersey: Paulist Press, 1990).

[10]　Ibid., 73–90.

[11]　Marguerite Porete, *The Mirror of Simple Souls*, ed. Ellen Babinsky (Mahwah, New Jersey: Paulist Press, 1993).

scene in Chapter 10 of the former text – a scene that is rooted in her affective piety – she sees in Christ 'a doubille thirste: ane bodilye, ane othere gastelye' (*A Vision*, 10, 13). She writes of Christ's suffering, including the 'blawinge of winde fra withouten that dried mare, and pined him with calde mare, than min herte can thinke, and alle othere paines' (*A Vision*, 10, 19–20). She also refers to the wind in the eighth revelation concerning the drying of Christ's flesh, and in the thirteenth revelation of the same text in prophesying tribulation for the Church. Watson and Jenkins speculate that Julian was drawing upon her experience of the local environment: 'a cold east wind from the North Sea might have been a feature of many Good Fridays in fourteenth-century Norwich'.[12] This visionary experience of the Passion occurs within the context of Julian's personal experience, thereby underscoring the union between Christ and the believer. With the words 'ilke saule, aftere the sayinge of Sainte Paule, shulde "feele in him that in Criste Jhesu"' (*A Vision*, 10, 22–23), the spiritual and the physical converge through Julian's affective piety and physical suffering.

Significantly, Julian interrupts this meditation of the Passion with an autobiographical interlude, providing a tantalising aperture into her familial life and fourteenth-century practices concerning the dying:

> My modere, that stode emanges othere and behelde me, lifted uppe hir hande before me face to lokke min eyen. For she wened I had bene dede or els I hadde diede. And this encresed mekille my sorowe. For noughtwithstandinge alle my paines, I wolde nought hafe been letted for love that I hadde in him. And towhethere, in alle this time of Cristes presence, I feled no paine botte for Cristes paines (*Vision*, 10, 26–31).

In this autobiographical description of the physical, contemporary sickbed scene, Julian's mother believes that her daughter is dying just as Julian experiences this vision of the late stage of the Passion. We learn that besides Julian's mother there are others present (line 24). These witnesses who believe they are observing Julian's death remind the reader of those at the foot of the Cross. This supposed deathbed is therefore a focal point in a communal event which Amy Appleford explores as she highlights the centrality of the medieval conception of the 'good death' – that is, preparing to die whilst being fully focused on Christ and at peace with God. The dying believer was to serve as a reminder of the transitory nature of life, the urgency of repentance and the interconnectedness of all believers.[13] The pain that Julian feels is the pain of Christ.

---

12   Watson and Jenkins, *Writings*, 82, n. 19.
13   Amy Appleford, 'The "Comene Course of Prayers": Julian of Norwich and Late Medieval Death Culture', *Journal of English and Germanic Philology*, 107, no. 2 (2008), 190–214.

The reference to Julian's mother at this point is also significant because of the subsequent lines concerning the Virgin Mary:

> Herein I sawe in partye the compassion of oure ladye, Sainte Marye. For Criste and sho ware so anede in love that the gretnesse of hir love was the cause of the mekillehede of hir paine. For so mekille as sho loved him mare than alle othere, her paine passed alle othere. And so alle his disciples and alle his trewe lovers sufferde paines mare than thare awne bodelye dying. For I am seker, be min awne felinge, that the leste of thame luffed him mare than thaye did thamselfe (*A Vision*, 10, 38–43).

Julian suffers from both her own and Christ's afflictions, identifying with him to the point that they almost seem to elide within the vision. The roles of the Virgin Mary and Julian's mother, tending her daughter, also appear to be conflated, recalling to the reader Mary at the foot of the Cross. Julian also joins the company of those at the crucifixion through her identification with both the Virgin and Christ as she transposes the scene from the Gospels onto contemporary Norwich and her evencristen through her illness and the vision.

In the earlier account, Julian's identification with Christ is intertwined to a greater degree with her own illness. Consistent with the reduction in number of such autobiographical elements in *A Revelation*, Julian omits the reference to her mother found in *A Vision* 10 in the equivalent chapters in *A Revelation* (17 and 18). Having developed the vivid imagery of the Passion and described her pain, which derives from her empathetic identification with Christ's pain as the wind dries his flesh, she moves directly to the section on Mary (*A Revelation*, 18). Julian may have omitted the personal reference out of humility, or else the earlier allusion and affective element had become an even deeper union with the divine that is consonant with a mystic's focus – her personal circumstances replaced by more intense focus on the Passion. *A Revelation* also displays Julian's mature theological understanding, giving precedence to spiritual autobiographical elements over references to her physical life.

Elsewhere in the *Revelations* we detect omission in two further interconnected doctrinal areas. Firstly, and unusually for her period, Julian makes no mention of the wrath of God, focusing instead on his compassion and love. One of the most enduring images of the showings is that of the hazelnut in the ninth revelation. We read:

> And in this, he shewed a little thing the quantity of an haselnot, lying in the palme of my hand as me semide, and it was as rounde as any balle. I looked theran with the eye of my understanding, and thought: "what may this be?" And it was answered generally thus: "It is all that is made". I marvayled how it might laste, for methought it might sodenly have fallen to nought for littlenes. And I was

answered in my understanding: "It lasteth and ever shall, for God loveth it. And so hath all thing being by the love of God" (*Revelation*, 5, 7–13).

This famous image which exhibits the act and character of a divine Creator caring for his creation typifies Julian's conception of a compassionate God which is prominent elsewhere in relation to Christ, where Julian focuses upon attributes which have traditionally been associated with motherhood. Julian was not the first to use such metaphorical language, but it is a major characteristic of her text. This motherhood topos, which is a key aspect of her conception of God, shows Julian making space for a feminine voice. Secondly, and in contrast to Margery Kempe, she sees no vision of hell – an omission that is consonant with her optimistic soteriology. We gain a sense that she may have wished to be bolder when dealing with material pertaining to soteriological matters and it is in such discussions that omission is most evident. In both versions Julian requests a vision of 'a certaine person that I loved howe it shulde be with hire' (*Vision*, 16, 13). In contextualising the passage it seems probable that Julian is concerned about the destination of the woman's soul, which in itself would indicate a belief in the possibility of purgatory and/or hell. Significantly she is given no such vision. However, she does receive an explanation for this omission, including the words, 'it is mare worshippe to God to behalde him in alle than in any specialle thinge' (*Vision*, 16–17). However, Julian's supposed universalism – that she cannot conceive of anyone being sent to hell by a loving God – may initially invite comparisons with Marcionism, which was a heresy deriving from the teachings of Marcion (c. AD 85 – c. AD 160), a bishop (in what is now Turkey) who rejected the Old Testament and sections of the New Testament and whose teachings created enough concern to hasten the formation of the Canon of scripture that would ultimately comprise 66 books. Nevertheless, Julian displays knowledge of and belief in the Old Testament, for instance the book of Isaiah. Whilst Julian chooses to ignore passages such as those in Matthew where Jesus warns believers about hell, she doesn't deny them, and it is important to stress that she was never accused of heresy during her lifetime. The views which she expounds are ostensibly orthodox and we cannot *automatically* read omission as implying lack of belief in such passages, even when a section which would naturally seem to require a reference omits it and/or replaces it with something else. We can however raise this implication of omission as a distinct possibility, and reading between the lines it is possible to detect an undercurrent of discontentment through her emphasis on certain passages and omission of others which, when combined, hint at a radical soteriology.

Julian is incredulous that anybody sins willingly and holds that nobody would sin if they appreciated its impoverishing effects, writing in Chapter 53 of *A Revelation*, 'in ech a soule that shall be safe is a godly wille that never assented to sinne, ne never shall' (*Revelation*, 53, 9–10). She regards sin as a punishment in itself, writing in Chapter 39 of *A Revelation* that 'Sinne is the sharpest scorge that ony chosen soule may be smitten with' (*Revelation*, 39, 1). Framing Julian's abhorrence of sin is her sense of unity with her community of evencristen – those within the body of Christ – upon whom she superimposes her own response to sin. Whilst she acknowledges Church teaching that hell exists – by definition, for Christ's incarnation, crucifixion and resurrection to have meaning it is through the presupposition of the existence of a hell from which people are saved – she sees no vision of hell. She does state that heathens, fallen angels and the devil are damned eternally (*Revelation*, 32, 33–38), so, given this, what induces the confidence of her famous and cryptic phrase, 'alle shalle be wele' (*Vision*, 16, 21) – a tantalising statement which seems counter-intuitive in the context of her professed belief in hell? In fact, she is unable to reconcile convincingly these beliefs in accordance with Church teaching. Indeed, Julian's soteriology and the absence of visions of hell convey optimism which is often highly suggestive of underlying universal salvationist tendencies – although I tend to agree with Kathryn Kerby-Fulton that these should be viewed more as liberal salvationist tendencies.[14] Julian seeks to overcome any friction with protestations of orthodoxy, leaving the subject hanging as a mystery to be revealed on judgment day. We can either take her words at face value, in which case her continued belief in defiance of a contradiction presents a problem, insofar as her belief would operate on the basis of a contradiction, or we can see it as a case of deliberate omission designed to avoid highlighting liberal salvationist beliefs. Either way we must account for the omission.

I would like to propose the following. In *A Revelation* Julian implies prophetically that there will be an ultimate salvific act and in doing so she cites a 'grete dede' that will make all things well:

> For this is the grete dede that oure lorde God shalle do, in which dede he shalle save his worde in alle thing and he shalle make wele that is not welle. But what the dede shal be, and how it shall be done, there is no creature beneth Crist that wot it, ne shalle wit it, till it is done, as to the understanding that I toke of oure lordes mening in this time (*Revelation*, 32, 46–50).

Whilst the 'grete dede' that she is alluding to is inextricably bound with the Cross, we infer from the text that the former will be an extension of the latter's salvific power – for how could all be well if any were damned? Julian cannot, however, state this, either because she is not sure what constitutes the 'grete dede', or more likely, because to do so would invite accusations of heresy.

---

[14] Kathryn Kerby-Fulton, *Books Under Suspicion: Censorship and Tolerance of Revelatory Writing in Late Medieval England* (Notre Dame, Indiana: University of Notre Dame Press, 2006).

Given that Julian acknowledges the presence of sin and suffering in the world and, from an eschatological perspective, the existence of an ultimate hell, the act of faith and belief in the statement 'alle shalle be wele' is based on an absurd notion, from a human perspective as opposed to a divine one. Within this context we might consider Søren Kierkegaard's definition of faith on the strength of the absurd, as found in *Fear and Trembling* (1843).[15] In this philosophical work Kierkegaard juxtaposes Abraham's thought process regarding the divine command to sacrifice his son, and his willingness to do so, based upon faith on the strength of the absurd, against societal norms and the future sixth commandment. Drawing on Hegel's concept of the universal, which in the context of human cognition does not recognise the deviant and transgressive thought process of Abraham, the latter's 'justification' (Genesis 22:8) for his position on Isaac in relation to society translates as whatever is in the best interests of mankind (the common good) and the structure of laws and society as a whole. Anything which transgresses the universal does not benefit society as a whole, thus it is outside the universal. Abraham stands in relation to the universal by way of the absolute, believing that Isaac will be revived or resurrected by God. To do this he must first obey the command to kill, thereby proving that he is willing to transgress the law and to sacrifice his son who, in an additional degree of paradoxical absurdity, is to be the progenitor of the race that had been promised and given to Abraham at the age of seventy. Yet he acts on the strength of faith and on the basis of faith and the strength of the absurd. The only way that the universal can be challenged here is by means of an overarching teleology – although even then it contravenes its own divine pronouncements (the future sixth commandment) in the case of Abraham, and the references to hell in the Bible which presented such a challenge to Julian's concept of God.

Despite the obvious differences between Abraham's willingness to sacrifice Isaac, as analysed by Kierkegaard, and Julian's intellectual dilemma, Julian's (what we would today term) 'cognitive dissonance' – in the case of a dual acceptance that hell exists as a place where heretics and heathens are sent whilst she sees no vision of hell and embraces a liberal salvationist view – is analogous to Kierkegaard's teleological suspension of the ethical. As Abraham believes God's promise regarding the future of the people, Julian believes, for example, the Apocalypse account in which, after all the suffering that is described, comes the promise of the new heaven and new earth and the new Jerusalem along with the words of 21:4 (directed to those who have come through the great tribulation) that 'God shall wipe away all tears from their eyes: and death shall be no more. Nor mourning, nor crying, nor sorrow shall be any more, for

---

[15] Søren Kierkegaard, *Fear and Trembling*, trans. Alastair Hannay (London: Penguin Classics, 1985).

the former things are passed away'.[16] However, humanly speaking, this appears to constitute faith on the strength of the absurd given the vivid description of hell in the same book. Julian's act of resignation is her acknowledgement of the presence of suffering in the world as the state of things since the Fall. Whilst Julian must be resigned to the presence of sin and suffering in this life, on the strength of the absurd what is humanly impossible is nevertheless divinely possible: she can believe that 'alle shalle be wele'. The implication is that God will somehow overturn this state given that, according to Julian, hell and suffering are incompatible with a perfect state in an afterlife. Julian too struggles with this paradox in that she conceives of a framework of society containing all her evencristen, who are included by a God who exhibits no wrath in her visions. Her faith thereby allows apparently mutually exclusive doctrines and rests in an impossible action, if what she has claimed is true. This outlook is encapsulated in her statement that what is impossible for human beings is possible for God. The key to this is her understanding of the hypostatic union and Incarnation which united Christ and Adam (mankind).

Julian's postulation of a 'grete dede' and the aforementioned precedent of Abraham's actions appear to offer a way in which to reconcile the Church teaching on hell (which she professes to accept) and the absence of a vision of hell. We might speculate whether Julian had in mind something similar to Uthred de Boldon's[17] (c. 1315–1396) *Visio Clara* – that is, a belief that every person on the verge of death experiences a beatific vision and is given the choice between good and evil. Although this borders on heretical second chance salvationist teaching, the operative word is *dying* – in other words, the subject is still alive when he or she witnesses the vision. An indication that Julian may have been thinking along these lines, either solely through her own meditations or through contact with other sources, is discernible from her allusion to the Harrowing of hell, as found in 1 Peter 3:18–20, 4:6; Matthew 12:40 and Acts 2:27 and the apocryphal *Gospel of Nicodemus*. The Harrowing of hell, which developed as a tradition within a tradition through representations in literature, such as the one found in the Chester Cycle of the Mystery Plays, refers to the time when Jesus, between his death and resurrection, descended into Sheol in order to preach to those who died in the Flood, thus offering them a chance to come to faith. Julian writes, 'And at this point he beganne furst to show his might, for then he went into helle. And whan he was ther, he raised uppe the gret root oute of the depnesse, which rightfully was knit to him in hey heven' (*Revelation*, 51, 254–256). Here she does not refer to the figurative hell of the

---

[16] 'Apocalypse 21:4 (The Latin Vulgate [Douay Rheims Translation])' in Vulgate.org, http://vulgate.org/nt/epistle/revelation_21.htm (accessed June 20, 2014).

[17] A Benedictine monk and theologian whose views on salvation were condemned in 1368.

Passion, but rather the place called 'Sheol', the word that the Vulgate uses. The Hebrews' concept of Sheol was a holding place between this world and the next; Christ's victory over death meant that Adam could be released. Julian relates how Christ released Adam, who 'fell fro life to deth: into the slade of this wretched worlde, and after that into hell' (187–188) from this place. Using hell in a figurative sense, she continues: 'Goddes son fell with Adam into the slade of the maidens wombe, which was the fairest doughter of Adam – and that for to excuse Adam from blame in heven and erth – and mightely he feched him out of hell' (188–191). Liberal or universal salvationist views were also influenced by non-canonical books, such as the *Apocalypse of Peter*, which holds that people could not learn about universal salvation, otherwise they would become even more sinful, and the apocryphal *Gospel of Nicodemus* which influenced Uthred de Boldon.

We are faced with a number of possibilities. By highlighting this apparent discrepancy in doctrine Julian may be positing such a liberal salvationist alternative, or else she may be exhibiting simple faith stemming from assurances which she gained from the visions. Although there is a sign of struggle in the text, there is not sufficient evidence to state categorically that she does more than problematise orthodoxy whilst covering herself against allegations of heresy. We should also bear in mind that she is writing to believers.

Julian's selection of tense when discussing soteriological matters is revealing. She invariably writes of those who 'will' be saved, or those who are 'being' saved. Her deliberate use of the future form conveys an eschatological view that accords with the biblical *Apocalypse*. The great salvific work is still under way and will not be completed until the day of judgment, which is why Julian begins the final chapter of *A Revelation* with the words, 'This boke is begonne by Goddes gifte and his grace, but it is not yet performed, as to my sight' (*Revelation*, 86, 1–2). Her eschatological awareness is also consistent with the many biblical warnings regarding the dangers inherent in backsliding from the faith. This is indicative of Julian's awareness that personal salvation cannot be assumed until Judgment Day. She asserts that there is a hell from which people need saving; the question is whether it will ultimately be populated by any other than the devil and other fallen angels. The possibility of choosing hell over heaven must exist if there is free will, and although Julian does not recognise sin's power, since it has been defeated by Christ, she acknowledges the active struggle and faith that is required in order to continue overcoming it.

A key section in *A Revelation* that is not included in *A Vision* and which omits any mention of the biblical aspect of God's wrath – and indeed states that his love is incompatible with wrath – is her parable of the Lord and the Servant in Chapter 51. When the servant, on an errand from the lord, falls and loses contact with the lord, the latter is described as displaying no wrath. Julian tells us that she omitted the parable earlier because she didn't comprehend its meaning and needed to reflect upon it further. Significantly, in this representation of the Fall there is no mention of Eve; rather it is Adam's sin that is foregrounded, although we must qualify this with the fact that Adam represents mankind as a whole (i.e. *Adama*, the Hebrew generic term for *man*). Indeed, in the parable, the servant represents both Adam and Christ, and through the servant's fall Julian simultaneously depicts Adam's Fall and Christ's incarnation and subsequent crucifixion. Nevertheless, Julian's omission of any reference to Eve may be viewed as an attempt to counter the tendency in the Middle Ages to blame Eve for the Fall, which is consistent with Julian's positive view of femininity elsewhere, such as in her references to motherhood and her depiction of the Virgin Mary. Julian focuses on two points in Mary's life, namely, her suffering during Christ's Passion, saying that due to her love she suffered more than anyone else, and Mary as an idealised mother. Whilst upholding a redemptive and pastoral view of Christ, Julian omits any mention of an avenger who is angered by sin. Her conception of the Trinity focuses on love and compassion for individuals. Sin is presented as almost a hell in itself that is suffered by the sinner, who whether conscious or not that he or she is suffering in sin becomes less than they could be in their true, full humanity.

With the words 'it is not yet performed, as to my sight' (*Revelation*, 86, 1–2), we understand that Julian neither claims to have been informed of the outcome nor has experienced it. Nevertheless, this omission of any direct reference to salvation conveys a comforting and hopeful soteriology which despite (or indeed because of) her many professions of orthodoxy, offers a glimpse of discontentment with certain aspects of official teaching, and posits an optimistic eschatological view. Such omission does not equate to a denial of sin and its consequences – on the contrary, the struggle against sin forges a closer unity with Christ and is suggestive of his empathy for the human condition which is conveyed through the metaphor of motherhood. Besides the deliberate omissions that we have examined, the doctrinal omissions concerning salvation may, consciously or otherwise, convey information that Julian either couldn't safely express in words, or felt were better left as allusions or messages. In her life (as on the page) Julian created and utilised existing spaces to express a positive message based on the showings. The physical space of the anchorhold facilitated the development of a creative space which led to an enhanced intellectual framework. Her writings are indicative of a liberal salvationist outlook and a highly empathetic and optimistic world view. By drawing on the life of Christ and Mary respectively, Julian offers the fruits of her meditative life to her evencristen – both her contemporaries and others who have read, and will read, her *Revelations* up to the present day and beyond.

Index